How W

T0307974

'Sian Lazar shows us anthropology at its best. She explores how different capitalist strategies for organising workers' productivity generate problems that encourage certain solutions that in themselves create more problems, and on and on. Lazar is remarkably imaginative in revealing how, in large and small ways, workers of all stripes can organise to create otherwise, generate new possibilities for resistance and lead more fulfilling lives.'
—Ilana Gershon, Ruth N. Halls Professor of Anthropology, Indiana University

'Sian Lazar's new book is as brilliant as it is useful. She manoeuvres lightly among the opposing schools of labour anthropology and shows with worldwide examples that how we struggle for better lives is deeply embedded in the type of relationships in which we labour, care and serve; relationships that are globally produced, intimately lived, and more often than not divisive. *How We Struggle* is a boon for analysts and activists alike.'
—Don Kalb, Professor of Social Anthropology, University of Bergen, author of *Expanding Class*

'With its fresh analysis of labour agency, *How We Struggle* is a source of tremendous inspiration and hope. I can't wait to share it with my students.'
—Dr Rebecca Prentice, Reader in Anthropology and International Development, University of Sussex

'With ethnographic flair, this book beautifully incorporates a wide range of contemporary contributions to the anthropology of labour, from the workplace to the home and the community, from collective action to individualised strategies of resilience and escape. It provides a highly readable and state-of-the-art analysis of the politics of labour, with a keen eye to gender and migration.'
—Luisa Steur, Associate Professor, Department of Anthropology, University of Amsterdam

'*How We Struggle* is marvellously expansive and generous in its conceptualisation as it allows us to think broadly about labour agency in a post-Fordist, post-pandemic world. Lazar has written a masterful book – a resource that makes anthropology matter.'
—Andrea Muehlebach, Professor of Anthropology, University of Bremen

Anthropology, Culture and Society

Series Editors:
Holly High, Deakin University
and
Joshua O. Reno, Binghamton University

Recent titles:

How We Struggle

A Political Anthropology of Labour

Sian Lazar

PLUTO PRESS

First published 2023 by Pluto Press
New Wing, Somerset House, Strand, London WC2R 1LA
and Pluto Press Inc.
1930 Village Center Circle, 3-834, Las Vegas, NV 89134

www.plutobooks.com

British Library Cataloguing in Publication Data
A catalogue record for this book is available from the British Library

ISBN 978 0 7453 4751 6 Paperback
ISBN 978 0 7453 4753 0 PDF
ISBN 978 0 7453 4754 7 EPUB

Typeset by Stanford DTP Services, Northampton, England
Simultaneously printed in the United Kingdom and United States of America

Contents

Series Preface

As people around the world confront the inequality and injustice of new forms of oppression, as well as the impacts of human life on planetary ecosystems, this book series asks what anthropology can contribute to the crises and challenges of the twenty-first century. Our goal is to establish a distinctive anthropological contribution to debates and discussions that are often dominated by politics and economics. What is sorely lacking, and what anthropological methods can provide, is an appreciation of the human condition.

We publish works that draw inspiration from traditions of ethnographic research and anthropological analysis to address power and social change while keeping the struggles and stories of human beings' centre stage. We welcome books that set out to make anthropology matter, bringing classic anthropological concerns with exchange, difference, belief, kinship and the material world into engagement with contemporary environmental change, capitalist economy and forms of inequality. We publish work from all traditions of anthropology, combining theoretical debate with empirical evidence to demonstrate the unique contribution anthropology can make to understanding the contemporary world.

Holly High and Joshua O. Reno

Acknowledgements

This book developed out of a lecture series, and so I would like to thank the many students who were test audiences. I am also very grateful to the public sector unionists of Buenos Aires and the street vendors' associations of El Alto for pointing me down the road of organised labour as a research topic. I would like to thank all the labour activists who struggle for better conditions for their inspiration, and who write about that struggle on Twitter, in newsletters and in the media. I hope I have done them some kind of justice and adequately expressed my admiration for their tenacity.

As I put together these acknowledgements, I realised that a whole series of workshops and conference panels were inspirational for this book, beginning with the AAA congress in New Orleans in 2010, the workshop on 'Regular and Precarious Forms of Labour in Modern Industrial Settings' organised by Chris Hann and Johnny Parry at the Max Planck institute in Halle in 2015; a workshop I organised at Cambridge in 2017 on Labour Politics and Precarity; the meeting of the EASA Anthropology of Labour network in Amsterdam in 2019; the panel on Social Reproduction at EASA 2020, and the 2021 workshop on the Politics and Ethics of Platform Labour in Cambridge. Both of the Cambridge workshops were supported by the Centre for Research in the Arts, Social Sciences and Humanities (CRASSH) and I am grateful to CRASSH for their financial and especially administrative support. My thanks to the organisers and participants for such stimulating events, all of which have been important sources of inspiration and insight.

Laura Bear, Deborah James, Don Kalb, Sharryn Kasmir, Geert de Neve, Rebecca Prentice and Andrew Sanchez have all been key sources of support and advice at various points in time. Don read a version of the manuscript and his comments were both encouraging and critical, influencing some key changes. Because this was such an ambitious project, I turned to colleagues to help fill gaps in my knowledge and I am hugely grateful to those who answered my questions and suggested references. I've especially noted down Catherine Allerton, Kate Boyer, Charlotte Faircloth, Kathleen Millar, Tom Neumark, Irene Peano, Miranda Shield Johannsen, Dan Souleles and Sofia Ugarte, but I've been pestering people over a period of about five years and my recording systems are not great. So, I have probably also forgotten some people, for which I am sorry.

Ilana Gershon read the entire manuscript incredibly closely. She gave me editorial comments and talked through my arguments with me, and I am amazed at and deeply thankful for her generosity. In my experience it has been rare to get that kind of detailed engagement with work of this length after the PhD and outside of the formal processes of manuscript reading at the publisher. I also thank the editors of this series at Pluto Press for their comments and insight, especially Holly High.

I want to acknowledge the continuing importance of Olivia Harris in inspiring me and shaping my thinking. I thank my colleagues in Cambridge for the time to think and to write, my students for requiring me to structure my thoughts better, and my friends in the Department of Social Anthropology and Clare College for being such a supportive academic community of care and intellect. Finally, Dave has kept me going on the many occasions when my self-confidence flagged, and Zakk and Milo are wonderful young men who make me proud to be me. Thank you.

Introduction

This book is about the day-to-day struggles that contemporary working people engage in to resist oppression or simply strive for something better. It draws on ethnographies of working life to explore the experience of labour and what that means for workers' political agency, putting that more intimate perspective into the context of how global capitalism has developed in recent decades. In a post-Fordist world, how should we think about labour agency? Using examples from ethnographies conducted all over the world and in multiple workplaces I ask: how do people strive to improve their life and work conditions? How are they constrained and enabled in that struggle by the nature of the work they do, and by their own personal experience and embedding in local histories, cultures, under-standings and networks? In asking these questions, I deploy a capacious notion of agency, that includes self-activity in the workplace (which may in turn be appropriated by the employer) as well as resistance and struggle, coupled with life beyond work and in the realms of subsistence and social reproduction.[1] This emphasis on holism derives from my anthropological commitment, as does my goal to achieve a radical compassion for what people do to try to make things better for themselves and for those they love. I offer this as an analytical and political contribution to the debate because often theorists on the left only see the most spectacular and oppositional protests at work; or they focus on organisational forms that are novel or ideologically uncompromised. In contrast, anthropology can bring to our attention other aspects of political life and, I argue, make a case for them as equally valid kinds of radical politics, at different scales of life, from personal to collective.

The Covid-19 pandemic brought the problem of work to the foreground of popular and political attention in unexpected ways. In March 2020, the UK government released its list of key workers who were permitted to send their children to school during the first lockdown. The list included, among others, frontline health and social care staff, teachers and nursery workers, those required to run the justice system, police officers, members of the armed forces, transport workers, utilities workers and those involved in food production and delivery.[2] For ten weeks, people stood on UK doorsteps at 8 p.m. on a Thursday to applaud keyworkers in the NHS. Government furlough schemes paid the salaries of people who could not work from home but were not considered key workers. Parents (especially mothers) homeschooled their children and attempted to juggle that with (sometimes) full time work from home. In the early stages of the pandemic, press articles and social media reported the pleas of doctors, nurses and care home workers who had not been provided with enough personal protective equipment. High infection rates in parts of Leicester were thought to be related to garment factories where employers were not observing safety protocols.[3] In Norfolk, meat-processing factories saw significant outbreaks, thought to be at least in part associated with working conditions of close proximity to others, lack of ventilation and low temperatures.[4] As the vaccine programme rolled out from late 2020, healthcare workers were vaccinated, and some union leaders and politicians began to lobby for teachers to be similarly prioritised,[5] although for men at least, the riskiest professions outside of healthcare were security guard, care worker and taxi driver.[6] White collar workers considered the relative merits of working from home versus going into the office and wondered how their workplace might change after the pandemic. In short, work was discussed as never before: how we value it, who does what, what do they need to do it safely, where must it happen, how might it change.

Such debates were of course not unique to the UK. On 30 March 2020, Instacart workers in New York City went on strike to demand protective equipment, hazard pay and sick leave, and on 1 May, workers at Instacart, Amazon, Whole Foods, Walmart, FedEx, Target and Shipt struck for basic health and safety provisions. Ununionised delivery workers struck in ten Brazilian cities in early July.[7] Workers protests went beyond purely pandemic-related concerns. In India, nearly a million farmers converged on Delhi in November 2020-January 2021, protesting legislation to liberalise agricultural markets. They succeeded in making the government freeze the implementation of the laws in January, and eventually repeal the legislation in late 2021.[8] In November 2020, gig economy unions campaigned to prevent Proposition 22 ('Prop 22') passing at the ballot box in California but were defeated by the better-funded campaign run by Uber, Lyft and their allies. Prop 22 was the companies' response to prior legislation that had required them to classify their drivers as employees, which would have meant enforcing a series of workers' rights. The companies instead proposed a minimum earnings guarantee and some healthcare provisions but maintained drivers' status as independent contractors.

Uber had been appealing a UK employment tribunal judgement on much the same question since 2016, and in February 2021, it lost its final appeal at the UK Supreme Court and was ordered to classify drivers as workers and pay minimum wage and holidays, among other rights. In May 2021, Uber agreed to recognise the GMB union, the first time Uber had recognised a drivers' union anywhere in the world, albeit with an agreement to collective bargaining on only a very limited range of issues (not including drivers' earnings). Back in the US, a group of Amazon warehouse workers in Bessemer, Alabama led a year-long campaign to achieve union recognition for the Retail, Wholesale and Department Store Union (RWDSU), culminating in a vote in March-April 2021. The workers voted against unionisation after a hard-fought campaign by Amazon. In December 2021, despite a similarly tough anti-union campaign from their employer, staff at a Starbucks store in Buffalo, New York, voted in favour of unionising, and established the first labour union at a Starbucks since the 1980s.[9] On 1 April 2022, after a nearly two-year-long campaign led by Chris Smalls, who was fired from his job at an Amazon fulfilment centre in Staten Island after protesting inadequate Covid safety measures, the independent union he founded (Amazon Labor Union) won a vote for recognition there, becoming the first labour union at Amazon in the US. That same day, Starbucks Workers United won their tenth vote for unionisation since Buffalo, with petitions under way in more than 170 Starbucks stores across the US.[10]

Meanwhile, across the world, unions were negotiating health and safety protocols, wage increases, redundancies, job openings and multiple other questions with their employers. Workers who are not members of a union were chatting with each other online, sharing worker IDs or platform profiles and giving advice about how to avoid a bad employer; they were supporting and teaching each other, finding out about new job opportunities and deciding to leave jobs that they didn't like; they were seeking out ways to combine their job with their caring responsibilities, building solidarities and political power through collective action; solving disputes, seeking amenable clients, getting angry, feeling resigned, getting ill, slowing down, speeding up, and so on. Collectively and individually, despite and because of the pandemic, people tried to make their working conditions better.

The upsurge of labour mobilisations in 2020–2021 was not actually that new, though. In some form, organised labour has been part of many of the most famous mass mobilisations in recent decades, from indigenous rights and anti-neoliberal protests in Latin America to the 1999 anti-WTO protests in Seattle, service delivery protests in South African townships in the 2000s, the Arab Spring and Occupy protests of 2011, and more recently, pro-democracy mobilisations in Chile in 2019. Labour played a crucial role in anti-coup protests in Myanmar in early 2021, and a general strike in Israel/Palestine in May 2021. While scholars from the 1990s to the 2010s bemoaned what they assumed was an irrevocable weakening of trade unionism and saw instead new political subjects rising up – indigenous peoples, the multitude, youth, environmentalists – we forgot that these 'new' kinds of mobilisations for democracy, against neoliberalism, or for urban services were also based profoundly in how people live, and that what people do to generate the resources to enable life is central to that fundamental struggle. Not to mention all the less spectacular day to day efforts, negotiations and strategising that working people engage in all the time, both individually and collectively, within and outside of formal trade unions. These struggles are the subject of this book.

Capitalism and labour: orienting narratives

While the most distinctively anthropological contribution to how we understand labour agency would be a focus on everyday experience, anthropologists of labour also usually argue that labour processes are embedded in local historical, social and cultural contexts and practices. That claim differentiates anthropology from alternative disciplinary approaches (principally from political economy) that describe labour in more abstract theoretical terms or on a larger scale, as part of global processes of capitalist accumulation and organisation. Anthropologists of capitalism combine the two approaches to varying extents; so, some emphasise the processes of political economy that shape labour in similar ways globally,[11] while others resist what they see as an imposition of a singular logic on deeply heterogeneous spaces, lives, understandings and subjectivities.[12]

Many contemporary Marxist anthropologists of capitalism put labour or class at the centre of their study and produce deeply textured local histories of labour that both identify local particularities and focus on common processes, such as accumulation through dispossession, extraction of surplus value, class formation, and the antagonism between capital and labour.[13] This is both a historical and scalar analytical position: a commitment to historical materialism and to understanding the local context within an interconnected world system. It draws upon a particular tradition of work in anthropology, including scholars such as Eric Wolf, Sidney Mintz or Jonathan Friedman. For example, Lesley Gill's book *A Century of Violence in a Red City* (2016) describes the interplay of paramilitary, state and corporate violence in the destruction of the organised working class in the city of Barrancabermeja, Colombia, over the 1980s and 1990s. She connects the local history of labour militancy in the oil industry and the Coca-Cola factory to global processes of class composition and decomposition, accumulation by dispossession, neoliberalism and counterinsurgency that led to the decline of the once strong labour unions and the diversion of their class-based militancy into human rights activism.

Another recent approach, exemplified by the Gens feminist manifesto for the study of capitalism, starts from a perspective of family, kinship and radical heterogeneity, and calls forth an understanding of capitalism that incorporates human-non-human relations, financialisation, temporalities and conversion devices. The Gens manifesto decentres classic topics of labour, value, or exchange; and argues that 'Class does not exist outside of its generation in gender, race, sexuality, and kinship'.[14] In an earlier article, one of the Gens authors, Anna Tsing, argued forcefully that 'diversity is structurally central to global capitalism, and not decoration on a common core'.[15]

Anthropology's distinctiveness as a discipline is that there is more than enough space for both treatments of capitalism. I do not mean to create an artificial antagonism between two camps, since Marxist scholars from Engels onwards have stressed the importance of local historical specificities and grounded their work in a study of class composition as generated through histories of kinship, gender and race relations as well as political economies that play out in both local and global spaces. Likewise, other contemporary scholars of labour integrate their focus on heterogeneity with discussion of linked global processes and political-economic structures, such as global supply chains.[16] However, the distinction I'm identifying does raise questions about scale and global interconnectedness. It makes a difference if we see the 'local' as a slice or segment of processes that operate both on a global scale and quite similarly across the globe; versus looking predominantly for what is distinctive about each local situation and how capitalism touches down differently from place to place, even if those places are understood to be linked globally. Anna Tsing goes so far as to articulate the difference as one between masculinist and feminist approaches to the study of capitalism.[17]

Ideally, we would do both, and so this book attempts to work with both kinds of perspectives, shifting scale continually to seek out similarities and differences across ethnographic contexts, while acknowledging the role of global processes of accumulation, dispossession, dislocation, racialisation, patriarchy, pandemic and so on. I try to contextualise without positing the global situation as entirely deterministic, but also to avoid what I consider to be the opposite sin of considering global context as mere background to local particularities. Therefore, in order to ground my argument about the distinctiveness of a political anthropology of labour agency, I move now to give brief overviews of the global development of post-Fordist labour and associated theories of labour agency and politics. I am summarising what I consider to be hegemonic orienting narratives in order to help me contextualise the chapters that follow. Readers interested in the finer details are invited to follow through the references in the notes section.

To understand the current situation, we can begin the story with the development of Fordist industrial processes in the US and Europe in the early twentieth century and the associated advance of organised labour under social democratic governments in Western Europe after the Second World War (especially in the northern European countries such as the UK, France, Germany, the Netherlands and Scandinavia, but also to some extent in Italy and then later in the century in Spain, Portugal and Greece). Fordism denotes a way of organising production developed in the factories of the Ford Motor Company in Detroit. It is especially associated with the 'standard employment relationship', which Jonathan Parry summarises as: 'premised on stable, full-time jobs. Maximum working hours were regulated; workers were paid not only for days worked but also for periods of recuperation, and were somewhat shielded from arbitrary dismissal. That enabled them to organize in support of their demands.'[18]

Notionally the norm, at least in wealthy Western countries, the standard employment relationship still holds an important affective charge as a way of defining decent work and organising social welfare. In the northern countries of western Europe it was associated with strong labour unions, who protected it for their (mostly male) members and defended the model of the male wage that could support a family. As a result of labour militancy and determined union pressure, channelled through the dialectic of collective bargaining and strikes, unions negotiated relatively good wage rates in what was in reality probably only a minority of workplaces, while strong shop stewards (workplace union officials) improved conditions and prevented the worst excesses of management demands for overwork. Or at least, that was the headline story.[19] Gradually over a period of thirty years, organised labour in northern Europe also gained concessions from the state, mostly run by broadly social democratic governments, and economic growth was accompanied by regulatory control and improvements in workers' rights. Elsewhere in Europe, workers organisations were often active and quite strong but rarely independent of the state.[20]

That period was followed by global retrenchment on the part of capital, starting in the 1970s in alliance with politicians and dictators including General Augusto Pinochet, Margaret Thatcher and Ronald Reagan. The retrenchment centred especially on economic policies of labour flexibilisation and capital mobility, a set of policy prescriptions usually gathered together under the umbrella term 'neoliberalism'. Neoliberal flexibilisation of labour means more precarity for workers, through measures like temporary contracts, use of piecework structures of payment, greater ease of firing, reduced benefits like pensions, holiday and sick pay, and so on. Much of the time, this flexibilisation happened through outsourcing, which enables companies to avoid responsibility for large numbers of those who work for them by subcontracting production to agencies or other manufacturing companies or even chains of companies. Sometimes privatised companies even subcontract to workers they formerly employed. Elana Shever describes the privatisation of the Argentine petrol company YPF, which led to the loss of 43,000 state jobs. A number of those laid-off workers were encouraged to start 'emprendimientos' (i.e. companies providing a service to YPF on a sub-contracted basis). They provided services that involved 'almost everything necessary for petroleum production – from geological imaging and well drilling to pipeline cleaning and paper filing'. The transition from state-employed worker to small business owner was not always smooth, as subcontractors lost salaries and welfare benefits that they had previously enjoyed and took on new responsibilities, like 'negotiating contracts, managing large cash flows, providing insurance, obtaining credit, and paying business tax.'[21]

Neoliberal policies to increase the circulation of capital and attract foreign investment have also been promoted as part of the same package of economic orthodoxy, contributing to the financialisation of the global economy. Financialisation has been characterised by the liberalisation of currency and commodities markets, the growth in financial services at all scales, and the emphasis on shareholder value in corporate governance, among other changes. That mix has created pressure for capital to continually move across the globe in search of cheaper and more docile labour forces; thus disciplining labour forces everywhere. In combination, these developments have resulted in the expansion of the global proletariat. Since the 1970s, two billion people have been added to the world labour market, both as a result of the entry of more women into the paid workforce and China's entry into the world capitalist system, as it developed its manufacturing capacity at an astonishing and seemingly unstoppable rate since the 1990s, and became a member of the WTO in 2001.[22]

In addition, companies have been incentivised to increase investment in extractive industries or agriculture for export, which they have done through evicting millions of rural people from their land, especially during the global commodities boom of the 2010s. These and other 'new enclosures of land, property, commons and rights' are contemporary forms of accumulation by dispossession.[23] In response, people have flocked to industrial areas and the peripheries of cities, seeking economic opportunity or escaping violence, or both. As a population, they form the reserve army in Marx's sense, an available labour force that subsidises capitalist accumulation in multiple ways, from cheapening reproduction so that wages can be kept low and conditions of employment precarious, to contributing to the expansion of the state as the target of state projects of development and violence (invasion, policing, incarceration). Some scholars argue that the urban poor are now a surplus population beyond even that; a population for whom capital has no use, 'cast adrift' and left merely to survive. Others point out that the 'wageless life' of the urban peripheries is how most people across the Global South have sustained life for decades, including in rural areas.[24] It should be said that these processes happen unevenly across the globe: in some regions, labour shortages have led to wage increases, expansion of opportunities for wage labour and betterment of conditions.[25] What we know for sure is that capitalism is a globally linked and spatially uneven system that has developed through dispossession, especially dispossession by means of colonialism. Today, it is experienced through local gendered and racialised histories and cultures of work, class consciousness, coloniality, legal environment, kinship and ritual.

What does this mean for workers? How might people improve their life and work conditions in the shadow of such large-scale forces? One might worry that these developments constrain ordinary working people to the point that resistance based on labouring identity becomes almost impossible, but is that true? These are questions that we must answer ethnographically, not only because the answers vary across geographical and economic context, but also because actions and strategies in search of something better are deeply connected to how people sustain life; their own and the lives of others for whom they are responsible.

Labour agency

The central problem for this book is how to think about labour agency outside of Fordism. I pose the question in those terms not just because Fordist labour processes and their associated politics are less common these days, but also because how we think about labour agency generally has been very strongly shaped by the nature of labour agency under Fordism.

Fordist labour agency is especially associated with trade unions. Indeed, when we speak of the labour movement (in Euro-America especially but not exclusively), we usually think of trade unions, especially industrial trade unions. There are two main sources for this starting assumption: first, the power of social democracy in parts of post-war Europe, and second, Marxist analysis. In northern Europe, industrial trade unions worked with governments of the post-war period to make real the model of the standard employment relationship and family wage, even if in practice the proportion of workers they covered was always quite restricted, especially along gender and racialised lines. Outside of Europe there were a few countries with similarly powerful unions in industrial centres, such as Bolivia, Zambia, South Africa, Argentina and India. Globally, though, work very rarely conformed to these models, and today even in northern Europe we are no longer in a predominantly Fordist economy.

Nonetheless, in those parts of the world where the standard employment relationship of Fordism did once exist, it still holds an affective charge as both object of nostalgia and aspiration for the future, far greater than its extent in reality as a modality of employment.[26] The thirty years of the post-second world war period are known as times when industrial and public sector unions of formal workers enjoyed considerable political power, both through political pressure on governments and in systems of corporatist co-government (including in some of the dictatorships of southern Europe). Known in French as 'les trentes glorieuses' or the 'glorious thirty', they were also years of economic growth in northern Europe at least.

A second contributory factor to the tendency to emphasise industrial labour and its trade unions is the role of Marxist analysis of the relationship between labour and capital. Marx formulated that problematic in writing that focused specifically on conditions in the factories during the first century of the English industrial revolution. He did not analyse how the workers might respond to such conditions in much detail. His most substantive discussion of worker agency is in *Capital* Volume I chapter 10 where he describes the struggle for the ten-hour working day; he also mentions moves against child labour. In *The Poverty of Philosophy*, one of his earlier political works, he ends with a discussion of 'combination' as resistance, through workers collectives that he defines as trade unions and political parties. In *Capital* Volume I, the struggle to shorten the working day is portrayed first as a struggle determined by the way that surplus value is extracted from the labourer by the capitalist (i.e. it is inevitable, structurally determined) and second as a problem that is resolved somehow through legislation. Marx grants a big role to the factory inspectors, from whose reports he got much of his information, but he stops at the point where legislation is implemented to reduce the working day. He does not ask whether capitalists actually follow the rules, nor does he explore the strategies they develop to evade the rules. In addition, he focuses on what we can think of as institutional political spaces – the factory, the trade union, the political party. That emphasis carries through to the political project of the *Communist Manifesto*, where it is accompanied by a sense of the inevitability of struggle as an outcome of (structural) class antagonism between proletariat and bourgeoisie. The *Communist Manifesto* also introduces the notion of the political agency of labour as revolutionary and the proletariat as the principal actor in the future revolution. The important points here are the emphasis on the male industrial worker as the key figure of political agency, on political institutions as the key channel for agency, and on revolution as the key modality of political agency.

Yet debates within Marxist analysis also provide us with ideas for how to displace the industrial worker as the central conceptual figure in our theories of labour agency. Orthodox Marxists tended to describe how capitalist development affected workers, creating the conditions for agency and putting workers at the mercy of capital. They were challenged by the autonomous Marxists in 1960s Italy, who instead focused on how workers' resistance provokes a response from capital and drives cycles of capitalist development. Their approach was to theorise through the triad of class composition, decomposition and recomposition. They argued that class composition is both technical and political: technical referring to the relation to the means of production and the organisation of the labour process, as with Marxism more broadly, while political 'names the formal and informal modes of organization and forms of struggle deployed by workers against this process, consciously or otherwise'.[27]

This approach underlined how class composition can change as a result of shifts in the economy (technical composition) but also how that will produce different kinds of action (political composition). To give an example, in regions where heavy industries disappear as major employers and are replaced by call centres or care homes, the working class will decompose as industrial workers are laid off, but then recompose itself into a new formation, with a new political expression. The historian Gabriel Winant describes this situation for Pittsburgh, where the steel industry dominant in the early twentieth century declined in the latter half of the century, shedding thousands of jobs. Because this happened through younger people not being employed and then outmigrating, rather than older workers being laid off, the population as a whole gradually aged, and because the steel jobs had been well paid, they were mostly well insured. As a result of the interplay between these demographic and economic conditions and the welfare state, the healthcare industry boomed; and the steel jobs were effectively replaced as working-class jobs by nursing assistants, hospital workers, home carers and so on. This new working class is more African American and more female than the steelworkers.[28] Their employment conditions are much poorer, their jobs low paid and precarious. Their political expression is more fragmentary and tentative than the steelworkers' was, channelled partly through service sector unions but also facing challenges of racism, dispersal and the need to survive.[29]

Following Gus Carbonella and Sharryn Kasmir, we could say that dispossession is one of the mechanisms that produces class decomposition, a form of class struggle from above.[30] Composition and recomposition are class struggles from below. One of the most important insights from autonomous Marxism is the call precisely to look at these struggles from below. Capital adapts to labour as well as labour adapting to capital. This unequal but two-sided struggle is a major part of what drives capitalist development. We can see this in Beverley Silver's description of the automobile industry, which spread across the globe over the twentieth century, from the US in the 1910s and 20s to Western Europe in the 1950s, Brazil and South Africa in the 1960s, South Korea and Japan in the 1970s and then to China from the 1990s onwards.[31] Geographical relocation of this kind is often called the 'spatial fix', a concept first developed by David Harvey, and it is motivated by capital's search for cheap and disciplined labour.[32] But

Silver argues that the moves were also – and perhaps mainly – a response to the emergence of strong and effective labour movements in each site.

The emphasis in Marxist analysis remains on class as the engine for workers' political agency. However, the decentring of the European industrial worker from our imaginations of worker agency has also changed how we think of class. In the 1970s and 1980s, Black Marxists pointed out the complexities of the racialised capitalist world system (which does appear as a hint in the very last chapter of *Capital* Volume I) and argued, in Cedric Robinson's words, that: 'Marx and Engels's theory of revolution was insufficient in scope: the European proletariat and its social allies did not constitute *the* revolutionary subject of history, nor was working-class consciousness necessarily *the* negation of bourgeois culture.'[33] Robinson argues instead that other revolutionary subjects emerged in the resistance to colonial oppression, especially in Africa. Importantly, anti-colonial revolts and slave rebellions were struggles against capital as well as struggles against colonialism.

Around the same time, Marxist feminists critiqued conventional Marxism's under-recognition of the role of social reproduction in the reproduction of capitalism.[34] That critique highlighted women's reproductive agency outside of the factory and incorporated gender into theories of labour and labour agency. Feminists of all stripes pointed out women's work not only in social reproduction but also in conventional production, in factories, fields and other workplaces. They challenged the organisation of society through heteronormativity and the nuclear family, and argued that resistance to those norms is also a form of resistance against capital, indeed that the two must go together.[35] Contemporary work focuses on the intersections between questions of race, class and gender in oppression and in our response to oppression.[36]

These developments are not just about pluralising our concept of who the agent is, but also about pluralising the kinds of agency that we see and acknowledge. To see the effect of this, we might turn to the debates in the 1960s–1980s about the nature of political agency among peasants, an early example of this kind of pluralising in anthropological scholarship. Most Marxist theorists, with the important exception of Maoists, had largely ignored peasant political agency because of their focus on the industrial proletariat. They thought that peasant societies simply lacked class consciousness and held deeply conservative values, a perspective shared by many conservative and non-Marxist scholars. However, the 1950s and 1960s saw multiple peasant-led rebellions in South America and Vietnam, as well as anti-colonial struggles more broadly, and so radical anthropologists began to argue that peasant rebellion and even revolution was entirely feasible.[37] Then, as the revolutions seemed to fizzle out by the mid-1980s, the anthropologist and political scientist James Scott argued that to focus only on rebellions was to miss much more widespread and everyday forms of resistance in the countryside, which he described at the outset of his book as a constant but not overtly defiant struggle against extraction, waged through 'ordinary weapons': 'foot dragging, dissimulation, false compliance, pilfering, feigned ignorance, slander, arson, sabotage, and so forth.' They were, he said, often a form of 'individual self-help', 'the tenacity of self-preservation ... the steady, grinding efforts to hold one's own against overwhelming odds' and he argued that we should celebrate them as 'a spirit and practice that prevents the worst and promises something better'.[38]

Scott was critiqued for his rather bleak prognosis for the prospects of rebellion and for peasant agency as capable of transforming rather than merely adapting to historical conditions.[39] But his call to acknowledge the very varied forms of resistance other than rebellion is an important one. We might not consider practices of 'individual self-help' or 'the tenacity of self preservation' to be precisely resistance in the way that Scott did, but I would argue that they are forms of political agency, especially insofar as they are mobilised in order to care for others. A complementary way of thinking about the different kinds of everyday political agency I am working with here is Alf Lüdtke's idea of *Eigen-Sinn*, which was developed more for industrial workers. Lüdtke summarised *Eigen-Sinn* in the glossary of an important collection he edited as 'denoting willfulness, spontaneous self-will, a kind of self-affirmation, an act of (re)appropriating alienated social relations on and off the shop floor by self-assertive prankishness, demarcating a space of one's own. ... [a] prankish, stylized, misanthropic distancing from all constraints or incentives.'[40] We can also think with the concepts found in the titles of two historical ethnographies: Don Kalb's 'everyday politics' and Susana Narotsky and Gavin Smith's 'immediate struggles'.[41] Both studies explore in depth how specific groups of workers have responded to structural economic developments over the course of a century or so. The challenge I take from all these ideas is to explore how autonomous and agentive action is present even if constrained by exploitative structures, and even if it does not look as we would expect it to look.

When thinking about labour agency in today's non-Fordist and mostly neoliberal world, we must acknowledge the often-overwhelming power of the long and varied processes of dispossession of the poor and class struggle waged from above. But if we seek workers' political agency only in relatively formalised and overt forms of resistance to oppression – in formal unions or political parties, collective action at the chokepoints of production, or in a specific understanding of class consciousness – we risk a kind of analytical foreclosure as well as political despondency. If instead we set out to examine the agentive possibilities in the everyday politics of workers' lives, what we find is a huge range, from resistance to accommodation to escape and everything in between. We see collective action in organised and disorganised modes, we see action by individuals or households, and by extended kinship networks. And we realise that much of what drives that is the desire to be able to sustain and care for others.

What is distinctive about an anthropological approach to labour agency?

This then is a commitment to look at what is there rather than what is missing. This is uncontroversial for anthropologists, and indeed probably the central methodological commitment of our discipline. If labour agency is more complex than a relatively predictable enactment of class consciousness, rebellion or resistance would suggest, if it does not always fit within a mould designed for a very particular European context, then ethnography can tell us what shapes labour agency in its political sense, both individual and collective, across the globe. An anthropological approach does not simply open up new spaces of action to scholarly scrutiny but is also shaped by a political commitment to pay proper attention to what ordinary people do and say, the stance of radical compassion that I mentioned at the outset of this introduction. The chapters that follow explore these questions for labour in multiple economic sectors. Before summarising them, I introduce some cross-cutting themes that emerge from an anthropological and ethnographic approach, and present the definition of work that animates this book.

The first cross-cutting theme is power, specifically the relation between social-economic structure and individual and collective experience. The sociologist Erik Olin Wright distinguished between working class 'associational power' and 'structural power'. He defined the former as 'the various forms of power that result from the formation of collective organisations of workers' and he did not confine that definition to unions and parties, but also included works councils, representation on boards, and some community organisations. Structural power, in contrast, 'results simply from the location of workers within the economic system' and can refer to things like tight labour markets or strategic location; as for example where workers can shut down an important mine, power station or network of roads.[42]

At a local level, structural questions such as labour supply and regulatory environment influence the possibilities for workers' agency. Where labour markets are quite fluid, workers might find it easier either to move to a different job or negotiate better conditions in their existing job (as happened in some logistics work in the immediate post-Covid period). Conversely, power flows the other way to constrain agency as capital's fluidity allows it to move to locations where labour is cheaper or more docile, or to threaten to move as a means of disciplining workers. Where unions can function legally and free from repression and cooptation, they are stronger than where that is not possible. In some parts of the world unions also have a long history of political power, which has translated into better legislation on labour rights and unions' own operating environment. Examples of places like this include Argentina and South Africa, although we must remember that legislation does not automatically grant on the ground power to improve or protect conditions. Conversely, unions might be entirely coopted, such as in the industrial belts of China, or legislation may make it very difficult to unionise specific workplaces, like in the US. Or protest might be violently repressed, and union leaders persecuted, making collective action almost impossible. In such instances, workers need to develop other kinds of agency outside of the trade union.

Another structural feature that shapes agency and that appears in different ways throughout this book is the nature of the workplace: large places that concentrate many workers like factories, steel plants, mines or government offices may enable more formalised kinds of collective organisation. Where people work in their own home (e.g. for piecework like garment stitching, or home-based digital labour), or in someone else's (in care work or other kinds of domestic labour), they are more fragmented and traditional unions have a harder job reaching them. In such contexts, kin or friendship networks might be other ways of channelling support and action. Other workers might be out on the streets on their own (e.g. an Uber driver or Deliveroo rider) or with others (in a street market), which creates problems of fragmentation but also particular possibilities for being collective, both in the streets and online. Workers' agency also depends a great deal on what kind of employment relationship they are in, another broadly structural factor. It makes a difference if you are formally registered with a permanent contract, or you are working as an independent contractor, for day rates, piece rates or on another kind of short-term contract. Informal and patchy income generation, unpaid work for subsistence or social reproduction, all shape opportunities for action.

Labour is also structured in gendered and raced ways, which enable and constrain agency. In this book I explore some of the multiple ways that workers are divided by gender and race, segmented into particular sectors of work, shaped by norms and expectations of what's appropriate, or in jobs that have specific employment conditions that are enabled by racialised and gendered vulnerabilities (e.g. care work). One of the most important themes here is migration, both transnational and from rural to urban areas, which interacts with capitalist systems at all scales to cheapen labour and shape what is possible in response. In most places, migrants are the most exploited sectors of the working class, and migrant labour is a particular example of how ethnography can help us understand how people navigate exploitative systems. One important insight, for example, is that migrants do not necessarily see themselves doing those most exploitative jobs for a long time, and that people's expectations shift according to where they are in their life cycle and what they hope to do in the future. This is often related to how people feel about their responsibility to their kin, usually as central to migration strategies as economic considerations are. All these questions of responsibility, life cycle and available economic opportunities are deeply gendered.

On a more subjective level, ethnography prompts us to look at feelings of autonomy and control as well as vulnerability and exploitation. What kinds of conditions of work do people want? Does everyone want a formal job based on the standard employment relationship or do they experience that as working for someone who controls how they use their time and their body, and therefore negative?[43] Of course, much depends on level of income, but that isn't the only factor. People's aspirations to own a small business or to work from home could be as much about their desire for autonomy in their working life as about a kind of neoliberal entrepreneurialism. Those we view as 'surplus population' expelled by capitalism might not wish to be incorporated into the capitalist system under the conditions that are open to them. For example, Franco Barchiesi argues that under colonial regimes, African workers sometimes preferred casual employment to wage labour, especially once they realised that the wage was not to be conferred on them under conditions of equality with Europeans. They resisted becoming the 'orderly and productive industrial men' that the colonial governments desired.[44]

Ethnography can therefore also show how prevailing cultural attitudes to work shape our agency. The philosopher Kathi Weeks argues that the demands of post-Fordist work in the US have made it especially necessary for workers to create a kind of subjectivity that sees work as self-realisation. Non-industrial work, she argues, requires more than merely workers' 'submission and sacrifice' but cognitive, communicative and emotional labour, as well as 'flexibility, adaptability, and continual reinvention'. In contemporary labour structures it is also harder to measure workers' compliance. When an individual's contribution to a collective production effort is difficult to make out, employers move to evaluating workers' 'character' and commitment as a proxy; equally when workers are dispersed across sites (e.g. in other people's homes) then a cultural emphasis on values of commitment to work make possible discipline without direct surveillance. As a result, over time, the Weberian work ethic that valorised work as a religious commitment has morphed into a work ethic that requires devotion to work *in its own right*. At least for some parts of the labour hierarchy (Weeks argues, at the top), 'work is expected to be the whole of life, colonizing and eclipsing what remains of the social'. This affects our subjectivity and our sociality: people develop their friendship and kinship networks through work, we work long hours, we blur the distinction between work and leisure spatially and temporally, and many of us at least tell ourselves that all this is because we identify so strongly with our professional identity.[45] The US is a particularly acute example of this ethic of work, but it may be recognisable to many of us, who could do well to remember the title of a recently published book: *Work won't love you back*, by Sarah Jaffe.[46]

What does this mean for how we understand work today?

An anthropology of labour agency must pay careful attention to how different people understand work, and I try not to fall in the trap I outlined earlier of thinking through Fordist, industrial assumptions. But what does that mean for the vision of labour that animates this book? To answer that, in this section I address two important distinctions: between paid and unpaid work, and between material and immaterial products of labour. I then suggest that we think about the politics of labour as producing relations of care.[47]

If, as I have argued, our archetype of work is industrial labour, one serious risk is that of missing or downplaying those kinds of labour that do not produce material goods and are not conducted within a relationship of employment. Although in this book I do at times distinguish between paid and unpaid work, I do not mean to suggest that unpaid work is lesser, or somehow not 'real' work. Quite the opposite. I use the distinction to highlight how much of human action I consider to be work. For me, work means those activities human beings undertake to provision themselves, their households and their communities to produce life.

Throughout the book, I use the terms 'labour' and 'work' interchangeably, as I have in this introduction. With both, I refer to what Susana Narotsky summarises so well as 'the forms in which energy is expended, co-ordinated and organised in order to sustain life and make it worth living'; to which I would add a phrase from another essay, where she and her co-author Niko Besnier speak of 'sustaining life *across generations*' (my emphasis).[48] Even if they do not involve the direct exchange of money, all of the types of work that I discuss in this book articulate in some way with capital. This means that they do, to some extent, also conform with the more restricted Marxist definition of 'living labour', summarised effectively by Kathi Weeks as 'a collective and creative human capacity harnessed by capital to the production of surplus value'.[49] But not all are waged, and only a minority are productive in the most conventional sense of producing use or exchange value in goods. Thus, I start not from how labour sustains capital but from how people expend effort to sustain their lives and the lives of those they love.

Given this intentionally broad definition of the nature of work, I find it helpful throughout the chapters that follow to retain a thematic focus on the products of labour. It is the products of our labour that shape the nature of our labour, and it is important to recognise their variety. In Euro-America today, more people than ever before work to produce immaterial 'goods', such as knowledge, affects, communication, collaboration or relations. Hardt and Negri described immaterial labour – which they divided into intellectual and affective – as 'labour that creates not only material goods but also relationships and ultimately social life itself'. In their discussion, they located the quality of immateriality in the product of labour not its process: affective labour might well be very material in the sense of physical (for example care work involves highly material tasks) but it mainly produces feelings of well-being, of being looked after, and the relation itself.[50] Both they and other key theorists of immaterial labour stress that the material and immaterial are always mixed together.[51] The anthropologist Silvia Yanagisako for example has pointed out how classically 'material' production in industries relies on communicational work including relationship building, intellectual design labour and so on.[52]

Nonetheless, I want to retain the distinction between immaterial and material labour because it helps to conceptualise what kinds of agency are possible for workers, especially since our classic understanding of labour agency has been so strongly associated with material labour processes and products. In material production processes it is easier to find chokepoints to strike at in order to halt production or distribution of goods, while immaterial labour relies upon non-linear relationships of distributed networks and production in common, and its time stretches outside of the workplace and working day.[53]

And, if your work is precisely about producing a relationship, especially one of care, it often goes beyond an employer-employee relationship. Affective labour can be deeply alienating, as you need to convince yourself that you feel the necessary emotions to care for your client, patient or student, or it can pull you in to those very relationships.[54] Where our work produces love, care, people and relations, we can't always just stop doing it in order to threaten our employer's profitability. If what we are producing is life itself, how do we pause that?

Except that curiously, some of us may not even be convinced that we are working to produce something of value. In a very popular essay and subsequent book, David Graeber suggested that large numbers of people are doing jobs that they consider to be largely worthless, what he called 'bullshit jobs'. He thought that these might include jobs in sectors like 'financial services, telemarketing … corporate law, academic and health administration, human resources and public relations' and suggested that their only purpose is to grow finance capital.[55] In Graeber's formulation, the bullshit job is a subjective category because it requires people to feel that their job is pointless, and subsequent empirical studies have questioned to what extent that is true.[56] But the essay makes an important point about how we value different kinds of labour, what we perceive to be labour that makes a 'meaningful contribution to the world' and how that is rewarded. Graeber suggests that in the North Atlantic at least, jobs that provide social value are usually undercompensated and often feminised. What they have in common, he argues, is that they are based in caring for others.

We might do well to see care for others as key to how we think about labour beyond its role as production for capital. On a personal level, relatively few of us see our labour as purely in order to produce profit for our employer or for our business if we are self-employed. For most except the very wealthy, our labour is the way we create the material conditions to produce our lives and care for those we love. As Andrew Sanchez argues, we may gain satisfaction with our work when it allows us to transform the world around us in some way.[57] We may also see it as a means to an end; at its most basic, the ability to continue with our life in this world, something that necessarily involves others for most of us. Human beings do this through multiple kinds of waged labour (from hourly rates to permanent contract), through piecework, welfare benefits, small enterprises. We make things, grow things, sell things, clean things, deliver things, write about things, meet people, clean people, feed people, manage people, entertain people, gather people, propitiate people, propitiate spirits, feed spirits, feed animals ... and so on. This book only manages to capture a small part of this variety, and it does so in order to explore the politics that arises out of the work we do – the effort we expend – in our everyday lives, even if we don't at first think of it as labour. I focus principally on the part of labour politics that revolves around trying to create better conditions for our work. Another very important labour politics that is, for now, outside the scope of this book takes shape as a politics of working less, like the campaigns for universal basic income, four-day weeks, or generous parental leave from waged employment.

I acknowledge that there is a danger in making everything into labour and expanding its definition so that in the end nothing falls outside. Still, my hope is that the risk is only (or mainly) a problem for my analytical and political goals if we imagine labour predominantly as a market relation, and do not allow ourselves to conceive of it as voluntarily given outside of the market. At any rate, my main aim here is to identify what kinds of politics arise from the different kinds of labour that I've identified. The idea of 'radical compassion' that I have presented as a methodological and political orientation for my writing might well also serve to name those kinds of politics that arise from relations of care in labour. That is to say, seeing labour insofar as it produces relations of care in a broad sense brings into our analysis different kinds of radical politics and worker agency from those that arise out of class consciousness and alienation.

The coronavirus pandemic has brought these issues to the foreground for many of us. Questions about the social value of labour became particularly prominent as in the UK we clapped NHS workers and classified jobs and workers as 'essential', 'critical' or 'key'. It seemed initially as though we might as a society be recalibrating the way we value different kinds of labour. Yet at the same time many people were made vulnerable to the virus precisely because of the conditions in their workplace or the nature of their job. Globally, billions of people were unable to shield themselves from the virus because of how they made a living. What will this mean for the future of labour? The chapters in this book are based on research conducted and mostly written up in pre-pandemic times. They should be read as a baseline to see what effects the pandemic might have on labour and workers' agency in the future: will it deepen already existing longer-term trends or be a catalyst for change?

Structure of the book

My exploration of contemporary workers' agency and its relation to global political economy, local conditions and labour process is divided across different sectors of the economy, from heavy industry to social reproduction. Thus, this book is an exploration of the different kinds of agency that emerge out of multiple and diverse kinds of work: formal and informal; employed and self-employed (and everything in between); paid and unpaid; physical, affective, emotional, embodied and reproductive. Throughout, I use ethnographic examples from across the world, although my own research expertise (in Latin America, especially Argentina and Bolivia) and personal experience does at times balance the book more in favour of anglophone literature and examples from Europe and the Americas. Further readings can be found by following the links at www.sianlazar.org where readers are invited to contribute their own suggestions.

The chapters discuss a series of dilemmas in each sector of the economy, exploring questions such as what are the consequences of the division between permanent and temporary workers? Is agency only found in resistance, or can we speak of accommodation and escape as forms of agency? How does gender shape labour agency? How do our preconceptions about what labour is shape our understanding of labour agency? Does it make a difference if workers are producing immaterial rather than material goods? Each chapter deploys different scales of analysis, beginning with an overview of the global political economy for each sector and exploring some of the most relevant interconnections and changes since the mid-twentieth century. The chapters then move to the more intimate scale of experience, reading ethnographies to tease out what they can tell us about embodied experiences of labour. At times, that has been the main aim of the ethnographic work that I discuss, but in other cases it has involved reading alongside the author's main argument about concepts like financialisation, debt, care, selfhood, class, global commodity chains, plantation economies, or bureaucracy; illustrating the beauty of ethnography as a method that opens up multiple avenues for analysis, not all of which were anticipated by the author. The final section of each chapter explores labour agency as I have defined it in this introduction, tying together political economy and embodied experience with ethnographies of collective and individual action.

My view of labour agency is thus expansive, referring simply to how workers act to improve their working conditions. My discussion does privilege collective action and resistance, but I also bring in more individualised and fragmentary forms of agency, as well as collective and individual action that is resilient or accommodating rather than directly resistant or revolutionary. My commitment to include these kinds of actions comes from the methodological and political commitment to a radical compassion for what people do in real life, acknowledging multiplicity and failure as well as moments of unity and success.

Chapter 1 begins with 'heavy' industry, the archetypal space for workers' political agency according to orthodox Marxism. Drawing on examples mostly from steel plants and mines, I start by telling the story of changes in industrial labour over recent decades and their impacts on people's lives. The question of precarity is key to resistant agency in the remaining industries of the post-Fordist period. It brings to the fore issues of generation and kinship as well as temporality. As the timescapes of industrial workplaces continually shift, work has intensified, and contracts are no longer open-ended and secure. Fathers have seen a decline in their earning power and their political heft, as unions have often focused on protecting those still in secure jobs. Their sons are in precarious, subcontracted employment which is increasingly scarce and vulnerable. These days, imaginations of escape, such as the dream of becoming small business owners, characterise agency as much as collective action through unions does.

Chapter 2 focuses on 'light' industry, another material production process, but one spread across factory sites and home work. The two industries I discuss are electronics manufacture and garment stitching. The distinction between 'light' and 'heavy' is rather artificial, and one might equally distinguish between industries seeing a decline in the size of their labour force and those growing. Alternatively, one might distinguish along gendered lines, as these 'light' industries are especially associated with women workers. A key theme of the chapter is how exploitation is made possible through gender, and – because the industries are also highly reliant on migrant labour – race and rural-urban relations. Those structural questions make resistance difficult, but not impossible, and the chapter highlights the complexities of agency under very exploitative conditions.

In Chapter 3, I shift focus to the rural regions that produce and reproduce the workers who migrate to cities or industrial areas for manufacturing jobs, and I explore the possibilities for resistance and other kinds of agency within agricultural labour. In most countries, agriculture is probably the sector of the economy that has historically seen the most exploitative labour and property relations, from feudalism through plantation slavery and debt peonage to contemporary agribusiness. Political economies of agrarian labour must consider questions of land concentration, migration and plantation economies, while ethnographies have explored local experiences of these broader structures and more subjective questions of how farming makes persons – and how that changes with different crops and according to gender – and how peasants live with uncertainty. The chapter responds to James Scott's call to attend to peasants' experiences between the two poles of rebellion and traditionalism, revealing a more complex picture of political agency.

I then move to less traditional subjects for anthropological discussions of workers' agency, with a focus in Chapter 4 on the service sector, in Chapter 5 on professionals and managers, and in Chapter 6 on platform labour. Chapter 4 explores workers' agency within immaterial labour through the examples of affective labour in call centres and paid care (including domestic work and sex work), work which is predominantly coded as female. Gender was largely absent from early theories of worker resistance, and affective labour shows how its consideration fleshes out our understanding of what is possible for workers. The often-fragmentary nature of care workplaces makes traditional organising difficult, and people can be utterly vulnerable because they are hired through informal relationships to work in intimate spaces. They are employed to produce customer affects and relations, and those relations are the medium of their labour as much as its product. Ethnographies underline precisely how material and physical this labour process is (it is the 'product' that is not material), and reveal how in producing relations, affective workers also produce particular senses of self. The combination can make collective organisation more effective, when workers can argue that they are defending community, and less effective if they are reluctant to harm their clients. Often worker agency is individualised, and a mix between accommodation, escape and resistance.

Chapter 5 explores a different part of the service economy, with a focus on more middle-class occupations. Professional and managerial work is also affective and immaterial labour, and relations are the medium and product of that labour. In this chapter I focus particularly on how highly paid affective labourers like financial services workers, management consultants, bureaucrats and academics produce knowledge, information and relations but also selves, outputs and processes. The story of agency is complicated by the nature of workers' identities as professionals, and their (our) overidentification with work, which might be the contemporary but dysfunctional opposite to alienation. Tenured academics and other professionals have a privileged status, which can mean that many do not see themselves as workers in a political sense and are content with their labour conditions, especially when they enjoy permanent contracts and high salaries. Yet it can also mean that, particularly in the public sector, a more secure legislative structure and employment relation enables collective action like strikes and union organising.

In Chapter 6 I move to a newer form of work, that organised through digital platforms. Although absolute numbers of digital workers are currently small, it is a type of labour that is growing in importance, and is likely to have significant influence in the future. Platform labour is the most recent iteration of piecework: the worker is ostensibly an independent contractor making multiple individual arrangements with clients mediated via the platform. Qualitative scholarship about platform labour, including some ethnographies, highlights questions of worker autonomy, alienation, fragmentation and algorithmic management, all of which shape possibilities for agency. Perhaps surprisingly, workers who have been able to join together in physical space have started to have an impact, through making alliances with traditional and newer trade unions and in some instances pursuing legal cases alongside strike activism and street mobilisation. Dispersed digital workers have found it less easy to press their concerns, but still make community and evolve strategies to 'prevent the worst and promise something better' in Scott's words.[58]

The theme of precarity continues through into the Chapter 7, where I examine the ways of sustaining life that are common in urban peripheries of the Global South, among the surplus population that has so concerned scholars. Michael Denning's statement that 'capitalism begins not with the offer of work but with the imperative to earn a living'[59] is my starting point here, and this and the following chapter turn explicitly to (mostly) non-waged work. I call this 'patchwork living', as people patch together different forms of making a living, including street vending, welfare transfers, waste picking, political work, loans, work for day rates, transport, the circulation of debt and so on. In doing so, they often evade regulation, either deliberately or because they cannot be regulated. Their lives are not necessarily entirely wage free but nor are they characterised by the model of a secure male wage that on its own supports a nuclear family until the children are old enough to move away; a model that was of course only ever available to a select few in the north anyway. They are a product of structural adjustment, migration and urbanisation in the Global South and punitive neoliberal welfare policies in the Global North. Ethnographies reveal concerns of temporalities, kinship and autonomy; and these labour identities produce a mix of collective politics and individual and family resilience.

The patchwork labourers of Chapter 7 are entangled in a politics focused not so much on the production of goods (material or immaterial) but on the circulation and distribution of goods and resources and the production of life itself. Chapter 8 takes the exploration of the production of life itself further, into the theme of social reproduction labour. Social reproduction is woven into all of the labour considered in this book; not least because most people work not for their employer's profit but to live well, feed, educate and care for their loved ones. My focus in this chapter is especially on the labour involved in mostly unpaid care, and I bring together ethnographies of care and a discussion of the work of care with a consideration of the ways that people act to improve their lives with others. I argue that social reproduction labour produces activism around care, urban life, the public sector, and for life itself. Unsurprisingly, the analysis is permeated throughout with a consideration of gender, constructed in particular racialised and heteronormative ways.

My main aim in this book is to explore the multiple types of action for something better that emerge out of different ways of structuring work, and so the chapters all in some way speak to the multiplicity of strategies and responses that workers create. The conclusion returns to some of the cross-cutting themes and dilemmas, and is followed by a coda that considers some of the ways that the Covid-19 pandemic might affect the labour of making life in the future, asking what that could mean for struggles to make work liveable in a post-pandemic world.

1

Heavy Industry and Post-Fordist Precarities

This chapter begins my exploration of the relation between global political economy, local conditions, labour process and labour agency in the archetypal proletarian spaces of large factories or plants. I focus on steel production and mining. Heavy industry is important because of the ways that we have conventionally thought of labour politics in Euro-American academia and public life; ways that are conditioned by Fordism, although not peculiar to the Fordist period. Since Marx, the industrial proletariat has been considered the key political subject, with male factory workers, miners and other industrial labourers imagined to be the most typical representatives of the European and North American working classes. Class consciousness has been understood most strongly through the experience of (Fordist) production processes and (male) manual labour in mines and factories, at docks and furnaces.

As I explained in the introduction, our expectations of labour politics and perhaps even democracy itself have been shaped by a specific strand of collective politics associated with those places where trade unions came to hold significant political power as social democracy developed in post-Second World War northern Europe.[1] With the decline of these manufacturing spaces and their associated trade unions, labour politics itself has seemed to be in potentially terminal decline. In fact, as the remaining chapters in this book show, there is plenty of labour-based political activity across non-industrial sectors. Still, in the centres of northern Europe the powerful trade unions of the post-war social democratic consensus have suffered significant decline since the 1970s, as have their industries. In eastern Europe the post-socialist period saw a similar decline in the power of workers' organisations. In the USA, unions that were powerful in industrial areas declined with deindustrialisation, and globally, similar processes took place with the implementation of neoliberal structural adjustment programmes. All this has in turn shaped how scholars and activists perceive possibilities for worker agency. The examples in this chapter include India, Zambia, Egypt and Kazakhstan as well as eastern Europe, and so constitute a view from the periphery.

Labour processes within heavy industries are embedded in different localised cultural, social and historical patterns, practices or structures, that have taken shape as a result of global reorganisations of heavy industries in recent decades. I ask how these processes have changed, what impact that has had on people's lives, and what that means for labour politics. Specifically, I examine the consequences of these changes for workers and their families through ethnographies of family and temporalities, followed by a discussion of class identity. The animating dilemma for my analysis of labour agency in this chapter is a political one that revolves around the division between permanent and temporary workers: how should workers act when the availability and quality of work is constricting? Is it a problem if the 'labour aristocracy' of permanent workers defend their position at the expense of temporary workers?

Global changes

Steel plants are symbolic of modernist government: for much of the twentieth century, nationalised or heavily subsidised; established to serve grand state projects of infrastructure development because of the role of steel in construction; and organised in company towns (e.g. Jamshedpur in India), or at least dominating male employment in industrial regions (as in the case of Teesside in the UK, or the Ruhr valley in Germany). In the UK, the decline of steel is, alongside coal mining, iconic of processes of deindustrialisation in the north of England and Wales that are especially associated in popular imagination with the politics of the 1980s. Elsewhere in western Europe, production has remained relatively stable (Germany, Italy, France) or grown somewhat (Spain), but as the global demand for steel has risen, the big story is the rise to dominance of China and India as production sites, and Chinese and Indian companies as global commercial operators.

The 1990s saw significant shifts in dominant international policy approaches to steel and other heavy industries. The global neoliberal dogma of anti-protectionism and labour flexibilisation was justified by the idea that reducing tariffs on imported steel (and other goods) would enable goods to be traded freely around the globe. In theory that leads to competition and therefore reduces costs, as those countries with a comparative advantage can produce steel more cheaply and export it at nearer to cost price, yet still turning a profit for the owners. In turn, the least efficient – and more expensive – steel plants would not be able to compete in such a global market and therefore go out of business, leading overall efficiency to rise and costs to fall, and resulting in economic growth. Neoliberal technocrats preached this gospel in international institutions like the World Trade Organization (WTO) and the International Monetary Fund (IMF), even for a time the World Bank. They advised governments on how best to manage their transition to liberal capitalism and promoted very similar economic policies across the world.[2]

The language of 'efficiency' and 'comparative advantage' deployed by these free-market economists obscures the real-world processes by which both were achieved, which included 'labour flexibility' – another technocratic phrase that hides a multitude of sins. 'Labour flexibility' refers to reduced protections for workers: making it easier to fire them, using outsourcing and temporary work contracts, reducing welfare benefits and unemployment protections, constraining what counts as legal political action and so on. In Eastern Bloc countries, steel plants were affected by the transition from socialism to capitalism, which brought with it pressures to retrench labour costs by reducing the numbers of the permanent workforce and making flexible the jobs of the rest. In India, economic liberalisation took off with a series of measures in 1991, prompted in part by the IMF; in Zambia, labour law reform in the 1990s was associated with the conditionality of structural adjustment loans.[3] In Egypt, structural adjustment programmes from 1991 were intensified in 2003 when a law allowing for temporary contracting in the public sector was finally passed, affecting nationally owned steel plants.[4] More recently, in the UK the steel industry saw a loss of 7,000 jobs in six months from September 2015 to March 2016, when Sahaviriya Steel Industries closed their plant in Redcar, Teesside and Tata reduced capacity at their Port Talbot plant and sold their Scunthorpe site.[5]

Neoliberal policy doctrine allowed steel companies to drop production in some parts of the globe and increase in others, making for a global rebalancing of steel production towards East Asia. In 1967, China produced about a tenth of the steel produced by the US or the USSR, while in 2016, it produced 50 per cent of the world's steel, nearly 8 times the amount of the second largest producer, Japan. This is in a context of overall growth of steel production over the last 50 years of over 300 per cent.[6] The global rebalancing can be viewed as a 'spatial fix' that took place over a long period of time. The 'spatial fix' is an idea developed by David Harvey to describe how neoliberal policies of capital mobility have enabled capital to cope with crises of profitability (or merely continue to increase profits) by moving manufacturing to parts of the world where production is cheaper (usually – but not only – because labour is cheaper).[7] In heavy industries the spatial fix has been a slower process than in manufacturing.

The spatial fix or global rebalancing has combined with what Beverley Silver calls the 'technological fix' of reorganising the production process using labour-saving technologies.[8] In particular, mechanisation has enabled bosses to employ fewer workers. For example, Tommaso Trevisani describes changes in the oxygen shop of the crushing and shorting factory at the ArcelorMittal steel plant in Temirtau, Kazakhstan: tasks were outsourced to a German company that installed a 'fully automatized air separation factory' that employed 15 highly skilled workers, compared to 227 employed before its closure and 450 in 1993. The process is now managed from headquarters in the Czech Republic, via the internet. In contrast, much of the rest of the crushing and sorting factory has resisted outsourcing and maintains reliance upon Soviet-era technology; workers' practical knowledge of obsolete machinery protects them from redundancies.[9] In the Estonian mine described by Eeva Kesküla, new technology enabled greater productivity and intensified the tempo of work for miners; it also created new relationships between workers, skill and machinery. Service workers previously employed locally to repair the machines began to, as Kesküla puts it, 'los[e] their role as the creative developers and carers for the equipment, the doctors of machines', as mine managers decided that the more complex machines required specialist maintenance better provided by the manufacturer of the machine under a licence deal for service and repair.[10]

Actual layoffs were not as common as other methods of reducing the labour force, at least not in those steel plants that remained in public ownership. Steel plants in places as different as Egypt, India, Kazakhstan and Bulgaria generally tended to reduce their labour forces by two linked methods: first, natural attrition, simply not replacing workers who retire, while second, replacing those jobs that remain necessary with workers on 'flexible', usually temporary, contracts. This second process is often enacted through subcontracting, as workers are provided to the plant through labour brokers, through companies that are subcontracted for specific tasks, or agencies who pay labourers to work on day rates or for short term contracts. As Jonathan Parry has pointed out, this leads to the creation of two kinds of workers – to the point, he argues, where they constitute two classes – one privileged class of those with permanent contracts and another of more precariously employed workers who can be redeployed or their contracts not renewed as necessary.[11] The seeming naturalness of allowing permanent contracts to disappear as their holders retire rather than making workers redundant was surely not the outcome of the bosses' benevolence, but a political decision that resulted usually from the strength of the permanent workers' trade unions. And trade unions have often been complicit in the enforcement of poorer employment conditions for temporary workers, even when those temporary workers are in fact often kin to the permanent employees.[12]

Chris Hann and Jonathan Parry have edited an important collection of ethnographic case studies of steel manufacturing and industrial labour at the peripheries of capitalism, which almost exclusively tells a story of decline.[13] Once proud plants teeming with workers now run on what seems to be a skeleton staff; children can no longer aspire to jobs at the plants and either leave or try to eke out a livelihood in the informal sector; the grand nation-building industry of the modernist vision is now cumbersome and corrupted, its workers fragmented, divided into at least two antagonistic classes, distinguished by different conditions of employment, by generation and often by ethnicity. Once strong trade unions have similarly retreated into a mentality of protecting their own, enriching the leadership and a privileged core at the expense of those who truly need political representation. Life is harder, work is more intense, the future is uncertain as all jobs are vulnerable to technological innovation or the decision to close the plant down because it is deemed unviable, or because of the threat of cheap imports manufactured in China. What has this meant for workers and their families?

Family, gender, ethnicity

Like other heavy industries, steel manufacturing tends to be gendered masculine, even though there are plenty of plants where men and women worked together, especially in the former Eastern Bloc countries. The retrenchment described above affected men and women differently. Dimitra Kofti reports that in the Stomana plant in Bulgaria, after privatisation in 1998 families were allowed to choose who would leave their job, so that at least one regular income could be retained per household; the same happened in a further wave of layoffs in 2001. Women were more likely to lose their job than men, and the workforce shifted from a gender balance of approximately 55 per cent male in 1992 to 70 per cent in 2014. Although with increased automation it would in theory be possible for women to take on the higher-skilled machine operator or maintenance jobs, in many places households took gendered decisions about income generation, and women turned to the informal sector, public sector and domestic economy.[14] Outside of socialist Europe, women were generally not employed in the plants in the first place, other than in some of the most quickly outsourced jobs such as cleaning.[15]

Not only are steel jobs mostly held by men, these days they are held by men of a certain generation. They form an aristocracy of labour, a small and very privileged group in a very different situation from the rest of the manual workforce.[16] This was not always the case. Ethnographies tell of how in the past, permanent jobs in steel plants used to pass from father to son on the father's retirement, or employees could nominate family members for work when jobs became available.[17] From the early twentieth century, Tata Motors and Tata Steel in Jamshedpur, Jharkhand, India, allowed employees to nominate a 'ward' who would be recruited to work in the same place as his father, meaning that some families have worked for Tata for over four generations.[18] In Egypt, the custom of family employment in the steel plant at Helwan became understood as a right, in order to ensure worker acquiescence to structural reforms in the plant, according to Dina Makram-Ebeid.[19] Since liberalisation, the key distinction became that between those fathers who had managed to get their sons a temporary job 'with value' that could progress to a permanent contract, and those who had only managed to get their sons onto the lists of day labourers.

As Eeva Kesküla shows for a mining town in northeast Estonia, the imbrication of kinship and the industrial workplace in socialist Europe was not only about employment or the organisation of the workplace, but also about a whole social life of work-related welfare benefits like holidays in the mine-owned summer cottages or healthcare in a network of sanatoria; housing, cars, garden allotments and food distributed through the company; socialising with one's colleagues or brigade; children's camps.[20] Kesküla describes the workplace as a 'total social institution' that was central to workers' economic and affective lives. The labour collective was their main social network and those family members not working in the company were incorporated through sports clubs and holidays, and the company held parties for New Year and Miners' Day. The miners built a sense of labour dynasties attached to the mine by these processes of embedding of the family in the mine as well as the practice of passing on employment from fathers to sons during the Soviet period. After the collapse of the Soviet Union, the leisure events were maintained for some time, while material benefits were cut and employment opportunities drastically reduced. Still, the mining families retained a sense that they and their fathers had built the industry with their hard work, claiming what Kesküla describes as 'moral ownership' of the company, through their role in 'producing light and warmth for the country.'[21]

This is clearly an example of how an economic process is embedded within society – in this case through kinship – and it is a feature not only of mining and the steel industry, but also of many other sectors of the economy. A similar although less formalised process takes place in parts of public sector administrative employment in Argentina, as jobs are distributed through networks of kinship and the workplace becomes a space of kin-making through sociability, mediated by the union.[22] The practice of nominating family members for jobs in Argentina has also been noted in the petrol industry, steel and telecommunications.[23] Similarly, from the 1950s on, multiple Argentine formal sector industries implemented the kind of social wage that was common in Socialist Europe, as by virtue of their job – and, especially, their union membership – workers could gain access to health insurance, leisure facilities such as hotels, even housing. The historical experience of being cared for by the union has much to do with union strength today. A national leader of the Argentine public sector union ATE, explained to me that what he called a 'unionising culture within the working class', came from these kinds of relationships:

> I think it's transmitted from our parents, grandparents. They taught us this. If you're a worker, you have to have a union, you can't be somewhere else. The worker cannot not be in a trade union. I think it's this transmission that we've been making between generations; and also because the best times that our class remembers have to do with the unions. Personal things. I went on holiday as a child, to the union's hotels. My father was a petrol worker, and so we went to the petrol workers' union hotel. That's to say, all the good memories [from my childhood] have to do with this organisation that they put together.

Today, Argentine unions are the main means by which formal sector workers have health insurance, they organise childcare for their affiliates during the long school holidays, and own recreation facilities and negotiate discounts on various benefits, as well as solving work-related problems and bargaining over wages.[24]

Julia Soul has described how in the Argentine steel industry these social provisions are understood both as union provision for the worker and his family (understood very much as the nuclear family) and as the union's nature at least partly as a kind of family itself. Steelworkers said that being a delegate (shop steward) meant being 'a bit of a lawyer, a bit of a psychologist, a bit of a friend, a bit of a father and very very patient …' and explicitly made the connection between union social services and solidarity networks to support workers in difficult personal situations. The language of kinship was important also in political terms, for example when one steelworker thought that during the privatisation process (under structural adjustment) the union leadership should have acted more as a 'head of the family', sitting down around the table with the workers and discussing the threat together.[25] Kinship links the social to the political in Argentine unions.

In contemporary Zambia, the nature of mining unionism as family is articulated through 'tribal' identities, especially those associated with Copperbelt personhood. Workers understood the union's role as enabling them to fulfil their own kinship obligations, what Robby Kapesea and Thomas McNamara call 'kin-driven political action'. One example was the negotiation by union reps of allowances for school fees, paid at the beginning of each term, described as a moral obligation, and shaped by understandings of the miners' responsibility as provider for his family which are – they argue – especially associated with Copperbelt ideas of masculinity.[26]

In post-Soviet Europe, ending the practice of passing (permanent) jobs in the factory to family members was presented as both the inevitable result of international economic transformations and morally appropriate, through the use of technocratic languages of efficiency and good governance. Eeva Keskküla describes how an Estonian mining company used ethical codes to break up units of family employment, arguing for example that being in charge of a family member constituted nepotism. One couple who had met while training to be mine surveyors and had worked together for ten years were split up as one – Katia – was transferred to another mine, due to be closed in two years' time. This was very upsetting for both, and the partner who was left – Sergei – felt that he had lost both his family routine of driving to work together and one of the best specialists in his department. The company also withdrew from the sphere of social reproduction by distancing itself from those family members not directly employed, by not inviting spouses to leisure events like the Christmas party, in contrast to previous practice. Kesküla suggests that moves such as these are related to an emotional distancing of workers from the company, and linked to the withdrawal of the company from other areas of reproduction, such as hospitals, kindergartens and children's camps. All these moves might be justified as cost-saving, but, as she argues, 'By pulling out of the sphere of welfare and reproduction, the burden was shifted onto families, further increasing the disembedding of the economic from the social, recommodifying labor as a purely monetary relationship, and removing it from the family as a sphere of reproduction.'[27]

Where fathers could no longer nominate a son to take their place, they often felt that they had to keep working as long as possible in order to maintain their family income. In some instances the retirement age was extended, so they also had to work for longer to qualify for a pension. They also sought jobs of any kind in the plant for their sons, which has meant that in some the split between permanent and temporary workers is a generational split within families: the father has a permanent job while the son has a temporary contract but aspires to make it permanent.[28] Similarly, in Jamshedpur, Tata wards have entered the labour force, but on short term contracts with very low wages, employed as apprentices. Andrew Sanchez argues that this keeps the arrangement going very much to the benefit of the plant owners – not only do the temporary workers subsidise the permanent workers' salaries by doing the same jobs at lower cost, but this relationship also makes the workforce more docile: the permanent workers do not want to jeopardise their sons' chance at a better contract of employment by engaging in labour unrest, while the sons' aspirations to be made progressively more stable and eventually permanent keep them from agitating.[29]

The possibility of moving to permanent or more long-term contracts is one important way that bosses control the workers and dampen down labour unrest; and this may well be what is attractive to them about precarious labour arrangements, even more so than any reduction in labour costs.[30] Family connections between the workers make this mechanism of labour discipline even more effective in another way: if workers fear that their activism will lead not only to them being sacked but also to their family members losing their jobs, they can often be more reluctant to participate in activities like strikes and demonstrations.

Yet these days, in many plants the children of workers cannot even aspire to a temporary contract, and so are moving into different economic activities. In Stomana in Bulgaria, the lack of prospects for regular and stable jobs makes parents encourage their children to seek employment outside of the steel plant, because, as Kofti says, 'the only mobility was downwards.'[31] But workers' children do not always find better jobs, and so – in Estonia – parents must support their adult children in three- or four-generation households, which has created new stresses and tensions for both groups. Parents worried about their children's futures, and took out loans to pay for their education or for entry into public sector employment.[32]

In other plants, the split between permanent and temporary workers falls along lines of ethnicity rather than kinship, and the role of migration is another way that employment in steel works is embedded in social organisation. In some circumstances, the steel works itself provides the infrastructure to attract labour migrants from across the country, who settle in the company town and develop a sense of collectivity based upon shared employment and residence. In Helwan, Egypt, the steel plant displaced a local town, whose former residents are now mostly employed in informal sector occupations based around the factory, such as brick kilns, vending, or illegal activities. They are the most precarious workers, more precarious even than the children of the steel workers working on short term contracts. In India, the Rourkela Steel Plant was founded in 1954 as another one of Nehru's steel towns, or 'temples of modernity' (the others were in Bhilai and Durgapur), and was designed to provide work for local people and migrants from across India. Within 15 years, employment started to be restricted to local workers from Odia and local Adivasi backgrounds, and recognised trade unions became almost exclusively controlled by Odia lowlanders. The largest recognised union even opposed heritability of jobs, on the basis that it would allow those non-Odia workers who had gained employment at the plant in the early period to establish themselves and permanently settle in the city. After liberalisation, Odia workers gradually became concentrated in the better jobs, with houses in the company township, while the Adivasis inhabited the outlying *bastis* (informal settlements) and resettlement colonies. The privilege of township residence creates particular possible labour futures for workers' children. Residents of the township aspired to their children working in the software industry, not steel. However, education for the new high-skilled jobs is only really possible if families have access to a permanent salary, company house or high-quality company-run schools.[33]

Precarity is shaped by gender, ethnicity and generation, and lived not only through the specifics of employment contracts but in the anxiety of parents about their children's prospects, or the stresses of living with three generations in a small apartment. Secure employment is no longer a kind of patrimony that passes from father to son, and so permanent workers seek other strategies, like taking out loans to fund their children's education or business endeavours. The freeing up of global markets in steel and other heavy goods from the 1990s on has combined with periodic intensifications of competition as a result of economic and financial crisis, in 1997–1998 and 2008–2010, to pressure local plants and states to bring in severe processes of retrenchment. As a result, over time the labour aristocracies of the heavy industries have been shrinking and their members have taken on increasing amounts of personal debt and uncertainty.

Temporalities

Permanent and temporary contracts are particular temporal orientations to work, albeit ones over which workers themselves usually have relatively little control or choice, regardless of the industry. It matters whether a worker is paid on day rates, piece rates, on a contract that needs to be renewed every one, three or six months or number of years; or whether they have an indefinite contract that is understood to come to an end on retirement. Further, it matters what the specific retirement age is, as in the case of the Temirtau plant in Kazakhstan, where the retirement age was changed from 55 to 63 on privatisation.[34] The length of the contractual relationship between employer and employee affects how people can make plans for the future, including whether and how they can take on personal debts, or how they can manage financially in the case of unexpected expenditures, for example on healthcare. For some people, it contributes to a sense of uncertainty about their futures, which they may seek to reduce by investing in other forms of livelihoods they consider to be more stable, such as their own business, or professional education (for them or for their children).

Thus, the historical time of big changes from socialism to post-socialism, or from public to private ownership, or before and after economic liberalisation, combines with the temporalities of individual lives and intergenerational strategising. As Laura Bear argues, the act of work 'has to mediate diverse temporal rhythms, representations, and technologies in an orchestration of human action towards their temporary reconciliation.'[35] Labour is a matter of the ethics and affects that emerge within overlapping timescapes; and the industrial workplace is a space of heter-ochrony, not defined by a single temporality.

The importance of the relationship between work and time has been acknowledged since E. P. Thompson's seminal 1967 essay on clock time and work discipline, where he argued that the imperative to measure time by hours was associated with the needs of the factories and workshops of the industrial revolution. Whereas peasants had engaged in agricultural labour as required by the season and according to natural units of time – like the length of the day – the labour discipline of the factory needed workers present and working for regular and measurable periods.[36] In the twentieth century, Fordist industrial processes were in large part about the management of time, specifically how temporal experience interacted with the action of labour on the assembly line in the course of the workday itself. Fordism is famously about the combination of mass production with the encouragement of mass consumption through the provision of relatively good salaries for industrial workers. This is also a temporal ori-entation that in theory spans years or even generations, while relying upon organisation of the assembly lines that was often broken down into units of time as small as minutes or hours.

In the 1920s, the 'efficiency expert' Frederick Winslow Taylor adapted the already existing principles of 'scientific management' to a system that was applied to Henry Ford's production lines in the Rouge plant in Michigan. The basic idea was to break down production processes into smaller and smaller units, and having workers repeat the same small process in order to create maximum efficiency. The workers became parts of the machines. Aspects of Taylorism caught on across large parts of the industrial world in the mid-twentieth century, including in socialist eastern Europe. Both Lenin and Stalin were admirers: Stalin invited Ford himself to design a model automotive plant, bringing over American engineers and skilled workers to train the Soviets in production administration, while Lenin wrote approvingly of Taylor's system. So, state socialist factories used Taylorism and Fordism as their models of modernised industrialisation, which would, it was hoped, instil labour discipline in the peasants who were becoming urban workers.[37]

The temporal arrangements for industrial work vary according to both political arrangements and the materiality of the work itself. As Parry argues, steel plants are quite different from factories based on assembly lines. In his study of the plant at Bhilai, Chhattisgarh, India, he contrasts the 'staccato character' of work in the plant with the different rhythms of agricultural labour. He describes the incredibly demanding nature of jobs at the steel furnaces, such as the work of the 'rod group', who work in intense heat on the tops of the coke ovens to clear obstructions and move the bricks at the bottom of the heating chambers that regulate air intake. Yet, he points out, 'although such jobs are extremely demanding, the amount of the working day spent on them is not', so that the tasks might take 1.5–2 hours to complete, but for the rest of the shift they 'sat about chatting, drinking tea, and going for a stroll.' Shirking, he says, is a social fact – and the steel works are considered to be more 'restful' than other kinds of labour, like agricultural labour or tailoring, which may well include backbreaking work that needed consistent effort over longer periods of time.[38]

Elsewhere, workers in similar settings report a feeling of the intensification of work; product of the combination of workforce retrenchment and new technologies on the shop floor or plant. Eeva Kesküla argues that the introduction of new machinery in Estonian mines in the 1990s led to a faster tempo of production. New wheeled trucks replaced the old underground rail transport, and were much faster:

> The loading machines, TORO s, drive along the tunnel connecting the face area and the conveyer belt in an incredible speed. Seeing the big machine driving closer, its bucket full of oil shale, pieces falling off under its wheels and then bouncing off in every direction, the machine kicking up dust, one would want to be careful and step away from their path, especially so when miners are driving back from the conveyer belt in reverse gear, not seeing what is behind them. … New machinery was not only more efficient but was also capable of moving faster and further, hence speeding up of work. Miners on loading machines drive back and forth for the whole shift, stopping only if the conveyer belt stops or the miner needs a little pause for coffee or sandwiches. Old miners who have visited the mine and looked at the new technology notice that although the work is physically easier, the tempo is morally draining, needing constant attentiveness and fast reactions.[39]

Technological change also means that fewer workers are needed to do the same job, which affects the temporalities of work. While the work has become less physically arduous, it requires them to be alert at all times to the maintenance needs of the machinery. Computer tracking of quality can be done by only one person where previous forms of documentation were done by several; but the work environment itself has not changed and workers who are on their own are thought to be consequently at greater risk of accident. In Bulgaria, there has been a rise in health problems, such as high blood pressure, strokes and cancer, which doctors attribute to work stress, fear of job losses, and undermanning of the plant.[40] Further, the introduction of new jobs such as those associated with the repair of new machines allows for those jobs to be introduced under poorer employment conditions, largely through outsourcing.

Several factors have come together to produce intensification of work in steel production in recent decades. The classical logics of capitalist accumulation – the desire for profit – leads to increased production through pressure on workers and where possible a shift to automated processes and machines that are more efficient than humans. People are still needed to operate and maintain them, but now the worker must attend to several different labour processes, often on his own. He then has less opportunity for sociability with other workers working on the same process, and so the feeling of isolation contributes to the feeling of intensification. Often in the same spaces, workers on temporary contracts are required to work longer hours than their forebears or contemporaries with more secure contracts (who as a consequence of their greater security are more able to defend themselves through organised mobilisation). That lengthening of the working day is another form of intensification. One might also speculate that the feelings of uncertainty about the labour contract itself could contribute to feelings of intensification in the sense of the need to work better to ensure renewal of the contract.

Responses to the experience of intensification or uncertainty also have a temporal character, in the sense that they often take the form of a particular orientation to the past and to the future. For example, ethnographers of post-socialist industry report a widespread nostalgia for the past, something like the post-Fordist affect that others have highlighted in western Europe.[41] Complaints and anxieties about precarity in the present often have their temporal grounding in a nostalgia for the 'standard employment relationship' ideal. Andrea Muehlebach describes how ex-factory labourers in northern Italy engage in voluntary labour in part as a means of coping with the loss of their job and the resulting lack of self-esteem and identity. They turn up for regular working hours, dressed in a suit and tie, and through unwaged labour re-enact a form of social belonging that was first cultivated during the Fordist period. She suggests that 'Fordism is thus less helpfully thought of as an era past than as a locus of sensibility and yearning that leaves crucial traces in the neoliberal present'.[42]

Jeremy Morris and Sarah Hinz report the nostalgia of workers in an automotive plant in Izluchino, near Moscow, for the socialist era when they felt they had greater autonomy over their working day, mediated through the collective organisation of the work brigade. For these workers, reduced autonomy was experienced as intensification with a strong temporal element. They lost autonomy in designing their work and solving problems, which had gone alongside greater control over the shape of their working day, and a shop-floor culture of personalised relations. In the new organisation of production, everything they did was prescribed, and they felt that the managers constantly monitored them and pushed them to meet targets they had not set for themselves. One worker said 'they really know how to get every ounce out of you all the time, every day, from the start to the end of the shift'. For most, this was experienced as new, and contrasted to the experience of the past.[43] Yet orientations to the past may not always take the form of nostalgia, as Michael Peter Hoffmann shows for workers in a Nepali brick kiln factory, who contrast their current highly precarious situation to their lives as bonded agricultural labourers and deeply value their present autonomy.[44] Autonomy and freedom are important aspects of how people relate to their economic activity, as the discussion in Chapter 7 on informal sector labour also shows.

Related to autonomy too, a common response to precarious contemporary work conditions appears to be a kind of entrepreneurial orientation to the future. People want to earn enough money to save up and maybe start a small business, or buy a house that they can then use as a base for a business or collateral for a loan. Ching Kwan Lee analyses this as mineworkers in Zambia 'preparing for an eventual exit' from the mine, and indeed from 2007 the most important function of the trade unions in the Zambian Copperbelt has been to arrange loans for their members, which varied in size according to the nature of the worker's contract. While some spent their loans on private cars, others established TV repair businesses, or companies that sub-contracted to the mines, restaurants and poultry farms.[45] In Izluchino (Russia) and Karaganda (Estonia), steelworkers commonly held second jobs as taxi drivers or in construction and associated trades.[46] There is a similar kind of entrepreneurialism in the response of those children or wives of permanent workers who no longer have access to employment at steel plants, and who therefore seek other livelihoods, in the informal sector and by pursuing higher education.

Some scholars consider this kind of strategising to be the outcome of neoliberal processes of subjectification, as individuals are encouraged to become 'entrepreneurs of the self' – self-reliant individuals who do not expect state support and who take responsibility for their own welfare.[47] In the economic realm, such individuals should expect nothing more from the company than their contracted wage, and must be flexible enough to accommodate short term work contracts, for different firms and even using different skills.[48] In some cases, religion is being introduced to buttress shifting expectations of work and of subjectivity. For example, Daromir Rudnycykj's work on 'emotional and spiritual quotient' training in Indonesia shows how changing economic conditions such as increased competition for steel are presented as a challenge from Allah, with employees encouraged to embrace uncertainty like early Moslems did.[49] The need for entrepreneurialism or flexibility is thus not only an economicist discourse of necessity, or a modernist discourse of progress, but it is something that is compatible with religious precepts.

The relation of entrepreneurialism to uncertainty is complicated: as Chapter 7 will show, entrepreneurial work in the informal sector is highly precarious, yet for many industrial workers it is seen in part as a hedge against the uncertainty of formal sector work. This is because the success or failure of small enterprises is often seen as more within the control of the businessman or woman. It is a matter both of autonomy (as control) and of a philosophy of self-reliance, but it may well rarely be a matter of choice. That said, it may not really be an especially new experience either. With the exception perhaps of the socialist company towns before liberalisation, presumably family members have always had to do something like this. Those sons and daughters who did not get the privileged job in the Tata steel plant of Jamshedpur must have earned their living somewhere, and as Jamie Cross points out in his study of a special economic zone in Andhra Pradesh, India, industrial areas are sustained by a wide variety of unregulated economic practices, from moneylending between colleagues, to vending, maintenance and construction work in the factory district.[50]

Labour agency: working-class and worker identity

The turn to self-employment and micro-entrepreneurialism might indicate that individual effort is imagined as the best answer to the economic predicament of reductions in employment opportunities and job quality. As such it operates alongside a hegemonic discourse of neoliberal bootstrapping. These attitudes, together with the structural changes I described at the beginning of this chapter, have a significant effect on the class consciousness of industrial workers and their families. Certainly, many ethnographers argue that there has been a decline in once-strong working-class identity, from Brazil to Kazakhstan, Egypt to India; to be replaced by an aspiration to middle class status, which is hoped to come about through enterprise or education. A theory of labour agency derived from Fordist assumptions suggests that these changes would result simply in a decline in trade unionism. Yet the picture is more complex, because alongside decline and weakening, we also see reconfigurations of unionism and worker identity.

The materialities of industrial processes continue to shape what is possible for workers both politically and personally, informed by changing local experiences of kinship, care, temporalities and class consciousness. Traditional industrial unions have suffered from processes of deindustrialisation and the fragmentation of the workforce, in particular the increasing division between permanent and temporary workers and the shrinking of the permanent workforce. Nonetheless, some of them have also been able to defend their privilege and draw on histories of political power to maintain influence. Working class identity has become less tethered to industrial spaces and the working class recomposed in others, as the rest of this book explores. What does this mean politically for industrial workers?

First, it is important to state that strong industrial working-class identity was not just a feature of Fordist Europe. Pockets developed across the world even in countries which were not terribly industrialised. Even after restructuring or deindustrialisation, worker identities are being reconstituted and reshaped, informed by industrial models but not limited to them. Across Latin America from the early twentieth century, the mix of anarchism, socialism and populism led to workers movements developing in locally specific ways, but usually on the basis of some kind of working-class identity. Peronism, for example, is a working-class identity from Argentina that grew in the slaughterhouses of Berisso and the automobile factories of Cordoba, among metal workers, petroleum workers, electricians and, in later decades, truck drivers, public sector employees, bank clerks and retail service employees; as well as in working class neighbourhoods of major cities. It remains a powerful movement even in the early decades of the twenty-first century, nourished by strong labour unions and neighbourhood associations. Its political power is derived from the combination of the industrial history with a reorientation towards new actors in peripheral urban neighbourhoods and among more middle-class workers who identify with Peronism because of kinship commitments and ideas about a strong public sector.[51]

In Zambia, the copper mining boom of the 1960s led to a widespread expectation of the development of a 'modern' urban working class, as labourers migrated from rural areas to the Copperbelt to work and live. Anthropologists of the period described how rural, ethnicised identities were being replaced by urban ones based on a mix of ethnicity and class, enacted in practices such as dancing as much as in work or residence.[52] By the late 1980s, as copper prices plummeted on international markets and international financial institutions enforced structural adjustment policies, James Ferguson found on the Copperbelt an experience of decline, and nostalgia for the 'first class' experiences and consumption goods of the earlier 'African Revolution'.[53] Some returned to their native villages, but many remained in the towns, working in the mines and the informal economy, as Ching Kwan Lee described for the 2010s.[54] This is a complex working-class formation, based on a history of urbanism, migration, worker pride and modernist optimism, combined with the privations of structural adjustment-induced poverty.

In India, where most estimates put the informal sector at over 90 per cent of the economy, working classes have been constituted in multiple historically contingent ways, based on cyclical patterns of labour migration between rural agriculture and urban industry, and rooted in neighbourhoods and workplaces.[55] Pockets of strong worker identity developed in some industrial areas in the early to mid-twentieth century. Ahmedabad, in Gujarat, was known as the Manchester of India for its textile industry. Before the decline of the textile factories by the 1980s, the Textile Labour Association (founded by Anasuyaben Sarabhai and Mahatma Gandhi in 1920) was very powerful and absolutely crucial to city politics.[56] It was a precursor to the Self-Employed Women's Association, which formed in 1972 and is now the largest professional association of informal sector workers in the world.[57] Company towns like Jamshedpur, Rourkela or Bhilai supported the labour aristocracies of the steel plants, organised into trade unions and sustaining powerful worker identities.[58] Unions drew their strength from the conditions of employment of their core, permanently employed members: they could agitate with less fear of being fired than those on short term contracts, they could draw on the daily practices of working together to build solidarity and collective strength, and they knew that if they called a strike in an industrial plant, the machinery risked serious damage. In turn, their power at defending their members' position and salaries attracted new members. The existence of a labour aristocracy with decent conditions combined with the materialities of the labour process to sustain traditional unionism.

However, processes like deindustrialisation in Ahmedabad and restructuring in Jamshedpur and Bhilai did lead to a decline in traditional industrial working-class identity and union power, often understood as a result of union corruption.[59] Like in many formerly industrial regions across the globe, large numbers of people have been shifted out of the kinds of workplaces that are amenable to the development of strong collective solidarity and the organisation of production in ways that grant power to workers. From a factory or steel plant where halting production can cause serious loss of profit or damage to machinery, work is now in textile workshops, small businesses, or via national and international migration. This fragmentation affects the possibilities for the development of collective consciousness and the precise configurations of labour agency. As the core of permanent workers shrank, union strength shrank with it, and union leaders rarely – if ever – turned their attention to the growing numbers of temporarily employed workers.

For many ordinary people, this decision alone is crucial evidence of corruption at the higher levels of union bureaucracy. Ordinary workers see union leaders as not only corrupt, but also often criminal, resorting to murder to stop opposition and repeatedly betraying workers as they failed to stop the processes of precaritisation.[60] In India as elsewhere, the language of corruption is often quite accurate, and the truth of corruption goes beyond just the decisions leaders made with respect to precarious workers into other questions of individual benefit and compromise with management on a broad range of questions.[61] Yet, ascribing the betrayal of temporary workers to individual corruption or criminality does also displace anger about the effects of structural economic forces and decisions of the bosses that changed their (or their sons') employment conditions onto anger against the individual union leaders who allowed this to happen. Such discourses are widespread across the globe: in Latin America, Africa, western Europe and eastern Europe, the leaders of 'traditional' industrial unions are often seen as corrupt and venal; accused of turning their eyes away from their class interest towards individual gain.[62]

Union leaders are not alone in abandoning the classic version of a working-class identity based in industrial labour. Another pressure on working-class identity comes from the aspiration to middle-class status, which is accessible to different extents for different kinds (and generations) of industrial workers. Permanent industrial workers in India have gradually become something more than a labour aristocracy, according to Parry.[63] They enjoyed a more middle-class lifestyle in their company town houses and invested in their children's education in technical schools and universities. Workers on temporary contracts may have similar aspirations for their children, but of course it is easier to achieve on the higher and more stable salaries of the permanent contracts.

In Europe too, families of the established working class aspired to middle class status through the education of their children. As Patricia Matos reports, the generation of working-class people born in Portugal between 1940 and 1950 were able to achieve permanent stable employment, and forged dreams of middle-class distinction for their children after Portugal joined the EU, making available various consumer goods, education and economic freedom.[64] The promised social mobility through educational attainment has not materialised as that generation hoped in Portugal, as is the case too for almost everywhere in Europe apart from Germany (and the former Western Germany at that). In some countries, especially Spain, Greece, Portugal, Italy and France, this thwarted middle-class ambition has translated for some into a youth movement of the 'precariat', as highly educated young people find themselves unable to find stable work, in or outside of industry.[65] Their political struggles do not appear to be based upon the link between trade unionism and the kind of working-class identity that was once strong in the industrial regions of Europe, both west and east.[66]

But the story is not a single-threaded one of the waning power and growing irrelevance of trade unions, as in some places unions have experienced reconstitution and adaptation. Not all stories of industrial labour organisation are stories of a decline into acquiescence, apathy or mere survival against desperate odds, as the materialities of industrial labour continue to produce collective worker action, and even the division between permanent and temporary workers can be mobilised politically by unions. Ching Kwan Lee describes a situation of decline in organised labour in the Zambian Copperbelt and yet also mentions that the miners strike for increased pay roughly every two years. For Lee, the strikes are characterised by violent looting, and vengeance acts against the mines, by 'violent and angry casuals and unemployed locals' rather than formal workers.[67] Yet the grassroots militancy allows the formal union representatives to use threats of wildcat strikes in their bargaining with management. Strikes are more fragmented than before, but union power has not entirely receded. Kapesea and McNamara studied mineworking unions on the traditional Copperbelt and in Zambia's northwest. They argue that the former are stronger than the latter because northwestern membership in the unions is limited by the embedding of the unions in (old) Copperbelt kinship structures. Still, unions are undoubtedly politically active in both regions, participating in wage negotiations and providing services to their members. They fight to improve their members' abilities to fulfil kinship obligations, and see unionism as a kind of activism based firmly in kinship and community.[68]

Unions not only adapt to new conditions of work but also to different formations of worker identity. Politically, working class identity is currently undergoing a series of recalibrations in most parts of the world: in some places fragmenting, often along ethnic lines, but in others shifting worker (if not precisely working-class) identities into new spaces. This may be associated with the shift of members of the same family into new occupations, like the children and grandchildren of industrial workers who gain their education and enter into software development or public-sector employment. As part of my research with Peronist union activists in the civil service of an Argentine ministry, I asked the members of a shop-floor delegation about their parents' occupations. Of the ten I asked, six had fathers from working-class professions: a trucker, taxi driver, railway worker and metalworkers; mothers had been a systems administrator, telephone operator, special needs teacher, social worker, or housewife. They weren't unusual: other civil servants and academics I knew also came from working class families. That family history and their political allegiance meant that people who were middle class in any ordinary sense of the term also saw themselves as workers, and this shaped their politics and understandings of the value of collective organisation. Argentine unionism – which is almost entirely Peronist – is informed by industrial unionism as a political modality, but it is currently being remade by other kinds of workers. For example, the Confederación de Trabajadores de la Economía Popular (CTEP) is a union that has adapted Peronist unionism for workers of the 'popular economy' or informal sector in the twenty-first century.[69]

New working classes are emerging in different economic sectors across the world. Beverley Silver makes this argument for the retail sector in the US: in 2013, five of the six largest employers in the Fortune 500 list were retailers (Walmart, McDonalds, Target, Kroger and Home Depot), and recent labour mobilisations among Walmart and McDonalds employees for a living wage would back up her argument that this is where the labour movement is reconstituting itself.[70] Along with the emergence of new working classes are new kinds of political action, which include but are not limited to collective action and new or reconstituted unionisms, as the rest of the chapters in this book describe. The heavy industries that informed hegemonic Fordist understandings of labour agency have largely seen a decline in employment conditions for workers, and a weakening in their ability to defend themselves politically; both of these resulting from technological change and the political decisions of the capitalist classes in favour of disciplining labour and extracting greater profits. Traditional trade unions have had to adapt to these conditions, not always successfully. Meanwhile, as the following chapters show, other industries and economic sectors are subject to similar pressures from structural forces of global capitalist accumulation and international politics but are experiencing different outcomes in terms of both the organisation of labour processes and the workers' political responses.

This chapter has described what has happened to the archetypal Fordist political subject, the male industrial worker, but from a perspective outside of western Europe. Drawing on ethnographies from eastern Europe, Zambia, Argentina and India, I've shown that you can find working class identities outside of the hegemonic centres, but that also working-class identity can no longer be the sole basis for how we understand worker agency (if it ever was in reality). That is in part because of how common global processes of deindustrialisation or restructuring have led to a decline in conditions for industrial workers, which have in turn affected precisely that identity construction and inhibited collective solidarity. Solidarity is especially challenging when conditions fragment along generational lines and even within kin groups, as younger workers can only get access to extremely precarious jobs. It is important for many workers and commentators that traditional unions did nothing to halt that decline, preferring instead to protect a smaller and smaller group of permanent, high-status workers. As a result, the leaders are now often seen as corrupt, venal and criminal, further eroding their standing (even though they would likely argue that they had no alternative). Yet, in some places industrial unions continue to wield political power, and they continue to defend their members, even if those numbers are reduced. Meanwhile, individual workers and their families strategise to better their situation, by looking beyond traditionally constituted worker identities and patterns.

They educate their children, aspire to middle class identity, explore entrepreneurial activities, migrate; and the working class itself changes and reconstitutes, creating opportunities for new kinds of action, both individual and collective. Some unions have been able to adapt to these newer conditions, as we will see in the following chapters.

2

Light Industry

Gender, Migration and
Strategies of Resilience

This chapter studies the relationship between labour exploitation, migration and gender in the industries of garment and electronics manufacture, and describes how gender combines with the materialities of particular labour processes to produce complex and contradictory forms of agency. One strand of Western liberal feminism tends to focus on gendered discrimination as the main problem of the workplace, as something that could be resolved if only women were treated equally to men. An examination of garment and electronics production reveals how exploitation in the workplace is enacted *through* gendered differentiation. The difficult conditions of work in some feminised spaces can be so *because* the workers in question are women, and especially because they are migrant women, bringing race or ethnicity into the mix. And because they are migrant women, their agency is constrained and enabled in distinct ways. In particular, in this chapter I explore the embodied and gendered dilemmas of workers' experience: of individual versus collective action, and of resistance versus adaptation, escape, or self-destruction, all of which are different forms of agency.

The chapter will proceed in three parts: the first section will describe the changing global circuits of garment and electronics manufacturing. The second discusses the importance of migrant female labour in both these industries, looking first at some experiences of migration to the city/industrial zones for work, and second at the working conditions that are made possible by the nature of the workforce. Age and life cycle are also important factors that feed into the intersection of gender and ethnicity in the experience of migrant labour, and to explore this I draw on ethnographies of Chinese electronics manufacturing, where workers are predominantly young women in their late teens or early twenties who have migrated from villages in the interior of the country, and of the Tiruppur garment cluster of Tamil Nadu, southern India, where migration from rural areas plays a huge part in a multi-layered picture. The final section brings both together to explore what all this means for workers' agency and resistance; and how to conceptualise resistance in these contexts.

Global circuits of production

Both electronics assembly and garment manufacture have travelled around the globe in the last 70 years, as multinational companies have been able to shift the location and organisation of production in order to secure maximum profit. These have never been publicly owned industries like steel production or mining were, and owners have generally found it easy to evade the fairly weak forms of state regulation that do exist. Meanwhile, garment production at least has resisted automation quite dramatically, and electronics manufacture still requires large numbers of workers.

Jane Collins describes how garment manufacture in the US moved around and then out of the country: from small artisanal production in tailors' workshops and at homes across the country in the nineteenth century to larger workshops concentrated especially in urban centres in the northeast, where low-cost immigrant labour clustered, and then to the southern states in the mid-twentieth century, followed by a move further south to Mexico, especially after NAFTA in 1994.[1] Her book was written prior to the 2005 expiration of the Multi-Fibre Arrangement – an international quota agreement for garment production – but while it was being phased out. She correctly predicted that the majority of garment manufacture for big global brands would subsequently shift to China, India and Bangladesh. These days, China is responsible for roughly one third of global garment exports.[2] One of the effects of this capital mobility is that along the way, workers in one place could be told that production could just move to the next cheapest place if they object to their working conditions. For example, Collins quotes one mayor of a small southern US town ruefully admitting that in 1998 he told a laid-off worker that he was 'mighty sorry … But years [ago] … companies came out of the north for cheap labor. Now they're going on south to Honduras and Mexico.'[3] Garment capital is globally organised, mercantilist and footloose.

Electronics manufacture also moved from the United States and Europe to Asia in the mid-late twentieth century, enabling similar processes of cost reduction and labour discipline. IBM was a pioneer. From the mid-1960s, it shifted microelectronics production from New York to Japan and its former colony Taiwan, to cut costs. At the same time, electronics assembly burgeoned in Taiwan, South Korea (another former Japanese colony), Singapore and Hong Kong; the so-called Asian Tigers lauded for their state-promoted export-led development strategies. Then the industry moved to Malaysia, Thailand, Indonesia, India, to the Philippines from the early 1970s, and from the late 1970s to China. The Chinese state set up special economic zones, in the Pearl River Delta and Greater Shanghai region. From the 1990s onwards electronics manufacture in the Chinese SEZs grew dramatically, fuelled by money from overseas Chinese citizens and investment from Japan, Europe and the US. Once China joined the WTO in 2001, its status as a globally dominant electronics manufacturing centre was assured. The scale of the industry there is remarkable: Foxconn, a Taiwanese-owned firm that became China's leading exporter in 2001, employed 1.4 million workers in 2012, spread over 35 locations in eastern China.[4] In 2014, ICT manufacturing in the Eastern region of China employed just over 6 million people, in thousands of firms: just the three coastal provinces of Guangdong, Jiangsu and Zhejiang each hosted over 1,000 ICT manufacturing firms.[5]

Today, it is possible that parts of the electronics industry have actually become less mobile than in the late twentieth century, as the Chinese government and local capitalists have deliberately consolidated supply chains into the region. The effects of this can be seen in the global chip shortage that resulted from Covid lockdowns in China in 2020. The production of electronic goods relies upon the assembly of multiple different components (e.g. motherboard, cables, casing, packaging), some of which contain very rare minerals. The production facilities for nearly all of these key elements are now located in eastern China, and so the comparative advantage of Chinese firms resides not only in the fact that they can pay their workers less than workers in many other parts of the world, but that the firm itself is embedded in the complex networks that allow them to source all the different components needed. The government has supported these developments and is in addition developing programmes to enable firms to relocate towards the interior of the country as wages rise in the coastal regions.

In contrast, clothing firms can produce almost anywhere in the world: the technology is remarkably little changed since the early twentieth century and remains very reliant upon a person to manipulate the material, a job beyond the capacity of robots at least for now. Sewing machines have got larger, but their basic design has not changed a great deal from the first machines of the mid-nineteenth century, apart of course from electri-fication.[6] Over recent years technological innovation has developed more in business processes than in the process of stitching itself: the discovery of subcontracting and 'just in time' production, and the rapid commu-nication of needs, contracts and production quotas to meet continually changing consumer demands.[7]

In concrete terms that means the growth of firms organised like Nike, which does not manufacture any of their goods but subcontracts out the production of T-shirts, trainers, shorts, sweatpants, and so on to factories around the world. Their manufacturing map available on their website shows the global extent of this.[8] According to this map, in May 2018, Nike products were made in 554 factories located in 42 countries and employ-ing 1,017,000 workers. Thirty-nine per cent of its workers were employed in factories in Vietnam, and of those workers, 80 per cent were female, and their average age was 32. Some of the factories are very large: one footwear factory in Vietnam had over 23,000 assembly line workers. Nike produces its brand, and does so principally from its world headquarters just outside Portland, Oregon, its European headquarters near to Amsterdam, and its Chinese headquarters in Shanghai (although this office does not have any design department listed on its website, it does have merchandising and marketing departments). There and in multiple other smaller offices and shops, Nike employs thousands of 'immaterial' labourers who design the clothes, logos and advertising campaigns, arrange sponsorship deals with footballers and football clubs, or manage the production process and con-tracts, run retail outlets and so on.

Sometimes, the subcontracted factories do not only produce goods for Nike, but also other big global brands and not so big local ones. They compete with each other for each contract. Nike is somewhat different from other retailers in that they do try to enforce some minimum labour protections as part of their contracting process. They were stung by a big global campaign in the early 2000s against sweatshop manufacture of their products (hence the 'transparency' celebrated on their manufactur-ing map website). However, subcontractors most commonly compete on cost, which, like in the electronics industry, usually means reducing the cost of labour. Buyers have the power to insist on lower prices, and they use multiple tactics to achieve this, such as requiring higher quality standards without paying for the extra work, shortening lead times from placement of an order to delivery, putting in an increasing number of smaller repeat orders rather than one large one in advance, and using sealed bids in their tendering processes.[9] All these place the burden of flexibility onto the sub-contractors, and through them, their workers.

The electronics industry is similarly constituted through subcontracting, and buyers have similar power to enforce intense production processes and lower costs. The most notorious example of this is Foxconn and its biggest client, Apple. At first, Apple produced its own computers, but it began to outsource production in 1981, when it contracted facilities in Singapore, then South Korea, Japan and China. In the 1990s it sold off almost all of its remaining in-house manufacturing capacity, and now the only manufacturing complex owned by Apple is in Cork, Ireland. Apple designs, retails and markets all its products but manufactures none of them, and it uses its power as a buyer to drive down costs and drive up production speed. This is a very profitable arrangement for Apple: in the third quarter of 2012, Apple's operating margins were 33 per cent, while Foxconn's were 1.5 per cent. Foxconn assembles electronic goods for several companies, including Amazon, Sony, Nintendo and Microsoft, but Apple constitutes around 40 per cent of its revenues.[10]

In clothing, the practice of subcontracting manufacture helps large retail firms to be flexible in what they sell. In the past, clothing stores changed their stock twice a year, but with the invention of 'just in time' processes – management techniques imported from the automobile industry and especially associated with Toyota – retailers can have six-eight fashion 'seasons' a year; and some retailers change their lines monthly. For example, Zara uses 'quick response' techniques to enable clothes to be commissioned, manufactured and shipped to retail outlets within three weeks, business journalists claim, although it owns the factories in Spain, Portugal and Morocco that manage the fastest turnaround.[11] If a garment factory is going to gain contracts from multiple buyers operating to similar time frames, that factory and its workers need to be highly flexible and skilled. One week they could be making cotton summer dresses, but then the demand might shift to a different design, requiring a different set of skills – say, the design incorporates pockets, or ruffles; or the buyer wants dresses in a different material. Maybe that factory cannot do both at the same low cost, and so the buyer will contract another factory or workshop, and the first enterprise must find another contract it can meet. Maybe a retailer wants to contract an individual workshop to produce 500 cotton sundresses at first, which might well be followed by an urgent order for ten times the amount of those sundresses: say, because the PR team in London or Los Angeles have persuaded a celebrity to wear that particular dress. Or, conversely, an unexpectedly rainy summer in Europe might dampen down sales of sundresses, and so orders will tail off. Or economic recession leads to consumers purchasing clothes from cheaper stores, and the workshop that produced goods for Marks and Spencer sees its contracts slow down while those producing for Primark must produce more, ever more cheaply. Or a pandemic halts retail purchases of clothes in wealthy countries almost across the board, or leads to consumers purchasing leisure wear instead of suits as they work from home.

Shifts in production demands in electronics manufacturing come from a different mix of fashion and consumer desire. Again, Apple and Foxconn are the best documented example of these. Apple's goal is speedy production and no inventory – by which they mean no iPhones or iPads sitting unsold in expensive storage facilities. Tim Cook is famously quoted as saying 'Inventory is fundamentally evil. You kind of want to manage it like you're in the dairy business. If it gets past its freshness date, you have a problem.'[12] Apple combines this desire to avoid stockpiling goods with the release of new technologies once a year, leading to huge peaks in demand at certain times. When a new iPhone is released, consumers keen to update their phones put in an order, and those phones have to be assembled and then delivered to those consumers. A product launch or increase in production in readiness for Christmas might require the manufacture of 20 per cent more phones than at other times of the year. But Foxconn has maybe 1 million workers working on the production of Apple goods. To ramp up production by 20 per cent either means hiring 200,000 more workers or making the existing workers produce 20 per cent more than usual. Even in the highly mobile world of Chinese SEZs, finding and training 200,000 workers in a short space of time is not possible. So, the pressure from buyers such as Apple at times of product launches or spikes in consumer demand translates into near-impossible production targets for factory workers, which translate in turn to overtime, and the intensification of work demands.

Jenny Chan, Pun Ngai and Mark Selden described some of the effects of this in September 2012 at the time of the switch from the iPhone 4S to the iPhone 5.[13] When security officers in Foxconn Taiyuan beat two workers for not showing their staff IDs, workers in the male dormitory assembled to protest, and when a squad of security officers turned up, the workers rioted: 'tens of thousands of workers smashed security offices, production facilities, shuttle buses, motorbikes, cars, shops and canteens in the factory complex. Others broke windows, demolished company fences and pillaged factory supermarkets and convenience stores. Workers also over-turned police cars and set them ablaze.' Underlying the outrage against the security guards' actions was the increased pressure associated with the production schedules for the new iPhone5; and about a week later, workers in Foxconn Zhengzhou also protested, this time against exces-sively strict controls on product quality, aimed at avoiding customer complaints about scratches to casings. New quality standards were set that allowed only defects under two-hundredths of a millimetre, which is – as workers pointed out in interviews – undetectable by human eyes, and 'impossibly strict'. Meeting these standards created eye strain and head-aches; made worse by the cancellation of days off in order to meet the production targets.[14] So it is unsurprising that the workers responded as they did.

Labour unrest is a problem for buyers if it slows production and/or tar-nishes their reputation. After a wave of suicides at Foxconn factories in 2010, Apple shifted some orders to another contractor, Pegatron. Apple had realised that they were very exposed to the practices of an individual contractor, and so decided to diversify because of the risk to production and their reputation. The relationship between buyer and subcontractor is complicated: on the one hand, buyer pressure pushes subcontractors to dangerous practices, while allowing buyers to deny knowledge of what is happening. On the other, if buyers come to rely on a small number of subcontractors, the workers there can gain some leverage by slowing pro-duction or reducing quality.

But capital is creative, and a fairly recent development in China that has enabled factories to meet targets at times of peak production is the widespread use of student interns. Students studying courses at technical or vocational schools have found that their course requires sometimes as much as a year as an intern on the assembly line. During the summer of 2010, 150,000 students were interning at Foxconn, about 15 per cent of its workforce. Student interns receive lower pay than ordinary workers, no social insurance or bonuses for skills development, and they are required to complete the internship as a precondition for completing their course. Provincial governments have supported this by requiring vocational schools to provide a certain quota of interns for Foxconn, including by threatening to withhold funds if they do not meet their targets.[15]

The development of the garment industry globally has also been shaped by relations with government, most particularly the international system of regulation known as the Multi-Fibre Arrangement (MFA), which was established in 1974. The MFA was a set of internationally agreed export quotas for each country, and meant that the availability of quotas shaped where clothes were produced, although not always straightforwardly. It could lead to strange arrangements, such as where garments might be cut and partially sewn in Sri Lanka, sent to the Maldives for more sewing, and returned to Sri Lanka for finishing, because that was the quota-rich country.[16] The MFA was phased out from 1994 and expired in January 2005, allowing production to land in the most in-demand places, which usually means where labour is cheaper. And some countries such as Bangladesh have as a result been more intensively incorporated into the new global circuits of manufacture. Other countries lost the protection that the MFA quotas gave their garment industries and became disarticulated from those circuits. This was the case for Trinidad, where a garment industry that once exported throughout the Caribbean and the US now cannot compete with Asian manufacturers who can achieve economies of scale and pay lower wages.[17]

In some places, these processes have led to an increase in 'putting out' systems, where stitchers are given their own sewing machines to work on at home, producing clothes for factory owners on piece rates. Other processes can be done at home without requiring the donation of technology. Stephen Campbell describes how workers on the Thai-Myanmar border trim threads at home, work that is viewed as low-skilled and easily combined with domestic labour. Other kinds of home work in his study include stuffing toy animals and stitching them closed, inserting foam into motorcycle helmet liners, and embroidery. Home work is a new mode of organising labour in the region, but, as he points out, it is the same as the pre-nineteenth century modes of garment production analysed in England by Marx. Campbell argues that this informalisation of labour responds in large part to the gains achieved through labour struggles of Thai and Myanmar workers in the 1980s and 1990s, along with the effects of the Asian financial crisis at the end of the 1990s. Both raised the costs of factory production and prompted owners to find cheaper ways to organise work.[18]

Home work is not always purely a mode of exploitative extraction. In some places, where stitchers have received a machine to use on a subcontracted basis, they can produce their own goods for sale locally in the times that they are not working for the factory. Rebecca Prentice describes how in Trinidad, Lena makes school uniforms for members of her community when she has completed her piece-rate contract for her employer, and appreciates the fact that homeworking allows her to save time previously spent in transport to work as well as to 'throw an eye' over her children. Another entrepreneur, Victoria, has a small business in a studio apartment that she rents, with four sewing machines and three employees, sewing clothes for sale to local clients. Such small-scale initiatives might be possible precisely because of the regional disarticulation from global production circuits.[19]

Thus, countries or regions that have been disarticulated from the global production circuits may not just see a dramatic reduction in apparel production; the picture is instead more complicated. After all, people wear clothes everywhere, not only in the wealthy countries of the Global North, and large retailers are not the only buyers on the scene. For example, a small enterprise I know in Buenos Aires is run by a Bolivian couple. I've known David (a pseudonym) since he was 14 years old. Over the course of nearly 15 years, he and his family have produced sweatpants, shorts, capri pants and T-shirts, which they used to sell to vendors in the huge informal market of La Salada in Gran Buenos Aires. Their story of enterprise-building takes in three countries – as David moved from Bolivia to São Paulo and then to Buenos Aires – and various family connections, as he worked first for an uncle in São Paulo, then for his brother-in-law in Buenos Aires. He then took over his brother-in-law's market stall at La Salada. David and his wife Laura buy the material, and cut it in rooms they rent from their brother-in-law, sometimes then subcontracting to stitchers who in the past worked for the same brother-in-law (he is married to Laura's sister). When times are tougher, they use their own sewing machines to stitch the clothes themselves. They are networked internationally. When the Argentine economy was going well relative to Bolivia, David was joined by some of his siblings, who came over from Bolivia to work for him and earn some money which they took back to Bolivia to invest there. When they sold their goods at La Salada, he or Laura would go there two nights a week to sell wholesale to shopkeepers who came on overnight buses to purchase clothes for sale across Argentina and sometimes as far afield as Paraguay or Chile. Luckily, before the 7-month closure of La Salada in 2020 because of the pandemic, David and Laura had already moved to digital marketing, and since 2019, Laura has managed the network of sales via WhatsApp. Their story is one of entrepreneurial migration facilitated through kin networks – and although there have been ups and downs, it is one mostly of gradual growth in autonomy, income and consumption power for them.

Gender and migration

David and Laura's business caters for local customers, but where manufacturing industries feed into global production, scholars have reported
much greater intensity and exploitation.[20] Here I discuss two examples:
electronics assembly in eastern China's special economic zones (SEZs)
and the garment industry of Tirrupur, Tamil Nadu in southern India. I
draw especially on the work of Pun Ngai for China and Grace Carswell
and Geert de Neve for India.[21] Both local industries are deeply connected
to global supply chain capitalism, to use Anna Tsing's term, and both rely
upon specific constellations of gender and migration to enable the organisation of production and the reduction of costs. They are a good example
of how contemporary global supply chain capitalism is organised through
diversity.[22]

Famously, the electronics industry has long extolled women's particular suitability for assembly work, encapsulated in the 'nimble fingers' story
identified by Diane Elson and Ruth Pearson 40 years ago. As they sum-
marise: 'Women are considered not only to have naturally nimble fingers,
but also to be naturally more docile and willing to accept tough work discipline, and naturally less inclined to join trade unions, than men; and
to be naturally more suited to tedious, repetitious, monotonous work.
Their lower wages are attributed to their secondary status in the labour
market which is seen as a natural consequence of their capacity to bear
children.'[23] Women's small fingers and 'sharp eyes'[24] make them more
naturally suitable, so the story goes, for detailed work assembling small
components on motherboards or electronic devices. Elson and Pearson
quote a Malaysian investment brochure from the 1970s aimed at foreign
investors: 'The manual dexterity of the oriental female is famous the world
over. Her hands are small and she works fast with extreme care. Who,
therefore, could be better qualified by nature and inheritance to contribute to the efficiency of a bench-assembly production line than the oriental
girl.'[25] Their point is that to the extent that it may be true that women are
made suitable for certain kinds of work and working conditions, there is
nothing natural about it. The casual racism of the language in the investment brochure underlines that argument.

Women have generally been seen as more prepared than men to submit
to the kinds of labour discipline necessary for factories to organise work
using an extreme version of Taylorism. This is especially so for the young

migrant women who make up the majority of the labour force in China's eastern SEZs. They are known as *dagongmei*, a word imported from Cantonese. *Dagong* means 'working for the boss', and *mei* means 'girls'; male workers are called *dagongzai*. The translation of *dagong* indicates the commodification of labour, and the word contrasts with the much higher prestige word for proletariat, a status of the Maoist period that was considered out of reach for Chinese peasantry. *Dagongmei* are mostly aged between 16 and 29, women with village *hukou*, meaning that their state-registered place of residence is their rural place of birth, not the urban industrial areas where they work. The *hukou* system entrenches societal expectations that young women return to their village to get married after working in the factory system for 4–5 years. *Dagongmei* therefore do not have roots in the urban factory setting, where they and their employers see themselves as temporary. Their job provides them with dormitories to live in, where they develop close friendships with fellow workers, often on the basis of coming from similar parts of the country, meaning they speak the same dialect. Their principal social networks are tied to their rural area, and factory work is something they must suffer, to support family at home, and until they are ready to return home to make their own families or open a business.[26]

As a result, the factories can extract their labour power without paying for the reproduction of labour in the long run.[27] This is the role of the countryside, and is what enables migrant labour to be so cheap. As Ching Kwan Lee argues, the village is the main site for the social reproduction of labour, not the city. Workers can subsist in the village when waged work is not available, and urban work enables rural residents to survive in cases where they need extra cash, or to invest in material improvements in their village. Urban workers spend on house construction and on education for their children – who are future workers. The children may be cared for in the village by grandparents or other relatives. The *hukou* system means that the state maintains this rural–urban subsidy, monitoring where women can be registered and ensuring that they are not able to stay in the cities beyond a few years, but must return to the countryside, usually to their husband's village or town if not their own.[28]

Women are socialised through family relations into particular sites of labour and forms of conduct. Social reproduction beyond the meeting of immediate worker needs is located firmly in the countryside. Patriarchal expectations of specific obligations to family align with industrial paternalism to create patriarchal structures of capitalist accumulation that link urban and rural areas and operate at multiple scales, from the intimacies of family lives and individual expectations to the demands of large-scale industry in SEZs.

These kinds of relations are not peculiar to China or East Asia. Don Kalb's book *Expanding Class: Power and Everyday Politics in Industrial Communities, the Netherlands 1850–1950* (1997) describes a system he calls 'flexible familism' in the Philips factory complex of 1930s Eindhoven, which manufactured radio sets and light bulbs. Philips employed and housed migrant families with large numbers of daughters – they required a father and a minimum of three daughters so that two daughters could be sent home at times when the factory needed to reduce production. The daughters were socialised to accept exploitative labour discipline both in the factory by Philips and at home by their parents and siblings. It was a highly productive system, which allowed Philips to outcompete other manufacturers of consumer electronics at the time. Company accumulation was aligned with domestic accumulation processes and the only way out for the daughters was marriage and a family of their own. Philips was an important investor in the development of East Asian manufacturing production in the 1960s–2000s.[29]

In such industrial areas, migrant women's lives are characterised by transience and liminality, shaping how they submit to the organisation of work. To return to China, Pun Ngai reports how their status as migrant women shapes cultural modes of direct discipline, as supervisors on the assembly line tell them to behave as women, who are 'submissive, obedient, industrious and tender'. She quotes one foreman saying, 'Mei, you're a girl, how can you speak to me like this? Didn't your parents teach you how to be a woman? Do you speak to your father like this?' Factory foremen and owners also see them as peasants without quality – '*suzhi*'. They are lazy, do not know how to work, have no sense of competition, leave their position on the assembly line at will or spit on the floor, and must be trained into modern forms of comportment; a discourse which justifies both harsh discipline and low wages.[30]

On the assembly line, the workers are somehow more the line itself than individual people. Pun Ngai describes the production line where she worked in the mid-1990s: 20 to 25 workers sit at the conveyor belt which delivers them the product. She and two other workers were assigned to assemble the main board, the display screen and the plastic case for a route-finder machine produced for a European car manufacturer. Their actions were meticulously described on a diagram of the steps they should follow and precisely timed. Once the workers learned the steps, they could perform them mechanically. One quality control tester told her 'I don't need to use my mind anymore. I've been doing the same thing for two years. Things come and go, repeating every second and minute. I can do it with my eyes closed.' The moving belt dictates the speed at which workers must work; if they are too slow, goods will pile up and cannot be moved on to the next production line or worker.[31] Although her research was conducted some time ago, the system does not seem to have changed significantly since then. Chan quotes from a Foxconn worker on the iPhone assembly line: 'I take a motherboard from the line, scan the logo, put it in an anti-static bag, stick on a label and place it on the line. Each of these tasks takes two seconds. Every ten seconds I finish five tasks' (interview, 15 October 2011).[32] Such tasks are repeated for ten-eleven hours a day, extending well beyond if overtime is required. In Pun's factory, workers on the day shift began at 8 a.m., had a lunch and rest break between 12 and 1 p.m., dinner between 5 and 6pm and overtime until 9 or 10 p.m., but could be required to work until midnight. The worker is not moved around but does the exact same job each day for months.

The work itself is, Pun says, experienced as pain: the effects of chemical fumes, headaches and worsening eyesight from the closeness of the work with such small components, the stress of maintaining high speeds over long periods of time in order to meet production targets, flu contracted in the shift from the cold factory floor to the warmth of outside, fainting, menstrual pain and irregular menstruation.[33] The garment workers in Rebecca Prentice's study similarly report health problems, such as those associated with the dust in the factory atmosphere, failing eyesight from the detailed work, stiffness and aching from staying in the same position and carrying out the same tasks all day, and stress building up in the body to cause chronic pain, anxiety, high blood pressure, heart attacks and strokes.[34] Both groups of workers see themselves as using up their bodies in the factory, earning the money while doing so, and then leaving when they are too exhausted or ill to continue.

In Tiruppur, Grace Carswell and Geert de Neve describe a mixed eco-system of production, where large export companies, smaller workshops and home work combine, each with different labour conditions. The larger companies have greater pressure to comply with labour codes and tend to produce clothing that does not change on quite such a quick cycle as the others. They have a bigger directly employed workforce, with more regulated working days, and often provide dormitory accommodation for their workers. The smaller workshops tend to employ people for the short term through labour contractors and on piece rates, as is the case for home working. The workforce itself is composed of several categories of workers: settled workers, whose parents maybe migrated to the town, and who have a relationship with their home village but do not invest there; long-distance migrants who send money home to relatives and intend to return home in the future; and commuters who live in the area around Tiruppur, up to about 50 km away, and commute in for work.

Different groups of workers seek different labour conditions. For example, unmarried female migrant workers might work in the large companies, where the pay is not as good as other jobs but the hours are more regular and accommodation is provided. They need to find somewhere safe to live, they say, because of questions of personal safety and propriety (what is expected of them as young women). Thus their spatial mobility is restricted in comparison with young unmarried male migrant workers, who often prefer piece rates, where they can earn more and also organise their labour around other aspects of their lives, such as the desire to return to their village for a particular festival. Married women who live in the town or its surrounding region often choose piecework at home, as they can combine that with domestic responsibilities. These distinctions are compounded by the fact that some of the male jobs are considered to be highly skilled, as is the case with power table tailors, and so they can demand relatively high piece rates and what they consider to be good conditions. A given household might have members with different combinations of these characteristics, and so combine different earning strategies.[35]

Global campaigns against sweatshop labour may not fully appreciate the complicated motivations and desires of individual workers. The factory that complies with the kinds of labour codes that large garment retailers are prepared – or forced – to countenance may not be as attractive to some workers as the kind of work that looks from the outside to be an extreme form of exploitation or self-exploitation. Yet, for some groups of workers in Tiruppur, garment stitching is an escape from rural ties that they did not experience as dignified, such as 'physically taxing agricultural labour, … bonded relationships at rural power looms, and … dependency on high-caste landlords and employers', in Grace Carswell and Geert de Neve's words.[36] The garment industry holds the promise of freedom and relatively good money; albeit fulfilling that promise differently for men than for women. As Carswell and de Neve also caution, flexibility tends to mean higher pay and status for men – although this is combined with longer hours; for women it means a 'slide down the hierarchy' and lower pay, as they work in jobs easier to combine with their reproductive labour.[37] The choices they make are of course not entirely free.

Some of the Shenzhen electronics workers interviewed by I-Chieh Fang saw their factory jobs as about '"seeing the world" (jian shimian), "opportunities of meeting love interest" (zhao duixiang) and "being independent" (duli)'. For them, factory work was an escape from the unfreedom of the countryside, an opportunity to experience the urban area before returning home to start a business or a family. Young migrant workers create networks of friendship and support, and engage in new forms of consumption – buying cosmetics, magazines, or smartphones. They can fund their or later their children's education and support their families in the village, both of which they see as positive.[38] And, importantly, they also move between different jobs seeking better conditions where they can.

The point is that this is a form of worker agency, as Carswell and de Neve suggest:

> When a worker decides to migrate or not, to start a garment job or not, or to swap factories or not, they are considering their own interests and acting on them, and this agency itself has far reaching impacts on the organisation of capitalism and its labour processes.[39]

The relationship between the bosses and the workers – between capital and labour – is heterogeneous and dynamic, and it is both exploitative and responsive to local understandings of the good life. These might include values such as the escape from rural bondage, for both men and women; the turn to the home, marriage and child-rearing – especially important for women; freedom, autonomy and flexibility to control your working day by contracting as a pieceworker; the possibility of earning more through hard work conceived of as temporary; or the potential to run a small business at some unspecified point in the future. That agency operates within multiple structural constraints: of gendered relations of production, buyer power and the circulation of migrant labour.

Labour agency: resistance where it seems impossible

This chapter has used the term 'light' industry to distinguish the production processes in garment and electronics manufacturing from those discussed in Chapter 1 and because the product itself is 'light'. But as my discussion of ethnographic material has shown, the processes themselves are actually anything but 'light'; they are hard, intricate and exhausting. The distinction between heavy and light industries is in itself a gendered one, associating heavier weight with masculine bodies, hard work, camaraderie and political radicalism, and lighter weight with intricacy, fragmentation and female bodies. The figure of the industrial proletariat in common theories of labour agency is thus a gendered hegemony, and in the case of the industries discussed here inhibits us from fully understanding the range of actions that workers take in response to their exploitation. While some workers in these industries do organise in trade unions or participate in wildcat strikes, most engage in other kinds of embodied agency that lie somewhere between resistance, escape, accommodation and pain. These young women's agency is shaped by many factors, including their experience of their physiology, the materialities of the manufacturing process, temporality and mobility.

Both Tirrupur and Shenzhen are located right in the centre of their respective global manufacturing circuits. Over the last two decades, both have experienced a deeper embedding in the global networks of production. The result of this is both an intensification of work processes and a proliferation of employment opportunities. Even if the conditions of employment have not improved, there is a kind of fluidity, and workers can to some extent move from job to job seeking better conditions or more money. For example, in eastern China, Chinese New Year is considered a dangerous time for employers, as their employees return home for the festival, compare their conditions and wages with others, and often do not return. Employers told Pun Ngai that they would expect their workforce to drop by 20 per cent after the holiday period. In a more recent publication, Pun reports how 'almost all' of the industrial workers she conducted her research with in the 2010s 'had experienced changing their job once a year or after less than a year'.[40]

In Tiruppur, managing labour mobility is the responsibility of labour contractors. They take responsibility for one of the operations in garment production, like cutting, tailoring, ironing, quality checking or packing. The contractor agrees to produce a certain number of garments for a specified deadline and brings in the labour to do so. The contractor, then, needs to find the workers, supervise their work and pay their wages at the end of the week, out of the fixed sum that the company has agreed with him or her. Contractors generally recruit labour from their kin and friends, and they work alongside their team, which might consist of a core group plus helpers who may be brought in if demand is high. Contractors often put in a lot of effort to keep the team loyal to them, but don't always succeed. One example given by De Neve is the contractor Senthil, whose three tailors suddenly left to work for another company, because they had decided they did not like the way that they were treated by Senthil's father (also part of the team). Senthil made sure that he kept in touch with the workers who left though, as relationships are fluid enough that he knew the three might need to return another time.[41]

As Carswell and De Neve argue, the forms of labour agency exercised by workers who leave to find alternative jobs do not conform with standard notions of labour agency, even in discussions of capital's 'spatial fix', where the kind of labour agency that is seen to compel capital to move to new spaces is generally seen in terms of formal trade unionism, workers' collectives and resistance. Nonetheless, mobility is one of the ways that labour shapes the organisation of production and creates 'unevenly developed geographies of capitalism'.[42] They point out that not only do workers develop agency within the conditions created by capital, but capital strategises in response too. Factory owners pay bonuses at the time of the festival of Diwali, to encourage longer shifts and help to retain people at least until they go home for the festival. Others provide onsite accommodation for migrant workers, which particularly responds to the needs (and 'unfreedoms'[43]) of unmarried migrant women. Some larger companies provide company vans to collect workers from surrounding villages, or they relocate to villages in the rural hinterland.

Labour mobility in Chinese SEZ regions has been partially enabled by demographic changes from the one-child policy implemented from the 1970s onwards, lowering the population available for work.[44] When combined with the hypermobility of workers and the growth in production, employers such as Foxconn are starting to face labour shortages, which at times gives workers slightly more leverage than they had in the past. In addition, Chan points out that the second generation of rural-urban migrants is more highly educated than the first, which may have consequences for worker mobilisation in the future. Pun suggests that the first generation of workers turned their distress inwards, experiencing exploitation as ill health (discussed below); while the second generation have been more ready to turn to collective struggles, partly because of education levels but also because of – paradoxically – a more individualist and urban perspective. In particular, they have been excluded from participating fully in city life, which was also the case for previous generations but not something that they had expected in contrast to these newer generations of workers. Their resentment at this exclusion has prompted 'the emergence of the workers' consciousness of their shared class position' and is linked to collective action.[45]

Environments of labour shortages are quite different to those of retrenchment and labour surplus described in the previous chapter. That said, although manufacturing jobs in eastern China and in Tiruppur are not scarce, employers have not on the whole competed for workers by improving their conditions. Instead, Chinese capital is responding with initiatives such as the widespread use of student internships to meet times of peak production mentioned earlier. Another strategy is unionisation across the sector but directed from above and favouring capital.[46] Chan reports that by June 2012, 82.7 per cent of non-state companies were unionised, and the Chinese Trade Union Federation had a larger membership than the International TUC countries of the rest of the world. However, Chinese trade unions are operationally and financially dependent upon management. For example, the Foxconn Trade Union was chaired for more than a decade by Chen Peng, special assistant to Foxconn's CEO.[47] They have therefore been less than radical when negotiating on behalf of workers. Workers are frequently unaware of their union membership, and if they are aware, have little confidence in the union leaders, who are appointed by management. Even so, and despite the lack of pressure from the unions, between 2009 and 2014 China's real manufacturing wages increased by an annual average of 11.4 per cent,[48] and official minimum wage levels averaged similar levels of growth over the same period, in part because of the government's desire to stimulate domestic consumption.[49]

The other driver for these developments in China was worker protests, which have taken place with increasing frequency since 2010, albeit not under the direction of the formal unions. The precise extent is not known, since reporting of worker unrest is censored by the Chinese state.[50] However, researchers have identified different waves of strikes, for example when student interns and co-workers went on strike in a Honda autoparts plant in Nanhai in May–June 2010, winning a pay rise as a result. In 2012, Foxconn workers angry at poor shopfloor conditions and the excessive requirements imposed on them in the shift to the iPhone 5 rioted, as I mentioned earlier in this chapter. These protests were experienced by the workers as informal and spontaneous, or at least that is how they were described to researchers (any hint of organisation could put organisers in danger). In the waves of protests at Foxconn in the early 2010s, some of the very young workers on the assembly line said they did not know they were striking, as one teenaged Foxconn Longhua worker told Chan, Pun and Selden:

> I didn't know that it was a strike. One day my co-workers stopped work, ran out of the workshop and assembled on the grounds. I followed them. They had disputes over the under-reporting of overtime hours and the resulting underpayment of overtime wages. After half a day, the human resources managers agreed to look into the problems and promised to pay the back wages if there was a company mistake. At night, in the dormitory, our 'big sister' explained to me that I had participated in a strike! (Interview, 15 October 2011)[51]

Garment workers in Bangladesh have also engaged in spontaneous unrest and wildcat strikes, often resulting from increasing work pressure. Hasan Ashraf and Rebecca Prentice describe how in 2011 workers in one factory worked overtime for 46 consecutive days without a day's break in order to meet a particular set of deadlines. The work became unbearable, and workers became sick, but felt they had little choice but to continue. Talking among themselves, they decided that they would halt production if not given a day off; and one worker said loudly:

> This cannot go on like this. We are human too. Everything has a limit. Don't we have family to give time to? We came here to work to feed our stomach with rice. This doesn't mean we are here to die. Don't we need rest? What do these motherfuckers think we are? Machines?[52]

The supervisors realised they had to discuss the situation with the managing director, and eventually the workers were given a half-day break each Thursday until the shipment was complete, a small but important victory. Unfortunately, even small victories are unusual. In the same year in another factory, slightly more organised worker protests demanding better conditions and the dismissal of a particularly disciplinarian manager were repressed by riot police with tear gas and rubber bullets and those perceived as troublemakers were forced to sign 'voluntary' resignations.

Workers also engage in everyday acts of resistance, such as slow-downs and sabotage. In 2011, Foxconn workers of the A1 line assembling Kindle e-readers agreed that quality checkers would slow the process down so that workers could handle the work. The following day, when they were ordered to meet the production quota, they decided – by means of smartphone messages – to leave out a screw on the casing, or not affix the bar code in the correct place. The speed of the line 'slowed to a crawl', and managers had to resort to dispersing the A1 line workers throughout the factories in order to reassert discipline and the speed of work they demanded.[53] Slowdowns might also happen in less obvious ways. Pun Ngai tells how 'Sometimes, especially at night, when the work speed was unbearable to overstressed bodies, or when a new speed was set for new products and the workers had not yet gotten used to it, all of the women on the line would suddenly slow down at the same time, demonstrating a silent collective resistance to the line leader and the foreman. Nobody would utter a word, but simply let the jobs pile up like hills while someone else was left with empty hands.'[54] In such circumstances, the foremen would usually try to cajole the women into taking up their work again, or in the end, s/he would need to adjust the pace they expected of the workers. As with the heavy industries of the previous chapter, work tempo is a source of stress and control but also a place of resistance.

James Scott also identified acts of thievery as forms of resistance,[55] and there are some indications that this takes place even in high pressure factories such as the Foxconn ones. In the less intense space of the Trinidadian garment industry studied by Rebecca Prentice, workers frequently subverted the labour process for their own benefit, a process they called 'thiefing a chance'. They would take material from the factory and between themselves assemble copies of the garments they were sewing, for sale or gifting, or just to be worn at parties. They saw it as a form of individual entrepreneurialism, diverting factory resources that would not really be missed to workers and their families. Prentice details the forms of exchange between individuals that were necessary for this, as one worker would ask another to complete a detail (e.g. sewing on a pocket) on an item of clothing for her in the midst of her other work and in return for a similar favour later on.[56]

Back in China, when production was speeded up through the imposition of new targets, Pun tells how workers might also become ill, and disrupt production through their experience of menstrual pain, or fainting. Supervisors gave out pills for menstrual pain, but they could not control it; nor could they control women's responses as they fainted from the pain or from malnutrition, stress, etc. These physiological responses to labour discipline are similar to the cases of spirit possession described by Aihwa Ong in a Malaysian electronics factory in the 1970s. There, free spirits (*keramat*) associated with special sites on the boundary between human and natural space occupied some of the factories and possessed the mostly female workers there. Episodes were triggered by apparitions, which materialised in spaces such as toilets, the locker room and the prayer room – what Ong calls liminal spaces, where 'workers sought refuge from harsh work discipline'. The workers suffering spirit possession often raged against their supervisors, sometimes becoming violent when they were restrained. For Ong, one of the key drivers of the possessions was female workers' reaction to male supervision, for example of toilet breaks; they felt the violation of appropriate social and bodily boundaries between men and women, and as a consequence needed to be 'spiritually vigilant' in the factory. Those who were not able to be vigilant were more vulnerable to seeing spirits. Struggles over the meaning of workers health – in this case, spiritual health – were part of 'workers social critique of work discipline'.[57]

These responses are intimately linked both to women workers' physiologies and to their cultural experience as migrants. In Malaysia in the late 1970s, menstrual blood was considered to offend *keramat* spirits, while the factory breaks down moral boundaries associated with the rural areas where the migrant workers came from. Factories were often built on areas vulnerable to spirits – as one operator said, 'this used to be all jungle, it was a burial ground before the factory was built. The devil disturbs those who have a weak constitution.'[58] In China, the experience of industrial time in the factories contrasted to the experience of time in the village especially because of the lack of sleep, Pun's interlocutors told her. Agricultural work was physically arduous, they said, but they found it very difficult to adjust to the factory work routine where they often had to work between 8 a.m. and midnight, and then eat, bathe and relax before sleeping around five hours a night.[59]

The wave of suicides of Foxconn workers in 2010 is an extreme version of the link between gender, physiology, psychology, migration experience and labour. Over the course of a few months, 18 young workers (aged 17–25) in the city of Shenzhen attempted suicide by throwing themselves out of dormitory windows, with 14 succeeding and four surviving but with crippling injuries. Jenny Chan interviewed one 17-year-old survivor at length, and her story is tragic. In March 2010 Tian Yu threw herself from the fourth floor of a Foxconn dormitory. She'd migrated to Shenzhen from Hubei province in central China, as she explained: 'Almost all the young people of my age, including my school friends, had gone off to work, and I was excited to see the world outside too. Upon completing a course at the local vocational school, I decided to leave the province to seek new opportunities, with my parents' support.' She had been working in Foxconn Longhua for just a few weeks, checking screens for signs of scratches, and had in that time been moved between twelve-hour day shifts and night shifts. She had made no friends, and found the work very difficult and stressful, especially when workers were punished for mistakes. She then discovered that her wage card had been delivered to another Foxconn factory, so had to take a bus there by herself to try and track it down, but did not succeed and never received that first month's pay. She said:

> By then it was the middle of March 2010, and after more than one month in Shenzhen I had spent all of the money my parents had given me. Where could I borrow money? At this moment of crisis my cellphone broke. I was unable to get in touch with my cousin in Shenzhen, my sole link to home and family. I could find no one to help me.

Her fall left her paralysed from the waist down. No official trade union staff members visited Yu in hospital or offered to help her.[60]

It may well be that it is the demographic pressures that will slowly change conditions for Chinese assembly line workers, rather than outright worker resistance. There is also little evidence of a developing sense of class consciousness, at least not in the conventional sense. The garment industry is little different. But is this a problem for the workers or for our analytical categories? Do our gendered assumptions about labour agency mean that we expect a kind of class consciousness and organised resistance that could not come out of the modes of production specific to these industries? In some contexts, gender works against organised collective action; perhaps separating women out from each other because it is so inscribed on bodies – it is about menstrual health and fainting, bodily processes that become a resource for resisting demands that are too great. And yet, although the actions are individual, they also draw women together through empathy and a recognition of similarity.

Gender combines with migration to make the experience for women transient, at least in terms of expectation: bodily because they expect to leave the factory or workshop to get married and pregnant, spatially because they are expected to go back to their village. If we continue to be locked into envisaging resistance as formal labour organisation, the fluidities of transient labour agency will never look like resistance. As an analytic imaginary it is embedded in a temporality that contrasts to the teleological one shaping formal (Fordist) unionism: of getting the permanent job and staying there until retirement.

It is important that scholars do not fall into the trap of either condemning these workers for not engaging in the kind of resistance we think they ought to, or conversely failing to see the kinds of resistance that they actually do engage in. In places of 'adverse incorporation' into global circuits of production like Shenzhen and Tiruppur, resilience followed by escape may well be the best or only form of resistance to exploitation for young migrant women. Can we blame them for putting up with these conditions for as long as they can and then getting out? This chapter has described the different kinds of agency that become possible in very constrained and exploitative situations; where the forces of constraint operate especially through gender and the specific relations between accumulation, production and reproduction developed through the use of an overwhelmingly migrant labour force. By engaging in a compassionate appreciation of what people do, we can see that their agency is very much about mobility, turning their transience to their needs as well as to the needs of capital. There is also collective resistance, albeit not usually overt and often quite tentative or easily squashed. And there are multiple deeply *embodied* agentive experiences, of resistance and of pain, of desperation and possession; but also of finding ways around their situation – by thieving, making friendships, seeking joy in new experiences, and dreaming about the future.

3

Agricultural Labour
Exploitation and Collective Action

In this chapter I turn to production in the countryside itself, the places that produce and reproduce the workers who migrate to cities or industrial areas for the manufacturing jobs discussed in the previous two chapters. In most countries, agriculture is probably the sector of the economy that has historically seen the most exploitative labour and property relations, from feudalism through plantation slavery and debt peonage to contemporary agribusiness. Here I explore themes of land concentration, migration and plantation economies to comment on contemporary political economies of agrarian labour. I then draw on a small subsection of what is a very broad anthropological literature to think about local experiences of plantation economies and smallholder agriculture, and how farming makes persons and communities. In the final section, I describe how together these create certain kinds of labour agency, both collective and at the level of the household.

In addition to exploring the influence of crop materialities on labour agency, I highlight the social dilemmas of household versus collective action and agency as resistance, accommodation or flight. Within existing literature, the latter has been debated through the ideas of overt or hidden transcripts of resistance, and peasants' tendency towards rebellion or conservatism.[1] The focus on industrial labour as the archetypal political subject of resistance was combined with an assumption that rural societies were dominated by conservatism and false consciousness. In response, radical scholars of the 1960s, enthused by the actual (peasant) revolutions of the mid-twentieth century, argued that peasant *rebellion* would be the only place one might find true resistance or political agency in the countryside. By the 1980s, James Scott critiqued both assumptions in his famous book *Weapons of the Weak* (1985), where he argued for an acknowledgement of everyday forms of resistance among peasants, in actions such as sabotage, mockery or slowdowns. As the examples I draw on here show, contemporary ethnographers have certainly taken on board his call to attend to peasants' experiences, revealing an even more complex picture of political agency.

A political economy of agrarian labour

Any story that one might tell of a global political economy of agrarian labour will inevitably be pitched at a very general level, given that so much of the world is rural, and each place has very specific local circumstances. That is as much true of urban labour as it is of agriculture. Yet, as with the urban kinds of labour described in previous chapters, there are a few common narratives that link rural parts of the world together. These commonalities might be summed up as a shift over time from predominantly subsistence farming to predominantly farming for cash, and the consequent concentration of land into ever larger blocks under the control of fewer landowners. Depending on the crop, geographical location, history and nature of the state, some parts of the world have seen very high levels of industrialisation in agriculture, while elsewhere smallholder farms remain common. All this is linked to migration, both because industrial agriculture in some parts of the world requires migrant labour to function and because agricultural change has driven people to migrate away from the countryside, affecting labour conditions for those who remain.

Across the globe, processes of land grabbing have dispossessed rural people of their land and prompted mass migration to cities.[2] In parts of Africa and Latin America, one of the most important waves of rural dispossession was prompted by the structural adjustment programmes of the 1980s and 1990s, which eliminated subsidies and encouraged cash farming for export to earn hard currencies for debt repayment. In some countries (e.g. in West Africa or Central America), the countryside was depopulated through war, by means of violence and forced displacement, allowing agribusinesses or extractive enterprises to take over.[3] This is not new as such: land concentration is a long-used geopolitical tactic of colonisation, as we can see in the establishment of plantation economies in sugar and tea cultivation in the Caribbean, northeast Brazil and India.[4] Needless to say, plantation economies were built through violence well beyond that of the original moment of dispossession, and depended upon the forced migration of labourers, systems of slavery and debt peonage. But they have mostly coexisted alongside varied forms of smallholder farming techniques. Some commodities were produced by a mixture of the two, like coffee and rubber, and the story of rubber in Latin America shows the potential for violence associated with the move from one to the other.[5]

The story of soya in South America illustrates the contemporary working-through of some of these processes, and the imbrication of global commodity circuits, local resistance, environmental degradation and national politics. Soybeans are one of the most important agricultural commodities today. They are grown in the US and in the so-called 'soy republic' of southwest Brazil, northern Argentina and Paraguay. Everywhere they are cultivated on huge farms, where the land is either owned or leased by large agribusinesses. Paraguay is today the fourth largest exporter of unprocessed soybeans, and soy is produced on nearly 75 per cent of its total arable land, covering more than 3.5 million hectares. In the country as a whole, only 6.3 per cent of cultivated land is dedicated to products consumed in Paraguay, the rest is grown for export.[6] While soy production took off in the US in the 1920s, and Brazil and Argentina shortly after, in Paraguay it followed (or precipitated) the collapse of cotton production later in the century. Initially, Paraguayan governments had encouraged the production of cotton as an appropriate crop for small-holder farming; and even when soy began to encroach in the late 1970s, it was largely as part of Brazilian agriculture, as migrants known as 'Brasiguaios' brought the crop to the eastern regions of Paraguay. This process sped up in the mid-1990s with the introduction of genetically modified Roundup Ready soybeans, created by Monsanto. Since it was still illegal to plant genetically modified organisms in Brazil, and the industry was more regulated (and taxed) in Argentina, the failing cotton economy in Paraguay provided the perfect opportunity. The collapse of the local textile industry, import of cheap textiles from overseas and colonisation by mostly Brazilian land speculators and farmers all meant that selling land for soy farming became an attractive proposition for peasants. Once they sold up, many then moved to clear more forest, opening up new frontiers for agricultural development.[7]

Soy cultivation today does not require much labour, but (partly because of the dominance of genetically modified varieties of soybeans) it does require pesticides and does degrade the land. Local peasants have found that rural employment has plummeted, deforestation has affected local weather patterns, making the region much drier, and their health and environment has been affected by the chemicals that farmers use. In response, some peasant communities have protested against dispossession and the effects of agrochemical drift, but landowners (or their agents) have not been slow to threaten or even kill the organisers.[8] In the early 2010s, President Fernando Lugo's proposal of a marginal 5 per cent tax rate on the export of soy products alongside failed attempts to control pesticide use and otherwise regulate the industry prompted rising tension between producers and peasants in the countryside and eventually what many consider to be a 'soft' coup against him. Disillusion with the government led to peasant land occupations, and in June 2012, the eviction of one group of occupiers became a massacre. When Lugo was deposed, his successor rescinded the tax plan and removed restrictions on GM crops.[9]

A similar situation occurred in Argentina in 2008 when the landowners organised mass protests against President Cristina Fernández de Kirchner after she raised the level of taxes on agricultural exports. Showing its embeddedness in a global market, today soy is a particularly attractive commodity because of its role in the growth of the Chinese livestock industry, driven by increased demand for meat (especially pork and chicken), associated with the general growth in the Chinese economy. Donald Trump's trade war prompted China to turn increasingly to South American producers for its soy, exacerbating an already important trend where Brazil had grown from 18 per cent of world soy production to 31 per cent between 1990 and 2014, at the same time as the US declined from 50 per cent to 31 per cent.[10] But this means that soy farmers in Latin America need to expand, which means they tend to look to already cleared land. In Brazil, forest clearing is generally associated with cattle ranching, and so as people sell cleared land for soy cultivation, they move on to clear more forest for ranching or directly for soy. Without effective enforcement of regulation to stop them, this results in the kinds of forest fires we saw in 2019 in Brazil and Bolivia. Like cotton in Paraguay, cattle-ranching is the frontier, but soy farming follows soon after.

Land concentration can also happen very gradually through multiple individual initiatives, associated with the combination of social organisation and the nature of particular crops. Tania Murray Li describes a process of enclosure in Sulawesi, Indonesia, which happened as over time people planted cacao trees on forest land they had cleared. The existing system of land tenure gave rights to the pioneer who cleared primary forest in order to plant a garden; and as the forest grew back when left fallow to become secondary forest, the pioneer's descendants could 'borrow' the land. The crops belonged to the person who planted them, rather like the land belonged to the person who cleared the forest and his descendants. As people borrowed land that their ancestors had cleared, and then planted cacao trees, their use of the land became more permanent because of the length of time it took for the trees to mature. Over time, those with the capacity to plant tree seedlings or to pay workers to plant them captured more land and developed what we might call more capitalist property relations. Those who had not acted fast enough or had got themselves into debt and had to sell land, or became adults after the wave of tree planting, then found themselves without access to land that had previously been common. Very little primary forest remained to pioneer, while on any given part of secondary forest all were related so had some claim to the ancestor who had originally cleared it.

However, while other crops could be rotated each year and people could then ask to be allowed to plant in secondary forest instead of needing to clear primary forest, the cacao trees were productive for ten years, potentially more with chemical inputs. All these factors joined to promote cacao planting. In 1990, 13,000 hectares had been planted with cacao, by 2009 the figure was 225,000 hectares. The result of this gradual enclosure of the commons was an increase in wage labour. Importantly, as Murray Li points out, this is what development specialists in institutions like the World Bank thought should happen: for them, she argues, desirable modernisation consists of people exiting small agriculture and moving to wage labour, either on larger farms or in cities. Any resulting inequality can and should be addressed through skills-training (e.g. financial, agricultural, entrepreneurial as well as academic), locating the responsibility for 'failure' and the search for solutions at the level of the individual.[11]

A common result of processes like these is out-migration from villages, which has complex consequences for those remaining behind. Ben Campbell illustrates some of these for a village in Nepal in his description of a conversation with a woman who herded yak-cow hybrids; as they talked together while chickens ran about the herd shelter, she explained her dilemma about whether to sell the herd or buy more milking animals. With one son having died in an accident in Malaysia, another son in Kathmandu and a daughter in Malaysia, she was concerned that there was not enough family labour to support such a business. She then said that even her chickens had taken on airs and graces; like spoilt children they had come to prefer rice instead of maize. Purchased rice is especially associated with those who have migrated to cities and have little interest in participating in the agro-pastoral economy when they come home. This is a cause of social tension, ritual anxiety and kinship worries as much as it is one of economic change.[12]

In rural Nepal as in many parts of the world, out-migration has resulted in a feminising and aging of rural populations as young men and women migrate to cities and then women return to the countryside when they begin a family, if they ever do. Adun's story, described in Chapter 7, is an example of this process: he met his wife Gai in a garment factory in Bangkok, and when they got married, she moved to Adun's village to raise their family. Adun remained in Bangkok, sending remittances back home, while his wife performed the unpaid care work that allowed him to stay in the city. Gai felt lonely in the village and missed her friends and the fun of city life.[13] But as Adun's example also shows, it is not necessarily the case that the young men have completely abandoned the countryside. They may return for periods of harvest, or alternatively base themselves there but leave for periods of seasonal migration. As is the case in urban spaces, rural households also strategise as multiple units: some members of a household engage in subsistence farming, some in seasonal labour migration, others leave to live in the city and return for celebrations or to help with harvest or sowing. The decisions about who does what are shaped by gendered understandings of care, responsibility and work.

Agricultural work on plantations is also informed by long term histories of strategic and involuntary mobility. The Darjeeling plantations in West Bengal studied by Sarah Besky are staffed by the descendants of Nepali Gurkhas brought to the plantations by British settlers from the 1850s on. They were attractive to British tea plantation owners because the British had been impressed by the strength, loyalty and endurance of those they called Gurkha soldiers in the Anglo-Nepal wars of 1814–1816. Nearly two centuries later, they continued to work on the basis of this 'cultural taxonomy of labour'. Networks of labour recruiters channelled labour migration from Nepal and did not need to rely on methods of forced or indentured labour as the plantations of Assam did. Migrants and their descendants became permanent, life-long members of the plantation workforce, living and working on the farm, and jobs were passed through personal networks, mostly kinship. In the 2000s, workers received not only monetary compensation but also 'land for cultivation, housing, food rations, medical facilities, schooling, firewood, and other necessities', provisions in theory protected by Indian labour law. By that time, most of the tea pickers were the women of the families. Some husbands worked in the plantation factories or on odd jobs around the farms, but most search for work in Darjeeling town or nearby, or they are chronically unemployed.[14]

In my final example of this section, the fruit farms of the US are one
of the most important contemporary versions of the plantation economy
reliant upon migrant labour. Migrants have been pushed to farms in the
southern states by wars in Central America (which were themselves
fomented by the US), economic restructuring and recession, and increasingly also the effects of climate change (drought and hurricanes in their
home countries). Agriculture in California has long relied upon unauthorised workers. Between 1942 and 1964 the Bracero Program was a
national guest worker program that set wages so low that white citizens
would almost never accept work there. A short period of labour mobilisation raised wages, but by the 1980s the relevant legislative achievements
had been rolled back and farmers had moved to labour contractors to keep
wages down. The influx of Central American migrants in the 1980s and
1990s (with NAFTA) produced a labour surplus, of unauthorised workers
who had little difficulty reaching the US but few rights once there, and
were compelled to accept low wages and poor conditions.[15]

Since the mid-late 1990s, cultural and legislative shifts have led to the
increasing criminalisation of migration, and migrants' 'deportability' keeps
them vulnerable to exploitation and allows growers to enforce labour discipline.[16] From the 2000s, the US border with Mexico became more and
more militarised, and it has become increasingly dangerous and expensive to cross. From the 2010s, US policy has been to deliberately channel
border crossers via the most inaccessible and dangerous parts of the
Sonoran desert, so that the hardship and deaths serve to deter others from
attempting the journey. Now, people only make the crossing if they are
in desperate need of work, and 'shoring up the border has therefore also
shored up worker compliance', according to Jennifer Guthman.[17] When
deportation is always imminent, who would complain about violations of
regulations? With Donald Trump's rhetoric, further militarisation of the
border and policies of family separation, those processes only deepened.
Paradoxically, more recently these policies may have begun to create a
labour shortage, or at least the perception among growers that a serious
labour shortage is imminent, leading some to propose a new kind of guest
worker scheme, or to explore the use of technology to improve field conditions or to mechanise labour-intensive processes.[18]

We can see common stories of geopolitics and political economy from
across the world, as fruit farms in the California/Mexico border area share
questions of migrant vulnerability with those in South Africa/Zimbabwe;
as agroindustrial development shapes the farming of soy in South America,

tea in India and berries in California; as peasants migrate to towns and cities in India, Nepal, Thailand; as wage labour grows relative to subsistence farming in Indonesia but rural employment plummets in Paraguay due to processes of land concentration. In the spaces between and at the edges of industrialised farming, smallholders engage in subsistence agriculture, growing themselves, their families, and their communities as much as their crops. Still, peasants today continue to face land grabs for agroindustry, resource extraction, special economic zones and even conservation (so-called 'green grabs'), in the rural version of accumulation by dispossession. Today, privatisations of common areas and expulsion of indigenous peoples from their land in Indonesia, Africa and Latin America are the contemporary versions of the processes of enclosure that took place as capitalism developed in early Modern Europe and through colonial invasion.

Local experiences: from plantation economies to smallholder farming

The striking commonalities should not distract from the fact that processes which look similar at one level play out differently in different places. One driver of variation is the nature of the crop itself. Ethnographies of agriculture increasingly pay attention to the relation between the specific materialities of each crop, the land in which they grow, and the social organisation of agriculture in each place. In this section I discuss these points for larger scale agricultural production and smallholder agriculture. For the latter, I pay attention to the ways that agricultural labour generates persons and communities amid uncertainty.

Agribusiness and plantation economies

Fruit harvesting in California is conducted by a seasonal migrant labour force, who work in extremely harsh conditions. Fruit will rot if it is not picked on time, and while some crops can be picked at night, others must be harvested in daylight, because workers need to see the ripeness of the fruit they pick.[19] However, temperatures in the Californian fields can reach 110°F (43°C) during heatwaves; and in recent years these have become more frequent as a result of climate change. Not everyone has to suffer in the direct sun, often people's gender determines where they will work. For melon-picking, Sarah Horton describes how women work as packers on the field-packing machines, so have some shelter, while men

follow the machine, picking melons and throwing them to the machine
for packing, or they work on top of the reflective metal trailer – without a
protective canopy – lifting boxes of melons onto pallets. Food safety regulations prevent the workers from bringing their own water bottles to the
fields, so they often go without a drink until a trailer is full up or they
can get to the water jugs on the machines at lunchtime. In breaks, they
self-medicate for heat stroke with salt and lime. Supervisors and piecework pricing structures push workers to complete fields as fast as possible,
and rarely allow additional breaks. Workers might also decide to forego
state-mandated breaks so that they can try to meet their quota before the
afternoon heat really takes off. Young male workers associate their work
capacity with their masculinity and take pride in their ability to with-
stand the harsh conditions and demonstrate their strength at picking and
stacking.[20]

The citrus farms on the South Africa–Zimbabwe border studied by
Maxim Bolt also rely on intense labour under piecework regimes. Pickers
climb into the trees on ladders and branches, and fill canvas bags with
fruit, while two team members run up and down the avenues of trees to
bring empty bags and collect full ones. They shout 'Waiter!' to indicate
that they have empty bags, and the pickers in the trees shout 'Waiter!' to let
them know that their bag is full. The runners take the full bags to a trailer
waiting at the end of the avenue. When that trailer is full, a tractor hauls
it off to the packing shed. Prior to that point, the labour process relies
purely on the physical capacity of the male pickers. The shouts of 'Waiter!'
are accompanied by other shouts of encouragement, imperatives to work
fast and to keep working, perhaps even through lunch. The key is to fill
as many trailers as necessary to earn a decent wage for the day, and that
requires a very intense work rhythm which in turn requires a 'dynamic
productivity' that is, Bolt argues, 'connected with a performance of virility
and physical power'. Generating manliness produces that dynamism and
collective sense, binding together those who come from different backgrounds. The driving machismo is created and enforced through particular
kinds of physicality in labour as much as verbally, as men tell jokes and talk
between themselves about sex, rape, sexuality and so on.[21]

In Darjeeling tea plantations, it is women who work with the plants.
Most of the year, they pluck the smallest shoots of tea from the tops of
the bushes, using both hands and tossing fistfuls of shoots into a basket
on their backs held with a cord around the tops of their heads. They move
along the rows of bushes, walking along a soft carpet of tea trimmings and

soil; the ambidextrous picking is highly skilled and hard labour. During the winter months, the women switch to pruning, which is even harder. When plucking, women work in the mornings from 7 a.m. until noon, when they take their leaves for weighing, and afternoon labour lasts from 1 until 4 p.m. In 2010 they received a daily wage of just above 1 US dollar, with a small per-kilo incentive of a few rupees.[22]

The history of labour recruitment to the Darjeeling plantations has been built upon the recruitment of families, and this is expressed in contemporary forms of labour organisation, from the use of kinship terms for fellow pickers in the group (e.g. *didi/behini* or elder/younger sister) to the bushes themselves (e.g. young bushes are called *nani* or children), to the organisation of life itself on the plantation. From the nineteenth century onwards plantation owners used the provision of land and what were known as 'facilities' to attract migrant worker families. Contemporary workers spoke nostalgically to Sarah Besky of the time when 'good' planters provided care in the form of 'facilities', such as medicine dispensaries, creches, community buildings, and so on. Although that time of '*industri*' has increasingly been replaced by planter philosophies of '*bisnis*', the history of facilities meant that permanent workers in the plantations developed communities that have now housed several generations of the same families. The provision of facilities enables farmers to pay piece rates that demand a great deal of work, because the facilities (including housing and land for cultivation) are understood as payment in kind, and also because several generations later, workers have nowhere else to go.[23]

In contrast, in California, the payment of piece rates and consequent intensity of work is linked to the temporary and seasonal nature of the labour force. In turn, this has significant health impacts. Seth Holmes describes how berry pickers report back and knee pain from bending down to pick low-growing fruits, especially strawberries. They also have headaches from being constantly insulted and pressured by the supervisor, while pickers who work during the days suffer from heatstroke. They must keep quiet about the conditions because they are vulnerable to immigration raids, and in debt from the border crossing.[24] Migrants in the US have a high incidence of hypertension and cardiovascular disease, which is itself aggravated by farm work because of the stress, exertion, heat and pesticide exposure. As Sarah Horton reports, farmworkers in California's Central Valley know that kidneys 'dry up', 'go bad' or 'finish' as a result of their labour; the labourers 'leave their kidneys in the fields'. Also just being an undocumented migrant in the US causes its own chronic social stress that makes workers vulnerable to ill health, partly because they are anxious about their conditions of life and labour, also because they rarely have good health insurance provision and so treatment of illness can be beyond their financial capacity.[25]

Smallholder farming: making persons, living with uncertainty

The story of agricultural labour is not merely one of wage or piece labour on large farms or plantations. Ethnographies have shown how in small-holder farming, political economy, cosmological significance, kinship, gender, and the materialities of seeds, trees, chemicals, leaves and so on combine with labour and landscape to produce persons and relations as much as commodities; relations that vary according to the crop itself. In Papua New Guinea, a clear distinction is made between the cash crop of coffee and the much more socially embedded sweet potato, according to Paige West. She explains how personhood 'is attained through transactive relationships between living people, mutual recognition between people and other species, and exchanges between living people, ancestors, and other species'. For women in particular, gardening is crucial to this rela-tionality. As a woman labours to grow sweet potatoes, the plants she grows feed her husband's family, and so through consumption her labour of cul-tivation 'literally makes his family, she becomes infused into their bodies, and they literally make her, the plants they grow turning into her over the years that she consumes them.' Cultivation merges the women's and plants' life forces, mediated through song as women sing to sweet potato plants, and chant incantations as they plant sweet potato cuttings. They chant about their husband's clan, its lands and the animals that live there, and urge the cuttings to proliferate and grow well.[26]

While the cultivation of sweet potato plants is a highly intimate relation, coffee is different. Although women are responsible for nurtur-ing coffee seedlings, they do not sing to them or recite incantations; they do not merge life-force with the plants, and they do not consume the end product:

> although coffee plants are of course the fruit of their labor, they are not the physical manifestation of the undying bond between past and present that is embodied in sweet potatoes and therefore do not bring Gimi into the world in the same ways as other cultigens. They do not make Gimi bodies and subjectivities that are fully and totally connected

to ancestors and to future offspring. Thus they interrupt the constant transactive cycle that is the Gimi world.[27]

Yet coffee beans are important for producing different kinds of personhood. For example, the first act of a marriage used to be sharing pork from a bamboo cooking vessel, whereas now working together in the coffee garden is seen as the 'seminal moment in sealing a marriage',[28] and the production – but importantly, not consumption – of coffee as commodity is how the woman becomes part of her husband's clan. Women and men work together to clear secondary growth and plant coffee tree seedlings. A tree raised from a seedling flowers after 4 or 5 years and can then remain productive for up to 20 years. The flowers mature into deep red cherries, which are harvested and processed by the whole family. Middlemen then buy from the small-scale farmers, pool the coffee beans together, and sell them in national and global markets. Thus, although personal and family relations are not made in the same way as with sweet potatoes, coffee does produce relations between villagers, coffee buyers, exporters and regional, national and global markets and consumers.

In the Andes, cultivation of plants and animals also generates persons, as much through the generation and maintenance of a particular relation to the land itself and to the process of labour as through the specificities of the crop that is cultivated.[29] Olivia Harris suggests that for the Aymara peasants whose lives she has studied, 'work is an affirmation of human personhood, and of the community to which they belong'. The relationship with the land and ancestors that is created and maintained through agricultural labour is both physically demanding and (often) joyful.[30]

Importantly, a big part of that joy is its collectivity, experienced in the Andes through structured forms of cooperative labour. Two important types of collective labour are *ayni* and *chuqhu*. *Ayni* is a reciprocal exchange of labour, where for example one party might borrow a bull for a few days ploughing in return for some work on their house or fields to be conducted later, or even a like for like exchange of agricultural tasks. *Ayni* also refers to a reciprocal system of exchange of goods at festivities, especially weddings, where great care is taken to record who brings what gifts, and to return gifts of equal value at a later festivity. *Chuqhu* is a work party, where people will be invited to work on someone's fields, usually in harvesting or sowing, in return for food, the preparation of which is the labour of the women of the sponsoring family or village. Miranda Sheild-Johannson describes one *chuqhu*, which involved a representative from almost every family in the village. She tells of the excitement at the prospect of the communal work party, of the hard work, smiles, high spirits, and how many of the women and men had dressed up, creating the festive atmosphere that Harris also mentions. The women prepared the meal, the couple who requested the work party provided coca leaves for people to chew, and at the end of the day the work party was taken to the sponsors' house and provided with quinoa soup, meat and potatoes, and barley soup, as well as cigarettes, coca and alcohol. The work party returned to their village late that night, walking for two hours by torch and flame light across the Andean countryside, with a sense of exhaustion and contentment, and of intimacy with fellow workers and with the land.[31]

Collective forms of labour exchange in farming are not peculiar to the Andes. In Sulawesi, Indonesia, collective work parties were common, but organised on the basis of the individuals' relationships with the person requesting the work party rather than the more communal basis of Andean village or ayllu exchanges. The requester was expected to provide food in return for the work party but was viewed with suspicion if he asked too many times, as if he were seeking to get labour more cheaply than through paying a wage.[32] In Papua New Guinea, Paige West describes how gardening of sweet potatoes is a complex relationship of exchange within the clan, but there are also labour exchanges in the harvesting of coffee, which is a cash crop. Sara and her family would go to help her brother harvest his coffee, and then he and his family would return to help with theirs. Sara enjoyed the visit to her father's land to help her brother because it gave her the opportunity to socialise with her own family, especially her mother. Her sister-in-law also enjoyed it and commented that although you are doing the work twice, somehow it feels like less work.[33] These comments partially reflect the joy of communal labour that Harris and Sheild-Johansson highlight. However, the negative valuation of hard work that this suggests (it is better that the work feels easier) does not quite chime with the positive moral valuation of work in the Andes.

Harris suggests that this positive moral valuation stands in contrast to a view of work as a form of bondage and coercion that is related to a particular Western tradition which views manual labour as servitude, going back to the Ancient Greeks and the biblical tradition, which has linked original sin with 'unremitting toil' since Genesis.[34] As the material from Papua New Guinea indicates, this might not be such an exclusively 'Western' view. Anand Pandian describes how toil is understood as both moral virtue and fate in Tamil discourse, where the term carries a sense of suffering. He links it to vulnerability and uncertainty, given that the toil of individual farmers is never enough on its own, and agrarian productivity is subject to much bigger 'cosmic forces'; 'chance, accident and fate' are all crucial to 'the celestial economy of gifts and penalties within which many cultivators work today', he argues. Hard work might be rewarded by the gods, but not necessarily, and in fact, cultivators experience agriculture as a 'game of chance'.[35] They are subject to unusual seasonal weather, outbreaks of disease, and unpredictable fluctuations in price. And so, it is necessary to appeal to the Gods, to ask them to reward your labour, by saying prayers, lighting incense, offering meat, alcohol and cigars. Yet the gods might still not respond. They must be fed: back in Bolivia, I was told that if you tripped up on your property it was because you had not fed the Pachamama there sufficiently. The rituals that feed the gods are requests, supplications to capricious beings, and there are no guarantees that they will succeed as intended.

The rituals respond to the uncertainties of life as an agriculturalist. Benoit de l'Estoile distinguishes between radical and relative uncertainty, where radical uncertainty is a structural feature of life, of the precariousness of living without health or life insurance, and the vulnerability of agrarian livelihoods to climactic conditions and international commodity prices. Relative uncertainty is constituted by a person's social world and their ability to predict and act upon a more or less stable set of (reciprocal) expectations of each other. In agriculture, he argues, radical uncertainty remains constant, but the constellation of relative uncertainty can vary, for example as the sugarcane industry in the Northeast of Brazil entered into crisis in the 1990s and peasants occupied land without the stability of the landlord's friendship to fall back on if people were in need: '"Who will send a car to take someone ill to the hospital?" was a repeated query, as the local landlords had always taken this responsibility on themselves.'[36] Subsequently, state-led settlement projects provided a new constellation of patronage and 'friendship'. People on a settlement project enjoy the security of more certain land tenure, but they must become small farmers rather than plantation workers with regular weekly pay. That leaves them open to the uncertainty of agricultural production and less access to interpersonal credit in shops and from employer to employee. In all these contexts, people sought to develop 'friendships', often with more powerful people, potential patrons who could loan them money or arrange hospital treatment, or assistance with state bureaucracy. Interpersonal relations – including with God – were a way to reduce uncertainty. Beyond that, they of course have value for people in themselves, and the work of ritual and of building social life is not just about reducing uncertainty but also about generating communities, persons, relations and life itself.

Labour agency: the multiplicity of collective mobilisation

The everyday forms of resistance that James Scott identified – 'foot dragging, dissimulation, false compliance, pilfering, feigned ignorance, slander, arson, sabotage and so forth ... the slow, grinding, quiet struggle over rents, crops, labor, and taxes'[37] – are difficult to find in the ethnographic record. Of course, that's the point. These are hidden transcripts and the situation as a whole is generally one of limited possibilities for revolutionary transformation, as Scott also acknowledges. As with agency in other kinds of labour, the story of agency in agricultural labour is complex, and agricultural labourers find their agency significantly constrained. It is shaped by the materialities of agricultural processes and their related social organisation, for example in the different experiences of dispossessed plantation labourers and smallholder agriculturalists, but also in the nature of collectivity as part of everyday life and the role of migration in providing labour forces and shaping individual or household strategies.

We can see agency at work even among those workers in extremely exploitative conditions. For example, farmworkers in California do not appear to develop much loyalty to their employer and seem ready to leave when another option presents itself. Employers were worried that migrant workers were looking elsewhere for better jobs: for example choosing farms where they could pick 'cane berries' (blackberries, raspberries, blueberries), that can be harvested standing up and so do not cause such terrible back pain. At least, the growers think this is the case, and responded by trying to improve field conditions, and on a very few occasions, even wages.[38]

Individuals might also fight for compensation for injuries and ill health sustained at work, as Sulema's story shows. Sandra Horton describes how Sulema had an accident at work planting tomatoes, which led to excruciating back pain, but the doctor from the company's insurers repeatedly declared her fit to work. She could not switch clinics because the insurance would not cover an alternative, and so after about three months she hired a lawyer and only that way managed to change doctors. The new doctor declared her in need of continual future medical care, but because he said that she had recovered from the accident as much as she would ever be able to recover, her employers concluded that they could stop paying disability benefits under their compensation scheme. Later, they said that they would stop paying for medical care. They offered her compensation of $20,000, although that would neither cover her medical needs nor compensate for lack of income while she recovered. Meanwhile, her family life suffered, as she was unable to care for her three young children as she had before, and she became more depressed. Her husband also lost his work as a mechanic, they think because the labour contractors in the area knew that she had hired the lawyer in her dispute with her employer. Co-workers stopped talking to them in supermarkets or corner stores, for fear that supervisors would fire them if they did. All these stressors eventually culminated in a stroke, provoked by acute hypertension. That prompted her finally to stop fighting and to accept the compensation settlement offered by the company, leaving her with $14,000 after paying the lawyer's fees. She was sure that her undocumented status was the reason the contractor initially waited four hours after the accident to come, and the reason also for her poor treatment by the company doctor.[39] In many ways Sulema's story is a difficult tale of constraint and the ill effects of the legal process on the worker and her family, but it is also the story of a woman who continued to demand what she was due, and who had the ability to take her complaint quite far, even if she did not ultimately receive what she deserved.

In Paraguay, communities affected by soy farming have joined with NGOs to fight the actions of the industrial farmers in law courts and highlight their criminality in the face of public opinion.[40] One such initiative was a case from 2005, when peasants decided to appeal to the criminal court after an eviction raid on a squatter colony ended with the murder of two peasants in a drive-by shooting by soy farmers. While the murder case was dropped before going to trial, it had prompted significant media exposure, locally and internationally. That media coverage helped generate support for another legal soy case, from 2003, when an eight-year-old had died after being covered in herbicides by a crop duster. Kregg Hetherington uses these cases to show how soybeans can kill, and how the understanding that they can kill became widespread across Paraguayan and international society.[41] His earlier work analyses the expertise that peasant farmers have to intervene in processes of information transparency in government bureaucracies, as they use official documents to press their case against certain kinds of agribusiness development.[42] Both are stories of dogged collective campaigning on the part of the peasants and their leaders, bringing in local NGOs and metropolitan lawyers to help their case.

Another set of more individual strategies is associated with migration, including seasonal migration, which ethnographies have shown to be an active choice for some proportion of agricultural workers. People do describe it as such, and some may well prosper from cyclical migration to wealthier countries or regions. Seeking off-farm jobs is a common strategy to reduce the uncertainty of crop cycles dependent on the weather and other environmental conditions. Undoubtedly, people are pushed into migration and wage labour by the difficulties of making a living by agriculture alone, and labour migrants to cities are super-exploited, through poor living and working conditions, political marginalisation and extremely low wages that do not take into account the cost of reproduction back home.[43] But on an individual or household level, it is often a reasonable, if not positive, response to the inevitable ups and downs of agriculture. Daniel Reichman gives an example from Honduras. There, the reliance upon volatile international markets makes risk a fact of life for coffee farmers. One relatively wealthy farmer, Javier, dealt with low coffee prices by migrating for between six months and a year at a time to Denver to work as an electrician. Over time, he had built a large US-style house on his farm, and even imported two streetlights that he had bought at a public auction. Stratification in the countryside shapes the ability to strategise and find labour opportunities off-farm, but in complex ways, as both the desperate and the wealthy seek to hedge against uncertainty.[44]

Another more tragic act of agency conditioned by the materialities of agriculture is the example of the wave of farmer suicides in southern India in the early years of this century. Some commentators have interpreted the suicides as either the response of victims of overindebtedness in a situation of agrarian crisis or a political act in protest against debt, globalisation and abandonment by the state. However, as Daniel Münster argues, both these analyses can only work in aggregate (if at all), since as he started to ask people about farmer suicides in their area, different conceptions of agency emerged.[45] Those who committed suicide were thought to be lazy or greedy, having taken on too much financial risk to feed conspicuous consumption and alcoholism on an individual level. They were also seen as participants in collective agro-ecological processes that have led to environmental destruction and the destruction of livelihoods, as respondents drew attention especially to overuse of chemicals. They often pointed out that it was no coincidence that the main method of suicide was the consumption of an insecticide used in banana production in the area, because banana cultivation is very capital-intensive and high risk. Initial high yields from the conversion of wet-paddy land were followed by crop failures, droughts and a resort to chemical use. Once fields were chemically destroyed, those farmers who leased land moved on to another field. It was easy to become caught up in this cycle and Münster found that talk about the reasons for suicides often changed shape into a discussion of agricultural production. If in the aggregate it might be possible to discuss farmer suicides in terms of victimhood and/or resistance, agency is a fractal phenomenon, and individual agency was often viewed through the lens of moral responsibility – both individual and collective. While it is important not to lock ourselves into a victim versus resistance model of agency, including political agency, equally the fractal nature of agency should not blind us to the multiplicity of responses to exploitation, ecological destruction and political marginalisation.[46]

To further complicate matters, there is also actually plenty of evidence of agrarian collective action, based in the kinds of collective agricultural production described above. In Bolivia, the so-called 'Gas War' of October 2003 relied utterly upon urban-rural connections, mediated through the city of El Alto. El Alto is an indigenous city, populated by rural-urban migrants with many links to the countryside. It was peasant blockades in Warisata in the department of La Paz that sparked off the mass protests that eventually led to the resignation of President Gonzalo Sanchez de Losada. 16 years later, Evo Morales' resignation was prompted by the conflict between middle-class urban protesters and the supporters of his MAS party, many from the countryside. Friends of mine from both the wealthy southern zone of La Paz and in El Alto told me of their fear at large numbers of MASistas coming to the city from the countryside to defend Evo. Both October 2003 and November 2019 were importantly (though not exclusively) founded upon a strong organisational structure of peasant unions, especially the unions of coca-growers. But these are not trade unions confined to an industrial workplace, rather they are embedded within local community structures, acting as the local government, overseeing land allocation and dispute resolution, controlling crime, and under MAS governments monitoring state-provided infrastructure.[47] They are the same community organisations that implement and are grounded in collective work practices like *ayni* and *chuqhu*, based in kinship and the relations to land, personhood and collectivity described earlier in this chapter.

In late November 2020, farmers predominantly from the Punjab region of India began to converge on Delhi in very large numbers, to create mass protests on the outskirts of the city that perhaps reached a peak of over a million people in January 2021. The farmers were protesting three laws brought in to liberalise agricultural markets by removing minimum prices for some grains, allowing contract farming, and removing restrictions designed to discourage large-scale hoarding. They argued that the new legislation would amount to the enforcement of corporate control over agriculture in India, leaving smallholder farmers unable to compete.[48] The protests built upon a tradition of mobilisation in the countryside, albeit one that until the early 2000s was dominated by the interests of rich landowners. In the early 2000s the peasants' movement in Punjab became more diverse and mobilised smallholder and marginal peasants as well as increasing numbers of women. The 2021 protests represent a moment when the rich landowners joined with these small, marginal peasants in the face of corporate threat, and their unions – while still responding mostly to the wealthier farmers – were firm in their rejection of the three disputed laws.[49] The laws were eventually repealed in late 2021.

My point is that despite conventional assumptions about workers agency that privilege the industrial worker, peasants and agricultural labourers are not necessarily unorganised. For example, globally, the Via Campesina is a collective of peasant organisations founded in 1993 that includes 182 member organisations in 81 countries, and, they claim, over 200 million individual peasant members. Their membership is concentrated in Central and South America, but they have 20 member organisations in Africa, 36 in Asia and 38 in Europe and North America.[50] The Self-Employed Women's Association of India is the largest trade union for precarious workers in the world, with roughly 1.5 million members, and around 72 per cent of its membership in Gujarat (its home base) is rural, meaning predominantly employed in agricultural labour.[51]

Even California has seen some waves of organised collective mobilisation of farmworkers and urban allies, such as with the rise of the United Farmworkers (UFW) union in the 1970s. Under the leadership of Cesar Chavez, the UFW spearheaded a wave of boycotts and unionisation that raised wages significantly. From the 1980s onwards their achievements in favour of farmworkers were defanged by the rise of neoliberal policy-making and increasing militarisation of the immigration regime. Migrant farmworkers became too vulnerable to criminalisation and deportation to mobilise actively, and farmowners relied on labour contractors to subvert the union. The UFW also experienced internal problems and its decline as a political force.[52] More recently, partly in response to the labour shortage brought on by increased criminalisation of migration, some of the more shocking labour provisions in Californian law have been ameliorated. For example, in 2016, overtime laws changed so that while previously fieldworkers could work up to 60 hours per week (ten hours per day) without overtime wages, the maximum hours per week without incurring overtime will gradually become 40. The law also mandated that the hourly minimum wage should become US$15 by 2023, although in the late 2010s that was achievable on piece rates for the very fastest workers, albeit at the expense of their health as described earlier.[53] The bill was sponsored by the UFW union and signed into force by the same governor who in his first term signed the Agricultural Labor Relations Act of 1975 that allowed farmworkers to unionise in the first place.

Sarah Besky describes a wave of strikes in the Darjeeling tea plantations in 2008. Union leaders affiliated to the leading political party in Darjeeling were told to mobilise workers to strike for higher wages. On the Windsor plantation, workers gathered in the morning at the gate of the factory and demanded that the owner let them in to begin a hunger strike. They organised a rotating occupation of the factory entry hall, planning to swap over every 24 hours. The workers complained that owners were failing to supplement wages with 'facilities', and eventually achieved an extremely small wage increase, from 53 to 58 rupees a day. Although very small and below the rate of inflation between the last wage talks and these, it was enough to disturb the president of the Darjeeling Tea Association.[54] In Kerala in 2016, 8,000 Tamil Dalit women workers engaged in a month-long strike to demand better conditions and increased wages, prompting other workers across the Kerala plantation belt to follow suit. That action took place despite the unions, and the workers even denounced the corruption of their leaders, bringing mainstream attention to their situation and prompting the government to announce a new inspection system for labour conditions on plantations.[55]

This shows that 'organisation' should not be seen purely in terms of trade unionism or other kinds of official membership organisation. In November 2012, protests and strikes erupted among farmworkers and the rural poor of the Western Cape of South Africa. The protests lasted three months and covered 25 towns. They mobilised seasonal workers in highly precarious employment situations, and eventually achieved an increase of more than 50 per cent in the minimum wage for farmworkers.[56] They were organised outside of the usual structures of political relations between farmworkers and owners, which Jesse Wilderman characterises as paternalistic. Locally based community activists used prior experience in service-delivery protests and networks with other social movements to become 'coordinating units' to extend collective action. This was enabled partially because of the move from on-farm to off-farm labour: farmworkers now lived in towns or rural settlements off-farm, where large numbers could concentrate and organise. The conditions of social reproduction shaped their activism around conditions of production. Their very clear demand for a salary increase could not be diluted by the promise of provision of better conditions on-farm, and they were not reliant upon the farmowners for housing and other services. The protesters found allies in traditional trade unions, such as the national trade union federation COSATU, but did not rely upon them for leadership and for negotiating with the farmowners.[57]

Finally, another form of collective agricultural activism has been land invasions; another mechanism deeply linked to social reproduction as well as production. The Movimento dos Trabalhadores Rurais Sem Terra (MST) in Brazil is one of the most celebrated social movements in the world. Since the early 1980s they have been organising the occupation of land left unused and building communities there. Hundreds of thousands of landless families have participated in occupations of public and privately held land, and now live on settlements where they have gained access to government services like housing, roads, agricultural technical assistance, roads, education and healthcare. The communities have developed innovative forms of self-government, cultural practices and education.[58] They have inspired similar smaller movements both regionally and in other parts of the world.

David Gilbert describes a movement of about 260 families that occupied a bankrupt cattle ranch and plantation in Sumatra in the mid-late 1990s. As they worked together to reclaim the land, they 'transformed themselves [from (mostly) rural labourers] into agriculturalists and the land into a smallholder agroforest landscape'.[59] They planted a diverse set of tree crops and developed forms of collective land control based on non-heritable usufruct rights. The process was complex and politically contentious, and the agribusiness that formally held the land retained their ownership rights, but the farmers have managed to defend themselves against dispossession and they have changed the agroecology of the land so that it is now both more productive and more sustainable. They have experimented with alternative forms of community, including informal credit groups and work groups. For Gilbert, these new relations are 'agroecological ways of being', that 'bring people into productive interaction'.[60] They combine collective land control with individual cultivation in a form of production that is not alienated and only partially commoditised (not at the point of production). The planting and tending of tree crops without the use of pesticides was, he argues, a return to a human-scale form of natural farming that has made possible new agroecological assemblages in the region.

Lest I paint too positive a picture, of course it is important to remember that land invasions and peasant protests are often confronted with violent responses from landowners. In another article, David Gilbert and Afrizal suggest that the most experimental collective initiatives provoke the deepest repression from landowners and their allies in the state.[61] In Amazonia, 33 mostly indigenous land and environment activists were killed in 2019, and environmental campaigners are especially at risk in Latin America more broadly.[62] Kregg Hetherington witnessed the shooting of two men who were protesting the soy harvest in Paraguay in June 2005.[63] The 'reactionary agrarian elites'[64] are – globally – adept at capturing the state, granting them the impunity to engage multiple brutal tactics of violence and counter protest, often using the language of nationalism, or even indigenous rights. Scholars of Paraguay speak of a 'sojización' of the state to describe the extent of state capture by agribusiness interests, especially since 2012. The Indian government was willing to use violence and internet blackouts to demobilise protesters in early 2021.

Like those of the past, today's peasant 'wars' are fought on deeply unequal territory and at multiple scales. The ways that they are fought are shaped by local political economies and the ways that the materialities of agricultural production influence social organisation and individual personhood. In this chapter I have described a vibrancy of collective action that is quite surprising given the deep inequalities that shape property relations in most parts of the rural world. Agricultural work varies enormously across the globe, but is often highly collective – of necessity, given the challenges of rural production and the kinds of labour involved. Especially – but not only – in the case of subsistence and smallholder farming, it is also deeply tied to modes of social reproduction, as I discuss in Chapter 8. This combination shapes the kinds of activism that become imaginable, as social relations of production and reproduction come together to produce action. Sometimes, that takes the form of individual campaigning, sometimes community alliances with NGOs or collective workers organisations, sometimes land invasion, and so on. As with the light industry workers discussed in the previous chapter, sometimes agricultural worker agency becomes manifest in pain, ill health or even suicide. Sometimes it takes the form of permanent or seasonal migration, flight from (rural) exploitation. Sometimes it is joyful collectivity or simply dogged persistence in place.

4

Affective Labour and the Service Sector
Work as Relations

In this chapter I discuss service sector work as a form of affective labour shaped by migratory flows and global mobilities. My emphasis is on work in call centres and paid care work, with examples of the latter drawn from domestic work, sex work and beauty work. Like agricultural work, affective labour of this kind takes us still further away from the male industrial worker as the hegemonic subject of labour politics. What does it mean for agency that part of someone's labour is managing other people's emotions and producing relations in a relationship that is understood as commoditised? This chapter explores what problems emerge when trying to encourage another person to feel a particular way is so fundamentally part of the job. Affective labour is deeply implicated in gendered notions of care and work, and the service labour I describe here is most often seen as the preserve of women, with the exception of call centre work in some places. The principal commodity that paid service work produces is customer affect, such as the sense of a problem solved, contentment, sexual enjoyment, or feeling cared for. If the product is mostly immaterial, the labour process itself is often very material and corporeal. The work is enacted through relations, between employee, employer and client (these last two might in some cases be the same person); and it is enacted in order to produce those relations. Here the animating questions are how does relationality affect action? What are the consequences for collective politics if we understand worker agency principally through the withdrawal of labour? What kinds of political collectivity are made possible for affective labourers and what are prevented?

I explore three aspects of that relationality: first, how the relation between client and worker is crosscut by class, gender and racial hierarchies, which are in turn shaped by the mobility and immobility of work and of workers globally. The Filipina sex worker in Tokyo serves her Japanese white-collar male client; the Central American nanny looks after the child of a wealthy couple in New York; the Indian call centre agent soothes an irate customer from London, and so on. Migration is an absolutely crucial aspect of how this kind of affective labour is organised globally, and therefore the focus of the following section. Second, ethnographies reveal just how much emotional labour is involved in managing customer affect, and just how material and corporeal that labour is. Third, affective labour can also produce a deep attachment between client and worker, which shapes workers' responses to material exploitation, both enabling and preventing collective mobilisation. It is important to note that this chapter discusses *paid* affective labour within the service sector. Affective labour is a cross-cutting theme for how we understand labour, and it is part of most of the other kinds of work I discuss in this book. In its non-commoditised form it is the core of social reproduction labour, discussed in Chapter 8. Of course, in real life, it is not always possible to make very clear distinctions between commoditised and non-commoditised affective labour, and an important theme of both this chapter and Chapter 8 is how they overlap and mix.

Global mobilities and immobilities

As manufacturing moved east, economies of the West became more based on service sector work. For example, censuses show that, in 1841, 22 per cent of the population of England and Wales worked in agriculture and fishing, 36 per cent in manufacturing, and 33 per cent in services. In 2011, the respective figures were less than one per cent, nine per cent and 81 per cent. The shift to services is part of what Hardt and Negri identify as a shift in the hegemonic type of labour, from 'material' to 'immaterial'. Material labour is the production of material goods, mapped in their theories largely to manufacturing, especially industrial manufacture. Immaterial labour is 'labour that creates immaterial products, such as knowledge, information, communication, a relationship, or an emotional response'. Hardt and Negri divide it into two forms: intellectual or linguistic and affective, although they warn that most jobs in immaterial labour involve both. Affective labour 'produces or manipulates affects such as a feeling of ease, well-being, satisfaction, excitement, or passion. One can recognise affective labour, for example, in the work of legal assistants, flight attendants, and fast food workers (service with a smile). ... A worker with a good attitude and social skills is another way of saying a worker adept at affec-tive labour.'[1] Their ideas about affective labour are grounded in feminist discussions of emotional labour and the labour of social reproduction and care, which I discuss in Chapter 8; although they do not fully acknowledge that debt and have been critiqued for producing an analysis of affective labour that is largely blind to gender.[2] Silvia Federici in particular has pointed out that much of what Hardt and Negri describe as affective labour is reproductive labour. She makes the important argument that we should not allow the identification of affective labour to obscure the rela-tions between production and the reproduction of labour power.[3]

Hardt and Negri suggest that immaterial labour has now become hegemonic in terms of how we think about labour even if on a global scale it has not overtaken material labour in quantitative terms. Federici argues that this has a lot to do with the fact that the bulk of industrial labour has moved to the 'Third World' and that much of the service sector growth (in Euro-America) has happened as a result of the commercialisation of reproductive work, meaning that this kind of work has 'spilled over' from the home, not the factory, as Hardt and Negri claim.[4] In some countries, like the UK, immaterial labour has become dominant quantitatively, as the census figures for service sector employment quoted above indicate.

'Services' covers an extremely broad range of economic activities, including legal, financial and educational work, hospitality, health, beauty, cleaning, care work, administration, government and so on; each of which bear a distinct relationship to global movements of labour and capital. Some service sector work is mobile in ways that parallel the mobilities of industrial labour: outsourcing plus relocation to areas where labour is cheaper. In those cases, the work moves across national borders, while if workers move it is from rural regions to urban centres and not across borders. Other parts of the sector are much more reliant upon workers crossing borders. In this section, I give a sense of some of these different flows, beginning with business services and moving to paid care work.

Some kinds of service sector work have become more mobile over recent decades, meaning that there is less need for the worker herself to be mobile, while other parts of the service sector are reliant on the global migration of workers. Since the 1990s, there has been a process of out-sourcing large firms' 'back room' services: accounting operations, data entry, production of journal articles and books (typesetting, copy-editing, proof-reading), legal services and call centres. Since telecommunica-tions technology enabled phone calls to a national number to be rerouted anywhere in the world, large multinational credit card, energy, telecommunications, tourist, loan companies and more outsourced their customer services departments. The majority of these were located outside of large urban centres in the same country or region, but significant numbers of customer service jobs were also relocated to agencies overseas, in locations such as India, the Philippines, Ireland, El Salvador and Portugal.[5]

The business process outsourcing (BPO) industry in India is one of the most important examples of this. As with the mobility of manufacturing, the growth of this industry in India has its beginnings in the discovery of outsourcing by large US companies. In the 1960s, they began to move back-office processes out from their headquarters in expensive urban centres first to small rural towns in the US and then overseas, a move made possible by technological developments such as the automatic call distribution system. India was an attractive location in the early 1990s. It had a government that was interested in liberalising the economy and telecoms, and plenty of young middle-class workers educated to a very high level in English-medium schools and colleges, a legacy of the colonial education system. There were software developers, engineers, accountants, lawyers and so on, all available for a fraction of the cost of those located in the US.[6]

Renaming BPO as IT enabled services (ITES) allowed companies to take advantages of tax benefits granted by the Indian government for those developing IT and software. The first outsourced call centre in India was opened by General Electric in 1999 and from there demand grew rapidly, fuelled in part by recession in US and European tech sectors after the end of the dotcom boom in the early 2000s. Just outside cities such as Bangalore, Mumbai, Delhi, Pune and Hyderabad, industrial parks were built to house modern-style air-conditioned offices for software developers, call centre agents or other kinds of back-office service workers. Pay is better than other jobs available locally. Companies can take advantage of the different cost of living to pay these Indian workers much less than they pay their US or UK-based workers – and the company can still move from centres like Bangalore to other cities if they confront labour shortages or worker demands for better conditions.[7] As with electronics assembly, surplus value extraction is increased by the relatively simple operation of moving the work to a cheaper location, the spatial fix.

These developments were prompted not only by the relative cost of highly educated labour, but also increasing constraints on worker mobility. For example, in the 1990s, the US government reduced the number of H1-B work visas available to Indian citizens, and so highly educated workers increasingly had to stay in India. Meanwhile, a number of those who had migrated to the US or UK prior to that moment were available to return to India to manage the firms there, where they were known as 'key agents'.[8]

A more extreme example of the effect of US immigration policy on call centre surplus value extraction is the employment of deportees in call centres in El Salvador and Mexico. A significant minority of call centre workers are people who have been deported from the US because they are illegal immigrants who have committed a felony. That could be gang membership – and indeed, that is the stereotype that many have to contend with once back in El Salvador or Mexico, especially if they have gang tattoos, or gang-like tattoos. In 2014 Hilary Goodfriend interviewed some workers in this situation in El Salvador who had migrated to the US as children, sometimes at a very young age indeed. For example, 'TJ' was five when his family migrated to the US to escape the civil war. In the mid-1990s, he lost his US residency because he stole a car, and he accepted voluntary deportation. He returned to the US two years later but was then deported again in 2006. He was surprised at his deportation: 'That was my problem. I thought that because I'd lived there all my life, I was already an American citizen. So, it was really I didn't even think that I was from another country. ... I said "Whatever happens it's like – why would they send me away if I'm from here?"'. Another call centre worker had migrated with his mother when he was two years old and when he grew up joined a gang in the US. He said that when he was deported to El Salvador: 'For me it was like a new country ... I don't know shit about here. I've got nothing in common with anyone.'[9]

Deportees are valuable workers because their time in the US has given them the cultural competence to engage well with US-based customers. But they can't go back home. Deportation is a kind of forced mobility that expels workers from the centre to the periphery and then turns into the immobility of keeping them in the periphery, in order to serve customers from the centre. Some call centres even send recruiters to airports to meet deportation flights. Rafael Alarcón Medina, who studied the same phenomenon in Tijuana, Mexico, argues that the call centre itself is a space of 'informational return' to the US for some workers, who experience their forced move to Mexico as exile rather than return or deportation. They create a sense of home in the call centre itself, as they can talk English, hang out with people like themselves, even joke about how the call centre is like the US prisons they were deported from.[10]

Specific types of worker mobility are also crucial for other kinds of service work, in forms that range from forced trafficking to voluntary migration. Ethnicity, nationality and gender combine in complex ways, developing into what seem almost like trade routes of people often constructed along (neo)colonial lines. Sex work and beauty work are both examples of this. As much as half of the foreign sex workers in Italy come from Nigeria, and the majority of them from Edo State in southern Nigeria, formerly Benin; many of the hostesses in Tokyo's nightclubs are Filipina women; many prostitutes on the Mexico-US border come from Guatemala and other poorer Central American countries.[11] Migration leads to ethnic niches developing in particular cities around particular forms of service work, as in the example of Korean-run nail salons in New York City, studied by Miliann Kang. Kang describes how the removal of the US national origins quota system for immigration in 1965 led to an increase in Asian migration in general, and South Korean migration in particular. Many highly educated middle-class women emigrated to the US, possibly desiring more freedom to engage in the labour market than they had been allowed at home. Once there, they faced both the effects of racial discrimination in blocking their entry into some high-status jobs like accounting and the ready availability of beauty-industry businesses built around community connections. This enabled some to become businesswomen, albeit in an area they had not anticipated, while others started jobs in nail salons at first to pay their way through college, but then they stayed. Meanwhile, the public perception grew that – in New York City at least – Korean women were especially suited to nail artistry, in something of a reworking of the 'nimble fingers' stereotype discussed in Chapter 2.[12]

Women move for work from poorer countries or regions to richer ones, just like the electronics assembly workers in eastern China or the garment workers in Tirrupur. These routes have long histories, which are enmeshed in racial and gender hierarchies, slavery and colonialism, as Barbara Ehrenreich and Arlie Hochschild point out for domestic work:

In the ancient Middle East, the women of populations defeated in war were routinely enslaved and hauled off to serve as household workers and concubines for the victors. Among the Africans brought to North America as slaves in the sixteenth through nineteenth centuries, about a third were women and children, and many of those women were pressed to be concubines, domestic servants, or both. Nineteenth-century Irishwomen – along with many Englishwomen – migrated to

English towns and cities to work as domestics in the homes of the
growing upper middle class. ... In the United States, African-Ameri-
can women, who accounted for 60 percent of domestics in the 1940s,
have been largely replaced by Latinas, many of them recent migrants
from Mexico and Central America. In England, Asian migrant women
have displaced the Irish and Portuguese domestics of the past. In
French cities, North African women have replaced rural French girls.
In western Germany, Turks and women from the former East Germany
have replaced rural native-born women.[13]

Domestic workers in the EU now come from all over the world: as long
ago as 1987 a study found that domestic workers were mostly from the
Philippines, Sri Lanka, Thailand, Argentina, Colombia, Brazil, El Salvador
and Peru.[14] The expansion of the EU in the early 2000s led to increased
numbers of domestic workers from eastern European countries in the
UK and other parts of the EU. Because the sector is so informal, data are
difficult to gather, but a report produced by the European Federation of
Food, Agriculture and Tourism Trade unions (EFFAT) suggests that in
Italy, nearly two-thirds of migrant domestic workers are from countries
of eastern Europe. In the Netherlands, Filipina and Indonesian migrant
domestic workers have developed their own organisations, while in the
UK, the organisation Justice for Domestic Workers has members from 'the
Philippines, Indonesia, India, Sri Lanka, Morocco and Nigeria'.[15]

Migration routes are shaped not only by colonial histories of connection
and demand in wealthy economies, but also in some instances by explicitly
designed state policy. Anna Romina Guevarra describes the state-spon-
sored system of migration of Filipino care workers oversees, to the US, UK
and Saudi Arabia for nurses, and to Hong Kong, Lebanon, Singapore and
Taiwan for domestic work. The system is highly structured and well organised. Employers must be accredited by the Filipino government's overseas
labour office in their country. They are then assigned to a relevant employment agency, which recruits workers and matches them to available jobs.
Employment agencies are private or government-run – the latter catering
for public sector employers. Migrating workers are celebrated by the
Filipino government, given status as 'heroes' for their country, and a great
deal of state-led effort is put into encouraging overseas migration and the
return of remittances.[16]

Once in the US, Filipino nurses are deployed to meet labour shortages
across the country. Since the 1980s, numbers of US-based nurses entering

the profession have declined, due to dissatisfaction on the job and shortages of nursing educators. Guevarra sums up the sources of dissatisfaction as follows: 'demanding workload, stagnant wages, lack of opportunities for career mobility, forced voluntary overtime, presence of a business model of health care delivery and stress-related illnesses'.[17] Filipino nurses speak good English and are often well educated in a US curriculum; like the call centre workers, this is a product of colonial histories from when the Philippines was a US colony. Nursing work is demanding, both physically and emotionally, but they consider that they are better than the US nurses, because they work more independently and with more care. Working provides reasonable material rewards that allow them to support the education of their families back home, and also consumption in the US and the Philippines. This process creates global care chains, forged as women move to another country to care for another couple's child, leaving their own children in the care of their father or other relatives and drawing on extended family structures at 'home'.[18]

Work and relations, work as relations

Most if not all service sector work aims to produce a particular affect in another person such as a customer, client, patient; the sense of a problem solved, of feeling welcomed, relaxed, happy with a purchase, or anxious and ready to make a loan payment, and so on. The work is conducted through relations and is often about producing further relations. This is the key insight of Hardt and Negri's definition of 'affective labour' as a subset of 'immaterial labour'.[19] The idea of affective labour is a capacious concept, able to name aspects of the work of flight attendants, retail workers and call centre agents, as well as sex workers, nurses and domestic workers. All are service workers, some provide intimate services (which Boris and Parreñas call 'intimate labour'[20]), some use a bodily connection to do so (which Kang calls 'body labour'[21]). Most from time to time need to engage in what Arlie Hochschild first identified as the 'emotional labour' of managing feelings, either theirs or their customer's.[22] Their labour practices are not truly immaterial in the sense of not being physical, but they generally do not produce a material good; instead they primarily produce an affect or relation. For example, the immaterial labour of call-centre work consists of problem-solving and communication labour combined with the affective labour of personal and customer management.

Call centre workers must develop a particular bearing, even subjecthood. They must become a certain kind of person, with cultural competence in the customer's language and behaviour. In Indian call centres, especially prior to the mid-2000s, agents were expected to pretend that they were located in the US (or UK, Canada and so on, depending on the client base). They changed their names while at work, introducing themselves with American sounding names – Victor instead of Vikas, Ruth for Radha, Tim for Tarun.[23] They learned about US weather, local laws, local customs such as holidays, and habits of politeness and hierarchy. Purnima Mankekar and Akhil Gupta even report on training sessions that taught the agents how to use deodorant and Western-style toilets, to become 'modern' bodies, even though their connection with customers was mediated through voice only.[24]

From about 2005 onwards, Kiran Mirchandani found that call centres started to allow agents to admit that they were located in India, and so the stresses of pretending were no longer required.[25] However, agency employers continued to emphasise the need for a 'neutral accent' in their employees' spoken English, requiring agents to smooth out the 'mother tongue influences' of Indian English.[26] This form of 'Global English' is not the same as sounding American (or English, etc.) but is shaped by American or British ways of speaking English. One of the key elements of this, according to A. Aneesh, was lexical stress – which syllable of a word to emphasise. He describes how his respondents found it strange to stress the second syllable in 'magnificent' or to pronounce Indianapolis with the stress on the 'a' before 'polis'. Creating agents who could speak with an appropriately neutral accent and the correct bearing and approach was achieved through a combination of demanding recruitment procedures and training. Training would take place over several weeks, and include accents, how to enact the phone conversations, how to deal with difficult customers, and how to understand cultural expressions including slang like different meanings of 'zip', 'yank', even 'love handles'. Agents are also taught that customer dissatisfaction might be expressed in culturally distinct ways; US clients are usually considered more direct and impolite than UK ones, for example. The agents learn to shift their expectations about how to cope with hierarchies, and what politeness means.[27]

Thus, simply having a 'neutral' accent and competence in the spoken language is not enough. As well as knowing the specific procedures for the business process they are making calls about, agents also need to develop a broader cultural competence, even if it does not have to go so far as convincing the client that they are just down the road. That must be combined with competence in emotional labour, as agents must cultivate 'attention, solicitude, empathy and intimacy', developing affective repertoires 'of courtesy, familiarity, friendliness, helpfulness, and, above all, caring', in Mankekar and Gupta's words.[28] This is not merely an effect (or affect) of having correct knowledge, but is in addition a very physical process, not least because agents must keep up remarkable levels of energy to conduct phone conversations one after the other over an eight-hour shift with very few breaks.

A key element that has struck many ethnographers of Indian call centres is how agents are encouraged to smile when they talk to customers.[29] They are told that if they smile, the customer will smile on the other end of the phone line. In one case, an agent was admonished for not smiling while talking, and therefore coming across as formal and strained, and whether she smiled became part of her performance evaluations.[30] The agents' job, then, is to manage customer affect, which can range from convincing a customer to book an airplane ticket that they've already decided on before calling to more challenging tasks like calming a frustrated customer who has repeatedly called to try to solve a technical problem with their computer, or coping with racial and sexual abuse over the phone. In training, agents are taught to listen to abusive customers, apologise, understand and try to soothe them, even when they are accusing the agent of taking American jobs. This is part of the work – as one of Mirchandani's respondents said: 'If [the customer] is irate ... at first, be calm and listen to him. Let him take out their anger. Let them be calm, and once they finish ... "Sorry for whatever problem you faced".' Another agent said: 'I had customers who at the beginning of the call, they start with the slangs [abusive words]. I make them calm down. Convince them I can do their job ... that's when they come into the same frequency, wherein you can communicate very easily. It's the way you put the customer across. It's the way you talk.'[31]

The affective nature of call centre labour is underlined by the fact that increasingly the metric by which agents are assessed is 'customer satisfaction'. Agents are producing contentment, and they are required to engage in a lot of emotional labour to do so. Kimberley Kay Hoang distinguishes between expressive and repressive emotional labour in sex work in Ho Chi Minh City[32] (discussed below), and the distinction works well for call centre agents: the smile in the voice, the friendly chat, the calming down are all expressive emotional labour. By contrast, the suppression of feelings of exhaustion, anger at racist abuse, or irritation at customer stupidity, are all forms of repressive emotional labour.

Call centre agents use their voices predominantly in the affective labour of producing customer contentment. Retail workers, beauty workers, domestic carers and sex workers must use more of their bodies. For example, Korean nail salon artists in New York City must sit in close contact with their customers, massaging their hands and feet, engaging them in conversation, helping them to relax and to feel better about themselves. They must repress feelings of disgust at touching people's feet, with their odour, cracked skin, or yellowing nails. They must ignore customers' post-lunchtime breath, while at the same time managing their own body odours and comportment. As a consequence of this labour, they often develop long term relationships of care, but it is hard work. Miliann Kang tells the story of one customer in her eighties, 'Gwen', who comes into the 'Uptown Nails' salon once a week for a manicure and pedicure. Over two to three hours, manicurists attend to her hands and feet, bring her a cup of coffee and a magazine while her nails dry, talk with her, help her to the toilet – a task which requires two people to lift her out of her chair and so on. One time, when she fell asleep and began to slump sideways in her chair, a manicurist noticed and slid the chair next to the wall so she didn't fall. Gwen appreciated the care, but did not really see the demands she placed on the manicurists; she considered theirs to be a good, 'fun' job.[33]

Making work seem to the customer like fun often requires much effort, physical as well as emotional. Rhacel Salazar Parreñas worked in Japanese nightclubs, where she and the Filipina hostesses in her study engaged in the expressive emotional labour of flirting with customers, encouraging them to gift money, spend money on drinks in the club and relax. In the clubs where Parreñas worked, the hostesses did not necessarily have sex with customers, at least not in the club itself; but plenty of them considered it appropriate to develop sexual relationships with clients outside of the club, which would include gifts of money to the worker; or they were happy with straightforward exchanges of sex for money. She suggests that this varied among workers: some were only prepared to flirt with the clients, and restricted physical contact to a hand on their thigh, or a kiss on the cheek, others would receive money for sex with clients outside of the club only, while others sold sex inside the club. Clubs varied in what they allowed, in part as a result of this moral economy of the workers, as well as – of course – their bosses, and consequently the club's reputation attracted customers who would largely conform to expectations of particular behaviours.[34]

Sex work is undoubtedly one of the most varied and physical forms of affective labour. In Tokyo, Gabriele Koch shows how the sex industry is often described as a source of healing, or *iyashi*, for male white-collar workers, who are suffering the effects of increased economic precarity, stress and exhaustion: 'Healing by women working in the Japanese sex industry produces feelings of well-being, pleasure, connectedness, recognition, and masculine distinction in their customers.' The sex workers in her study saw this as a contribution to male economic productivity, placing quite a different value on their work than the usual stigmatisation, albeit still subordinating their own labour to male white-collar productivity.[35] Many sex workers need to repress their revulsion for their clients, perhaps by distinguishing between the acts that they perform as work and acts of love or sexual desire within non-work relationships. Often, they see their work as precisely that (i.e. work), making a distinction between the work they do and who they are; between 'doing sex work' and 'being a sex worker', or being non-professional sexworkers (*shirōto*), ordinary women who happen to be engaging in sex-work at that moment in time.[36] Koch stresses the diversity of women working in the Japanese sex industry, but suggests that a significant number of women find that sex work provides them with more autonomy and higher income than other possibilities open to women. Nonetheless, the vast majority do not reveal their profession to family and friends and the labour of managing that stigma is significant. They also expend effort (which increases as they get older) to appear *shirōto*, fresh and youthful, without too much experience but with genuine feelings.[37]

Some acts of labour can involve little emotional effort, as in the encounters described by Kimberley Hoang in a barbershop in Ho Chi Minh City, where three women take it in turns to provide sexual services to clients on a bed behind a curtain. The interaction usually takes around 20 minutes, unless the woman is having difficulty 'finishing off' her client, in which case another worker comes to assist. In contrast, in the same city, Hoang describes how women accompany visiting tourists or businessmen. Their working relationship is on the surface informal, the transaction disguised by the language of short-term relationships. The man is expected to give the woman money, and to buy her expensive items. Hoang quotes one Vietnamese client who was visiting family at home for two weeks: 'It's implied, you know, that as a Vietnamese guy that I buy her jewelry, clothes, and give her money to spend while we are together.' When asked how much money he thought he had spent, he answered:

> I don't know. I bought her a lot of things, and I probably gave her two hundred dollars here and there ... probably six or seven hundred dollars on the low end. ... These girls are expensive because they are young, pretty, and other guys want them. ... I knew if I didn't give her enough money she would move on to another guy.

The workers themselves are extremely adept at assessing which clients to associate with and managing their emotions so that the client pays the correct amount of money.[38]

Elsewhere, such as in the US, a similar kind of expressive emotional labour is encapsulated in the commercialisation of the 'girlfriend experience', which includes services of emotional support, usually through attentive listening, in addition to sex and other forms of physical engagement like massage. According to Elizabeth Bernstein, this can require the emotional labour of 'manufacturing *genuine* (if fleeting) libidinal and emotional ties, endowing their clients with a feeling of desirability, esteem, or even love'.[39] No one could argue that this labour is not material as well as emotional, and indeed the usefulness of the concepts of intimate and body labour lies precisely in the attention they give to the physicality involved.

A complementary way to think about this and other forms of care work is another theoretical contribution by Arlie Hochschild, namely 'marketized private life', which speaks to commercial exchanges in the work of social reproduction that might be considered intimate or domestic, traditionally carried out by women as unpaid labour: cleaning, childcare, elderly care, sex and so on.[40] As Viviana Zelizer argues, paid labour in intimate settings raises fundamental questions about social relations; what we owe each other, and what happens to affective connections when money enters the equation or vice versa, what happens to commercial relations when affect enters the equation.[41] This kind of reproductive labour overlaps with affective labour but is not subsumed by it; as Silvia Federici argues, it is important to keep the two conceptually distinct.[42]

Caring work is often very demanding, placing physical strain on the workers. Nurses and home carers report fatigue, back strain and burnout from stress.[43] Their work is often rendered invisible, their labour erased as we talk about how elderly people live 'independently'. Lynn May Rivas tells a powerful story of that invisibility. She was conducting an interview

with an elderly man, Bill, about his relationship with his personal attendant. Although after a while he was finding it hard to continue talking,
he would not allow her to hold a cup for him to drink from. As he struggled to speak, she eventually persuaded him to allow her to go and find
his personal attendant, who had gone outside to wait until the end of the
interview. For the remaining twenty minutes, Joe, the personal attendant, 'stands next to Bill, offering him a sip of water every few minutes,
seamlessly'.[44]

Although their work is often invisible, physically taxing and poorly paid,
home care workers nonetheless routinely go beyond the official requirements of their jobs – staying longer than their formal hours of work, using
their own money to make small purchases that ease their client/patient's
life, answering calls outside of work hours to reassure and so on. Like call
centre agents, they must often soothe angry, irritated or confused clients,
absorbing the aggression and mood swings that can accompany dementia
and other conditions of old age. They must also manage the family's
emotions, perhaps coping with family members who attempt to control
what they do, or conversely helping the client to cope with what they
experience as abandonment by their family.[45] Carers often develop strong
attachments to their charges. Maria de la Luz Ibarra calls these 'deep alliances', especially powerful for end-of-life care. Of course, one of the most
profound emotions involved in elderly care is grief for the client who has
died.[46] As emotional labour goes, this is one of the most highly skilled
occupations there is.

The US-based home care workers interviewed by Claire Stacey mostly
responded to the emotional demands of their work by incorporating them
into a self-identity strongly formed by their ability to care. An important
aspect of that was their sense of autonomy to do the job as they wished,
to 'provide care on their own terms' and to their own standards. Acts like
buying medicines out of their own money, or working out of hours were
not for them a sign of the exploitative nature of their working relationship, but something that they do because that is the kind of person they
are. This is what makes them good at their job. That is not to say that
they were operating under false consciousness; they acknowledged poor
working conditions. But they also took pride in doing their job well, and
some argued that they could seek other work but chose not to.[47] Similarly, the Filipino nurses working in the US who were interviewed by Anna
Romina Guevarra took pride in their hardworking and caring attitude,
contrasting it to the attitude of the American nurses, who were, they

felt, much more likely merely to do the physical aspects of the job, the minimum required.[48]

The imbrication of love and relationship-building with work is often summed up in the phrase that a care worker is 'like family' to her/his employer or client. The contradictions of this in practice are especially acutely felt in home-based childcare. Nannies, whether live-in or live-out, occupy an often stressful place within households. As Seemin Qayum and Raka Ray point out, they are 'like family' until something happens and they're not. Their interlocutor Ruchira brought her cook Kanchan back with her family when they returned to New York from a stay in South Asia. Ruchira had grown up with family servants in Kolkata and saw in Kanchan someone she knew well and who shared a cultural background, so would be a good nanny for her child. Ruchira and Kanchan's relationship ended after Kanchan asked not to work after 5 p.m. or at weekends, and prompted by Ruchira's second pregnancy, requested that she only cook two days a week, to allow her to focus on her nannying duties for the rest of the time. Ruchira felt this request as a betrayal, because it brought the employment relationship too much to the foreground.[49] Pierrette Hondagneu-Sotelo describes some of the 'blowups' that abruptly end employer-nanny relationships, as nannies ask for a raise, or are asked to add one more duty to their list without extra payment, or are accused of not caring properly for the child. Because the employer-employee relationship is so intimate, its ending cannot always be professional; and so both sides come up with excuses – for example, the nanny who wants to leave for a better job says she must return to her home country to look after a sick relative, or the employer says conditions have changed and she needs to rehire a previous nanny.[50]

Meanwhile, nannies come to love the children they care for, sometimes displacing the emotional labour that they might otherwise expend on their own children, who are being cared for by others (often overseas, in the country from which they migrated). If the nanny works for a heterosexual couple, it means that the father can continue to avoid housework and childcare duties while the mother is able to enter the labour market without exhausting herself on the 'second shift'.[51] This is a matter of class privilege, but it can also bring with it a complicated gendered relationship between the two women who are mothering the children. Mothers might feel threatened that their child has become closer to the nanny, or consider that the nanny is not bringing the child up correctly. Women who are strongly invested in the idea that their identity is closely attached to their role as mother and manager of the household do not always want to completely outsource that, even if they also work outside the home. And so they try to control what the domestic worker does and how she does it. Ana Ramos Zayas outlines some of the racial tensions surrounding this with regard to parenting, using the example of middle-class parents in Rio de Janeiro and San Juan, Puerto Rico, who complain that their nannies teach the children to speak in the language and accents of the favelas and the Dominican Republic, respectively.[52]

Conditions for nannies and other live-in domestic workers vary in different countries and different households. In La Paz, Bolivia, domestic workers are often indigenous migrants from the countryside who live with wealthy mestizo or white families and clean the house as well as care for the children of the household, whether the mother works outside the house or not.[53] This fits into a tradition of domestic servitude on haciendas in the past, where '*pongos*' had to provide both agricultural and domestic labour for their landlord. Particularly with older employers, the relationship is still structured as one of servitude. I have heard women describe how they had to teach their maid to cook or clean properly, while complaining that their maids never stay for very long; and I've heard stories of employers screaming at domestic workers who have not ironed their shirts properly. In another case, a live-in domestic worker I know stayed with a family for more than twenty years. When she became pregnant, she hid her pregnancy from her employers, thinking that they might fire her, as is often the case. But instead they accepted the situation, and she lived in her room in the house with her child, whose education, healthcare and other costs of life were paid for by her employers. She and her child ate the same food as the employers' family, but not at the table with the family. In other instances, this time in Argentina, families have live-out domestic employees who work only weekdays (but often have a very long commute to the wealthy districts where they work). They are called 'the lady who helps us with the children' (*la Señora que nos ayuda con los nenes*), and in Buenos Aires are usually migrants from Paraguay. In the UK, cleaners might come to middle-class households for a few hours once a week or fortnight, like babysitters, who might be local teenagers paid cash in hand; while nannies tend to be employed on a live-out basis by relatively wealthy households.

Domestic work is based in histories of slavery and peonage, which, along with the intimate setting of the workplace, makes the employee especially vulnerable to verbal, physical and sexual abuse. Globally, the maid has been seen as sexually available to her male employer, in some cases to the point of being the person to whom the young men of the household lose their virginity. The updated version of this story is that of the father of the household who has an affair with the nanny, a story which both participates in the old traditions and manages to blame the nanny – for being younger, more attractive, more impressionable, etc. Nannies need to be close to the parents and of course the children, but not too close. They participate in the most intimate of family relations but must not overstep the line. Similarly, other caregivers must pay attention to how intimate they become with their clients and how that is received by other family members.

Affective labour produces relationships but is also produced by complicated relationships, from wider histories of colonialism to the intimate relationship between a couple and the woman who cares for their children or an elderly dementia sufferer and the person who cleans up their incontinence. Some of those relationships are mediated just by voice, as in the case of the call centre agent, but all of them are very physical, both in the sense of often necessitating heavy physical labour and in the sense of requiring the worker to develop a particular physical bearing and energy, even self-identity. It is therefore a material labour process, that produces goods both physical and affective: a clean person or house, artistic nails, a well-behaved child; and customer satisfaction, a peaceful death, or a 'girl-friend experience'.

Labour agency: collective action and everyday strategies

Given the intimate nature of the workplace and the emotional valence of relationships and the labour tied up in them, one might expect limited opportunities for worker agency or resistance to exploitation, and even fewer possibilities for collective politics in affective service sector jobs. Hardt and Negri argue that the hegemony of immaterial labour creates a figure of resistance completely different from that created when material labour was dominant: specifically, the multitude rather than the industrial proletariat. The multitude is 'all those who work under the rule of capital and thus potentially ... the class of those who refuse the rule of capital.' It is composed therefore of all kinds of labourers, all those who are exploited, and expands the concept of the proletariat to 'all those who labor and produce under the rule of capital'. In the place of traditional forms of worker mobilisation, such as industrial trade unions, the fragmentation and precarity of immaterial labour and the multitude itself would also demand new kinds of collective practices, perhaps focused around mobilisational forms such as the neighbourhood assembly rather than the workplace strike.[54] Critics have argued that Hardt and Negri's claims about the political subject of immaterial labour are overblown, and that there is nothing intrinsic about affective labour that leads to greater cooperation or worker autonomy in actual practice, either in the workplace or as political expression. Indeed, affective labour can be just as alienating, surveilled and mechanical as other forms of labour.[55] Nonetheless, affective labour does present difficulties for labour-based organisation, because of the essential relationality of the work. When work is mixed up with personalised relations of care and even love, and workers are precariously employed and isolated from each other, it is challenging to create traditional kinds of labour mobilisation, like strikes, legal cases or demonstrations.

That said, and although I agree that we need to theorise new political subjects outside of the industrial proletariat, I think that Hardt and Negri have dismissed the trade union form itself a little too quickly. There are many examples of trade unions organising successful campaigns for service workers. For example, Steven Henry Lopez described the successful campaigning efforts of the SEIU branch in Pittsburgh to resist union busting efforts at for-profit nursing homes in the mid-1990s; and in 1999, the SEIU achieved a significant victory in California as public authorities recognised their right to collective bargaining on behalf of home carers. That led to higher wages and other improvements in working conditions.[56] Significantly, both campaigns were successful when they managed to turn their economic, labour issues into questions of social justice, and create a connection in public perception between better conditions for the workers and better conditions for their charges.

Since the 1980s, the SEIU has also organised the 'Justice for Janitors' campaign for subcontracted cleaners in California. Christian Zlolniski tells the story of one group, who worked for the 'Bay-Clean' agency to clean 'Sonix' buildings across Silicon Valley. Predominantly migrants from Mexico and Central America, half a dozen cleaners unhappy with their working conditions went to a local union in the early 1990s to see what they could do. They recruited fellow activists using their own kin and social networks, and with the support of the union managed to reach the majority of janitors working for Bay-Clean. They threatened a strike to bring their direct employers (the agency Bay-Clean) to a meeting, but when that meeting did not produce clear results, the union organised a public demonstration in front of Sonix buildings, supported by community allies such as non-profit organisations, religious groups, students and other union members. Sonix responded by removing the cleaning contract from Bay-Clean and giving it to a larger, unionised company, although keeping the same personnel. Wages were higher, and workers were entitled to healthcare, sick leave and one week's paid vacation. This was a victory, although as Zlolniski pointed out, not all was positive, as the larger company then placed slightly fewer workers on each site, leading to increased workload for the cleaners.[57]

The SEIU is an example of a well-established union that has been able to act creatively, adjusting their understandings of what organisation means and how it can work for the benefit of service sector workers in all kinds of workplaces.[58] Other campaigning organisations work in alliances, as Miliann Kang describes for workers' rights and occupational health campaigns for nail salon workers in the 2000s, which included the Asian American Legal Defense and Education Fund (AALDEF), a Korean American community organisation, National Mobilization Against Sweatshops, Chinese Staff and Workers Association and 318 Restaurant workers' Union.[59]

In the UK, some recent mobilisations of service sector workers have been channelled through independent unions, especially the IWGB and United Voices of the World (UVW), despite a very hostile legal environment. Their work has been organised around cleaners and gig workers. Recently, the UVW organised outsourced hospital cleaners, caterers and porters to campaign for parity with NHS staff.[60] During 2020–2021 they led a campaign at a nursing home in North London, explicitly linking their demands for better pay to their vulnerability as care workers during the coronavirus pandemic and to the celebrations of carers and key workers during the weekly doorstep applause in the first lockdown. Their campaign website simply says: 'Thousands of people have clapped for care workers and NHS staff all over the UK. It's time to turn this support into action'[61] and a news article quotes leading workers describing the weekly applause as a 'performative display of national gratitude served alongside their below-liveable wage and life-threatening working environment'.[62] After a strike in October 2021, the nursing home employers capitulated and agreed to pay care workers the London Living Wage, which represented a pay increase of eleven per cent for some of the lowest-paid workers.[63]

Across the world, unions organise domestic workers, and an international alliance of organisations successfully campaigned for an International Labour Organization (ILO) convention on domestic work, achieved in 2011.[64] Collective organising in this sphere of work is very difficult, as domestic workers are generally isolated from each other and subject to the intimate relationships discussed in the previous section. Nonetheless, some actions are possible, sometimes, even if the informality of conditions means that collective mobilisation will likely only ever cover a very small segment of the domestic workforce. As Dorothy Sue Cobble points out, it was once thought that women were unorganisable, and what she terms the 'factory paradigm of labor organizing' continues to hold sway, convincing us that collective organisation is only really possible in large, bureaucratised workplaces of traditionally male working-class jobs. In fact, even in the reasonably highly industrialised United States, millions of non-factory workers unionised before the peak of 'mass production unionism' in the mid-twentieth century.[65] Service workers have always joined collective organisations, from waitresses in the 1950s to McDonald's and Starbucks workers now.

Sex workers also have professional associations or trade unions at national and international levels globally, with the exception of the Middle East. Examples include the African Sex Workers Alliance, the Asia Pacific Network of Sex Workers, the Plataforma Latinoamericana de Personas que Ejercen el Trabajo Sexual and the International Committee for the Rights of Sex Workers in Europe.[66] That said, while scholars concur in arguing that sex workers should be understood in more complex terms than either criminals or victims of trafficking, the combination of illegality, violence and stigmatisation limits what is possible.[67] If sex work is not seen as ordinary work, fights for labour rights are easily foreclosed.

The precariousness of much affective labour can mitigate against collective action. Like domestic work, call centre work is based usually on short term or informal contracts. In contrast to the Indian call centre workers described earlier, who view their work as high status, in Portugal, the precarity of call centre employment produces feelings of 'shame, resentment and failure' among the workers. In the midst of the European recession of the 2000s and 2010s, they feel that they have failed to fulfil their parents' hopes of middle-class distinction, and their own hopes for more secure employment consistent with their status as university graduates.[68] They are reluctant to engage in serious organising efforts in the workplaces they see as temporary. Yet this is not always the case, as the example of grassroots organising in Greek call centres shows. In 2013, the young and precarious workers of a large telecommunications company in Athens held two days of four-hour work stoppages, combined with rallies at the office entrance. The management responded with tactics such as changing the shift schedule, moving shifts to other buildings and pressuring young workers to work; but they also halted the wave of lay-offs that had prompted the stoppages. Notably, the grassroots organisers worked through general assemblies of the workers but coordinated with the company union to give themselves legal cover for their actions.[69]

Although resistance to poor working conditions is very difficult for most affective labourers, especially those in precarious employment, it is not impossible. With due creativity, aspects of the job that might at first glance seem to constrain workers from pushing for better treatment can be used to argue in their favour. Care workers can mobilise their caring relationship with their charges to argue that they should be valued for their contribution to the community. Even precarity itself can become a source for mobilisation. Still, the conditions of much service work make collective organisation hard to achieve. The short-term nature of contracts in call centres is a means of reducing the capacity for collectivisation, the fragmented workplaces and exhausting nature of all of the work described in this chapter leave little time, space and energy for collective action. It can be necessary to make alliances with student groups, migrant associations, not for profit organisations, and religious and other community groups; all of which is very hard work.

Yet, in practice it is not the case that the only options available to affective labourers are always either complete subservience or collective organisation. Ethnographies and personal experience tell us that workers also engage in everyday acts of resistance and accommodation, perhaps taking extra breaks when their boss is not around, or working especially slowly when unhappy. The maids who do not stay long in jobs where they are yelled at for not ironing clothes properly exercise their agency by leaving to seek better conditions elsewhere, like the Chinese electronics assembly workers who leave their factories at New Year or the Tirrupur stitchers who go home at Diwali and don't return. Filipina hostesses in Japanese nightclubs negotiate over just how much and which parts of their bodies are available to the customer at a given moment. Call centre agents learn how to manipulate their metrics so as to give themselves a small break between calls. And so on. None of these negotiations happen within a relation of equality, but Claire Stacey makes a good point when she cautions us to consider that 'emotional exploitation does not necessarily follow from material exploitation'.[70]

Caring and affective relationships interact with worker agency and resistance in complex ways. Unlike factory workers, affective workers have a relationship with a client or clients and with their employer. Sometimes they are the same person, but more usually they are not, as when agency-employed care workers look after elderly clients on government run schemes, or a nanny looks after her employer's child. The workers' feelings of attachment to the client may blunt their ability to demand better conditions from their employer because if they remove their labour power the employer might not directly suffer, but someone they love will. In some cases, those attachments can mask exploitative labour relations, but rarely are they examples of fully false consciousness. Instead, they might well be seen as the interpersonal negotiation of relationships as a form of managing the work so that it is a more positive experience for both sides. Workers reach multiple individual accommodations with their clients, and – if they can – leave when that is no longer possible. Still, although individual acts of agency might be most common, collective organising is not impossible, and can even occasionally be successful.

5
Professional and Managerial Work
Producing Selves and Processes

Professional and managerial work forms part of the service economy and is also a form of affective and immaterial labour, but is generally better paid and afforded higher prestige than the service sector work described in the previous chapter. It too is aimed at producing relations, especially hierarchical ones, and is often enacted through relations. Like the workers of the previous chapter, these relations affect what people see as politically possible or desirable when it comes to their employment conditions. As well as relations, professional, managerial and academic workers produce the immaterial goods of knowledge, processes and outputs. The government of the production processes for these goods creates tensions around the measurement and commodification of immaterial goods, which shapes the experience of labour. Furthermore, one of the most important immaterial products they produce is the worker themself, although importantly it is rare for them to be produced as *workers* as such, preferring instead other professional identities. Again, a labour politics designed for the hegemonic figure of the industrial labourer producing material goods must be rethought for these workers. Like the previous chapter, one animating question of this chapter is what does immateriality do to labour agency? This is not to say that the labour *process* itself is immaterial, it is often very corporeal and at times exhausting. But when the (main) products of labour are immaterial, and even include the worker herself, then what kinds of agency are possible?

The examples I discuss come mostly from four groups of workers: financial services workers, management consultants, bureaucrats and academics in higher education. They (we) produce the immaterial goods of knowledge, information, relations, and selves, outputs and processes. In producing selves, many become an example of what I call 'overidentification', where the worker becomes the work, a counterpart to the alienation experienced in industrial labour. That overidentification is an important aspect of this kind of work, and it conditions labour agency and the possibility for collective action. Another conditioning possibility is the labour process itself: how labour is structured and evaluated, and what are the nature of working conditions, especially with regard to the distinction between secure and precarious employment (a characteristic that academia in particular shares with the industrial labour discussed in Chapter 1). Therefore, the second animating question for this chapter is: how might we analyse worker mobilisation (or its lack) among immaterial labourers, beyond the observation that the privileged ones are well paid and therefore content? This chapter is one of the two in this book with which I most identify personally, as an academic who defines myself very much through the work I do.[1] In part as a result, the weight of examples here tends to skew towards the US and Europe.

Changing values in management

Unlike the work I have described in previous chapters, much of the managerial and professional labour I discuss here has stayed put over recent decades. You can find bureaucrats and academics all over the world, and all of the kinds of workers I discuss in this chapter are to some extent internationally networked. But most bureaucrats work to run government in one country[2] or agency, investment bankers and stock traders are located in a few world cities and their financial centres, and higher education academics are mostly (for now) connected to universities, even if they move between them internationally. Management consultants move but their main offices are usually based in global centres of business and finance, like bankers and traders.

Geographically, significant parts of the university sector are very stable in physical terms: the University of Salamanca is 800 years old, for example, and eight of the nine Ivy League universities in the US were founded before 1770 (the ninth, Cornell, was founded in 1865). However, the past fifty years have seen a rapid expansion in tertiary education in most countries of the world. This is mostly from increased numbers of private universities, but in recent years a few countries, like Argentina and Brazil, have even established new public universities. In the UK, private universities are a recent development, as from 2010 private colleges were allowed to run two-year courses for which their students would be eligible for state student loans, like the public universities. This has brought new global corporate players into the UK system, like

Global University Systems, Pearson and the private equity fund Sovereign Capital.[3] Meanwhile, established and usually very wealthy US and UK universities have expanded by developing online courses or new campuses, especially in east Asia and the Gulf. These initiatives may come to have more significant effects in the future, but for now, much university work retains its location in global, regional and national centres. Indeed, cities become these kinds of centres in part because of the presence of a significant university.

Globally, government administration is often the biggest or most stable employer in all but the largest or most industrial towns and cities; and despite the policy prescriptions of international financial institutions (on which more later), this shows little likelihood of changing in practice, especially as private sector employment becomes more and more precarious. The global financial services sector has seen a rise in the power of centres in Singapore and Shanghai, but the old ones of New York, London, Tokyo and Hong Kong remain strong.[4] Similarly, over the last two decades management consultancy has experienced an expansion from its previous concentration in the classical financial and business capitals into new cities, especially in China.[5]

So, the geography of professional and managerial labour has expanded in scope but not (yet) changed quite as dramatically as, say, that of garment or electronics production. However, what has changed quite dramatically over time are the philosophies (or ideologies) of how to organise this kind of work. For bureaucracies, especially in the public sector, the most influential model has been 'new public management', introduced in OECD countries from the 1980s onwards. Christopher Hood distinguishes it from previous public sector approaches by first, the shift in focus of accountability from process to results and second, the bringing of private sector processes and agencies into the public sector, breaking down the differences between them. New public management is neoliberalism for the public sector, a rendering of efficiency and value for money in market terms. It does not necessarily mean employing fewer people, but often does mean reducing job security and shifting the overall balance of employment towards administration via the need to manage performance as outcomes (that's to say, meeting targets).[6]

What does that mean? One of the clearest examples of this in practice is the experience of the BBC in the 1990s. Georgina Born's ethnography documents the frustration of programme creators at the weight of administration brought about by management restructuring under the director general John Birt.[7] In response to the political situation of the 1990s, when the BBC was under considerable attack from its competitors and the government of the time, the corporation brought in management consultants to introduce new auditing processes, at every level. Born describes the situation:

> Of all the managerial initiatives, it was these [auditing processes] that creative staff found most onerous and that obtruded most on their work. They included periodic Programme Strategy Reviews throughout the corporation lasting a year or more, sometimes involving workshops for all staff; Annual Performance Reviews for all departments, which took several months and required the production of exhaustive documentation; and monthly and quarterly statements of purpose and account by each programme editor.[8]

Reviews and statements of purpose are quite standard practice in many institutions now, albeit not necessarily at such frequency; in my own university, departments need to prepare documentation for internal strategic research reviews or learning and teaching reviews every few years, combined with external government audits and reporting for research funders. Born goes on to point out:

> Audit encompassed even the mundane. The BBC toilets were audited by a Toilet Housekeeping Checklist hanging on each door, on which cleaners had several times a day neatly to note the details of their visits by time and task. On every table in the BBC cafeterias sat a card on which customers were enjoined to offer assessments and criticism, the better to improve services.[9]

Today, these sorts of audits are so normalised that it seems quaint to include them as the kind of ethnographic detail that is at the very least intended to make readers roll their eyes.

Such techniques are not confined to OECD countries. Political shifts in the conception of overseas development assistance have seen similar techniques exported to non-OECD countries, and like the BBC, they are often accompanied by management consultants. Since the turn of this century, development has been increasingly conceptualised as large scale, sector wide interventions with development partners, an evolution from previous varieties of development as enacted directly by donor agencies or Northern NGOs. This was fuelled by the recognition of the need for country ownership of development programmes, and the greater participation of beneficiaries – stakeholders – in design and implementation. So far, so good, but in its enactment, it has created complex arrangements of differently involved agents that require multiple reporting processes and meetings to organise and monitor the successful completion of various performance targets.[10]

Universities also moved gradually towards a form of administration focused on performance targets and their linked audit processes. This has been driven both by an ideological commitment to this form of management and cuts in state support for universities, especially research,[11] coupled in some countries with a shift to private financing through student tuition fees. In the UK, the introduction of performance measurement is associated with (and to an extent enacted through) the government audits of higher education research and teaching, known as the Research Excellence Framework (REF), and the Teaching Excellence Framework (TEF). The REF takes place every seven years and requires departments to submit a certain number of publications by eligible staff for evaluation by their peers. A good score in the REF often translates to increases in funding over the next few years, or to smaller reductions in funding perhaps, since the precise link between the REF and funding on the ground is usually rather opaque. The REF is still ostensibly a qualitative process, but elsewhere in the sector Cris Shore and Susan Wright argue that audit processes of performance management have come to rely on numerical indicators that were initially treated as proxies for excellence but have in many institutions taken on a life of their own. For example, in 2016, for promotion to Professor in the Social Sciences in the University of Auckland, New Zealand, candidates needed to have published over fifty articles in leading peer-reviewed journals, supervised eight MA and eight PhD students, and generated three external research grants of over NZ$100,000.[12]

Around about the same time that new public management was coming into vogue in the UK, financial services were undergoing the 'shareholder revolution', the latest cycle in the rise of the concept of shareholder value. Shareholder value is the idea that a corporation's value lies in its share price, rather than other possible measures like employment, the wellbeing of its workers, or its contribution to social welfare. Karen Ho tells how investment bankers on Wall Street described shareholder value as something beyond just increasing the price of stock: it 'signified a mission statement, a declaration of purpose, even a call to action. Creating or reclaiming shareholder value was morally and economically the right thing to do; it was the yardstick to measure individual as well as corporate practices, values and achievements.'[13] As Ho describes, with the increase in corporate takeovers in the 1980s, corporations shifted from their post-war identities as social institutions with multiple participants to become more like 'liquid networks of shareholders'. Symbolised most famously by the movie *Wall Street* (1987) and facilitated by the invention of junk bonds and changes in financial regulation, the takeover movement meant that investors could buy up enough stock to launch hostile takeovers, then control corporations to do whatever was necessary to increase their share price. That could be mass firings of workers, asset stripping and so on; all measures aimed at making companies 'leaner'. Over time, this led to an alignment between corporate values and the interests of the stock market in the US. Kimberly Chong's more recent work shows how the goal of increasing shareholder value shapes management consultants' work in contemporary China. Consultants often see their role as educating corporations in shareholder value in order to make state owned enterprises investment-ready, so that they can be listed on western stock exchanges. This is so even for those enterprises where two-thirds of the shares are owned by the Chinese state.[14]

Meanwhile, a technological revolution has taken place over the last two decades with the rise of automated trading in stock market exchanges across the globe. Public and private trading markets in the financial sector have, in Daniel Souleles's words, 'electrified, anonymized, sped up, and gone mostly automated', leading to an exponential increase in the number of trades. This has created a situation where market actors often feel a sense of powerlessness or confusion in the face of market illegibility, and where technological skill defined as computational expertise is the most valued characteristic for workers in the sector. By the 2010s, financial traders were more likely to be what Souleles's interlocutor Enos Millfield calls 'rock star programmers' with PhDs in computer science or mathematics than they were to be finance majors; and market exchanges no longer consisted of trading pits filled with humans making deals, or even banks of computers with humans executing electronic trades.[15] Instead, they are server centres where competitive advantage is established through the microseconds gleaned when firms are able to locate their computers as close as possible to those of the exchange, or along as straight a set of cables as possible between the two sets of servers.[16] The glossy offices in Wall Street, New York or Paradeplatz, Zurich are now where financial services firms meet clients; actual trades take place in places like Mahwah, New Jersey and the outskirts of Zurich.[17]

Another important development, especially in public sectors across the world, including universities, has been the expansion of unstable jobs, both as a result of outsourcing and as a structural change within institutions. In Argentina, structural adjustment policies of the 1990s were justified by the need to reduce public expenditure and resolve the fiscal deficit in order to gain the confidence of international credit organisations. This meant privatisations of state enterprises, and downsizing the number of agencies, state infrastructure and, importantly, the number of employees.[18] The reforms moved people off the (national) books to other employers – mostly provincial or municipal governments or private enterprises. Crucially, they were moved to jobs where employment conditions were poorer and protections were weaker. The move from secure employment conditions to a more 'flexible' and insecure employment environment gradually happened across the public sector. Although some administrative workers retained their secure, permanent jobs, with full access to benefits, when they left or retired they were replaced by employees on short term contracts. Unionists of state employees understand fixed term contracts as a kind of informalisation of state employment. Importantly, while permanent state employees can only be fired after a lengthy disciplinary process, it is relatively easy not to renew short term contracts, something often done for political reasons as a new functionary, Minister or President takes up position.[19]

Universities have also seen increases in the proportion of staff on short term contracts. In the academic year 2017–2018, 33 per cent of academic staff in the UK were employed on a fixed term contract, according to the government agency HESA,[20] while the union UCU has calculated that 68 per cent of research staff in higher education are on fixed term contracts.[21] In the UK, academics can be employed on contracts of nine months to three, sometimes five years. In Germany, around 85 per cent of academic staff below the rank of Professor are on short term contracts.[22] Adjunct faculty in the US are often hired per course that they teach, a system common in Latin America and Europe too. In the US, 73 per cent of teaching positions were not tenure-track in 2016, down from 55 per cent in 1975.[23] In the UK and the US, doctoral students might also be hired as teaching assistants, to run seminars or give some lectures (and in the US, grade course assignments); in the UK, according to UCU, 46 per cent of universities and 60 per cent of colleges use zero hours contracts to deliver teaching, and significant numbers of staff are on short term contracts across the sector.[24] All this means that tenured academics are a shrinking labour aristocracy, and contract workers the 'lumpenproletariat of the academy' in Theresa O'Keefe and Aline Courtois's words.[25] Work on the Irish higher education sector suggests that notably this lumpenproletariat is feminised, as women tend to remain stuck in precarious work for longer than men. O'Keefe and Courtois suggest that female academics do the 'housework' of the academy: the teaching and student support that does not get rewarded in dominant mechanisms of performance management.[26] This makes escape into higher prestige permanent positions less likely over time.

The neoliberal policies that drove new public management and public sector casualisation of labour are one of the strategies of accumulation pursued by capitalists alongside the spatial fixes described in earlier chapters. The push to shrink public expenditure through making the public sector more 'efficient' is justified by now familiar arguments about the need for austerity. The resulting policies represent (at least) two opportunities for accumulation: tax cuts for corporations and the already wealthy on the one hand, because public services are cheaper to provide, and on the other hand, opportunities for profit for big service providers like the accountancy and management consultancy firms, the consultancy arms of firms such as IBM or Hewlett Packard, and educational service providers such as Pearson Education or schools academy trusts. Jane Collins draws on scholarship from the 'New Enclosures' school to suggest that austerity policies in the US are ongoing primitive accumulation strategies; she is not alone in making the point that they are active strategies rather than merely the operation of economic common sense.[27] Arguably, at least in places where the public sector could be viewed as a kind of commons, shrinking public expenditure is another form of accumulation by dispossession via the appropriation of the collective.

Productive labour in the knowledge economy

One of the most important commonalities across these developments is the measurement and (attempted) commodification of the products of this kind of labour. This is a complicated political question with respect to immaterial labour and is profoundly shaping the experience of workers in these sectors. So, what exactly are professional and management workers producing? The most obvious answer is knowledge and information, and this makes sense because these workers are often widely thought of as part of 'the knowledge economy'. Academics produce knowledge through research and communicate it through writing and teaching. This is what most of us are most proud of, and much of the resistance to the incursion of new public management into universities goes along the lines of defending what is perceived to be an older version of that mission: namely, knowledge that is not commodified through performance indicators and tuition fees, but that is associated with values of freedom, autonomy and intellectual discovery.[28] Bureaucrats also produce non-commodified knowledge, in the form of regulations, policies, legislation and interpretations of legislation, codified in documents.[29] In the case of stock market traders and investment bankers, the knowledge they produce is more clearly commodified: financial instruments like trading algorithms, derivatives, collateralised debt obligations and so on are all forms of information. Financial analysts research markets and companies, hunting out the unpriced information that allows them to make investment recommendations; private equity investors seek to create profit in firms through balancing accurate assessment of value with correct market timing.[30] Like financial workers, management consultants deal in commodified knowledge as social process. Their job is to recycle 'best practice', which they learn about from one client and then sell to another.[31] They produce expertise. Although immaterial, expertise is nonetheless commodifiable, in the form of management processes, models, software programs, reports, PowerPoint presentations, Excel spreadsheets, and further afield in business books and MBA syllabuses.[32]

In addition to knowledge and information, ethnographies tell us that professional and managerial workers also produce outputs and processes, they produce relations, and they produce their own selves. These are all crucial for understanding labour agency in this sector.

Process and outputs

Management consultants produce 'best practice' as both knowledge form and process, and it can be encapsulated in different artefacts. One would be software systems such as systems of 'enterprise resource planning' (ERP), which turn information about a company into decisions about how best to maximise the use of its resources (human and other) to reduce costs. This might involve monitoring and documenting how long workers spend on a given task, or more broadly the status of purchases, invoices, accounting, customer services, etc. To implement ERP systems, organisations usually need to change their structures, ways of management, and collection of data; and people need to be trained in this IT-aided form of decision-making. This is where the consultants come in; and although each system is supposed to be implemented individually to the corporation, in practice consultants tend to rely on industry-standard models. The resulting standardisation is not usually a problem though, because the value they confer may not always take the form of profit maximisation. For the Chinese state-owned enterprises studied by Chong, the key was to implement ERP systems as an indicator of their modernity – their ability to compete in the contemporary global knowledge economy.[33]

Much of professional and managerial labour is organised around producing outputs as indicators of process, a practice long understood by ethnographers of development assistance.[34] New styles of public management based on targets and outputs also affect academics, as they face the challenge of turning immaterial products like knowledge, critique, democracy, etc., into quantifiable outputs. An important mechanism for this process is the production of metrics as measured by government audits, like 'impact' as defined in the UK REF process[35] or student satisfaction measured by responses to the National Student Satisfaction Survey. As with the commodification of knowledge, there is often significant cynicism about such understandings of what academic performance is and how it can be measured, or whether it should be measured at all. But one of the significant effects of the predominance of output-based performance indicators is the way that they lead to individual and collective self-government. So, if increased individual contact between students and academics is thought to increase student satisfaction as expressed in the NSS, departments might respond to a relatively poor result one year by increasing academics' office hours. That may or may not improve their score the following year, but it is difficult to tell. If universities are doing their job, students ought to be learning how to think critically, including about their own course and department, and so it is probably a good thing if students take a critical approach to the NSS. Part of the problem is that student satisfaction as affect is much more complicated than we can quantify through a survey. Perhaps it is not possible to measure the success of a mission to promote critical thinking and democratic disposition.

The proliferation of measurement in a competitive system can also produce considerable anxiety, especially for those on short term contracts. Vik Loveday has investigated the 'anxious labouring' of academics who must teach many hours a week on very demanding contracts, publish articles in respected journals and apply for multiple jobs, all at the same time. They work to build the best possible CV, and when they leave academia, they are encouraged to see themselves not as victims of structural insecurity but as having failed because they were not good enough or not able to cope at an individual level. She asks whether anxiety is a symptom of contemporary university governance or a tactic; really, a good way to produce multiple outputs (teaching hours and publications), by making academics responsible for the self-management of their anxieties, and in the process preventing them from engaging in critical political activity.[36]

Selves

Thus, one of the most important products of the kind of labour I am discussing in this chapter is individual selves. This is not an unusual dynamic today: Ilana Gershon has described how US job-seekers must produce themselves as a business, or personal brand, in the search for work.[37] Here I refer to a production of self as the outcome of labour. That self might be the neurotic academic described by Loveday, the arrogant trader in Caitlin Zaloom's work, or the embodiment of the state as in Nayanika Mathur's work. Mathur suggests that public meetings between state representatives and local political leaders in the Indian Himalayas are part of the 'public theatre' essential to construct the affect of the state. That affect was also a personal quality of bureaucrats that needed to be learned as well as performed, 'through the capacity to pen letters, to scold subordinates, to handle politicians, or ... to perform amongst one's colleagues as one who is cognizant of the system within which all are working and living'. It was performed in meetings through 'the monotonous recitation of figures, head-nodding, or even ... silence'.[38]

In contrast, the futures traders of Chicago and London in the late 1990s and early 2000s dramatised themselves as hypermasculine, belligerent, competitive; embodying the role of the brash trader who shouts out his deals, shoves others out of his place in the pits, curses and 'make[s] a point of displaying [his] threadbare moral fabric' according to Caitlin Zaloom. In practice this requires considerable labour of self-management, the other side of which is self-destruction. Market traders told Zaloom stories of colleagues who could not manage the risk and lost too much money, leading to self-collapse into drug or alcohol addiction, homelessness or suicide.[39] The combination of aggressive and outrageous behaviour with collapse is a common trope in popular culture, like the characters in the film *The Wolf of Wall Street*, or *Liar's Poker*, Michael Lewis's popular autobiography of his time trading at Salomon Brothers in the 1980s.[40]

Karen Ho's ethnography of investment bankers in Wall Street, also based on fieldwork from the late 1990s, points to another side of the self-production of financial workers. She argues that they came to produce themselves as 'liquid workers' who were coeval with the market. New employees quickly became used to three key aspects of their labour market: first, that they were part of an elite – mostly identified as such because they were graduates of Ivy League universities, principally in her case Princeton and Harvard; second, that they were very hard workers who could sustain long working days; third that they could be fired at any time if their bank decided to downsize their department. All these aspects were compensated for by high salaries and even higher bonuses, which became measures of people's self-worth. The combination made for a highly fluid labour market, as people were frequently downsized and therefore looking for other jobs or just decided to move once their bonus had come through. It was rare for people to stay in one workplace for longer than two or three years; and the workplaces also changed as banks merged, split, renamed themselves and so on. All this would be a peculiarity of this particular and relatively small working environment if it did not have a wider impact. But Ho argues that the traders' acceptance of their own liquidity as employees was part of what led them to see value in the liquidity of the firms that they bought and sold stock in. So, they valued firms that could react rapidly to market shifts – just like the banks that downsize departments as soon as they are no longer making money. The social effects of large numbers of downsizings in labour markets that were much less fluid than their own did not feature in their analyses of stock market value.[41] As previous chapters have also shown, flexibility is a key feature of how labour is organised under contemporary capitalism, and it is easier for some than for others.

More recent ethnographies describe financial workers who are less sure of themselves than those in the bull markets of the turn of the century. With the digitalisation of financial markets, bankers look very different from the brash stock market traders of popular culture. They are more likely to be machine learning programmers or data scientists, 'quants' with mathematical and statistical training rather than training in finance and accounting. The heroes of Michael Lewis's 2014 book *Flash Boys: Cracking the Money Code* are misfits who understood the importance of microseconds and communications technologies, and the impact of high frequency (algorithmic) trading in a way that classic Wall Street brokers did not.[42] Traders today are more like tech sector workers than old school financiers or the 1980s cockney yuppies that feature in Lewis' earlier books. They are also less likely to be from the US or Western Europe, at least according to Enos, Daniel Souleles's interlocutor mentioned above. He was deeply anxious about his future as a trader because he lacked computer programming skills, and he felt left behind by the highly educated Russian and Chinese programmers with computer science PhDs that he saw coming into the industry. Souleles suggests that Enos might end up managing the quants and the programmers (and I think this is probably quite likely, given what we know of the persistence of social hierarchies in sectors like this), but Enos certainly felt somewhat at sea in the new technological world of finance.[43]

That said, even though the social composition of finance workers has changed since the turn of the century, many remain graduates of elite universities; it's just that more hold PhDs in computer science and machine learning than before. The situation also varies across types of work in finance, and one of the important aspects of the new ethnographies of finance is their emphasis on the heterogeneity among financial services workers. The financial analyst is very different from the legal and compliance specialist, who is different from the private equity investor, the wealth management advisor or the trader of options, commodities or futures, and so on. Stefan Leins argues that workers in Zurich produce that distinction through the characteristics that they ascribe to themselves (e.g. of private bankers as trustworthy and discreet, while investment bankers are louder and take more risks) and in dress codes, where differences as small as the type of shirt and use of cufflinks index membership of one or another group (although they are still predominantly male, as these codes also indicate).[44] Souleles argues that among workers in US private equity firms, elite undergraduate education is not as dominant as in Karen Ho's earlier study. Nonetheless, a Harvard, Columbia or Wharton MBA remains a (very expensive) key to an enhanced career trajectory in both private equity and management jobs in finance and the tech sector.[45] This matters both because it serves as a way to filter for those kinds of people who can afford to enter these jobs but also because elite universities in the US and Europe continue to promote neoclassical understandings of the proper functioning of markets in the education of their students.[46]

Academics share some characteristics with financial sector workers: they are often the products of elite universities, they are encouraged to work long hours, and the systems of performance management encourage them to identify their selves with their job. Those who move through several short-term contracts before either getting a permanent job or leaving academia must constantly present themselves for evaluation in job or grant applications. They produce themselves as their CV, their academia.edu page, their Facebook or Twitter timeline, as quotes from student evaluations of their lectures, maybe their h-index or i-index and Google Scholar profile. Those with tenured jobs must also produce themselves as authors, keynote speakers, teachers, experts, representatives of their departments or universities and so on. It is highly individualised, especially at the most prestigious levels of employment. Within the field, rarely do we speak of someone as a Professor of Anthropology without also giving their name; indeed, usually the name of an anthropologist is more meaningful for the practice of our labour than their job title. (I have been discussing Karen Ho and Daniel Souleles's work, not the work of two professors of anthropology.) Citational practices exacerbate this, excluding those located on the peripheries of the global intellectual economy, and creating a canon skewed towards metropolitan elite institutions in certain parts of the world. At the top levels of recognition, people might well be head-hunted for a university job on the basis of their reputation and their publications profile more than their ability – or willingness – to engage in other aspects of the work like teaching and administration. Across academia, early career researchers rely upon the networks and personal recommendation of their supervisor or Principal Investigator when applying for jobs; and on their own networks when applying for promotion or tenure.

Affective relations

This points to another of the most important products of professional and managerial labour, which is relations, often hierarchical ones at that. Academia is an especially good example of hierarchy as both a product and a symptom of the organisation of labour. Vita Peacock's research on the Max Planck Institutes (MPIs) in Germany describes a particularly extreme version of that. In the MPIs, the only permanent staff are the professors, who direct teams of researchers on fixed-term contracts. Today, each institute has around five directors, and they each lead a stream of research that they alone can shape, employing research staff under conditions that they dictate. Research staff are group leaders, postdoctoral researchers and doctoral students. Group leaders are usually expected to stay in position for around five years, unless they have a particularly strong relationship with their director. These are relations of hierarchical dependency, forged through the history of a system and set of values akin to kingship, Peacock suggests. Directors often feel a sense of responsibility towards their team members, for developing their careers. Yet even for the 'intermediate tier' of group leaders and those past immediate post-doctoral status, the time-limited nature of their stay in the institute constrains autonomy and makes them entirely dependent upon the director. They must then seek to develop their own scientific trajectories while negotiating their status and the area of science they will concentrate on with their director, while also looking after their post-doctoral researchers and students.[47] For many it works very well, but it is clearly a delicate balance to maintain. Other academic systems are similarly hierarchical in the sense of being based around significant individuals, as Bourdieu famously showed for France,[48] and as critiques of the US 'star-system' also reveal. The hierarchy is maintained by keeping those at the bottom in temporary contracts, waiting ever longer for a secure and stable job, which does not arrive for everyone.

The distinction between permanent and contract-based workers affects bureaucracies as well as academia. In Argentina, short term contracts in state institutions are the only real means available to open up state jobs to new entrants, which happens on the basis of familial and political networks. The latter in particular is especially vulnerable to downsizing, as new political regimes take over and need to find space for their supporters. The entrance of temporary workers into state bureaucracies in order to carry out a specific project can also disrupt established hierarchies and understandings of what it is to be the state, what Nayanika Mathur calls state affect, or 'sarkari' affect, using the Hindi term. In Uttarakhand, state-employed 'young professionals' with MBAs, computer programming or engineering diplomas, were brought in on mostly three-year contracts to help implement the NREGA rural employment guarantee program. While delighted to have secured a job and hopeful of future permanent government employment, these young professionals were also desperate to escape from what they viewed as a rather backward rural area of the Himalaya. Their older colleagues on permanent contracts thought that they lacked a knowledge of state culture. They wore different clothes, were not suitably deferential either to those higher up than them or to the established rules and procedures, and were careless with documentation. This had significant repercussions for the work of the NREGA implementation because of the perpetual conflict between the two groups.[49]

The point is that bureaucracies rely upon the (ideally smooth) operation of relations for systems to function. Documents and procedures will only get you so far; there are always less formal and explicit aspects to how things get done. On the Hooghly River in Kolkata, the relational aspects of these informal systems are known as *jogajog kora*, or 'practices of useful friendship'.[50] For one port official followed by Laura Bear, this involved a whole range of activities, from advice about state procedures or ritual remedies for illness, to the use of official inspections to prompt the settlement of a conflict over the correct price owing for a boat. Friendship is a form of bureaucratic labour in systems such as this, and a crucial element for those engaged with the state, at all levels and in all countries. In India, Bolivia, South Africa, the UK, China, etc., to build public infrastructure requires relationships at all stages, to first convince politicians and bureaucrats that the infrastructure is needed, to manage public consultation processes, then to get the contract and once the contract is in place, to find subcontractors, employees and so on. Mechanisms to depersonalise the process, like official tendering schemes, rarely avoid the downsides of more overtly corrupt processes; and can anyway clearly be manipulated or just vulnerable to monopolies. All rely on relational labour.

Ensuring that corporations can operate also requires considerable relational labour. Silvia Yanagisako points out that a significant part of the ostensibly material labour of production relies upon just this immaterial labour of network management and communication. She studies the textile industry in Italy and China, with Lisa Rofel, and their ethnography shows how highly skilled the Chinese managers are at code-switching, able both to manage Chinese suppliers and foreign executives, not to mention relations with the state. They had to shepherd Italian executives through short- and long-term visits to their city, showing them around and helping them to establish their families in expat communities. They also laboured to develop the *guanxi* or relational networks that are necessary to link state and party officials with factory owners and managers along the supply chain, smoothing the production process and its regulation through the exchange of favours. They mobilised their cosmopolitanism to create relations both locally and with the Italians, who brought to the relationship a sense of '*Italianità*', or fashion sensibility and appreciation of a particular understanding of quality in clothing.[51]

The whole point of management is to manage other people, which is to say to produce relations. Management consultants work at least partially on the basis that this can be made into a technical process – that of installing ERP systems or 'customer relationship management' software systems, which seek to narrow the range of workers' actions that are positively incentivised. Yet Kimberly Chong shows how even these mean different things in practice for different clients, producing different affects accordingly. For the corporation she calls GlobalCo, the consultancy connected them to a globalised modernity, enacted also in their other work practices, the architecture of their offices, the dress of their workers and so on. In contrast, the management of a formerly state-owned enterprise saw the ERP system as increasing the workers' *suzhi*, or (personal) quality. At heart, though, 'developing close relationships with clients to find out what was most important to them, and then deciding how they could calibrate their actions to fulfil these requirements was ... the mainstay of consultants' expertise.'[52]

Labour agency: self-management and the challenges of collective mobilisation

The nature of professional and managerial work at least in part producing certain kinds of selves/selves-in-relation-to-others might well lead to a kind of over-identification between the worker and her job, which we can think of as the conceptual opposite of alienation. And if alienation produces a particular kind of politics, then its opposite does too. Labour politics within these spaces are shaped by the distinction between those who can tolerate labour liquidity and those who cannot; by the nature of governance through the production of anxiety; and by the hierarchical division of labour and employment conditions via the division between secure and precarious work.

Depending on the labour market, flexibility and liquidity are more or less tolerable for workers. Financial workers or management consultants who earn large salaries, and bonuses that they can use to cover their cost of living while they are not earning are more able to be flexible about leaving jobs or being fired than those who cannot. As Karen Ho points out, they may even develop a notion of labour liquidity as a value in itself which can be projected onto others. The bonus payment structure on Wall Street not only enabled bankers to look past the effects of enforcing flexibility on others far away from them but also led to what Ho calls 'a frenzy of deal-making', because bonuses were allocated based on the numbers of deals a banker made, regardless of whether the deals were successful or not. In bull markets like the dot.com bubble when she was conducting her fieldwork, this creates a dynamic where the market continues to speed up and promote these practices in a feedback loop until the bubble bursts.[53]

The post-2008 recession and further digitalisation of trading created a new dynamic for workers in investment banking. Still, the sector (or parts of it) expands and contracts at surprising speed, and during periods of expansion, it is common for workers to use job offers from other companies to increase their compensation, either by moving employer or by negotiating a raise in their existing job. In the first quarter of 2022, the labour market at the top end of the tech sector was a good illustrative case of this dynamic. People remain with one employer for short periods of time before they move on (usually less than two years), and employers respond to the resultant competition for workers by raising compensation, sometimes at eye-watering rates. In April 2022, Amazon pay rates in the US were expected to increase by 10–30 per cent for the most highly paid software engineers and managers, and the firm more than doubled the amount of salary it paid in cash rather than in shares.[54] In this kind of labour market, there is little space (or need, arguably) for systemic contestation, even if the workers feel dissatisfied with their employment conditions. They can just move jobs, especially if they do not have families to feed, and because of the structure of incentives, the main employment condition that bothers them is the size of their compensation package. The most common form of resistance is simply to leave, and there are multiple ways that people do so, from early retirement to the self-destruction described by Caitlin Zaloom's informants.[55]

The brash behaviour also described by Zaloom and perhaps the nerdy drive for greater technical knowledge that Michael Lewis describes might also be a form of self-management that protects against governance through anxiety. Arrogance is perhaps a prophylactic for the anxiety that is provoked by continuous evaluation. Vik Loveday points to Engin Isin's work on 'neuroliberal governance', which he defines as 'a rationality of government that takes its subject as the neurotic citizen'.[56] Loveday suggests that the creation of neurotic citizens in academia is an effective mechanism for promoting the politics of paralysis, where no solution to the structural problem seems possible and so mobilisation is foreclosed.[57] Where almost all are subject to similar processes of performance management, prestige (which is measured) is indicated by being asked to evaluate others (sit on an appointments committee, review an article or a grant proposal, write references, etc.), and so the system is maintained as people work their way up from mostly being evaluated to mostly evaluating. Even if they consider themselves impervious to others' evaluations (either because they're arrogant or they've reached a certain point of the pyramid), then withdrawing from the system of evaluation itself is morally difficult because it creates an added burden on others. Also, if all who are sceptical withdraw their labour then that leaves those who are less likely to question the system itself, maintaining the dynamic.

Vita Peacock reports the sense of responsibility that tenured academics felt towards 'their' post-docs, whom they tried to position in secure jobs.[58] Academics on permanent contracts can also allow themselves to slip into a paralysis induced by a sense of guilt at their inability to help those for whom they feel responsible, and at their role in upholding the system itself. Of course, one might argue that this inaction is often just what labour aristocrats do, leaving militancy to others. Yet academics do engage in collective action to defend their employment conditions or in alliance with others. Lecturers' trade unions are reasonably active in the UK, for example in the 2010 protests against rises in student tuition fees, or the 2018 strike against pension cuts.

Nonetheless, worldwide, where unions are reasonably present, unionisation tends to be higher in the public sector than in the private.[59] A relatively high proportion of public sector workers, including bureaucrats and academics, have secure employment; they work in offices where it is easy to share information and to strategise with colleagues; their employers are vulnerable to reputational damage at least in part because of a common ethos of public service; they can make alliances with the public (e.g. students) based on conceptions of the public good and ideas about the moral responsibilities of the state. All these factors facilitate union-based politics.

Still, unions of public sector workers are vulnerable to the ideological position of whichever government is in charge – even in places like Argentina where there is usually a very close relationship between politicians and union leadership. In periods of structural adjustment, such as in the 1990s and from 2015 onwards, Argentine state employees' unions sought to protect their affiliates from redundancies. Elsewhere I have discussed how the two main unions did so from a position towards the government of negotiation or contestation.[60] In the 1990s, one union (UPCN) participated in the committee that decided precisely what form the restructuring

would take and used that position to defend its affiliates from redundancies – and thereby to condemn non-members to job losses. Union leaders
were quite open with me that this was their strategy, describing the
reforms as a 'tsunami' that was simply inevitable, but activists from the
rival union (ATE) thought this was a betrayal, the ultimate form of cooptation by the state. Similar tensions emerged during the right-wing regime
of 2015-19, as UPCN were accused of collaborating with the government
to decide who would be fired in a round of IMF-prompted restructuring,
while ATE protested on the streets again.

Permanent state employees could not be fired, at least not easily. The
most vulnerable workers were those on temporary contracts, and the
unions had to decide how (and if) they would protect precarious workers.
ATE especially prided itself on its position towards this group, campaigning strongly against '*precarización laboral*', and pointing out that UPCN
would not even affiliate many temporary workers. While this is true,
UPCN activists do consider achieving the renewal of short-term contracts
to be one of their aims at the end of each financial year; and the union
was very influential in the negotiations of the early 2000s which brought
together temporary workers under one framework that gave them all of
the rights enjoyed by permanent workers except for permanence itself.
When they have to make a choice, though, they defend their affiliates, who
are the permanent workers. They condemn ATE's contrasting stance as
ineffective, because its absolutism means that nobody is saved.

In Europe, traditional unions have on the whole not been especially
prominent or effective at defending precarious public sector workers,
and so different kinds of collective organisation have emerged. The collective organisation of precarious academics has gained ground in recent
years. One initiative by anthropologists, #PrecAnthro, established itself
at the annual meeting of EASA in 2016, and has been active in EASA
since.[61] In Europe, the language of precarity suggests that it is partly
influenced by precariat activism, which we can trace to the EuroMay-
day protests from the mid-2000s, and the prominence of precarity in the
2011 protests of the Indignados in Spain, and other anti-austerity movements across Europe since then.[62] The focus of #PrecAnthro was at first
mostly on consciousness-raising and building networks among precarious
academics. Subsequently they carried out a survey of employment conditions for anthropologists in Europe[63] and they have been instrumental
in the development of good practice guidelines in collaborative research
for adoption by EASA.[64] Recently, conventional trade unions in academia

have begun to address the casualisation of academic labour in part because of the less formalised organisational efforts like this. In the US, unionisation initiatives among graduate student teachers have been organised through United Auto Workers.[65] The problem is that if precarious academics go on strike, they lose their income and may jeopardise their future careers. They are acutely conscious of the reserve army of labour waiting in the wings to pick up contracts that become available. The challenge is to mobilise tenured academics in solidarity.

Finally, the nature of the work discussed in this chapter as a production of the self means that unions can have trouble mobilising professional and managerial workers because they do not see themselves as workers: they are academics, doctors, lawyers, nurses, teachers, bankers and so on. My research with unionists in the Colón Opera House in Buenos Aires is a case in point. In 2009, the workers faced a management that wanted to 'neoliberalise' the theatre: reduce staff numbers and reorient the theatre so that it became a space which sub-contracted cultural productions, rather than produced its own (a model the workers called the 'factory theatre'). The management carried out their project in part through what the workers considered to be a bungled refurbishment, which paid more attention to commercial imperatives than production needs. However, activists found it difficult to get the ballet dancers, opera singers and musicians on board. Most of the active unionists came from technical jobs in the theatre. They were stage managers, janitors, props and scenery constructors, or lighting technicians. They produced or repaired stuff, while the dancers, singers and musicians saw themselves as artists, not workers. When they danced, they expressed themselves; they did not see themselves as working for others.[66]

In addition to professional identification, the fact that strikes affect the public can make mobilisation challenging. Some public sector employees are not allowed to strike, depending on the country, and bureaucrats often see themselves as public servants, identified with the state or the citizenry. One said to me that he was his own employer, because he was both Argentine and a civil servant; collapsing the triangle of state-capital-labour that lies at the heart of most current political understandings of what labour *is*. The material metaphors of labour that are still dominant demobilise large groups of people, especially those who identify so directly with their work.

Yet, when they do mobilise, public sector workers can be very powerful. One of the most moving and effective recent strike waves in the UK was that of junior doctors, led by their section of the British Medical Association (in September–October 2016). Teachers' unions across the world defend both their labour rights and their communities, arguing that their working conditions are children's learning conditions.[67] Since 2018, North American public school teachers have held strikes in Chicago, Los Angeles, Oakland, and the states of West Virginia, Oklahoma, Arizona, North Carolina and Kentucky, mobilising thousands of people in collective action in a society that we tend to think of as one of the most individualistic in the world.[68] In fact, these are not exceptions. In countries where public sector workers are not prohibited from striking, as in Argentina, they are often more likely to strike than workers in the private sector.[69] Where the withdrawal of labour affects day to day society, workers are more powerful than they often realise, and it might help to join the dots and realise that these struggles are both more numerous than we often think and linked to each other. Perhaps more of us could take inspiration from those Argentine state employees I know who realise that they may be 'middle class' rather than 'working class' (although this is actually highly contested) but that whatever their class position they are *workers* and entitled to defend themselves via collective organisation.

Professional and managerial work turns out, then, to be not too different from the other kinds of work I describe in this book, despite the stories we might tell ourselves. Like the heavy industry workers of Chapter 1, those with secure jobs with good employment conditions are better able to defend themselves collectively than those on precarious, short-term contracts, although the latter are engaging in significant acts of self-organisation and critique of the traditional unions. Like garment stitchers, in some sectors (like financial services and management consultancy), conditions of relative labour shortage mean that workers can leave one job for another one quite easily, reinforcing a dynamic whereby compensation is the main differentiator between jobs and motivator for workers, fluidity is inherent, and mobility is the main expression of worker agency. Like care workers, professionals often construct their self-identity through their work, encouraged through forms of control and measurement in the workplace that focus on anxiety, targets and individual characteristics and capacity for affect. As a result, the over-identification with their job inhibits collective action. And yet, especially in the public sector, collective organisations such as unions are surprisingly active, motivated by the desire both to improve working conditions and enact the workers' vision of the public good.

6

Platform Labour
Digital Management and Fragmented Collectivities

In this chapter, I consider what happens when the job as conventionally understood no longer functions to organise work, using platform labour as my example. Instead of the 'job' based on contracted hours or days that dominates labour imaginaries in the West, platform labour organises work into multiple fragmented tasks where one worker has multiple clients mediated through a digital platform. Sites connect clients to workers, organise payment and take commission, while mostly seeking to avoid the responsibilities that an employer might have to its employees. Digital platforms are increasingly important forms of organising work today, from the physical labour of driving, delivery, cleaning and other tasks organised through platforms like Uber, Lyft or Deliveroo, for example, to freelance digital labour through sites like UpWork, Amazon Mechanical Turk or Fiverr. Although absolute numbers of those engaged in platform labour are still relatively small in comparison to more conventional kinds of labour, arguably this is a new frontier for how labour is structured; it is creating a different labour process from that of industrial labour. Hardt and Negri argued that the hegemony of immaterial labour ought not to be understood necessarily in quantitative terms but in the sense of how influential it might be in the structuring of all kinds of labour. Similarly, the structures and methods currently associated mostly with digital labour are likely to have a much broader influence in the future. And given that as of July 2020, as much as 60 per cent of the world's population were online, even absolute numbers of digital labourers are likely to increase.[1]

Platform labour has developed out of the evolution of business process outsourcing described in Chapter 4, and it relies on communications technology that is relatively new, or newly accessible to more people. However, it is also essentially technologically enabled piecework, and in that sense not especially novel. Thus, many of the issues I describe in this chapter are similar to those discussed in other chapters on precarious labour, and much platform labour is affective and/or associated with social reproduction, so there are significant overlaps there too. Platform labour is also mostly about the production of immaterial goods and services. Like other types of immaterial labour, it involves particular kinds of physicality: for example, the bodily (and especially ocular) experience of hours sitting in front of a computer screen, or of being sat in a car for hours to drive passengers around or deliver goods. New in this chapter is the role of the labour of circulation and delivery, which is especially key for important groups of platform workers.

I begin with a discussion of the political economy of digital labour, and then move to a consideration of the experiences of platform workers, with special focus on questions of autonomy, alienation and algorithmic management. The final section of the chapter explores the possibilities for worker agency, individually, informally and in alliance with more traditional trade unions. One of the most important questions for platform workers' agency is how do you identify who is the boss? Where the boss is ephemeral, algorithmical or hidden, what it is that makes for resistance rather than accommodation, flight or escape? Furthermore, when workers are dispersed and isolated from each other, how do you create collective action? These are dilemmas that thread through most of the chapters in this book, but they are especially acute in precarious places of work.

The political economy of digital and platform labour

Scholars distinguish between 'geographically tethered' platform labour, where workers and clients come into direct contact on city streets or in people's homes, and remote digital labour, which can be further subdivided into 'microtask' and 'macrotask'.[2] Digital labour at the 'microtask' level is sometimes called the 'hidden labour of AI', or 'ghost work', where digital labourers pick up work from platforms such as Amazon Mechanical Turk (AMT), or Microsoft's internal equivalent, to improve the AI algorithms underlying all our digital lives. They do so by tagging pictures, moderating content, transcribing text, checking information and so on. Although this kind of remote labour is by now quite well studied, and Amazon's Mechanical Turk more so than any other platform, it counts for only about 10 per cent of remote digital work.[3] The rest, mediated through sites such as UpWork, Fiverr or ProZ, consists of tasks set for freelancers. The range of these 'macrotasks' is very broad, and includes search engine optimisation, writing reviews, writing content, designing logos or marketing materials, generating leads for businesses, personal assistance, software development and quality assurance, data entry, copywriting, copyediting, translating, etc.[4]

The growth of digital labour is an extension of the same kinds of processes that produced call centres in countries such as the Philippines and India subcontracting services for clients in the US or Europe, which also relied upon improvements in communications technologies since the mid-twentieth century. Digital labour moves the physical location of work from the call centre to the worker's home. As Ursula Huws powerfully points out, this is as much about disciplining labour at home as it is a global spatial fix in Harvey's sense. She says:

It is often assumed by workers in the developed economies that the point of moving work offshore is to eliminate the jobs back home. But this is to miss the point. The purpose of a reserve army is not to take over all the work but to act as a disciplinary force. ...

While not denying the real misery caused by the unemployment that is certainly taking place, it is nevertheless important to remember that the most powerful effect of offshoring is not to eliminate jobs in the United States or in Europe – it is to cheapen them.[5]

In August 2020 nearly 80 per cent of active AMT workers each day were based in the United States, a proportion that had probably increased as a result of the pandemic.[6]

In her book *Labour in the Global Digital Economy* (2014), Huws argues that the development of capitalism in the economies of the centre since 1945 has been punctuated by moments of crisis and reorientation, and digital labour plays an important role in the most recent ones. Since 1990 we have seen rapid growth in the global outsourcing of manufacturing and, increasingly, service labour. This was prompted by a wave of deregulation from 1990 to 2008 combined with the boom in stock markets based on technological firms and financial services in the centre and bolstered by the increased outsourcing of manufacturing away from the centre. Together, these produced processes of deskilling and reskilling, such as when specialists design systems for 'lower-skilled' call centre operators to provide technical support or customer service (or to take an example that is perhaps closer to home, as professors put content online for 'e-learning'). The financial crash of 2008 ushered in even deeper austerity than the 1980s and 90s, with poor labour conditions in the centre enabled by high unemployment and high personal debt. Concurrently, technological developments lead to a dissolution of the boundaries between work and non-work as well as increased use of internet and smart phones. Large tech companies were able to consolidate and grow, contributing to increased investment capital attracted to tech startups.[7]

Since 2008, we have seen the further development of technologies of outsourcing towards the fragmentation of labour into ever smaller digital tasks such as those found on AMT.[8] As I drafted this chapter during the Covid pandemic, it seemed clear to me that 2020 will mark a new phase in the development of labour more broadly and digital labour in particular. Even more labour will become digital, especially in the context of hybrid working arrangements. We may also see a greater digitalisation of sociality, through the more widespread use of platforms such as Zoom, WhatsApp, or Facetime for recreating offline forms of social communication, coupled with the further growth of social apps like TikTok and Instagram as distributors of creative labour.

Over the course of this century, the organisation of digital labour through platforms has created what Mohammad Amir Anwar and Mark Graham call a 'planetary labour market', organised spatially along neocolonial lines.[9] Thus, requesters for remote digital labour are predominantly located in the US, especially on the West Coast, and those who carry it out are concentrated in former colonies, especially India and the Philippines. In the Global South there is a rapidly developing global reserve army of digital labourers, located in places with very different minimum wage levels and cost of living to those of the Global North, with resulting downward pressure on the cost of labour. Freelancing platforms like UpWork often require workers to bid for work, so they frequently find themselves having to work at a lower hourly rate than even they consider to be ideal. Digitally organised labour is an especially low friction spatial fix for capital, and available to ever smaller employing entities, even individuals. There is no need for employers to account for the costs of moving physical infrastructure like factories, ports, or roads; capital can seek lower labour costs simply by travelling across optic fibre cables and wi-fi frequencies, once these physical infrastructures have been installed.

Global labour arbitrage is made possible by the specificities of *local* labour markets. What look like very low wages from the perspective of the country where the employer is located can be attractive to workers elsewhere. Pay rates may well compare favourably with salaries in the civil service, higher education, and other white-collar sectors. It is not just a question of pay rates, as working from home can mean that workers can also avoid long and often costly commutes, and create working hours that fit around their other responsibilities. The unregulated nature of platform labour means that opportunities in both remote digital labour and geographically tethered platform labour are also attractive to migrants who do not have the necessary papers for other kinds of jobs.

These factors are not only relevant to workers located in the Global South. The years since 2008 have seen a sharp rise in the availability of workers in the US, related to increased unemployment and personal debt, including student debt. Most platform labourers in the US are relatively young, in their 20s and 30s. Many turn to the gig economy to work their way through university or to supplement income from a poorly paid conventional job in a warehouse or factory. Especially with regard to the more geographically tethered platform work, some are attracted by the language of entrepreneurship or the chance to leverage an asset they own (such as a car or a house) for additional income, or they become ride hail drivers because that is the only way they can afford to run a car.[10] Many of them take out loans to buy the car or a taxi licence where required, thus closing the circle that connects platform labour to personal debt and the financialisation of the broader economy.

But in another way, platform labour is not especially new. The emphasis on micro-task digital labour in much of the current literature on the global political economy of platform labour might obscure the fact that Care.com is the platform with the largest number of listed workers worldwide. At around 6 million its numbers are well beyond the 500,000 registered on AMT. Care.com is essentially an online labour brokerage for domestic workers. Its success indicates that platform labour might be thought of as a way of organising labour that at least initially has intervened in sectors that were already highly informal. In similar fashion, Uber, Lyft and other ride hailing apps have deregulated already-existing taxi driving and private vehicle hire businesses, but we should recognise that large parts of these were already operating in the shadows of formal regulation.

This points to the fact that another important condition that has affected the development of platform labour is the regulatory environment. It is easy for digital labour platforms and employers to evade local regulation because the networks are so footloose: clients are in one place, workers in another, potentially anywhere in the world. In the absence of global labour regulation, it is extremely difficult to control for questions of minimum pay, discrimination and so on. For geographically tethered platform labour, like ride hail and delivery, the picture is different, and very gradually improving in some parts of the world, with some key legal cases focussing on platform workers' rights.

Autonomy, alienation and algorithmic management

One of the main challenges for regulation turns on how to categorise platform workers, since they usually have the status of independent contractors or some other category of self-employment, leaving them with few legal rights. Yet workers do not always wish to become employees. Autonomy also matters to them on a more experiential level. In this section, I explore what's at stake for platform workers who have to balance the flexibility and responsibility of controlling their own time with the supervision via algorithm to which they are subjected. I begin by considering the importance of the language that surrounds platform labour, and the different cultural claims it reveals.

The concept of 'platform labour' covers a wide variety of jobs, and the experience of different workers depends on how reliant they are on that particular job for their income. Even within the same category, such as Deliveroo delivery person, workers have different expectations of what the job will provide. Callum Cant describes how in Brighton the Deliveroo riders divided into two groups, between the cyclists and those on mopeds. The cyclists were mostly students or people riding for Deliveroo in addition to another job, while the riders who had invested in a moped tended to be older and were on the whole more dependent on the platform as their main source of income. Many were migrant workers, from South America, eastern Europe, or southeast Asia. Some were working using someone else's account so that they did not have to present a passport and valid work visa, or so that they could work while their asylum requests were being processed. They often had greater financial commitments than the cyclists did, such as families to support or hire-purchase agreements for their mopeds to pay off. So they tended to work longer hours, and were both more vulnerable – since it was difficult for them to find another job – and had a greater incentive to push for decent pay, or to object when pay rates changed for the worse.[11]

Alex Rosenblat identifies a similar differentiation within Uber drivers across several cities in the US: some have decided to drive for Uber in order to bring in additional money on top of their regular job, or to plug a gap between jobs, while others are more locked into the platform because they have bought cars on loan purchase agreements or made other investments. As with Deliveroo, there is a very high turnover of workers: more than half of Uber drivers quit within a year of starting. According to Rosenblat, Uber has been quick to take advantage of this stratified workforce, 'actively weaponising' the existence of those who were driving for a bit of extra money to undermine the ability of drivers who relied more upon the platform for income to assert their power to demand better conditions.[12]

Alexandrea Ravenelle divides the gig economy workers she researched into three different categories: 'Strugglers, Strivers, and Success Stories'. The few 'success stories' she found made a comfortable living in the sharing economy, through renting out multiple properties on Airbnb for example. The 'strivers' worked through platforms in addition to another job, sometimes full time; while the 'strugglers' were only just managing to pull together enough work to live on. Platforms like Uber and Airbnb hold out the promise to prospective workers of recreating them as entrepreneurs – 'success stories' – infusing their adverts with promises of high income and flexible working. An advert on the back of a bus in NYC reads 'Drive with Uber. No shifts, no boss, no limits.' The companies' PR speaks to several kinds of potential workers, although never the 'strugglers'. One set of potential workers they address is those for whom the work is an additional help; a bit of extra income when you need it, made accessible by financialising an asset you already hold (your car, or the spare room in your house) through participating in the community of the sharing economy, as in the following example from an ad in 2015: 'Drive with Uber and earn great money as an independent contractor. Get paid weekly just for helping our community of riders get rides around town. Be your own boss and get paid in fares for driving on your own schedule.' Another set of messages suggests that potential workers could earn impossibly large amounts, although stays quiet on the expenses that they have to cover, and the hours they must put in to achieve those amounts.[13]

In practice, more common than the Uber driver who decided to use their car to generate some extra income were those who had taken out loans to pay for the right kind of car, and in some cities – like New York – a taxi licence. Sometimes they rented a car with taxi licence plates, for as much as $2,000 a month. Rates like these mean that drivers have to work for around two full days a week just to pay off their rental or loan expenses; not to mention costs of insurance (vehicle and health insurance), petrol, phone data, etc.[14] Uber drivers, like Deliveroo riders and remote digital workers, provide their own means of production – the car, the bicycle or moped, the laptop and internet connection – meaning that the platform can outsource almost all costs to the workers.

Platforms lower costs also by avoiding certain kinds of regulation. Companies are careful not to describe the providers of services advertised through the apps as workers or employees. In most cases they are categorised as independent contractors, 'users' of the platform as much as the clients are. According to the companies, the platforms exist to put the service provider in touch with the client, and they tend to studiously avoid any kind of relationship that looks like employment. Some sites can make this case easier than others: freelancing sites like UpWork do appear to be coordinating contractors and employers, but more geographically tethered platforms like Uber or Deliveroo look more like they are employing people. Somewhere in between are the platforms that serve as labour brokers for slightly longer tasks, like TaskRabbit, or KitchenSurfing – where someone is hired for a few hours to complete a task or cook a meal for a client. What many of the platforms have in common is a tendency to stress their identities as a 'tech company' rather than a labour company. If Uber's value lies in a combination of the connective technology that it uses to match drivers and passengers with the data that it collects in the process – that's to say, in the app itself rather than the actual provision of the service – then it can enjoy being associated with other Silicon Valley technology startups, similarly 'disruptive', innovative and too new for old forms of regulation.

Even terms such as 'gig economy' or 'sharing economy' avoid associations with the standard employment relationship and old-fashioned notions of work and labour. Especially in the North Atlantic context, they bring with them cultural associations of individual freedom: you can choose your clients, you work for yourself, and you don't have a supervisor telling you what to do. The gig economy is a new way of organising, emphatically not the factory production line, but something much more fragmented and autonomous.[15] As Rosenblat argues: '"sharing" also points to how culturally undesirable it is to think about gigs as work: it's as though we can't change the conditions of labor, so we change the way we think about it instead'.[16]

Yet, it isn't all propaganda from platform companies: workers do report a positive sense of autonomy and appreciate the flexibility that does exist in this way of organising labour. In a study of remote digital workers run by Alex Wood and colleagues, their interviewees appreciated the ability to choose among a diverse set of clients, to take on new and stimulating kinds of tasks of increasing complexity, and to work when they chose. The extent to which they could enjoy flexibility of hours was constrained by the frequent need to work very long hours, as people competed for tasks and responded to insecurity by taking on multiple clients if they could, making the work more intense.[17] Still, undoubtedly digital labour can be organised in such a way that it can fit around other kinds of responsibilities that are important to people, as in the case of 'Joan', as described by Mary Gray and Siddarth Suri. Joan left a full-time job as a technical writer to care for her 81-year-old mother, and turned to AMT as on-demand work that she could do while still being able to cook and keep house for her mother, and drive her to hospital appointments.[18] The move to working from home as a result of coronavirus lockdowns has taught even more white-collar workers than before that home working has its own challenges, including feelings of social isolation and blurring distinctions between work and leisure so that work extends through more of the day. However, digital workers on the whole thought that working from home was a 'major benefit', not least because it meant they could avoid long and expensive commutes.[19]

Further, not having a supervisor matters to people: Mark, a Kenyan writer, said to Alex Wood and colleagues, 'I don't have someone supervising, telling you: "you have not done this, you have not done this", yelling at you',[20] and Deliveroo riders also told Callum Cant that they appreciated not having a (human) boss. Platforms have taken (human) supervisors out of the equation, but the ways they have done so do raise questions around both automation as process and control or autonomy as personal experience. It is paradoxical that platform technology, which could be a clear driver of automation, does not remove the human worker from the process of service delivery entirely, despite fantasies of drone deliveries and self-driving cars. What it does do is remove humans from the layer between client and worker: automating the taxi dispatcher or line manager.

'Middle management' is, it turns out, less necessary and more amenable to automation than workers themselves, giving rise to the development of 'algorithmic management', where the platform itself manages the workers.[21] At its heart the phrase refers to the ways that apps match client and worker, allocating certain jobs to particular workers or presenting the list of available workers to clients in a particular order. To take the example of Uber: when a driver logs on to the app to show that he or she is available for work, s/he is offered a job based on how close s/he is to the client, where the journey is to, and what kind of tariff the client wishes to pay (for different kinds of cars, from shared rides to more luxury or larger vehicles). The driver has a period of time within which s/he can choose to accept or decline the job, but s/he is not given the full information about the job. Most controversially for drivers, they are not told where the passenger wants to be driven to. This helps Uber avoid discrimination, as they found that drivers would decline jobs where passengers wanted to go to notoriously rough areas; but it also means that drivers cannot, say, take a job that takes them nearer to home at the end of their shift, or decline journeys that are so short that they won't earn any money after costs and Uber's fees are counted for. Uber also requires drivers to accept a certain percentage of jobs offered to them by the app, enforced by 'deactivating' them if they fall below (i.e. preventing them from full access to the app). Drivers may also be deactivated if the star rating they are given by passengers falls below a certain level, usually around 4.6 stars out of a possible five. In addition, drivers are encouraged to work in particular areas in the city at certain times of the day by 'surge pricing', when the app raises the fare in response to passenger demand, but also – according to the drivers – in response to other factors that are hidden from them. For example, drivers wonder whether they are offered good surge pricing opportunities when they are new to the app but not once they are locked in as regular drivers; or whether the notification of high demand is just manipulation to make a driver go to a particular district simply because there is a passenger there.[22] Algorithmic management relies upon the withholding of information and as such generates suspicion.

Deliveroo does something similar to Uber, albeit without the rating system. Each job is broken down into stages, and each stage revealed to the delivery rider only when the previous stage is completed. So, riders are at first only told which restaurant they should pick the food up from, and only when they have picked up the order are they given the address of the customer.[23] Callum Cant explains how this stage by stage revelation was particularly important for Deliveroo cyclists in Brighton. Since it is quite a hilly city, some journeys are more difficult than others, especially for cyclists. It mattered when Deliveroo pivoted from paying an hourly rate to paying per drop off; so a long, steep delivery suddenly became more consequential for the rate of pay the riders could earn. In order to earn a reasonable hourly rate, the shift to piecework also led to work intensification, as riders pushed themselves to make more deliveries in peak times to compensate for the slower pace of the rest of their shift. Cant describes how he learned to cycle somewhat more recklessly than before, finding short cuts through the city and learning ways to speed up the time he spent at the restaurant.[24] Like Uber's surge pricing, Deliveroo also runs 'promotions' where they pay a higher rate per drop off at some times of the day or in particular parts of the city to attract riders to where they are needed. Riders also received regular emails detailing their performance as measured against specific targets. Management through metrics draws upon processes that are familiar across the tech sector, and management consultancy, as well as even academia, as described in Chapter 5. Management through the offering of variable pay is one process by which human labour is commodified beyond just the provision of a wage.

Applying algorithmic management to humans fuels and relies upon two key characteristics: the fragmentation of the work and the importance of reputation, the latter usually expressed through ratings. With remote digital work, the fragmentation can be even more extreme than the Deliveroo or Uber experience. Much online work is moderation: tagging pictures or sentences that have been reported for offensive content; or tagging pictures to train AI systems. It consists of small tasks and is often repetitive. Workers do not know exactly who is hiring them and where their contribution fits in to a broader production process. One data entry job advert on UpWork identified by Mohammed Amir Anwar and Mark Graham was explicit about this, giving only the following details: 'This job does not require any technical skills. I need your help to do some repetitive work. It's very simple.' Other jobs, such as writing reviews for hotels or tourist sites, or putting in links on websites for search engine optimisation, might involve longer work but don't necessarily require an understanding of the bigger picture. For example, a US-based client asked for articles about health supplements that included specific keywords, and links to their product, in order to boost search results. A Kenyan worker who produced this did not know what the point of the job was, all he knew was that 'he had a lot of job'.[25]

As Valerio de Stefano argued in a paper for the ILO, this kind of work represents the 'severe commodification of work', resulting in a 'just-in-time workforce'.[26] The founder and CEO of Crowdflower put it more bluntly:

Before the Internet, it would be really difficult to find someone, sit them down for ten minutes and get them to work for you, and then fire them after those ten minutes. But with technology, you can actually find them, pay them the tiny amount of money, and then get rid of them when you don't need them anymore.[27]

Another CEO described his platform as 'an eBay of jobs', indicating his view of labour as commodity. When Polanyi discussed the commodification of labour, it might have meant relatively identifiable and stable wage rates, either by day or longer term. Today, remote digital work, especially 'microwork' is work for payment by not only piece rates but piece rates that can vary from hour to hour, with a reduced unit of calculation: the 'piece' of work at stake takes seconds or minutes.[28] Sometimes clients simply don't pay for work done. This is a well-known feature of AMT, where requesters can choose not to pay if they are not satisfied but nonetheless retain ownership of the work.[29] Digital labour is very alienated and at the extreme end workers have no real sense of who they are working for, what the end product is, or how their effort fits into a wider project.[30]

One effect is, as Ilana Gershon and Melissa Cefkin argue, that 'platform driven work acts to transcend and even displace forms of workplace sociality',[31] with fairly obvious negative consequences for horizontal sociality between workers, but also an altered vertical relationship between client/employer and worker. The UpWork or AMT way of organising labour demands a change in management so that requesters have to segment and describe the work in much smaller steps than would be necessary with a more conventional team structure. Fragmentation is then made more acute by re-outsourcing, which is common across platforms. Re-outsourcing is when workers split up tasks into smaller chunks and re-outsource to family and friends, embedding the labour in personal networks. Facebook groups can also serve as networks for re-outsourcing. The re-outsourcer takes on the risk that the other workers might not do the job as well, but according to Wood et al, those who re-outsource to others are usually able to bid successfully for a job because they have a high ranking as someone who has successfully completed more jobs and so therefore appear higher up the search results for clients and is more attractive to clients. It is a self-reinforcing circle. As Abaeze said to Wood et al., 'It's just like a chain. He employs us as his freelancers. We do most of the calls for him ... [He has] a very good profile ... [he] just appl[ies] for multiple jobs ... and get[s] jobs because ... he has a very good account.'[32]

On remote work platforms, algorithmic management operates through reviews and rankings that shape where someone appears on the list of available workers and how attractive they look to potential clients. It means that often workers must work further down the chain of re-out-sourcing, and put in long hours for low pay to build a reputation and a series of completed tasks. Remote digital labour also involves emotional labour, mostly on unpaid time. Workers must bid for jobs on freelancing sites by maintaining a good profile and reviews from past clients, producing a strong narrative about exactly how they would do each task offered, and how well it matches with their past experience; and pitching their hourly rate correctly, all the while paying attention to what rates people in other – cheaper – parts of the world are proposing. Job searches take time, and bids are often unsuccessful because several workers are bidding for the same task.

For geographically tethered platform labourers, ratings are vulnerable to capricious clients (or at least workers often feel that to be the case) and algorithmic management does not do dispute resolution well. For example, Uber drivers in the US complained to Rosenblat that they must submit to the rating system even when passengers are intoxicated, rude, or abusive. Their vulnerability to customer ratings creates the need for emotional labour to preserve a good ranking. Lyft even promises a friendly relationship between driver and passenger as part of the experience, advertising itself as 'your friend with a car' and encouraging its drivers to fist-bump passengers, who can sit in the front seat and chat if they wish to.[33] Achieving good ratings also requires repressive emotional labour, where workers need to suppress distaste, discomfort or pain in order to maintain customer affect and sense of getting a five-star service, like the sex workers in Chapter 4. They can find themselves supressing pain from injuries and putting up with potentially dangerous situations for the sake of the review, or deal with clients hitting on them or otherwise making them feel uncomfortable.[34] In the fragmented world of the gig economy, legal regulations about workplace safety and sexual harassment are easily sidestepped.

Labour agency: creating new forms of collective action

Like other precariously employed workers, it is difficult for many platform workers to improve their work situation but not impossible. Opportunities for agency vary depending on the type of labour, worker and employer. Workers develop individual strategies, come together in social media groups, and even engage in collective mobilisation, although this last tactic is mostly open to geographically tethered platform workers.

Together, these amount to some remarkably creative responses to the dilemmas of how to act when the employer is mostly absent and how to act when workers are isolated from each other.

For remote digital labour on freelancing sites, workers are very conscious of the structural challenges created by global oversupply of labour and lack of regulation. Clients are perceived to be almost completely footloose, not caring if their freelancer is in South Africa or the Philippines (although there is some evidence of discrimination against those who come from countries perceived as less well educated, or less able to speak good English). This pushes wages lower, as freelancers are conscious that they must bid for tasks accordingly. They may also be pushed to accept poor treatment or work longer hours to complete tasks in a competitive timeframe, especially those who are new to the platform or have not built up a strong rating.

Freelancers with a good profile are more able to filter jobs, negotiate with clients and decline tasks from unreliable employers. Occasionally, they can threaten to stop working for a client. For example, 'Ben', from Nairobi, worked for a Canadian client as a virtual personal assistant, managing the client's diary, for over a year. When he asked for an increased hourly rate, the client refused. Ben then cancelled the contract and made the client rehire him at a new rate, on two occasions, managing to increase his hourly rate by 50 US Cents/hour. Digital freelancers have several ways of improving their conditions, which Anwar and Graham call 'hidden transcripts', following James Scott. For example, freelancers might avoid automatic monitoring systems on UpWork by having two monitors, allowing them to watch YouTube videos on one while the screenshot monitoring function focusses on the screen where the work is taking place; or they design applications to alert them to a task being posted on a site like AMT, so that they do not have to be in front of their computer waiting for tasks at all times; or they share their accounts (for commission), buy highly rated pre-approved counts with locations set in Europe or the US, buy client reviews, set up multiple accounts, participate in re-outsourcing – all to subvert the effects of the rating system.[35]

WhatsApp and Facebook groups are extremely important in enabling these strategies. Freelancers also use them to warn others about scams or clients who don't pay. Experienced workers use social media networks to advise those who are new to the platform, as well as sometimes to find people to re-outsource to. Internet-facilitated collective collaboration is even possible for digital microworkers. Gray and Suri's research in India showed how workers shared news with friends and family about good tasks as they were posted, recruited them to AMT and shared tasks. Through a mix of Facebook forums and one-to-one communication (by SMS or phone) they supported each other with advice on the cultural and technical knowledge needed for tasks (such as how to interpret US street addresses, or phrases in American English); and helped them to feel less isolated while working at night – necessary for workers in India since most tasks were posted from US timezones.[36]

Internet forums have been especially important for US AMT workers. Mturkforum[37] has 69,700 members. Given that current estimates suggest that around 10,000 of AMT's 500,000 workers are actually active, the numbers are significant. Each day, there is a space for users to post about good HITs (human intelligence tasks). The entry for 'Finding Great HITs 09/09 Whimsical Wintry Why Not Wednesday' from September 2020 includes different questions about tasks, postings about specific tasks, and a user describing their experience with a 'rejection', when a requester refused to pay for the work: 'Wow, I got my rejection reversed. I struggled real hard to keep my emotions out of the message I sent them and it appears to have worked. :)'. They copied the letter from the requester: 'After reviewing your submission we have decided to reverse our decision. It appears that you did make a good faith attempt at answering our questions. Apologies for the mistake. Thank you for your work. The approval has already been submitted. Ben.'[38] There are similar initiatives for other platform workers especially in the US, such as the very popular Rideshare Guy forum[39] for Uber and Lyft drivers and other gig workers for food delivery platforms. The site claims over 60,000 subscribers to its regular email and has a podcast and YouTube channel with thousands of subscribers. It is incredibly comprehensive, providing resources for drivers, including advice on setting up, paying taxes and maximising income, directing people to Facebook discussion groups, accident lawyers, finance and insurance deals and so on. The blog has an influential media presence and even a consulting arm, which offers advice to policy makers and startups. Of course, most of the internet forums and Facebook groups are not really examples of worker agency as resistance. Arguably, given their role in training, advice and support, they are a way for platforms to outsource the activity of social reproduction in the workplace to the workers' own time. But the forums and groups do allow for the sharing of complaints about the app, and some like the Rideshare Guy have become quite powerful as a result.

Sharing information about unreliable clients is one of the most important roles of social media groups for remote digital workers. One activist software initiative, 'Turkopticon', sought to turn this aspect into collective action, as Lilly Irani explains. Turkopticon is a browser extension that allows AMT workers to rate requesters, on four different characteristics – communicativity, generosity, fairness, promptness. Workers can give a rating for each of these four and are also asked to provide some free text comments. Their website says that 'Turkopticon helps the people in the 'crowd' of crowdsourcing watch out for each other – because nobody else seems to be.' They designed the characteristics based on what they called a 'workers' Bill of Rights' for AMT, elicited by posting a task on the site asking workers what was most important to them in a good requester. By 2013, Turkopticon had been installed over 7,000 times.[40] The same group of researchers at University of California San Diego later worked with discussion forum leaders to develop the 'Dynamo' site, which aimed to be a 'virtual union hall of sorts for MTurk's international worker base'.[41] Members could 'upvote' suggestions, and so they built a campaign in Christmas 2014 that encouraged AMT workers to write letters and emails directly to Jeff Bezos, to make them visible to him and to the public. Bezos famously urged customers to write him directly if they were dissatisfied, although he didn't reply to any of the emails from the AMT workers. As of September 2020, Turkopticon remained available but the wearedynamo. org site had lapsed.

Organised collective action is more feasible for geographically tethered platform workers and indeed has grown over time as the platforms employ more people. Riders for Deliveroo organised a wave of strikes in the UK and Europe in 2016–2017. Callum Cant participated actively in the mobilisations in Brighton in 2016–2017. In his book *Riding for Deliveroo* (2019), he describes how Deliveroo took on significant numbers of new workers in Brighton in late 2016, meaning that pay – calculated per delivery – dropped, but also that more workers than before were waiting for orders in what the app called 'zone centres' at any one time. Gradually, impromptu meetings started happening in zone centres, as riders discussed their conditions, argued, messed about together, and shared more and more militant ideas about possible action. Inspired by activism among Deliveroo riders in London earlier in the year, he and another Deliveroo rider decided to produce a news bulletin, which they called the 'Rebel Roo'.[42] The bulletin reported on conditions, wage rates and activism in cities across the UK and Europe and was supported by the two UK unions that were organising Deliveroo riders at the time, the IWW and the IWGB. Cant began to distribute the bulletin among riders in Brighton, while a network of riders covered other cities in the UK. Meanwhile, riders continued to discuss issues – including those raised in the bulletin – on their WhatsApp groups and in the informal meetings.

In January 2017, Cant and a few others organised a meeting in a community centre, with the aim of forming a union branch and organising for a demonstration. An IWGB rep came from London and shared their experience of organising outsourced cleaners.[43] They shared information from the Rebel Roo, and discussed strike legislation, potential plans of action and so on. They were particularly pleased to note that they could turn their lack of status as employee to their advantage, since it meant that they did not have to hold a postal ballot, or otherwise meet the restrictive conditions of the 2016 Trade Union act before holding a strike. They could just decide to strike. This initiative was led mostly by the student cyclists. However, the Brazilian moped riders had heard of the meeting and the union branch, and simply decided through their WhatsApp group to go on strike in early February. Discussion on WhatsApp grew, union and non-union riders agreed and coordinated, the IWGB gave its backing, and momentum built. The strike itself was remarkably effective, with some deliveries three hours late, and order volume halved. Deliveroo responded by holding one-to-one meetings between managers and riders in a café by the zone centre, but without actual concessions to the riders' demands. Other demonstrations followed, including a May Day demo. In response to the mobilisations Deliveroo temporarily instituted an unofficial hiring freeze. Orders and therefore pay went up, but opportunities for gathering in the zone centres went down, and gradually prospects for union activism started to look bleak to the student riders. Student workers returned to their parents' houses for the summer, and new non-unionised riders began on the job. People suspected that those cyclists who had been particularly prominent in the organising were forced out and the IWGB lost an important court case about their right to represent Deliveroo riders in London. Still, in parallel the moped drivers had been organising among themselves, and they called a second strike for November 2017. Cant found out about this from WhatsApp group messages.

What's striking in Cant's discussion is the mix of more formal union-based forms of organising, discussions at zone centres and other physical spaces, WhatsApp group messages and other kinds of social contacts. All combine to produce what feels like almost spontaneous – wildcat –

strikes and demonstrations, without it being completely clear to anyone how exactly they combine. The 'invisible organization' in Romano Alquati's sense[44] behind the wildcat protests is invisible even to someone as active and interested as Cant. Also, organisation is shaped by the labour process and regulatory environments: the physical spaces of co-presence that enabled discussion were the zone centres where the app told riders to wait for orders. These are, according to Cant, quite gender-differentiated spaces, as women tended to avoid them, perhaps making the demonstrations and strikes more masculine affairs even than Deliveroo is normally (riders are predominantly male). The differentiation between the student cyclists and the Brazilian migrant moped riders mobilised different understandings of labour militancy, at key moments prompting more radical action. The migrant riders had dependants to support and relied on their Deliveroo work for the majority of their income, so when that fell, there was more at stake for them than there was for the students. They also came from a region with a strong tradition of labour activism, which informed their decisions about what to do, for example to strike as opposed to just hold a demonstration. The legal environment actually facilitated wildcat strikes, precisely because Deliveroo refuses to grant its riders employee status. But organisers must learn to fight for what the workers demand. For example many delivery riders for Deliveroo and Uber Eats were more concerned with the length of waiting time at restaurants and reductions in wages than the formal question of their legal status as employee, worker or independent contractor, even though activists argued that the three were related.

The question of legal status came to the fore in a recent employment tribunal case against Uber in the UK. Yaseen Aslam worked with Jamie Woodcock to tell his story as a leading organiser for Uber drivers in the UK. Like the Deliveroo riders, their mobilising originally happened in meetings and on WhatsApp, especially as Uber began to change its fees around a year after it launched in London. This is standard practice; Uber gains market share in a city by starting with good conditions for drivers, such as a bonus per trip (of £10 in London) and commission fee of 15 per cent, to attract them from other private hire firms. Aslam was earning about £1,000/week initially. Then, the bonus stopped, and the fee was raised to 20 per cent, then 25 per cent. He and other drivers began to discuss these changes on a pre-existing WhatsApp group of 50–60 private hire drivers, who had used it to warn each other about traffic jams and exchange information about demand. They formed an association, which then joined the GMB, one of the UK's largest unions. The GMB offered to support Aslam's legal challenge to Uber, taking the firm to an employment tribunal to claim minimum wage and annual leave, both of which rely upon Uber recognising the drivers' status as employees rather than independent contractors. But the GMB also represented taxi drivers, which created a conflict of interest, as they campaigned to revoke Uber's operating licence in the city, in collaboration with the taxi firm Addison Lee. The Uber drivers wanted better conditions from Uber, not to lose their jobs entirely, and so formed a different association, which eventually split from GMB and joined the IWGB instead.[45] They won their case at first, but then Uber appealed successfully, so it went to the UK Supreme Court, which ruled against Uber in February 2021.

Legal activism and alliances with traditional unions have also borne some fruit for Uber and Lyft driver activists on the West Coast of the US, although the companies did fight back. In California, Assembly Bill 5 came into force at the beginning of 2020, partly as a result of union lobbying. AB5 required specific tests for whether workers are employees or independent contractors, one of the key ones being whether workers are 'free from direction and control'. As a result of this, in August 2020, the Californian supreme court ruled that Uber and Lyft must reclassify their drivers as employees, which means paying for sick pay, unemployment insurance and holiday pay. The companies appealed and began also to lobby for a state-wide vote to exempt them from AB5, so that they could keep the drivers as independent contractors, known as Proposition 22 ('Prop 22'). In return, they promised limited health insurance and income protection, but not the full labour rights that AB5 required. Both companies used their apps to prompt customers to lobby for their desired outcome; and they threatened to suspend services in California in late August 2020, forcing an extension to the deadline for reclassification of drivers.[46] In the California state election in November 2020, Prop 22 passed with 59 per cent of the vote, after the Yes campaign had spent $200 million.[47]

In Europe, traditional unions have begun to pay attention to platform workers more broadly and start the process of building towards what could eventually become a broader regulatory environment. The German union IG Metall produced a manifesto for decent platform work (the Frankfurt Declaration) and has joined with Swedish and Austrian labour federations to campaign for fair crowd work. Their website reviews platforms and directs people to unions for crowd- and platform-workers.[48] Outside of union structures, the academic researchers Mark Graham and Jamie

Woodcock proposed the establishment of a Fairwork foundation, modelled partially on the Fairtrade Foundation and inspired by the London Living Wage campaign.[49] This promises a certification scheme for job quality. There have also been experiments in the design of ethical labour platforms by social enterprises and the small but growing movement of platform cooperativism.[50]

It is difficult to tell how influential initiatives like web-based review or certification schemes can be, and platform coops today are still small in size and often short in duration. While on the ground action is absolutely essential for collective organisation, the experience of the Uber drivers with GMB shows that traditional unions are not always up to the task. Most app-based work is structured so that workers remain isolated from each other, making collective solidarity difficult. Still, workers fight that isolation using social media and communications technologies, mobilising their existing social networks and creating new ones. Sometimes a group of workers can come together either physically or over social media, and if it is at a moment when they are in a relatively powerful position, they can organise collective action. A good example is the 2020 coronavirus strikes in the US. Mobilised through social media and drawing on the recognition of delivery workers as essential workers, Instacart shoppers made an alliance with workers at Amazon and Whole Foods fulfilment centres, and at Target warehouses, and held strikes on 31 March and 1 May 2020. The strikes and campaign were very focused around the claim to safety at work in the context of the pandemic, including claims for hazard pay, like the young Instacart shoppers who risked infection on behalf of bourgeois city-dwellers who sometimes did not even pay the tips they had promised.[51]

During the pandemic, delivery workers were increasingly in demand. In April 2020, as countries locked down and people turned to internet shopping, Amazon announced that it was recruiting an additional 100,000 workers for its fulfilment centres and delivery network in the US. They paid fulfilment workers an additional $2 per hour at the height of the crisis, although rescinded it after a few months, presumably once their recruitment process was complete. Public opinion acknowledged that these workers were needed, indeed essential, and the fear of the virus and desire to be protected from infection became a cultural truism. The strikers could then take advantage of an unusual confluence of workplace and marketplace power with what we might think of as cultural power. Who can blame them for claiming hazard pay, or a large tip? In this instance, we see a good example of collective action arising out of the combination of ongoing organisational efforts with the ability to recognise and take advantage of a political opportunity.

Usually, the labour process encapsulated in platforms mitigates against collective action for platform workers, because of the global oversupply of labour in remote digital work as well as the general fragmentation and isolation of platform workers organised as individuals isolated from each other. Yet, as I've explained here, digital workers create social ties outside of the platform but about the platform, and geographically tethered platform workers can create physical spaces of co-presence and even opportunities for withdrawing their labour. Workers are developing new techniques of resistance as they learn from each other and connect globally. Although the structure of platform work as organising labour outside of the job role makes it hard to identify the boss in conventional terms, platform workers are overcoming that problem through their activism. They do so by pinpointing the algorithmic management that shapes their labour and identifying the entity that suffers most from the withdrawal of that labour (i.e. the platform) as their employer. Platform labour is the most recent example of the axiom that throughout history it is not only capital that is creative, but workers too.

7

Patchwork Living

Doña Gregoria[1] lived in El Alto, Bolivia, until she died at the age of about 69 in early 2017. She had migrated to La Paz from the countryside at the age of 13, worked as a maid, and then married Don Lucio. In El Alto, she lived with her brother and her six children across two sites in the same neighbourhood, in houses they had built themselves from adobe. Don Lucio was away most of the time, working in his job in road construction. Doña Gregoria's brother worked as a knife sharpener in one of the markets in La Paz, and from 2008 collected his state retirement pension. Her children are now all adults, and four have children of their own. Her eldest son has worked as a mechanic locally, and then in Brazil and Argentina as a garment stitcher. He returned to his mother's property in El Alto, to stitch clothes, but after her death and the death of her brother soon after, he fell out with his brothers and sisters and left. Her eldest daughter worked for the local catholic church, mostly stitching. She also lives in her mother's house with her own son, and a few years ago was joined by her fiancé, now husband, who has a construction business that works on government contracts. The next son now has a business producing garments in Buenos Aires, for sale at the informal La Salada market, or via WhatsApp. He learnt his trade in São Paulo first. The next two sons work occasionally for their brother in Buenos Aires, and occasionally on construction jobs and other unskilled work they can pick up in El Alto, although one of them is gradually building up a business as a tattoo artist. The youngest daughter became a nun for a while, then worked on odd stitching jobs for the church, but has been back and forth between El Alto and São Paulo. When I first knew her, Doña Gregoria earned small amounts of money for jobs she picked up as one of the leaders of the parents' association of her school, and for conducting rituals to the Pachamama and local saints. The last time I visited her, she was selling second-hand blankets at one of the city markets as well. Over time, the family managed to save enough to build a three-storey building on their compound, to be apartments for the older children, with a view to later developing their other property (that belonged to Doña Gregoria's brother) in a similar way. With the exception of Don Lucio, no one has had a formal job that brings with it stability, health insurance or retirement benefits.

In this chapter I explore the precarious ways of making a living that are characteristic of life for urban majorities in the Global South. They have mostly been analysed in the language of 'informal' economies, or what Michael Denning calls 'wageless life'.[2] As Denning suggests, 'capitalism begins not with the offer of work but with the imperative to earn a living', and that happens in multiple ways, not all of which include a wage relation. People sell goods on the streets, stitch garments for piece rates, borrow money, live from cash or food transfers from governments and NGOs, and so on. They also make bricks, labour in others' fields, mine metals, carry goods, build offices, dig roads, clean houses, tend gardens, for day rates; or live from the salary earned by the one member of their household with a government job (whether short term or permanent). Their livelihood strategies involve multiple labour processes, and the overall patchwork might include industrial labour in the very short term (e.g. some piecework, or two weeks work in a petrol field, a short term contract in a workshop), but this 'patchwork living' is far away from the Fordist ideal of relatively stable material labour.

Amid changing global and national conditions, ordinary people focus on 'sustaining life across generations', in Susana Narotsky and Niko Besnier's terms.[3] In doing so, they often evade regulation, either deliberately or because they cannot be regulated. Their lives are not usually entirely wage free but nor are they characterised by the model of a secure male wage that on its own supports a nuclear family until the children are old enough to move away; a model that was of course only ever available to a select few in the North anyway. While the previous chapter explored labour agency when the job role does not organise work, this chapter focuses on ways of making a living when the *wage* does not organise work. The dilemma for workers' agency is between action for individual or household survival or betterment versus making broader alliances for collective action. What makes for the shift from one to the other (and back again)?

In the first section I introduce some of the changes in global political economy that have pushed people into a wageless or patchwork life, focussing in particular on the relation between structural adjustment, migration and urbanisation in the Global South, and on neoliberal welfare policies in the North. Then I discuss everyday experiences of this kind of work, using examples from ethnographies of waste pickers, motorcycle taxi drivers, street vendors and welfare recipients. I emphasise questions of temporalities, kinship and autonomy. The final section examines the collective politics that emerge out of these labour identities. Throughout, I try to balance out the need not to romanticise people's actions into a narrative of initiative, micro-entrepreneurialism, resilience and so on, but also not to produce a dystopic vision of bare survivalism. The economic activities are an 'effort to make life', again using Narotsky and Besnier's words.[4] Unlike those discussed in the chapters to date, they are focused not so much on the production of goods (material or immaterial) but on the circulation and distribution of goods and resources. Like the social reproduction labour discussed in the following chapter, what they produce is life itself.

Precarious livelihoods and global changes

Making working conditions and the payment for work as 'flexible' and precarious as possible has created a very profitable regime of accumulation enforced by governments from colonial times, that became more acute since the 1980s under the latest phase of global neoliberalism and population growth. Precariousness is intimately related to urbanisation processes, as structural adjustment programmes consolidated landholding in rural areas in the hands of agribusinesses, prompting mass migration to cities, especially in Sub-Saharan Africa and Latin America.[5] Once settled in peripheral city neighbourhoods, workers became available to work for low pay and to invest their labour power in autoconstruction of their houses and neighbourhoods, and in caring for relatives in the absence of state social or healthcare provision.

The city of El Alto, in Bolivia, is a case in point. Located on the edges of the crater that contains the major city of La Paz, El Alto began as a slum. Rural-urban migrants were attracted there first in the 1930s after the War of the Chaco against Paraguay, and another wave followed the agrarian reform of 1953. The city continued to grow through migration, especially with the construction boom of the 1970s, fuelled by foreign debt and US aid. But the real impetus for its growth was the structural adjustment policies of the 1980s, especially the 'Ley Maldita' (Evil Law), Decree number 21060. Decree 21060 enabled the privatisation of the state-owned mines. It was partly a response to the crash in tin prices on international commodity markets, and partly an effect of the economic ideology of the time. Twenty thousand miners lost their jobs. Many went to the coca-growing region of the Chapare, in Cochabamba to supply the cocaine boom in the US and Europe. Thousands of others moved to El Alto, where between 1976 and 1992 the population grew by 9.23 per cent annually, and then by 5.1 per cent each year until 2002 and then 2.34 per cent a year until 2012.[6] As a result, El Alto is mostly self-constructed, literally. People built their own houses, roads and neighbourhoods with very little government intervention, and started small trading and transporting businesses to generate an income for their households.

El Alto is sometimes thought to be a 'dormitory city', housing those who worked in La Paz, but that varies across neighbourhoods. In 2000, I found that only about 12 per cent of residents of a middling neighbourhood in the city worked in La Paz. The rest transported goods across the rural hinterland, worked as taxi or bus drivers, or for the local or national administration, as mechanics, shopkeepers or teachers; or in short-term jobs for political parties or NGOs.

Most households, however, seemed to be involved one way or another in selling in the city's markets. The largest markets in the areas known as the Ceja and 16 de Julio stretch across whole neighbourhoods of the city, and you can buy almost anything there, from a small bag of limes or second-hand nails to a TV or a sofa. Goods are brought in from the countryside or smuggled across the borders with the neighbouring countries of Peru, Brazil, Paraguay and Chile. The markets are governed by a mix of formal and informal regulations and negotiations between vendors' organisations and the municipality. Like other markets in the region, the vendors there trace a fine line between legality and illegality; as Cecilie Ødegaard says for traders in Arequipa, Peru: 'the successful trader is the one who manages to keep a certain balance between activities that are sufficiently formalized/legalized so as not to get caught too often, and enough informal/illegal to actually earn money'.[7]

Following Caroline Schuster, we might consider this a form of arbitrage: trade makes profit in the small differences in price from one place to the next – from informality to formality, countryside to city, one currency to another, or across national borders. That is especially acute in the Triple Frontier Region, where the borders of Paraguay, Brazil and Argentina meet in one of the most important free trade zones of the world.[8] In the late twentieth century, Ciudad del Este, the Paraguayan city there, became a node in global commodity chains that stretched at first to Taiwan, prompted by the migration made possible by the Paraguayan government's diplomatic recognition of Taiwan's sovereignty in 1957. Taiwanese migrants set up businesses importing cheap manufactured goods, for sale mostly in Brazil. In 1975 the Friendship Bridge between Paraguay and Brazil was opened, smoothing the importation of goods via Paraguay into Brazil. Following Deng Xiaoping's 1978 reforms that opened up the region of Guangdong to export-led manufacturing, most production shifted to mainland China, and Cantonese migrants began to settle in Ciudad del Este. By the 1990s, the city housed approximately 20,000 Chinese immigrants (Cantonese and Taiwanese). They mostly focused on importing, of cheap gadgets, watches, toys, etc., which they sold wholesale to Paraguayan and Brazilian traders.[9] Small-scale Brazilian traders cross the border multiple times in a week, with bags of goods. They are called 'sacoleiros', or 'bag men'. They register their tax-free allowance (of $300 worth of goods in 2010) or avoid customs duties by sending their goods over on skiffs or just floating in the current.[10] At the other side, they embark on long haul buses to towns in Brazil to sell in informal markets there.

People develop their income-earning strategies in dialogue with the big changes wrought by globalisation, urbanisation and structural adjustment. Claudio Sopranzetti tells the story of Adun, who migrated to Bangkok from the Thai border with Laos in 1981. Having worked on the family farm and as a seasonal labourer for sugar-cane agribusiness in his region, he moved to Bangkok at the age of 15, as soon as he got his national ID. Once there, he worked in a small shoe factory, a job he found with the help of a friend from his village. Adun moved around different factories, contributing to the export-led boom of one of the four Asian tiger economies and gradually accruing consumption goods for his urban base and rural family. He got married and his wife returned to live in their village to bring up their children, while he sent home remittances from his work in the city. Then, in the early 1990s, the Thai government liberalised national capital markets on advice from the World Bank, in the hopes that it would help the economy to grow even faster. Investment flooded into the country and real estate became highly profitable. Adun, sensing a shift in opportunities and frustrated by the hierarchies and discrimination of the factory floor, moved to construction work, building tourist resorts across the country. In 1997, the Thai currency was hit by speculative attacks, and capital flew out of the country (helped by the financial liberalisation), sparking the Asian financial crisis. Adun and his work colleagues lost their jobs, and while some returned to agricultural labour in the countryside, Adun drifted into driving a motorcycle taxi in Bangkok. Numbers of these grew seemingly

exponentially at that time: in 1994 there were around 37,500 motorcycle drivers; by 2003 there were 109,000. Adun's story, then, is one of the
intertwining of individual desires and strategising with global policy-making processes and their consequences, as he tracked through multiple
informal and precarious jobs in the countryside and the city. For him,
ending up as a motorcycle taxi driver was something of a triumph.[11]

Similar processes have happened across the Global South, as mass
deindustrialisation occurred in the mining belts and industrial areas of
countries that were once thought to be on the way to increased economic
formalisation, while large agribusiness companies bought up huge tracts
of fertile land, displacing the peasants from their source of livelihood. The
resulting mass migration to cities has not been sustained by an expansion in wage labour in formal businesses, but rather a proliferation of
income-generation strategies.

In the early 1970s, this kind of work was captured by the concept of the
'informal economy', an idea first coined by the anthropologist Keith Hart
in a paper in 1971. He outlined the variety of informal economic activities
undertaken by the urban sub-proletariat in Accra, Ghana, both licit and
illicit.[12] The informal economy is probably the most influential concept
to come to the mainstream from anthropology, as the ILO took it up to
describe unregulated parts of economies globally. It has sparked a whole
series of debates, as scholars pointed out that it is inaccurate to describe
informal and formal sectors of the economy as if they were separate and
not mutually constitutive, or how parts of seemingly 'formal' sectors have
considerable informalities (and vice versa), or that as you get up close
to how people actually make a living you see that you can't possibly disentangle the two from each other. For some, this means that we should
discard the binary in favour of other ways of describing economic activities, while others think that it might best be thought of as a continuum,
or as processes of formalisation and informalisation that interact with
each other.[13]

Part of the problem, as Kathleen Millar points out, is that the binary
is rooted in modernist concepts of the economy, where informality first
appeared as excess, the surplus that ought to disappear with modernisation.[14] Although few would agree with such a teleology these days,
informal activities are still often described through the 'form' that they
lack (i.e. regulation) with a sense that people resort to such activities
when they are not able to find formal waged labour. The geographer Mike
Davis for example, describes informal workers as the 'new wretched of

the earth', and a 'surplus humanity', who engage in 'informal survival-ism'. They are, he says, best considered as 'the "active" unemployed, who have no choice but to subsist by some means or starve'.[15] An alternative approach to informality emerged in the late 1980s, influenced by the work of Hernando de Soto. It is a more neoliberal one that celebrates infor-mality as micro-entrepreneurialism, held back only by the unnecessary red tape of southern bureaucracies.[16] Yet neither of these focuses really capture the range of activities and approaches to making a living in urban peripheries, reducing them instead to, as Franco Barchiesi puts it, 'images of hopelessness and victimhood – from the left – or initiative and oppor-tunity – from the right'.[17]

Instead, it may help to draw inspiration from James Ferguson's analysis of the case of southern Africa through the prism of a political economy of distribution. He argues that now that the majority of people are wholly or largely excluded from wage labour, the distribution of goods or resources happens very differently. People engage in what he calls 'survivalist improv-isation', which often takes the form of very small businesses that consist of buying a relatively small amount of a product and then breaking it up into even smaller units (e.g. selling individual nappies, or small quantities of fruits at the roadside).[18] Other kinds of 'distributive labour' include living from social welfare grants – from the state or NGOs – or working for pol-iticians and making claims on them through clientage. For Ferguson both are ways to put oneself into the position of dependent; and this kind of labour happens at all levels, including in the ways that members of house-holds make claims on each other for support.[19] Politics in particular is an important distributive flow to tap into, because of the idea that politicians should support their people, by giving them jobs, tenders, welfare plans, or just goods in return for votes and other kinds of support.[20] These distrib-uted flows are themselves broken up and distributed within households, like a stream breaking up into multiple rivulets.

In parts of Europe and North America now, waged labour is similarly either hard to come by, insecure or poor quality. In the absence of jobs, many turn to welfare schemes, another form of distributive labour. Sveta Roberman describes labour activation schemes for Post-Soviet Jewish migrants to parts of the former Eastern Germany, where she says that work 'has become an entity without substance'.[21] Among middle-aged migrants, 40 per cent were unemployed, and so participated in seemingly endless rounds of job-creation schemes, retraining courses, and jobs known as 'one-euro jobs' because they were paid one euro an hour for unskilled labour for the local government. Post-Fordist models of welfare across the Global North subsidise low-pay economies, assisting the working poor and punishing the unemployed by forcing them to take part in workfare programmes.[22] Since the 1990s, welfare programmes have been oriented away from a model where welfare was thought to provide a safety net for when the breadwinner of a family dropped out of the labour market – through sickness, retirement or losing his job. Now, the emphasis on the labour market remains, but welfare recipients are urged – through punitive surveillance – to accept any job that becomes available to them, no matter how insecure or low paid it is. If they do not attend job meetings or participate in state-organised work schemes, they lose their welfare benefits. Meanwhile, an increasing proportion of welfare expenditure is directed to those in jobs but earning below the poverty line, such as food stamps programmes in the US.[23] This is nothing less than a subsidy to those employers who are not prepared to pay a wage that covers the full cost of the worker's reproduction.

The labour of welfare

Welfare is one of the most important types of income for those living 'wageless lives' on global urban peripheries, especially (but not only) in the Global North. Welfare is one of the most important distributive flows from the state, but we rarely recognise the distributive labour associated with gaining access to those resources. By this I mean the work of collecting welfare that includes qualifying, waiting, developing expertise and behaving in morally appropriate ways. Welfare income relates to other precarious incomes by smoothing out the lumpiness of payment for short term work contracts or enabling women to provision their households without relying on men. It is an opportunity for income, an important and relatively reliable patch in the patchwork of household strategies, even if it is not often viewed as *work* in a conventional sense. Because welfare payments are usually targeted at women, the labour associated with them is gendered. Indeed, not only is welfare frequently targeted at women, but it is targeted at women specifically as mothers or carers, to help them provision their households and 'sustain life across generations'.[24]

Studies from the US, Argentina, Chile and Kenya all show the extent of the labour of waiting involved for those who qualify for welfare to process both their qualification and the payment. Clara Han's Chilean interlocutors told how they needed to '*tramitar*' their welfare payment – a word that describes the process of taking a case through a bureaucratic procedure.[25] When I applied for a research visa in Bolivia I could hire a 'tramitadora' to *tramitar* on my behalf, but those who cannot afford to pay others must wait in line themselves, often at multiple stages of each process. Javier Auyero documents how welfare applicants in Argentina will usually have to return a few times before they have pulled together the correct paperwork; they may be given appointment times when offices will be closed and must maintain their file with all the documentation that could possibly be required, with the correct stamps and signatures, and so on. They wait at the welfare office for hours on multiple occasions, being 'kicked about' like a ball in their effort to meet the variable and seemingly arbitrary requirements set by the officials and keeping their patience in the face of frustration and bad treatment (a kind of repressive emotional labour).[26]

Take for example 'Marta', an assistant in a New York dental office, whose case is described by Maggie Dickinson.[27] She was experiencing problems recertifying her eligibility for food stamps. Although for five years previously all she had needed to do was provide a copy of a letter showing her income, that year the caseworker had requested extra documentation because he suspected her letter to be fraudulent. Marta was nervous about asking her employer for a printout of her earnings in case he reacted negatively to finding out that she was applying for food assistance. She was also very anxious that she would be fined by the food stamp office for fraud. She decided to try though, as she found that her wage really did not cover all of her expenditure. The process of working through her case involved at least two visits to the food stamp office, one visit to the advice centre, and a request to her employer for a printout of her earnings, despite her nervousness. Still, she agreed to ask and was very relieved when it worked out. Dickinson also describes the situation of 'Jeff'. He is a freelance sound engineer who also had to work to make his employment legible to the welfare office. He is paid quite well but not every week, and not via pay stubs, and his income varies from month to month. He had to attend an interview with a caseworker, then reapply, attend the advice centre, followed by a work-assessment appointment to check that he is working 20 hours a week. He said, 'I have a job. I don't need to go to this. I had to sit there all day to show them paperwork that I have a job. They really give you a hard time. You know, it's demoralizing to not be able to support yourself, and they don't make that process any more ... you know, they add to the stress of that.'[28]

Marta, Jeff, and Han and Auyero's interlocutors were all entitled to their benefits, but they all had to labour to receive them, and of course many others drop out along the way. Even universal welfare payments can require regular attendance to collect the money. For example, in northern Argentina, if recipients of the universal child benefit do not have ATMs in their community, they must travel each month with their identification to a post office to wait in line for their payment.[29] In Nairobi, the government social grant for orphans and vulnerable children was collected at first every two months through the post office, later through a bank card. An NGO-run cash transfer scheme was run through M-Pesa, as SIM cards were allocated to recipients, allowing them to collect their money at an M-Pesa agent kiosk.[30] Bank cards and mobile money distribution systems cut down on the labour of waiting for payment, but recipients must still work to qualify (as I discuss below) and if payments are stopped for any reason, there are usually many hours of problem-solving labour to get them started again. This is not peculiar to Argentina or Kenya, being a characteristic of any bureaucratic system anywhere in the world. In addition, learning the welfare benefits system anywhere is a labour of expertise, as evidenced by the proliferation of non-governmental advisers who help recipients navigate its waters.

Although often onerous, welfare labour results in relatively small payments, as governments tend to set welfare levels well below the level of income that could be achieved through paid work. But those payments are at least relatively regular, in contrast to the punctuated payments of insecure work. Agustin Díz has studied the gendered effects of this in the Chaco region of northern Argentina. There, he argues, paid employment has all but disappeared for young Guaraní men, with the exception of occasional well-paid stints of work in construction or oil exploration for a few weeks at a time. The rest of the time, they wait, play football and engage in job-seeking activism through a local Unemployed Workers Centre. Young women, however, qualify for universal child benefit, which is set at a rate of ten per cent of the minimum wage for each child, up to a maximum of five children. Once cash transfers become the only source of regular income in Guaraní households, Guaraní men become dependent on their female kin. This has two main effects, Díz argues: first, that dependency is hidden within a regime of value that associates male income with abundance and therefore politics, but also hides the way that income (and the ability to make a claim on that income) relies on intrahousehold ties of dependency and care. Second, although he finds no evidence that young women are deliberately getting pregnant in order to gain access to welfare payments, once they do, many no longer feel obliged to live with the father of their child, and fathers do not feel very responsible for their children. Young men often do not officially recognise their children, and the young women stay with their parents, contributing to the income of that multi-generational household.[31]

The cash transfer is payment for their labour of care for their children, and Díz's interlocutors are very clear that they should spend it on provisioning the household for the benefit of the children. The child benefit payment is universal, but in theory requires that parents (mothers) ensure their child attends school and gets regular health check-ups and vaccinations. Other cash transfers are conditional on specific behaviours: for example, in Bolivia the Bono Juancito Pinto is an annual payment to mothers of children with an 80 per cent school attendance rate, while the Bono Juana Azurduy is given to pregnant women and mothers of children up to two years old who must attend health appointments in order to qualify for each payment. Women must also refrain from becoming pregnant again until their child is two years old.[32] In some countries welfare recipients must literally work for their payments, as in the US work assignments programmes which employ them in unskilled jobs for well below minimum wage and on pain of losing their benefits.[33] Even where the transfer is ostensibly unconditional, people understand it as requiring a particular set of behaviours, especially in the education of their children. In Nairobi, Tom Neumark argues that people saw cash transfers as facilitating women's existing caring work, and resulting from their status as poor people. The transfers weren't seen as payments for particular activities, but were seen as creating an obligation to behave correctly, which means to attend to their children's education and healthcare in ways expected by the government and NGO.[34] Thus, welfare labour involves both the labour of collection and the labour of appropriate behaviour, the 'correct' use of the benefit. Because welfare payments are usually targeted at women, the expert labour associated with collecting welfare money is gendered. It's (mostly) women's work.

There is also work of self-presentation that must go into qualifying for welfare in the first place. Clara Han recounts the story of Pato and Valentina, who were working as a taxi driver and street vendor respectively when she first met them. Pato had previously worked in textile and lighting manufacturing, then transporting goods from warehouses to stores. When the company he worked for hired a labour broker who offered work at too low a salary, he resigned and became a taxi driver, but that work proved unstable and inadequate to support his family. While he was out of work, Valentina had applied for a welfare subsidy to help pay for water and electricity. This required a visit from a social worker, to assess eligibility, but Pato and Valentina did not know that they should have hidden the consumer goods they had bought on credit when Pato had a reliable income, so they were denied the subsidy. Women told Han how dehumanising they found having to fulfil a particular image of poverty for the social worker's visits.[35] Neumark describes similar assessment processes in Nairobi, as possession of consumer goods are taken as proxies for income in the evaluation of eligibility for welfare payments.[36]

While petitioning for benefits, individuals have to present themselves as needy but also deserving. Like 'Marta', their poverty needs to be documented and legible to case officers. Their income must conform to an expectation of regular but small payments, and they must certainly not use money that they earn or borrow to buy large consumer items like TVs or washing machines. They must become experts in the welfare system and learn how to describe themselves and their situation in the correct way. Scholars have discussed these processes as processes of creating particular subjectivities among welfare recipients,[37] but here I want to point to the ways that they involve a labour of self-presentation, if not necessarily of self-creation.

Relational autonomy and the temporalities of patchwork living

Welfare bureaucracies expose the erratic nature of ordinary people's income generation strategies, even though they are not designed to take it into account. Eligibility criteria are predicated upon a smooth definition of poverty, one of a regular income below a certain level, whereas people mostly earn sporadically. Their poverty is punctuated, lumpy. In moments of relative abundance, they might be able to afford a particular consumer item, or they might buy on credit, itself a kind of smoothing process.[38] When the welfare application is successful, regular payments can help to smooth poverty, and facilitate credit arrangements. People manage the different temporalities of their livelihoods strategies, balancing them out and patching them together. One of the most important values that animates this strategising through variety across different places is autonomy, understood not in individualistic terms, but as shaped by our insertion into networks of care – 'autonomy [that is] always already woven into relationships and forms of social belonging', as Kathleen Millar defines her concept of 'relational autonomy'.[39] 'Relational autonomy' is perhaps best thought of as the autonomy of the 'encumbered self', to use a version of an older concept from Michael Sandel's work, which describes the self as defined by and embedded in relations.[40]

With both cash transfers and wage labour the main experience of work is one of subjection to another – the state or the employer respectively, especially when considered in temporal terms. You must be patient and wait for the government agent to decide your eligibility, or be prepared to submit yourself to the demands of employers that you work certain hours or shifts. Having control over your own work is an important value for people in all sorts of jobs, and it might partly explain the fairly common aspiration to have a small business. For some scholars, the desire for a small business is a result of the hegemony of neoliberal entrepreneurialism, while for others, it is a mechanism of survivalism in the political economy of distribution of ever decreasing amounts of goods.[41] However, it might also be experienced as a positive choice for a different and more autonomous relation to work.

Ariel Wilkis tells of 'Marga', who owns a small store in her house in Villa Olimpia, Buenos Aires. She kept her store open for unusually long hours, often all night on Fridays and Saturdays, selling beer and cigarettes to a group of friends who gathered outside her store to play cards and drink. She worked very hard indeed, often feeling utterly exhausted by Mondays, and she said frequently that she was a 'slave to her store'. But her hard work also gave her independence, in her case from her husband. He had wanted her to stay at home to look after their daughter when she was born, so she left her job in a beauty school and set up shop with her savings. He was happy while her business did not compete with his position as breadwinner, but their marriage broke down when her earnings exceeded his. Their daughter now lives with her and is expecting her first baby. Marga values her economic independence and her obligation to her daughter, and her business enables her to live according to these values of relational autonomy.[42]

For Kathleen Millar, relational autonomy is also bound up in questions of temporality. Her example is the rubbish dump of Jardim Gramacho, Rio de Janeiro. The trash pickers she worked with told her that they found it hard to adapt to working for a boss, and to the different rhythms of that kind of work. Their critique of the boss's power was often articulated through a temporal critique, albeit one that placed blame on themselves as being unable to adapt to regular work schedules or to being present for a certain number of hours even when the necessary tasks had actually been completed. 'Rose', for example, left a formal job as a domestic worker because her boss required her to stay for the entire day even when she had finished the cleaning. The problem for her with this arrangement was first, that she wanted to be able to return home to care for her children, and second, she could not get used to these formal temporal arrangements. Others said that they left jobs because they were 'restless'. The trash pickers' response was to create a different temporality of labour that suited them better. Sorting rubbish from the dump was a way to work when they needed money, and the landfill was a resource available 24 hours of the day, seven days a week, until it was closed by the municipal government after Millar's fieldwork. Workers would come to the dump according to their own rhythms, and if they needed to earn more money, they would stay longer than usual. Periodically they left the dump for other jobs, but they almost always returned. The dump was a source of refuge and even stability, despite the work being precarious, dangerous and utterly informal. Patrick O'Hare found similar attitudes among trash pickers in Montevideo, Uruguay, who called the landfill the 'mother dump' because she was always there for her children. O'Hare suggests that the dump is an urban commons, available to pickers when they need it, and 'a refuge from wage labour'.[43]

In Bangkok, the living map of the city could also be seen as a commons available to the thousands of motorcycle taxi drivers working there. Whereas the rubbish-pickers of Rio expressed their turn away from wage labour and towards autonomous work in terms of their inability to adapt to normal work, Claudio Sopranzetti's interlocutor Adun explained that motorcycle taxi driving was a source of freedom or independence for him. He said 'It is a free life. You can come and go from home anytime; you can get money fast, every day, without waiting for the salary.'[44] The word he used was 'itsaraphāp, which he defined as follows:

I can go home whenever I want. I don't have to take leave. Don't have to ask anyone. I don't have to come to work if I get sick or get drunk. If I earn enough money for the day and I want to go home to sleep, I can do that. This is 'itsaraphāp. I used to work for a company, I went home often and I was never promoted. I have to go back home to the village regularly: my family is there, my farm is there ... I was offered to go back to work in the company I used to work for, but that job in Bangkok is bad for a countryman like me. The boss always looks down

on you, always orders you around, always insults you. In the construction company, the boss's son kept insulting me, shouting at me, treating
me like scum. A twenty-year old kid with no experience, just out of university; I could not accept that. So I am happy now, I am my own boss.[45]

The long working hours required to make enough money to live on
show that both motorcycle taxi driving and rubbish picking also represent the freedom to self-exploit, but that freedom can be experienced as
positive and a source of pride. When Sopranzetti pointed out that Adun
works more hours than he would in a factory, he responded 'Yes, but it's
my own decision.' Rather than a story of informal entrepreneurialism,
this is more like a refusal of waged work and its attendant discrimination
and bad treatment. For Adun, control over his own work meant temporal
control, as well as the freedom to return home as often as he wanted to. It
was also a work arrangement that enabled Adun to care for his family back
in the countryside as he wanted to.

Other informal workers organise their work through kinship in the city.
In the dump in Montevideo, many of the trash pickers were connected
through kinship. Most important were bonds of siblingship: brothers and
sisters worked together and with their husbands or wives, caring for each
other through waste. Materials found on the dump would be split between
family groups, small recycling yards were run and staffed by single families.
O'Hare suggests that in contrast to an image of waste workers as either
individualistic or organised in formal associations like cooperatives, the
extended family was the primary social group on the dump. Trash picking
is a family enterprise.[46]

Trading businesses are also frequently family enterprises. In Latin
America, street vending is predominantly associated with women, especially in the Andes. As Cecilia Ødegaard points out, it enables them to
'engage in the economy in a way that does not depend on a rigid separation of the home from the workplace'.[47] Stock can be stored at home and
markets are held only on specific days in a week. Vendors do not need to
go to the market to sell every day if they do not want to and do not need
the money at a given moment. As a profession, vending can be compatible
with childcare, as traders bring their very young children to the market, to
help or to play while their parents sell; although frequently they do leave
young children at home in the care of older siblings.[48] Husbands often
come to work at the stall, especially when the family holds more than one;
or they participate in the vendors' associations, engaging in the political

work associated with trading. They might also help by driving the truck or taxi that takes goods to the market.

Business owners also often contract family members to work at stalls or as ambulatory vendors, although that can bring problems of its own. Astrid Stensrud tells the story of Isabel and Wilfredo, a wife and husband who had a business selling mobile phone calls on the streets of Cusco, Peru. They employed their nephew to sell the calls, but after a few weeks found that he had spent mobile phone minutes calling his girlfriend and mother back in their home village in the countryside, and dialled incorrectly for national calls, which then cost more than they should have. Because he was their nephew, they could not recover any money from him, and importantly they did not expect to, however irritated they were. But he did stop working for them and returned to the countryside. As Stensrud points out, running a small business allows people to achieve the independence they value, but it is not an individual independence, rather one that is 'entangled in bonds of relatedness'.[49] Kinship is at the heart of entrepreneurialism, in small businesses as much as in large family-owned multinational conglomerates.

Labour agency: networks and the state

The networks and relations that enable income generation in situations of patchwork living require labour to maintain. On an everyday basis, this might be as simple as keeping records of credit arrangements with a customer, holding a purchase for a customer to collect later, or having a beer with a particular scrap dealer. It may also take the form of collective organisation, like cooperatives of trash pickers, associations of motorcycle taxis, associations of market stallholders or ambulatory traders. The existence of collective organisations and mobilisations does not mean that all of those who patch their livings together in this way participate in a collective politics. For many, the aim is just to earn enough to contribute to the provisioning of their household, or if they are a migrant, to support themselves and send some home to their families. Workers might compete with each other for contracts, inhibiting the possibility for solidarity between them. Alternatively, they might consider the leaders of the relevant organisation to be corrupt and out for their own interests; they might just not have the time for collective political action; or they might consider it too dangerous. Most people do not participate in this kind of politics most of the time. Nonetheless, collective organisation of some sort is not unusual, and can become especially important – and bring in more people – at times of threat.

Juan Thomas Ordoñez describes the work of day laborers in Berkeley, who stand on a seven-block corridor of Hearst Avenue from sunrise to about 3 p.m., waiting for employers to drive by and offer them a few hours work on a construction site, gardening, clearing a home renovation, or other kinds of manual labour.[50] Mostly undocumented migrants, they competed fiercely between each other for work, to the point that Ordoñez argues very strongly that there was no form of collective politics possible among the group. Yet he also documents a kind of collective action to set a preferred minimum hourly rate. When a prospective employer offered less than ten dollars an hour, most of the workers would object and refuse to get in his or her vehicle. Although eventually someone would take the job, it would provoke vocal objections from the others and thereby communicate the normative expectations to both workers and employers. Somehow it was usually respected, too. Labourers also used their networks to get jobs, developing – if they could – relationships with particular employers, who would ring them to offer repeat work, and ask them to bring others along when necessary. There were also a few local non-governmental institutions who could provide advice when something went wrong.[51] For example, 'Francisco' was bitten by his employer's dog, and incurred hospital bills and lost income that he could not afford. The local NGO tried to help him, and sent him to another NGO, and then – at the suggestion of the men on the corner – Ordoñez got involved. Their attempt to get compensation for Francisco involved visits to the courthouse, to the dog owner's house, to a *pro bono* lawyers' office, and calls to Animal Control and to the dog owner herself. Ordoñez found himself in the uncomfortable position of interpreter, and his friends among the other day labourers teased him that Francisco had become his boss. At times he felt that Francisco was taking advantage of his help: having unrealistic expectations of him, and repeatedly calling to chase the money. Problem-solving networks do not always work smoothly.

Collective networks are more formalised for street vendors. They are based upon problem-solving like price-setting and negotiating relations between vendors and with the state. Like traditional unions in factories and the public sector, the labour of networks is made particularly evident in their investment in social events. In Bolivia, the principal festivals for market vendors are Gran Poder in La Paz (24 June), 16 de Julio in El Alto, and for the Virgen de Urkupiña in Quillacollo, near Cochabamba (15

August). The parties and religious processions associated with the festivals are moments for collectives of traders to come together, to assert their presence in the city, and to demonstrate their wealth and success through expenditure, as well as to honour the supernatural sources of their business fortunes.[52] The mostly Bolivian traders in the market of La Salada in Buenos Aires celebrate the Virgins of Urkupiña and Copacabana, and the Argentine folk saint, Gauchito Gil, each year.[53] The interplay between alcohol, ritual expenditure and cash expenditure is similar across the sites. None of the festivals happen spontaneously, but they require months of organisation, for example in practicing the dances for processions.

Ritual action is at the base of the strength of the collective associations of vendors, whose role is to resolve disputes between members, and between their members and rivals. Collective organisation in street vending is a politics of territory: often, traders who hold fixed market stalls or locations for their business join together to protect their territory against ambulatory vendors, while associations of ambulatory vendors seek to negotiate with the fixed stall holders over pavement space, or open up new spaces so that they can gain a fixed position themselves.[54]

For fixed and ambulatory vendors, the state is a major interlocutor, one that can be both relatively benign and highly aggressive. Again, it is often a politics of space, as municipal governments seek to formalise markets or 'clean up' the streets. Unlicensed vendors might be directly targeted by the police, as in the case of the fish sellers at the station of Cais do Sodre in Lisbon, studied by Kesha Fikes.[55] Periodically subjected to police raids, the women had to be highly mobile, ready to move on at any point. Some developed friendships with licenced vendors there, who looked after their merchandise out of the view of the police if there was a raid. However, ultimately the fish sellers were cleared out by the relocation of their wholesale market to a new terminal further out of Lisbon, purpose built with money from the EU, and designed to meet EU regulations on hygiene and safety. Few of the small traders could afford transport there, and so gradually they sought other sources of income. Fish selling is a particularly vulnerable trade, because the products must be sold quickly and kept in hygienic conditions, and they smell, meaning that residents are rarely happy to have a fish market on their doorsteps. In El Alto, I followed the negotiations of a group of fish sellers with the local government over proposals to build a wholesale terminal for fish selling further out from the centre of the city. This involved meetings with municipal and prefecture agents (two different levels of government), both of which meant hours of waiting before being granted an audience. There were also meetings with rival sellers' organisations, assemblies to decide tactics, mobilisation of connections between the leaders of traders' associations and local councillors, and many rumours and accusations of financial irregularities as part of the political work of legitimation and delegitimation.[56]

It is common for governments to try to displace vendors from city streets. Although vendors are clearly selling their wares to someone, other residents of the city are supposed to object to informal trade because their transit through the city is blocked, or they find the vendors to be aesthetically problematic. The mayor of the city of Lima in the mid-1990s, Alberto Andrade, ran a campaign to 'recuperate' the city centre, to recover its colonial identity and wrest it away from the migrants from the countryside, a deeply racialised endeavour. He employed a troop of city agents to raid brothels, illegal discotheques, pickpockets, drug dealers and vendors selling their wares on the streets surrounding the Central Market.[57] In Rio, too, street vendors found themselves targeted by police as part of Mayor Cesar Maia's 'clean-up campaigns' in the 1990s, as Kathleen Millar's friends recounted. Rose said: 'A new mayor took office and the guarda municipal (a police force) began taking our merchandise in the street. We had to run from them. You must have seen this on television. How the *rapa* – we call them the *rapa* – come and take vendors' merchandise.' Officers of the guarda municipal do not carry guns, but do use clubs, handcuffs and sometimes attack dogs against vendors.[58] Both mayors were influenced by Rudy Giuliani's broken windows policy in New York, as well as the authoritarian conservatism of the local upper classes, who are in reality the main group of city residents opposed to informal street markets.

Repressive policing on the streets may be accompanied by the offer of alternative market locations. Where this causes conflict is usually because they are either inconveniently located or too small for the number of vendors the government wants to displace. It is complex political terrain for vendors associations to navigate. In Yogyakarta, Indonesia, Sheri Lynn Gibbings followed a traders' association that attempted to oppose relocation to an enclosed marketplace. The association underwent a series of damaging splits between those who wanted to relocate and those who didn't. Leaders were accused of being bought off by the mayor, seeking their own personal interests, or even being an agent provocateur working undercover for the mayor, an accusation that eventually turned out to be true although nobody correctly identified the real culprit. A bewildering number of organisations, factions, leaders, interests and government agents were involved in the struggle, which took place in municipal offices, during night-time police raids, demonstrations, press conferences, rumours and mobile phone calls.[59]

Rubbish pickers must sometimes organise themselves too in order to negotiate with state agencies or their sub-contractors who want to formalise waste management or reorganise it in some way. Across the world there are associations, organisations, trade unions or cooperatives of rubbish pickers. Sometimes they form to run recycling centres set up by municipalities or NGOs, or to coordinate trash collection between themselves and fight for their right to continue their profession. Both Millar and O'Hare show that this formal organisation is not necessarily a very smooth process, and perhaps even incompatible with the work rhythms and subjectivities of the dump.[60] As cooperatives or other more formal organisations take shape, tensions often arise over their attempt to regulate trash collection, and people leave. This contrasts with street vending, where collective organisation of some sort is often integral to the organisation of work. In Bolivia, you must be a member of an association in order to be allowed to sell in a given location, and this provides strength in numbers for demonstrations and other acts of visibility to the state.[61]

But even where membership is more fluid, associations are not necessarily weakened politically, as long as leaders can maintain their credibility with the larger community. Rather, collective organisations constitute themselves, fragment, disappear and then reconstitute; this is the stuff of politics. Together with other less formal kinds of collective identity and action, they are available to be the foundations for more spectacular mobilisations when those become necessary. When scrap dealers in Rio took advantage of currency fluctuations in the mid-1990s to reduce prices they paid for recyclables, the waste pickers convened a meeting and agreed not to sell to the dealers until prices improved. In the meantime, they lived from the food they collected from the dump, so no one went hungry. The strike lasted three weeks, after which time the dealers gave in and began to raise their prices. Another time, the municipal waste agency contracted an engineering company who redesigned the spatial layout of the dump so that the staging area where the waste pickers put their sacks was a kilometre away from where trucks unloaded. After someone was run over by a bulldozer on the long trek between the rubbish and their sacks, a group of waste pickers demanded a meeting with the engineer, but they got nowhere until they organised a blockade of the trucks arriving at the dump, insisting that if a truck unloaded before there was agreement to relocate the staging area, they would set it on fire. That time, they were successful, and the staging area was moved back to its original location. While the mobilisations took place, the waste pickers acted as a collective, and then, when completed, they returned to their usual ways of 'labouring in common'.[62]

From time to time, groups of informal workers can find themselves holding political power, and when that's the case it's no real surprise that their organisations look to leverage that power. In Thailand in early 2010, prodemocracy protesters known as the 'Red Shirts' took over the Ratchaprasong intersection in central Bangkok. Motorcycle taxi drivers participated as occupiers, messengers and rescuers; they 'slowed down, filtered, and arrested the movement of people, commodities, and information in the area', according to Sopranzetti.[63] In early April, a group of leaders of the Association of Motorcycle Taxis of Thailand (AMTT) pledged their support for the protest at a public meeting. This brought them to the attention of the army, a faction of which then sought to neutralise their influence by offering to be patron to the AMTT. Prior to the crackdown of 19 May that year, the AMTT held a meeting with Army envoys, who promised cash support for the organisation and assistance against the 'people of influence' from the post-2006 regime who extorted money from the drivers. The AMTT saw an opportunity to play one faction of the state against another, and while they did not actively support the crackdown on the protesters, as a collective presence they melted away when the Army moved in. Individual taxi drivers continued to help the protesters and to participate, and some left the AMTT in disgust. Many thought it had sold out to the army, and the weakened organisation then moved into a period of factionalism over the next few years.[64] Such is the danger of realpolitik.

Patronage networks are crucial for the politics of the urban poor and informal workers. In some states of India, organised informal workers form themselves as voting blocs available to politicians in return for the promise of social welfare policies. Rina Agarwala argues that this is most effective in states where populist politicians compete for the votes of the poor, like Tamil Nadu.[65] Elsewhere, welfare often goes along explicitly with hierarchical patron-client relationships.[66] In Argentina, government social grants for housing and other forms of welfare have under different regimes been channelled through neighbourhood organisations, especially those supportive of the party in power at the time. They might be direct client networks of local politicians, or neighbourhood-based associations with strong connections to those politicians and/or the governing party. They involve a lot of work, organising support, pressuring the state, distributing goods, putting together project proposals for funding, keeping people onside, conducting research and so on.[67] A related form of welfare is what Ariel Wilkis calls 'political money', namely payments from politicians to the people in their network in return for gathering supporters at rallies, affiliation drives and, of course, elections. Those payments could be a small regular salary, or some kind of assistance: help with fixing a broken pipe, building a house, getting access to land, a scholarship for school, job on a construction contract, or – the best – a job in the civil service. The relationship is one of exchange as much as dependency. People view it as a kind of work: they might even use the language of a salary, or talk about their *jefe político*, their political boss.[68]

Patron-client networks are one of the places where the politics of distribution links professional collective identities with neighbourhood politics and allows for mobilisation around neighbourhood infrastructure. Welfare recipients do not generally organise themselves into political associations based on that specific identity, but they are often the same people as the clients of a communal kitchen, the members of a street vendors association, or the residents who are mobilising in order to gain utilities infrastructure for their neighbourhood. In Latin America, the self-construction of peripheral urban districts is grounded in collectively organised mobilisation for water, sewage, electricity, roads, health and education infrastructure.[69] In South Africa in the last two decades, residents of many peripheral neighbourhoods and townships have mobilised in multiple spontaneous protests for service delivery. In both cases, the demand for better infrastructure is both a demand for better services and a demand for jobs. It is usually the work of the local government to organise the installation of the infrastructure, and even if the work itself is done by private companies, the tenders for that work are directed through patronage networks linked to the state. Local people with the right networks can then expect work digging ditches, or constructing health centres, or other public works.

The work of patching a living together is, then, often linked to the political work of mobilising clientelistic networks. The politics of this flows through a combination of professional identities and identities based upon place and belonging. Welfare is both a piece in the patchwork of strategies to 'make life worth living', in Susana Narotsky and Niko Besnier's words,[70] and a form of often politicised labour in its own right. Households combine their members' various income strategies, expertise and networks in creative ways which change over time. Their political action is similarly dynamic, changing according to opportunity, desire and necessity. In the next chapter I explore some of the political strategies I have described here, but from the point of view of social reproduction as labour and as a political goal: the politics of making life.

8

Social Reproduction Labour

Andrea explains: 'You have to do anything for your children ... You have to take care of them, make sure they eat and go to school, but you also have to give them hope and make sure they are loved and that they grow up to be good people who will take care of their own children.'[1]

Tatsanii's diaper is changed four times a day – in the early morning, midmorning, afternoon, and night – and she receives three meals (two with medication).

... First, preparation. Ying lays out a small pink floral plastic sheet on the floor and a larger one near the bed, later to be stretched underneath Tatsanii (called Yāi, 'Grandmother'). Next, two tables are placed on top of the first sheet, which will protect the floor from the inevitable bathwater spills. Additional materials are brought over – small plastic bins holding necessities like cotton balls, powder, lotion, and bedsore medicine. Then three plastic tubs are filled with water – one large and two smaller – and lifted onto the plastic floor sheet.

... The second plastic sheet converts her air mattress into a bathtub. Then begins the process that will be repeated for all clothing and diaper changes, as well as all mattress adjustments – a series of rolling her to one side, shoving materials underneath her, rolling her to the other side, straightening, and easing her back to center.

... We start with her eyes. The smallest tub – about the size of a soup bowl – is filled with plain water without soap. Cotton balls are soaked and used, one per eye, to clean the yellowish mucous from the old woman's eyelashes.

... After wiping her face, we replace the tap water with drinking water in the small tub. More cotton balls are submerged, this time for the mouth. Ying brings a wet bud to Yāi's lips. Then, as with so many motions of this process, she begins a subtle bodily negotiation. She wipes across the lips, then begins to coax the jaw open, pushing the cotton in while encouraging Yāi to open her mouth. 'Ah, ah, ah' – Ying makes sounds with her own mouth wide open, and, whether by the force of Ying's fingers or by directive, the old woman's mouth opens, allowing her daughter to push the cotton inside to wipe her palate, the insides of her cheeks, her tongue.

We pat the old woman's now-clean face, neck, and ears with a dry cloth. Then Ying and I position ourselves on either side of the bed for exercise and massage tasks.

… Overcome by what I have just experienced, I launch into a speech about how impressive their work is. Aom answers without blinking an eye: 'Impressive? Come every day, four times a day, and then it will be impressive.'[2]

EASA 2020 took place virtually. On the Friday I was in the room that served as my home office during the pandemic, listening to a panel and watching the video presentations. My partner and our two teenaged sons were working from home too (the boys' school was online). Over lunch we discussed how we would collectively clean the house that week: we agreed that my two sons would clean the bathroom and their bedrooms and my partner would cover the downstairs, while I would do the downstairs toilet and hoover the upstairs, apart from the boys' rooms. During the afternoon session of the conference, I decided to get ahead with my normal weekend duties and went into the adjacent room to take down dry laundry and fold it in piles ready for distribution to each family member, while listening to a presentation on social reproduction. After the session, I hoovered the stairs and upstairs. While doing so, I reflected on a discussion I had had over private chat with another female participant in the panel on just how open we feel we can be about how our social reproduction labour interacts with our anthropological work.[3]

Social reproduction labour, as the maintenance and production of life, is woven into all of the kinds of work discussed in this book. In reality, it is probably the reason that most people work: not for the capitalist's profit but to live well, feed, educate and care for those they love. Marx distinguished production from social reproduction, but for him, 'social reproduction' meant the reproduction of the capitalist system as a whole. Feminist social reproduction theorists added to that the importance of the production of people as labour power and beyond.[4] Hegemonic understandings of labour politics as derived from material or industrial labour have mostly ignored social reproduction, despite feminists pointing it out from early on. We still have some difficulties in thinking about social reproduction labour as *labour* per se. In this chapter, I discuss social reproduction labour by drawing on the anthropology of care and examining the ways that social reproduction integrates with other kinds of work discussed in this book. Although it is perhaps the archetype of affective labour, the labour of social reproduction is also profoundly material, because it produces and nurtures persons and bodies, and it is corporeal, because it involves bodily and emotional processes and is even often thought to come from our biological instincts or affinities. The final section of the chapter explores the politics of territory that derives from social reproduction, both from the labour of social reproduction and from social reproduction as a goal. I argue that neighbourhood-based movements for urban services and infrastructure should also be conceived of as labour movements for social reproduction. Unsurprisingly, the analysis is shot through with gender, constructed in particular racialised and heteronormative ways. The analytical dilemmas animating this chapter are, first, can we call political actions at the household and neighbourhood level *labour* agency, and if we don't, then why not? Could we be still falling into the trap of our (gendered) assumptions about what work is?

The political economy of social reproduction labour

Human labour is the motor of capitalism, and the reproduction of human labour power – 'capitalism's human subjects' – is essential to capital accumulation.[5] However, as Tithi Bhattarcharya reminds us, the labour of sustaining and reproducing the worker is 'naturalised into nonexistence', being the realm of kinship, care, love, 'women's work'.[6] The emphasis on 'productive' labour over reproductive work in economic governance, politics, social thought, academia and so on, can be thought of as a kind of dispossession, of (mostly) women's energy, time, sleep and physical capacities.

Even early struggles for limits to the working day suited capital because some leisure or rest time was necessary for workers to rejuvenate. But the experience of that time as rest has always been more available to men than to women, for whom 'non-working' time away from the factory was time when they shifted to a different kind of labour, that of cooking, cleaning and so on, to rejuvenate the male workers and the future workers in their households (i.e. their children). Feminists call this the 'double shift', as women work both domestically and for pay.[7]

The reliance on women's social reproduction labour creates a basic contradiction at the heart of capitalism according to Nancy Fraser, because 'capitalism's orientation to unlimited accumulation tends to destabilize the very processes of social reproduction on which it relies'.[8] Different regimes of accumulation have arranged this contradiction in historically specific ways, which she outlines from the perspective of the North Atlantic, beginning with the liberal capitalism of the nineteenth century, which relied upon industrial exploitation and colonial expropriation and left workers to reproduce themselves outside of the 'circuits of monetized value' and of state regulation. Key to this regime was the creation of a bourgeois ideal of domesticity and the private family as a separate realm of social reproduction and of women; even though most people were actually deprived of the conditions needed to realise that ideal.

Then came twentieth century 'state-managed capitalism' premised on industrial production and domestic consumerism in the core and colonial and post-colonial expropriation in the periphery. In Europe and to some extent North America, this regime managed social reproduction through the provision of social welfare and the modern notion of the breadwinner's wage – the 'family wage' – that was, again, achievable for only a few. As Eileen Boris elaborates, post-Second World War welfare states in Europe provided some public services of social welfare (education, preventive healthcare, childcare) while also expecting family security to come through the wage of the breadwinner and the benefits that accrued to him, like pensions, unemployment benefit and so on.[9]

In theory this arrangement freed women to devote themselves to domestic labour but it also made them dependent upon their husbands and reinforced heteronormative understandings of family. Further, it was possible only because the surplus labour and resources extracted from former colonies went to the core and not to the colonies themselves. Families in the colonies faced a very different experience.

The 'male breadwinner norm' in the North Atlantic started to become inadequate in the 1970s, both culturally as second wave feminism emerged in the US and Europe, and economically as Fordist models of mass production gave way to neoliberal hegemony and the new global division of manufacturing labour. As Nancy Fraser says:

[The resulting regime] has relocated manufacturing to low-wage regions, recruited women into the paid workforce, and promoted state and corporate disinvestment from social welfare. Externalising care work onto families and communities, it has simultaneously diminished their capacity to perform it. The result, amid rising inequality, is a dualized organization of social reproduction, commodified for those who can pay for it, privatized for those who cannot – all glossed by the even more modern ideal of the 'two-earner family'.[10]

Concurrently and globally, a series of political-economic developments (market fundamentalism, financialisation, structural adjustment, labour flexibilisation and conflict) have contributed to the dispossession of people from their land and the growth of urban peripheries where social reproduction faces the challenges of precarious earning strategies, crime, drug addiction, violent policing and more.[11]

These economic processes have also prompted transnational migration, as the crisis of care in wealthy countries with shrinking welfare states provided employment opportunities for women migrants. As more women in core countries entered the paid workforce, they hired other women to cover domestic labour. Long-standing histories of racial servitude as well as contemporary inequalities mean that domestic workers are often migrants or from racialised minorities. Françoise Vergès argues that the question 'who cleans the world?' is at the heart of decolonial feminism.[12] As women migrate to care for other people's children, they create global care chains as they seek out alternative ways to care for their own children back at home. This task usually falls to female relatives, especially grandmothers, who care for their migrating daughters by mothering their grandchildren.[13]

Global care chains also mean increased commodification of care work and other aspects of social reproduction, as the earlier quote from Fraser pointed out. In 2010, the ILO estimated that the domestic workforce globally reached 53 million, accounting for 7.5 per cent of women's labour across the globe; although as with other kinds of home-based labour it is impossible to get a truly accurate count. The increased numbers in domestic labour, coupled with political activism by multiple organisations, did open up possibilities for global labour standards, and the ILO agreed a convention on domestic work in 2011. Ironically, but probably not surprisingly, this represents an attempt to govern an employment relationship based on the standard employment relationship just when it was breaking down even in those few sectors where it did apply.[14] Domestic labour – like agricultural labour – was always protected from the standard employment relationship by employer resistance to labour regulation.

Discussing the commodification of care labour exposes some of the complexity of analysing the labour of social reproduction, because of the balance between paid and unpaid care work. First, because that balance varies across contexts, households and time, and it can be difficult to disentangle commodified from non-commodified social reproduction work, as Chapter 4 attested. A care worker might not be paid for the time that she looks after the family of her elderly charge as they organise the funeral arrangements and for the time that she attends the funeral, but it is painful to her to be excluded at such moments.[15] Second, the naturalisation of social reproduction as acts of love and of kinship obscures the hard work that it can actually entail and enables governments to avoid regulating this labour even when it is quite clearly commodified. For example, employer representatives argued against the ILO convention on the basis that domestic work was different because it was 'to help in the household', and that employers (i.e. housewives) would not be able to fulfil the legal requirements that would result from a convention.[16] Yet, on the other hand, much of the work that we do for social reproduction is done for love and emotional attachment, or as a moral project of care or socialisation, or for desire, worship and joy, and we often instinctively resist the implication that it is equivalent to a paid job.

Women's work

Social reproduction labour produces life itself – labour power in the Marxist sense, but also life more broadly. Arguably, most people work for a wage in order to reproduce life, but we also engage in labour that does this unmediated by the wage. In this section I focus on how that unpaid (or unmediated) social reproduction work is woven through the other types of labour discussed in this book.

A crucial aspect is the way that the labour of social reproduction is usually understood as women's work and naturalised as driven by women's role in biological reproduction, or as an act of love, or helping. Describing domestic activities like this is one way to make invisible the labour of social reproduction. Even in anthropological analysis, when the importance of feeding and commensality in the making of kin is central, the actual labour involved in preparing, cooking and cleaning up on the day is rarely attended to in as much depth as are the symbolic aspects of the food, the ritual aspects of consumption, or the processing of crops or hunting of animals.[17] Similarly, it took one of the reviewers of this book to point out to me that I should also discuss the bodily work of pregnancy, breastfeeding and early infant care.

Women's domestic labour makes families and people, both literally and figuratively. Where women are wage labourers, social reproduction labour must fit around their work. Sarah Besky describes the daily routine for the workers on Darjeeling tea plantations in northeast India: they wake before dawn and make the trek to collect water from the nearest spring, which might be an hour's walk away. On their return they make tea for themselves and their family, and prepare the morning meal and tiffin lunches for everyone. Then they walk to the fields and at 7 a.m. they start work picking tea leaves. On their return home after the workday finishes at about 4 p.m., they prepare dinner of lentils, green vegetables and rice. They may also take food to sick relatives in hospital and buy medicines for themselves and their families. On Sundays, when they do not have to work in the plantation, they send their children to watch the local youth football games while they do the laundry, cooking and cleaning, and maybe spend some time with their husbands or visit with friends. The provision of facilities like football pitches is an incredibly important responsibility of the plantation owners as far as the workers are concerned, and workers distinguish between contemporary times of 'bisnis' and the older times of 'industri' when owners provided good 'faciliti-haru' like recreational spaces, community houses, schools, creches, garden spaces. Today, the 'faciliti-haru' remain and are highly valued by the workers as the plantation's contribution to general social reproduction; but investment is declining, and the facilities are deteriorating. Still, the plantation owners' responsibility is to care for the workers by providing faciliti-haru and in return the workers care for the landscape. Social reproduction is thus woven into the fabric of the plantation and the exchange of picking labour for a wage is only part of the landscape of care, labour and exchange there.[18]

Clearly the women tea pickers work a double shift of paid and domestic labour, a situation familiar also to office workers. Both Reena Patel and Kiran Mirchandani found that the consideration of domestic labour as 'ladies' work' remains powerful in parts of India where women have entered the labour force as call centre workers.[19] Married women reported that they were responsible for getting their husbands' clothes ready, preparing his food and getting children ready for school, all of which they had to fit around their paid shifts. Academics also find it challenging to combine paid work with social reproduction labour, in their homes and at the workplace. Theresa O'Keefe and Aline Courtois reported that women were concentrated in the more precarious academic jobs perhaps because of their responsibilities for social reproduction.[20] As office workers including academics become more established in their careers, they often choose to outsource domestic labour and hire a cleaner or a nanny or both. As already discussed, these domestic labourers are often migrant women or women of colour, and domestic labour in Europe and the US at least draws on very longstanding histories of racialised servitude.[21]

During the pandemic, lockdown meant that new kinds of workers had to grapple with how to fit their domestic labour in with paid work, but of course this has been a problem for homeworkers in industries like garment stitching or on digital platforms for a long time. For many of the workers, the ability to combine their paid work with caring responsibilities has been a positive aspect, as discussed in the previous two chapters. Other workers can bring the home to their workplace, like the street vendors in Cochabamba, Bolivia, described by Daniel Goldstein.[22] Agricultural workers bring their children to the fields. Workers involve the children in the work itself as a form of childcare and help. These are spatial arrangements that enable the combination of paid work with social reproduction labour.

Alongside those spatial arrangements are temporal management strategies. Office workers negotiate part time hours that match with their children's school day. Homeworkers combine their work times with the times when their children are asleep or at school and organise to break off when they need to prepare meals. Uber drivers work night shifts so that they can attend to their children during the day. Street vendors arrange the time that they will leave the house in order to leave the children alone for the shortest length of time possible.[23]

Finally, I think it is important to acknowledge the social reproduction labour that takes place at traditional workplaces like factories, docks, offices and so on. Where workers live in dormitories on site, social reproduction and production take place under the eye of the owner. Also, most factories and industrial plants do not just extract productive labour from their workers but provide opportunities for social gatherings and ceremonies to mark important dates, all of which regenerate the workers to some extent. Ritual work associated with the workplace is another form of social reproduction labour that regenerates the workers, the workplace and the product, and this is an extremely important feature of agricultural work, too.[24]

In my work on Argentine public sector unions, I have argued that ritual serves as a means to reproduce the labour force and their commitment to their work, through honouring important political figures and moments of time. Both ritual and political action resolve problems of work and develop workers' sense of belonging to a collectivity, which is both the union itself and the Argentine state. That reproduces them as moral individuals who share a perspective on what a state should be, and can embody the strong state, with the capacity for good policies of public health, justice and social welfare. Ritual celebrations require labour to organise: someone must put out chairs in the room and sort out audiovisual equipment, make video presentations, prepare the food, advertise the event, give the speeches. They produce conviviality and relations, which are the stuff of bureaucracies the world over, alongside paperwork.[25] On a more day to day basis, union leaders pay considerable attention to affiliates' health, through their management of the civil service health insurance scheme but also in some cases leaders arrange for tests, treatment, sick leave, or leave to care for a sick child, and so on. They advise affiliates struggling with personal problems, developing relationships with them that the leaders describe as therapeutic. The union organises a childcare scheme over the summer school holidays and provides school materials for affiliates' children. In these and other ways, the union cares for the worker and his or her family, paying attention to the realm of social reproduction as part of its own political work.

Care

The idea of care enables us to further draw out how social reproduction labour appears in contemporary ethnographic writing. The anthropology of care is rapidly developing into a new sub-field, one that crosses anthropology of kinship and medical anthropology. Here I focus on the unpaid labour of care (Chapter 4 discussed paid care work). I examine the care of children and the elderly, which mostly falls to women and girls, and is mostly naturalised as inevitable. Care usually takes place through multi-generational arrangements, criss-crossing between children and adults, between grandmothers and grandchildren, between parents and adult children, and so on.

Children and care

Caring for children involves all sorts of daily activities of feeding, cleaning, dressing, playing, talking, educating, disciplining, waking up and putting to sleep, and so on. As we care for them, we build them into particular kinds of moral persons and we engage in projects of moral becoming ourselves. Cheryl Mattingly and her team researched the experience of care for African American families of very ill or disabled children in Los Angeles. Mattingly argues that caring for medically vulnerable children through the long arc of their treatment for terminal illnesses or ongoing physical disabilities is a moral project. Parents, and mothers in particular, undertake the labour of care as projects of self-making and making others, making a good life through virtuous action. Care includes the day-to-day care of feeding, bathing, looking after a child, taking the child through their home exercises of physical and occupational therapy, and organising special events like birthday parties or funerals.[26] It also involves negotiating medical settings which are deeply racialised, products of long histories of differentiated care and perceptions of need. This has been especially well studied for the case of antenatal care in the US, as shown in the work of Khiara Bridges and Dana-Aín Davis.[27] They show how Black mothers' concerns are repeatedly overlooked or dismissed in medical settings, and their care is compromised by structural and individualised racism leading to excessive medicalisation of their birth experience and a greater likelihood of premature birth. Health workers and the attendant structures of expertise often perceived Black women as especially 'hardy' in childbearing (a legacy of slavery), but also – particularly since the moral panic of the 1980s about 'welfare queens' – as 'wily patients', engaged in ('immoral') activities such as addiction, overwork, single motherhood or poverty, all of which put them 'at risk' as a population. Medical 'care' around pregnancy and birth is a common locus of racialised treatment globally, at the extreme including forced sterilisation programmes such as that targeted at indigenous women in 1990s Peru.

Mothers in Mattingly's study of medically vulnerable children changed their lives when their child had an accident, often reorienting themselves from previous goals of self-becoming into a different kind of moral becoming so that they could be a good (or good enough) mother. In the process, they developed significant skills and expertise, including nursing. Andrena did physical and occupational therapy exercises and administered chemotherapy to her daughter at home. She even cared for her daughter there while she was in a coma for the last two weeks of her life. Parents became experts in medical care as they came to understand their child's need, and pressured clinicians for particular kinds of treatment, or debated 'do not resuscitate' orders in neonatal intensive care. For some, this seems to have become a kind of activism. Activism on behalf of their child was not limited to medical spaces, as they attempted to get suitable educational provision for their children; or worked out how to include a child with cerebral palsy in children's soccer games. And parents also moved into a more general kind of activism, turning their experience into knowledge and help to support others in a similar situation.[28]

These and many other kinds of activities are clearly very time intensive, a kind of moral labour for producing life. They might well be undertaken in very difficult contexts of poverty and violence, both structural and occasional. Mattingly tells the heartbreaking story of Leroy and Delores, his grandma, whom Mattingly meets when Leroy is six and must have repeated operations for a congenital hip problem. Delores takes Leroy to the repeated hospital appointments for surgery and then recovery, does his physical exercises for his recovery, and brings along his mother Marcy (who is trying to recover from an addiction to crack). She also supports her other daughter Sasha when she must care for her toddler, Willy, who tipped burning cooking oil over himself when 18 months old. By the time of Willy's accident, Leroy had recovered from his hip problems and his mother had been clean for three years. Delores managed to hold her family together and Marcy managed to stay clean; but then in the space of six months, Sasha's partner (Willy's father) was shot and killed, Delores died, and Sasha was imprisoned for drug dealing. Just a year after Delores's death, when Leroy was 16, he was shot dead in an altercation with his sister's boyfriend, while nine-year-old Willy was standing next to him. The labour of building lives is hard when drugs and guns circulate freely.[29]

Clara Han describes a similar situation of entangled care for multiple generations amid addiction and poverty, this time in Santiago de Chile. When we first encounter Señora Flora, her daughter Florcita is living on the second floor of her house with her partner Kevin and their two children. Both Florcita and Kevin are addicted to alcohol and *pasta base* (cocaine base paste), and Kevin suffered from manic depression, panic attacks, and waves of anger and fear, made worse since a stroke. He is violent towards Florcita. Han describes the ups and downs as Señora Flora tries to encourage her daughter to leave her partner, or tries to calm Kevin down, once by buying him a music player on her credit card. Mostly, she

waits patiently for her daughter to leave Kevin, or to get clean; and meanwhile she cooks for her grandchildren when she can. Over time, Florcita
appears to improve at times, but then relapses. At one moment she's found
unconscious in a street after being raped while selling sex. Eventually
Florcita moves out with her children, but she never leaves Kevin. During
that time, Florcita and Kevin's addiction shows in Señora Flora's house as
they steal and sell consumer goods, or – in a good moment – as Señora
Flora manages to buy tiles for her kitchen floor, but then must sell them
again as Florcita's condition deteriorates. The house recovers again when
she makes Florcita and Kevin move out.[30]

Señora Flora's ability to invest in her house is shaped by a combination of the nature of her daughter's addiction at any given time and access
to consumer credit, which funds all of her major consumption. As well
as affecting her house, the situation with her daughter affects her relationship with her second husband, not least because he is responsible for
earning the money for credit card payments. I would imagine it to be a
really difficult situation, but Han does not report Señora Flora particularly
complaining about it; she takes it in her stride because to care for your
child is simply part of life. The tragedy of this story is perhaps related to
how we think about reciprocity between parent and child. It shows how
children, even when adult, do not always repay their mother's care as we
might hope. Señora Flora's story is made more morally complicated by
the existence of grandchildren. She must mother her daughter, and to an
extent her son-in-law, but also her grandchildren, where she can.

Delores too must care for both her ill grandson Leroy, and his mother
Marcy, her adult daughter. The first time we meet Delores and Marcy,
Marcy remains seemingly disengaged from her son's medical condition
and his appointment. She has her head down, she is reading a book, and
does not answer questions or engage with the medical staff, who think
that she is an irresponsible mother. But it took an immense effort for
Marcy even to be there, given her struggles with her addiction at the
time, and the book she was reading was in fact her Narcotics Anonymous
manual. Delores's choice to mother both her daughter and her grandchild
was something that she also experienced as inevitable – partly because of
lack of resources to pay someone else to do the work, partly because of
gendered expectations for care labour, but also just because that's what
you do for your children if you can. She said: 'But I said [to myself], sometimes we just have to deal with situations. And we know we gotta put up
with it no matter what. It's the rest of our lives. We gotta deal with it and

adjust ourselves to dealing with it. I had to adjust myself ... and adjust to these children.'[31] Inevitability is constitutive of the experience of the labour of social reproduction.

Responsibility for grandchildren is especially important in the context of the global care chains mentioned earlier. As women migrate to engage in domestic labour in wealthier countries, they often leave their children in the care of their mother. For Nicaraguan grandmothers this is an act of care for both their daughter and their grandchildren. They look after their grandchildren so that their daughter can migrate (usually to Costa Rica or to the US) and build a life for herself and her children, eventually. Kristin Yarris describes this as a kind of solidarity with their child. Solidarity is both political and interpersonal, an emotional alignment with the other and social action in support for their struggles.[32] They also understand their actions as a sacrifice, both in a daily sense where they sacrifice themselves to care for others, but also because they sacrifice the care that they might otherwise have received from their daughter as they aged. At some point also they must sacrifice the child they have cared for when that child is sent for by its mother. Some of the grandmothers have been caring for their grandchildren for many years, and so this is emotionally very difficult for them. However, all agree that the children's place will be with their mother when she is ready. So, the grandmothers lose both their daughter and eventually their grandchild, with whom they develop very close relationships. Still, feeling that this should happen, they try to nurture the child's relationship with their mother, which can become difficult when the mother has a new family in her country of residence. They manage the remittance money sent by their daughter, ensuring that it can cover the key expenses of (in order of priority) schooling, more varied food, debts and eventually possibly a house. Meanwhile, each day they wake the child(ren) up, feed them, wash their clothes, clean up after them, take them to the doctor when sick, take them to school, ensure that they do their homework and so on. All the daily tasks of domestic care. For the grandmother, this is labour as sacrifice, and it is inevitable. Marbeya has been looking after her grandchildren for more than 10 years while her daughter is in Costa Rica. She says 'I wash, cook – I do everything for them ... If they get sick, I have to run around to take care of everything. And maybe ... I have to go to the doctor with them. So I say, whatever, I have to do it because if I don't, who else is going to?'[33]

For the daughter, the remittances she sends symbolise her parallel sacrifice and her continuing responsibility for her child(ren), they maintain the affective tie. The main point of all these sacrifices – for the grand-mother and the daughter[34] – is that the child should go to school. Investing in children's educational opportunities is the highest priority for remittances. For the children, their contribution to the 'intergenerational sacrifice of transnational family life' is that they should study well and succeed in school.[35] Indeed, schooling is a key part of how we understand care for children in many societies these days; as well as being a central site of social reproduction itself. Marisol Verdugo Paiva describes how in the Chilean town of Concepción, mothers who worked very long hours tended to take on as much of the household reproductive labour as they could, so that their children could attend school, and – crucially – study well for their homework. The mothers would rush to clean the table after cooking and having dinner, so that their children could have it for studying; and cook up stew so that their children only had to heat it up in the microwave when they were on their own in the house. These examples do represent a change from past years, in that girls are expected to study just as much as boys, and not to forfeit their education in order to undertake reproductive labour. Yet in the inevitabilities of domestic labour, it does seem that the only alternatives were that either the children (especially daughters) would do this kind of labour or the mothers. The fathers or other male adult members of the household were generally thought to be exempt from that responsibility.[36]

Perhaps fortunately, children usually appreciate the labour of care they receive, from mothers, grandmothers, schoolteachers, fathers, aunts, uncles, big brothers and sisters, and so on; often attaching it to feelings of love, pride and admiration. Wendy Luttrell's beautiful book *Children Framing Childhoods: Working Class Kids' Visions of Care* (2020) depicts this through children's photography, conducted as part of a research project in Worcester, Massachusetts. She and her team asked children to take photographs of their lives at the ages of 10, 12, 16 and 18. The children's photography showed the importance to them of all the care undertaken by the adults in their lives, from the schoolteachers 'who make learning fun' and are always smiling in the photos, to the pictures of the food their mothers cook for them and for school events such as bake sales. One of the key visual tropes was what Luttrell calls the 'mom-in-the-kitchen' photo of their mother usually looking up from some task, caught in the middle of a routine moment. The children related to these photos with incredible tenderness, holding them carefully and speaking emotionally of their love for their mother, and their gratitude to her. They spoke of how their mothers looked after them and other family members, feeding them, helping with homework, 'keep[ing] the family going' in one girl's words. The children were proud of their mothers, of their intelligence, the amount they read, the way that their cooking was appreciated by others as well as by them, and of how hard they work. One really sweet ten-year-old boy told a researcher, 'I love her so much I could explode from too much.' His mother, he said, helped him 'with being a child'.[37]

Children are also important social reproduction labourers, labour which is often made invisible as 'help', or their natural obligation as part of the family. Olga Nieuwenhuys argues that this relates to adult surplus value creation by directly contributing to goods produced, by saving costs on adult labour as the adults are freed from reproductive work to engage in paid or otherwise productive labour, and by saving on the social costs of bringing up new generations of workers.[38] Pamela Kea adds that children may also contribute to money generation, for example by selling goods in the market. She argues that in Gambia the contributions of children are underpinned by a moral economy which values hard work as tradition, the Mandinka way, linked also to Muslim ethics.[39] All over the world, children's tasks are perceived as help and naturalised as socialisation. They change over time as children grow and are capable of more complex tasks, or tasks requiring greater strength.

At some point, children's participation in 'choreographies of care' and social reproduction becomes more recognisable as child labour, and from there as potentially exploitative. Systems of child circulation bring these questions to the foreground. 'Child circulation' refers to when a child goes to work as a domestic labourer for (usually) more wealthy kin. Jessaca Leinaweaver's ethnography of the Peruvian Andes describes how girls 'accompany' elderly relatives, to whom they are often linked via ties of godparenthood. Their duties can be quite varied, usually an extension of the activities that they are expected to do when at home – cooking, washing clothes, minding younger children, cleaning. In return, they may be able to attend school, and the person they are 'accompanying' will pay for school supplies. Their move to a wealthier household is usually a move to a more urban environment, and so it is a form of social mobility, and a way to '*salir adelante*', or 'get ahead' socially and educationally. It is a particularly gendered mode of social mobility because of the close association of girls with domestic labour. Girls get room, board, the occasional 'tip' (in cash), and the hope of social mobility in return for 'the gendered performance of household labour, gratefulness and humility'.[40] Mélanie

Jacquemin describes a similar fosterage system in Abidjan, Ivory Coast, where 'little nieces' live with wealthy 'kin' and cook, clean, etc. For her, this system of child circulation is essentially the provision of free maids cloaked in the language of kinship.[41] In both the Ivory Coast and Peru, conceiving the labour as 'family labour' obscures its more exploitative sides. The affective charge of the language of 'helping' and 'accompanying' contrasts to work and obscures the fact that the young women are 'mobile and gendered labourers'.[42] They can feel homesick and lonely, but they also report becoming accustomed to the city, and not fitting in when they return to their birth villages. Some do genuinely get opportunities for education that they would not have had in the countryside.

Care for the elderly

Thus, relationships of care are as much generational as they are gendered, and care flows in both directions, towards children and towards the elderly. Migration makes elderly care both possible and complicated. Cati Coe shows how female migrants in southern Ghana coordinate their life course and migration movements with their responsibilities for elder care. Migrating women might initially leave their children in the care of their mother, but then somewhere between the ages of 40 and 60, they return to look after now elderly parents. They can do so because their employment situation is more precarious than that of their male siblings, meaning that they are available to return. But they are also simply expected to be the ones to provide caring labour. The men of the family ask the eldest daughter to take on this job and so she does. As Abena Oforiwa said to Coe:

My elder brother, the one I come after in birth order, said that no one was at home and the cousin also was alone at home, so if anything happened, no one lived here. So I should come with my children so that she would be happy. This is why I came to live here.

Her elderly cousin said: 'The men go out to work, the women stay at home. You who are the eldest female will come home [to the hometown], and the children will go [to] work hard [in the cities] to look for something to make their living.' Between them they look after eight grandchildren, and Abena also expects to care for her older cousin, whom she considers to be a sister.[43]

This is the 'care slot', the role of the woman who cares for both the children and the elderly in a household at the same time.[44] Women who grew up expecting to take care of their husband and their children often have very little time before they then must care for elderly parents. As many of the quotes in this section indicate, they (we) tend to view the labour of care as inevitable, unavoidable, although with a moral tinge of kinship obligation, and it is remarkable how consistent that sense of inevitability is globally.

Felicity Aulino analyses the way that two middle aged daughters look after their elderly mother in Thailand as ritual action and without heavily loaded moral overtones. She outlines the extremely labour-intensive bathing process (part of which was quoted at the opening of this chapter), which had taken place four times a day for two years by the time she conducted her fieldwork. Aulino argues that, as with ritual action, it is not necessary to seek any particular internal state of mind on the part of the daughters. The action itself is enough, they don't need to believe that they are doing it out of love, kinship obligation or something else. They do consider that it is related to karma and merit, but mostly – again – it seems largely inevitable, moral destiny.[45]

The inevitability of care is important for the analysis of social reproduction labour in commodified as well as non-commodified modes. Where people have the money, they can choose to hire a care-worker, nanny or maid, or pay for a nursing home or kindergarten place. Yet, precisely because of the association of the labour of social reproduction with kinship labour, such work is generally undervalued; it lies in the realm of help even when delivered as part of a commodified labour relationship. This means that the labour of social reproduction is paradoxical because it is on the one hand seen as inevitable (the natural result of gender and kinship) while on the other it requires a lot of affective overloading to get people – usually women – to do it for free or for low pay. We are told it's about love, the reciprocal attention to those who cared for you, emotion, moral goodness and so on.

But while this might work as a mystification of what is really just exploitation, the relationships between caregiver and the receiver of care are also real, deeply powerful and often experienced as love, even when they are commodified, as the discussion of paid care work in Chapter 4 shows. Moreover, care also expands well beyond kin or those relationships that are parsed through the language of kinship, without necessarily becoming commodified. Ethnographies repeatedly show how neighbours care for each other through small acts of kindness. For example, in Santiago de Chile, one of Florcita's neighbours buys marmalade from her even though she already has plenty; in Rio, Rose told Kathleen Millar in passing how she had filled up her neighbour's water jugs for her because she'd noticed that the children hadn't showered in a while; and she had informally adopted the child of another neighbour, who was suffering from addiction to *pasta base*.[46] Care also extends out beyond humans, as people care for their animals, plants, their ancestors, earth-beings and other deities, often through ritual.[47] In the workplace and at home, ritual is a central form of social reproduction labour, which builds the relations that make humans, propitiates potentially capricious non-human entities (spirits, gods, landscapes, etc), and protects human life, as described in Chapter 3.

Labour agency: political activism for family, community and life itself

I suspect that the sphere of social reproduction produces more political activism than all the other kinds of labour discussed so far in this book. There would be many places to begin a section on the relationship between social reproduction and political activism, but I choose to start with a very brief historical-theoretical discussion of feminism, especially second wave feminism. The naturalisation of a particular notion of womanhood and its violent effects has fuelled feminist struggles worldwide, from white liberal feminists who critiqued the confinement of women to the position of housewife to decolonial feminists today. When we think about political agency for those who carry out social reproduction labour, this naturalisation plays a huge role in inhibiting resistance to oppressive relationships. Feminists have been key in challenging that situation both theoretically and politically.

One important movement that explicitly took on the question of social reproduction labour was the wages for housework campaign, associated with Italian autonomous Marxist feminists in the 1970s. They argued that women in heterosexual relationships had been naturalised into the role of housewife in order to serve capital:

> In the same way as god [*sic*.] created Eve to give pleasure to Adam, so did capital create the housewife to service the male worker physically, emotionally and sexually – to raise his children, mend his socks, patch up his ego when it is crushed by the work and the social relations (which are relations of loneliness) that are reserved for him. It is precisely this peculiar combination of physical, emotional and

sexual services that are involved in the role women must perform for capital that creates the specific character of that servant which is the housewife, that makes her work so burdensome and at the same time invisible.[48]

By demanding wages for that work, they articulated its value and (artificial) separation from spheres of production, emphasising that reproduction subsidises production and pointing out that keeping it unpaid is necessary for capitalism.

Liberal feminists (in the US and Europe) focused on improving conditions for women's entry into the paid workforce through advocating for measures such as maternity leave, improved childcare provision and labour standards, especially on anti-discrimination and equal pay. This recognises the entanglement of reproduction with production, but largely benefits only very privileged women, who may only be able to enjoy their privileges because of their reliance upon other women for domestic labour. More recent feminisms are starting to argue that the emphasis on the workplace itself may be the problem, while also trying to avoid taking a position that returns women to domestic spaces only. Kathi Weeks advocates for a social reproduction feminism based on the refusal of (paid) work. She takes a feminist perspective on the arguments for universal basic income, which, she suggests, would free men and women for labour that they enjoy, including that of social reproduction.[49] Recent social reproduction feminisms in the US such as that expressed in the *Feminism for the 99%* manifesto by Cinzia Arruzza, Tithi Bhattacharya and Nancy Fraser are a welcome move away from the complacency of liberal, 'lean-in', feminisms there, because they bring back the explicit link between feminism and anti-capitalism.[50] This has been an important feature of decolonial or 'Third World' feminisms elsewhere in the world and among US women of colour for decades now; which of course is also grounded in the importance of anti-racism to feminism.[51]

It would be madness to attempt a survey of feminist, anti-racist and anti-capitalist politics globally, especially now, when we are in the midst of another wave. But through ethnography we can identify some important interlinked ways that social reproduction labour as I have described it produces activism: around care (including medical care), around urban life, around the public sector, and around life, violence and death.

Medical care produces social and political activism at multiple levels. As Cheryl Mattingly shows, illness can lead to activism on very personal levels as people seek treatment for themselves or their loved ones.[52] More collective campaigns have also emerged, one of the most famous being the ACT UP campaign advocating for HIV/AIDS research and treatment. The US and South Africa were hotspots for this multi-faceted movement. At first, activists campaigned against stigma and for effective preventive public information campaigns and provision of condoms. As treatment became available, advocates turned to questions of accessibility and cost, which especially highlighted global inequalities. Anti-retroviral (ARV) treatments for HIV initially cost thousands of dollars per person, highly profitable for the large pharmaceutical companies but well beyond the reach of those countries most affected in Sub-Saharan and southern Africa. In a series of well-publicised protest and lobbying actions, campaigners successfully advocated for the manufacture of generic ARV medication. Vinh-Kim Nguyen shows how alongside the political activism, social activism around HIV in West Africa became institutionalised into a development space consisting of NGOs, capacity-building workshops, community programs, experimental research, project applications and so on. That is to say that activism for social reproduction (health) also involved a lot of social reproduction labour in that professionalised space. One very important aspect of that in the earlier years was the building of networks that could enable access to medication, including through travel to Europe once France stopped deporting HIV+ asylum seekers after a powerful local campaign.[53]

Experiences of pregnancy and early maternity have also produced activism. In the US, campaigners target the medicalisation of birth, with particular focus on its racialised effects. Dána-Ain Davis describes the work of radical Black birth workers, most of them doulas, who accompany pregnant women through their antenatal care and during labour. Their goal is to support the women, and in particular to help them be more in more control of their experience. Davis argues that this is a way to 'navigate structures of oppression within the medical environment'.[54] The doula mentors the mother during pregnancy, and supports her to maintain her birth plan, for example being able to refuse an epidural or medicalised induction of labour and to labour at home for as long as possible. The doulas that Davis worked with saw their 'birth work' as an extension of other kinds of social and political activism. For both them and the parents, movements for natural birth practices are linked to the right to parent children in a safe environment in the context of racialised oppression, for example violent policing, a point I return to later.

Other forms of activism have been linked to infant feeding, including boycotts of the manufacturers of infant formula as well as the promotion of breastfeeding. The boycott of Nestlé for its aggressive advertising of infant formula in the Global South started in 1976 and advocates have campaigned globally for the effective regulation of the marketing of breast milk substitutes as well as for the promotion of breastfeeding in international and national health policy.[55] In the US, Australia, Canada and the UK a movement of public 'nurse-ins' in recent decades has sought to de-stigmatise breastfeeding in public. Kate Boyer calls this 'care-work activism' and it makes explicit the nature of breastfeeding as a form of labour.[56] Public campaigns are combined with a more personal form of collective action as organisations such as La Leche League (LLL) provide support for breastfeeding across much of the Global North through group meetings and advice sessions.

Conscious political movements sometimes called 'lactivism' (lactation advocacy) interact with personal choices and feelings about parenting as labour. Charlotte Faircloth's ethnography with LLL groups in the UK shows how some mostly middle-class mothers choose to stay out of workplaces that they see as dehumanising in order to pursue motherhood as a career. She names the first decades of the twenty-first century in the UK as a period of especially intensive mothering that in itself is a form of identity work. Whether following prescriptions for routine-based early infant care or attachment parenting (or some uneasy path between the two, as in my case), professional mothers in particular came to see parenting activities as tasks to be achieved for successful infant development.[57] Parenting was child-focused, and choices about something as seemingly natural as birthing and caring for young babies became tied up in what Boyer calls a kind of 'activist mothering' for many. Others of us struggled through trying to meet the demands of societal pressures for intensive mothering at home and rational efficiency in the workplace, feeling like we were doing neither 'task' as well as we ought to.

My second space where we can see very clearly the link between social reproduction labour and activism is the politics of urban life. Here I think especially of land invasions and struggles over urban service delivery. Urbanisation itself is both a labour of social reproduction and a sphere of political activity. The expansion of cities, especially in slum areas, does not happen magically but involves people settling on previously unsettled land, often but not always at the edges of cities and often in areas that are unsettled precisely because they are risky.[58] Occupation of available peri-urban land requires community organisation and leadership, both of which demand a great deal of labour from the most active. They must coordinate the collective of settlers: decide on when and where to invade, how to allocate land initially or resolve disputes when commercial landholders sell overlapping plots, they must fight evictions and organise legal cases to regularise ownership. This last activity can take years, as James Holston describes for a peripheral zone in São Paulo, involving multiple private landowners, the judicial system, municipal, departmental and national state departments, and many other actors. He calls this push for legal status 'insurgent citizenship' and it is a crucial part of urban settlement.[59]

When a new neighbourhood is created and property ownership is not yet legal, it is usually important to occupy your plot of land, preferably in a reasonably permanent structure. This then implies the labour of construction – including making the bricks (adobes in the Andes), building fences to mark out the property, and staying on the property to guard it from squatters.[60] People need also to join together to build roads and other facilities like football pitches. When I conducted fieldwork in a neighbourhood of El Alto, Bolivia, people often told me that the zone was 'puro pampa (just prairie)' before they came and built their houses. They were proud of the work they did clearing stones from the football pitch – which served as the neighbourhood's principal square and gathering place – and setting out roads, pavements, as well as building the school and other community buildings.

As settlements become more established, community leaders petition the state and commercial entities for services like electricity, sewerage, water, roads. In El Alto, this involved gathering quotas from the residents to pay for installation labour, as well as a great deal of work in city government offices following up on bureaucratic processes and convening political support within the neighbourhood at times of elections that they hoped to exchange for service provision later on. They also negotiated with NGOs for funds to build a health centre, community centre, school classrooms. Usually, donors gave money for the building materials and required members of the community to provide the labour – either through quotas or as volunteer labour. This is quite standard practice for development programmes of 'empowerment' or 'community partnership'. Elana Shever describes the experience of a community organisation in Dock Sud in Buenos Aires. Their core activity was a communal kitchen that provided food and warm milk to children, but out of that developed a community organisation that came to the attention of Shell, which runs a refinery in the area. As part of their CSR scheme, 'Creating Bonds', Shell gave money for building materials but expected the community to provide voluntary labour.[61]

Considerable labour is also required for community organisations to manage the relationship with donors and in the case of the Dock Sud group, balance out its different roles as communal kitchen, community CSR partner and explicitly political movement. Shell's 'Creating Bonds' organiser underlined that empowerment meant that the community 'would not only be asking for things, but also offering what they know how to do and the resources that they might have' and distinguished the approach from a philanthropic donation because the latter served only immediate needs and maintained a link only through the provision of money. In contrast, her new approach implied 'un conocerte' – a 'knowledge of you', which also, perhaps ironically, meant greater monitoring, for example tasting the food at the soup kitchens to ensure that it would be suitable for the children.[62]

In Argentina, communal kitchens are both a kind of social reproduction labour in their own right and the basis for organisation of what is known as the *piquetero* movement of territorial organisations mobilising for the benefit of their communities. The *piquetero* movement began with a strategy of protest that developed in the province of Neuquén, Argentina, in June 1996, as residents of Cutral-Có and Plaza Huincul blockaded the roads entering their cities. They were responding to the cancellation of a project for the installation of a fertiliser plant, jobs that were sorely needed given the reductions in jobs since the privatisation of local installations of the state oil company. They maintained the blockade (*piquete*) for a week and influenced other blockades in the provinces of Salta and Jujuy. Virginia Manzano suggests that these events sparked off 'a new identity – the *piqueteros* – a new form of protest – the road block (*corte de ruta*) – a new organisational mode – the assembly – and a new kind of demand – for work'.[63] Although the newness of the *piquetero* strategy and movement is a matter of debate, their importance in the subsequent economic and political crisis of 2001–2002 is not. They were central to the unrest sparked as social reproduction was threatened by a severe economic recession, currency controls and massive dollar devaluation, which in December 2001 prompted widespread riots and a succession of five presidents over the course of ten days. But they did not only organise themselves at these extreme moments, instead they built their organisational capacity slowly through patient engagement with the state for local urban services and welfare plans. Like the systems of party political clientelism studied by Javier Auyero, the *piquetero* movements also became a means by which state resources were distributed to the urban poor.[64] This became even more important in the period immediately after the crisis, as the new government used them as channels for the delivery of welfare. Like the community leaders of El Alto, *piquetero* leaders in Argentina laboured to make clientelism work for themselves and their neighbourhood.

The service delivery protests in South African townships are another example of social reproduction labour unrest channelled through demands for better urban infrastructure. Since 2004 there have been multiple waves of road blockages and strikes, as residents decide to escalate from petitioning to radical political action.[65] Luke Sinwell describes the 2015 protest in Thembelihle, an informal settlement 25 miles from Johannesburg. Residents decided that after twelve ineffective years of engaging local government officials, they should target instead the provincial officials to demand upgrading of the settlement. Knowing that their protest would attract heavy policing, they nonetheless decided to barricade the roads (used by residents of a nearby and wealthier settlement to commute to Johannesburg). The protest was hard and dangerous work:

> We started singing there, burning tires, putting stones on the road, you know, big rocks, anything you can find, you know? Put [it] on the road, burn [it]. And then obviously some cars were stoned there, I mean when they tried to pass. Until the police came and then they started to patrol the traffic on our side, like the cars had to pass [on] this [other] side. Then we keep on protesting until the early hours. Where the police came and just [told] us to move. And they were shooting [rubber bullets], you know? ... They'd throw tear gas and stuff. And [stun] grenades. Throughout the day.[66]

Seventy-five residents were arrested, three hospitalised and one murdered during the three-week-long struggle, but eventually the provincial government official did respond to the residents' request for a meeting and electricity finally came to the settlement a few months later.

The demand for urban infrastructure is about producing urban life, but it goes beyond the infrastructure itself, since it is also about mobilising for jobs in the road building, sewage installation programs and so on. People want the services in their neighbourhoods, partly because they know that it will also mean local jobs, usually distributed along political lines. Community leaders are responsible for the work of network-building with government officials that might result in jobs and infrastructure. Ordinary people engage in this kind of political work on a daily basis: attending political rallies, helping to campaign for particular candidates and so on, in the hopes of a future job.[67]

Labour struggles link with social reproduction struggles in multiple ways, unsurprisingly given the entanglement of social reproduction and production. Trevor Ngwane argues that the 2012 and 2014 strikes by the Lonmin miners in Marikana, South Africa, were not just a struggle for higher wages but against the 'oppression and misery of substandard living conditions in the shantytowns of Rustenburg'. Workers committees independent of the formal trade union (the NUM) organised a wave of strikes in 2012 to demand a living wage, which was brutally repressed in the Marikana massacre of 16 August 2012, when 34 miners were gunned down by the police. Subsequently a more formal but still insurgent unionism developed in the region, and workers then engaged in strikes in 2014 under the banner of a newer union (AMCU). The waves of strikes and protests coincided with and fed into service delivery protests, and the anger at the Marikana massacre fuelled widespread unrest. The unrest and strikes were organised in workers' living spaces and joined together workers and community struggles. The Marikana miners organised themselves outside of the structure of the traditional trade union, and built radical unions of their own, premised, Ngwame argues, on precisely the connection between workplace and living place.[68]

That connection has been very important also for other social reproduction struggles, especially of paid social reproduction workers, like carers, public sector workers, or teachers. Paul Johnston and Steven Henry Lopez describe labour mobilisations among public sector and nursing home workers respectively in the US in the 1980s and 1990s. They both point to the importance of 'social movement unionism', also known as community unionism, which is a form of trade unionism that seeks to mobilise beyond specific labour struggles for wages and so on, seeking alliances with the wider community it serves.[69] Some of the most radical groups to follow these kinds of strategies have been teachers, emphasising that their working conditions are children's learning conditions, and developing alliances with their communities in their struggle. For example, in Oaxaca in 2006, a teachers' strike for union democracy, resources and labour rights broadened out over 6 months to incorporate demands for indigenous rights and wider anti-neoliberal struggles against dispossession, as teachers occupied public squares and mobilised whole communities.[70] Similar waves of teachers strikes in Chicago in 2012, and in West Virginia, Oklahoma and Arizona in 2018, have challenged traditional unions and achieved significant successes by framing their struggle as a community problem and a fight against austerity.[71]

These struggles go beyond a matter of political strategy that links workers together with those they care for in an alliance to demand better conditions from capital and the state. They are also a symptom of the crisis of social reproduction that Nancy Fraser describes, as unlimited accumulation undermines conditions for the survival and rejuvenation of people. Here then is the final space of social reproduction activism that I want to mention: the struggle for life itself. This is the most varied space of action and includes the global waves of anti-austerity and anti-neoliberal protests that have been especially acute over the last two decades and most recently in Chile in 2019–2020, along with recent movements such as Black Lives Matter, #NiUnaMenos and Extinction Rebellion. All of these in different ways protest the danger of death and of life made unliveable. Black men and women who are murdered by the police have their lives cut short, and those who live in fear of that happening to them or their loved ones face a life made contingent upon the violence of others. So too do women victimised and killed for their gender. Climate change means that the whole earth faces a truncated horizon of social reproduction. Those who protest tell us that life itself is at risk. Like all protests, they both represent a struggle for social reproduction and involve labour themselves, as activists create blockades and occupations of urban streets and squares, building self-governing communities that take care of food, infrastructure, medical care, media, etc. as well as political strategy. They protect each other from violent policing, and work to organise and disseminate their struggle across global and national media. They create knowledge and art for social justice; and experiment with new ways of living ethically, drawing on historical experiences of activism and transnational sharing of strategies and ideas. The protests, then, both defend and produce life.

Conclusion

The story of labour agency is one neither of clear and inexorable decline over the last fifty years nor of straightforward progress towards equity. It is deeply uneven, as workers collaborate to pressure employers and the state, sometimes successfully, often not. Across the globe, workers are usually dispersed and very often precariously employed, making activism difficult to initiate and sustain. In this book I have explored a few of the many kinds of collective labour mobilisations studied by anthropologists. But collective organisation is not the only kind of labour agency available to us, and I have also tried to take into account more individualised and fragmentary strategies. In addition, I have sought to explore agency beyond resistance, including strategies of accommodation, escape and resilience. I have also tried to think about agency at household and community level, not only at the level of the individual and their workplace collectivity. The investigation, through ethnographies that discuss the *experience* of labour in contemporary economies, has produced a complex picture, one that goes well beyond the story of union decline that we might expect from within the traditional labour imaginaries grounded upon industrial and material labour and outlined in the introduction to this book.

As workers, we experience labour in the context of shifting conditions of exploitation within global capitalism and local histories, which interact with particular constellations of class consciousness, ideology and social relations. To make sense of that picture, in this conclusion I reflect on questions of labour process, the outcome or 'product' of different kinds of work, and workers' understandings of their selfhood. My argument is that these three elements of experience are key to shaping our agency at work. I begin with a discussion of collective action and move into more personal acts of agency.

Collective action, trade unions and community

Traditional industrial unions have lost power globally, especially as workers have become more precarious and less able to organise collectively. Yet unions have not completely disappeared, and in some countries, some sectors of the economy have seen maintained and sometimes even growing mobilisation, not only in formerly industrialised regions. In many cities, even informal sector workers organise collectively, creating forms of association based on economic activity but very different from industrial unions. The organisation of labour processes shapes collective action differently in industrial spaces and the less 'traditional' spaces for trade unionism in the public, service and informal sectors. Across sectors, anthropological work shows us that collective labour politics are deeply embedded within community politics and the labour of social reproduction, as workplaces and home are linked together in multiple ways.

Trade unions are especially associated with industrial settings: manufacturing, mining, steelwork and so on. Although we might think that heavy industry is a feature of Western economies, anthropologists like June Nash showed that strong industrial working-class identities were not just a feature of Fordist Europe; pockets developed across the world even in countries which were not highly industrialised.[1] Workers on the Zambian Copperbelt developed similar and equally complex formations of identities; and company towns in India supported strong labour aristocracies organised into trade unions and with powerful worker identities. But in many places across the globe, including those just mentioned, deindustrialisation has meant that large numbers of people have been shifted out of the kinds of workplaces that are most amenable to the development of strong collective solidarity and the organisation of production in ways that grant power to workers.

Instead of a factory or steel plant where halting production of a material good or preventing it from leaving the site can cause serious loss of profit or damage to machinery, work globally is now organised through subcontracting in factories, textile workshops, small businesses, or via national and international migration. Industrial workers are now more precariously employed than when unions could draw much of their strength from the conditions of employment of their core, permanently employed members. These kinds of workers could agitate with less fear of being fired than those on short term contracts, they could draw on the daily practices of working together to build solidarity and collective strength, and exploit the risk of serious damage as a result of a strike in an industrial plant. As the core of permanent workers shrank, union strength in many industrial spaces shrank with it, and the unions failed to speak to the growing numbers of temporarily employed workers. It was often the sons (usually) of the permanent workers who became these more vulnerable workers, and so neither group wished to risk temporary workers' jobs by engaging in too overt oppositional organisation. Union leaders repeatedly betrayed ordinary workers as they failed to stop the processes of precaritisation; a failing that for many ordinary people was evidence of corruption and even criminality at the top of the union.

Yet, even if overall membership numbers have declined, the story of unions is not entirely one of loss or corruption of power, for three reasons. First, 'traditional' unions, even in industrial spaces, have not necessarily lost their ability to mediate between workers and employers, even if they are often compromised. Second, the relative decline in industrial unionism has exposed the continuing – and in some cases growing – strength of unions in different sectors of the economy, especially the public sector. Third, alternative labour organisations have come to the fore, in multiple formats: for example, as new, independent unions, as professional associations, or as collective associations that straddle the workplace and the community (productive and reproductive labour). The story of these organisations is one of continual struggle and repeated failure, but also some successes.

Public sector workers for example often have reasonably secure jobs, and they work in workplaces where coordination between employees is quite easy, like government offices, hospitals, or schools. They can mobilise public support through shared ideologies of public duty, as with teachers, who often argue that their working conditions are children's learning conditions. That is to say, the product of their labour of communication and education is deeply entwined with the relations teachers develop with their students.

Some unions in the service sector have campaigned to make similar connections in public perception, arguing that better conditions for the workers mean better conditions for their charges. Unionisation is difficult in the service sector because so much of the work is precarious, workers are not connected to each other in large workplaces, and many are migrants with attendant racialised vulnerabilities to exploitation. However, as I discussed in Chapter 4, some well-established unions have responded to the challenge to adapt. The SEIU in parts of the US mobilised subcontracted migrant labourers and community allies in the Californian 'Justice for Janitors' campaigns and healthcare workers and their communities in Pittsburgh and California.[2] Significantly, both campaigns were successful because they managed to turn labour issues into questions of social justice, connecting community and labour concerns.

Newer, independent unions have been important for mobilisations of service workers, such as in the UK, where the Independent Workers of Great Britain (IWGB) have successfully campaigned to improve conditions for outsourced cleaners at the University of London and elsewhere. IWGB has recently turned its attention to organising workers in the gig economy and a range of other usually precarious sectors, such as foster carers, nannies, game developers, couriers and yoga teachers. And there have been some significant victories, especially in the gig economy. In February 2021, the UK Supreme Court ruled that Uber must classify its drivers as workers, albeit from the time they accept a driving job on the app rather than for the whole time they are logged on. Similar legal cases have taken place in California, where unions have allied with gig economy workers to promote favourable legislation and fight the companies' response.

So, workers have made alliances with traditional unions or turned to more radical independent unions in their attempts to improve conditions. Others have created newer non-union forms of organisation, an important example of which for anthropology is #PrecAnthro, active in EASA, whose work is mentioned in Chapter 5. Workers also mobilise outside of clear institutional forms, taking matters into their own hands despite corrupt or complacent unions. Some of the most spectacular events have been wildcat strikes like those of the garment workers in Bangladesh and the wave of strikes and slowdowns in electronics factories in China discussed in Chapter 2. Workers simply stopped producing the goods they were told to make or slowed down parts of the intricate manufacturing process where multiple small components must be fitted together extremely quickly. They used their control over the material process of manufacture to disrupt profit – so closely related to production targets because of the structure of sub-contracting (i.e. the risk that Apple or another buyer would turn to an alternative subcontracted factory if targets were not met). Both waves of action were suppressed by violent state repression, and official unions have been unable or unwilling to take up the concerns very actively. Nonetheless, from time to time, worker discontent has emerged in the form of seemingly spontaneous riots and protest, and we could assume that actions like sabotage and slowdowns take place under the radar. The wave of strikes that took place in the South African platinum belt in the early 2010s is a hybrid of all the tendencies just described: a traditional union that was seen as corrupt, new insurgent unions, seemingly unorganised wildcat strikes and the importance of the relationship between workplace and residence.

As I argued in Chapter 8, service delivery protests in South African townships and land invasions in Latin America lie at the nexus between work and territory, as residents engage in protest labour to produce a certain quality of life locally. In the cities, the demand for infrastructure is about producing urban life, but it goes beyond the infrastructure itself, since it is also to mobilise for jobs in the programs of road building, sewage installation and so on. Thus, labour struggles are deeply linked to social reproduction struggles, and workplace is linked to community, a point that June Nash made over four decades ago.[3] This point goes beyond the discussions of strategies to link union action with matters of public concern as with the teachers and health workers, known as 'community unionism' or social movement unionism.[4] As anthropologists have shown, unless it is an empty company union, trade unions in most places are fairly well embedded in community life. For example, in Zambia and Argentina, kinship obligations shape workers' demands, their access to jobs, and therefore their unions;[5] in South Africa and Latin America, organised workers are the same people as those who engage in community activism for urban infrastructure; in some places, unions or other labour organisations may even be the collective entities that run self-governance, at the interface between labour and territory, as is the case for street vendors or taxi drivers across the world.

To understand collective labour politics today, our conception of the workplace must expand beyond the factory, plant, mine, hospital or office. The city itself is workplace for street vendors, day laborers waiting for jobs at street corners, taxi drivers, electronic scooter collectors, delivery drivers, sex workers. That is also the case for homeworkers on piece rates, for those who make their living from welfare payments or by access to NGO schemes, and for political workers whose job is to mobilise their neighbours for project funding or to provide support at a rally. Through all kinds of actions people try to improve their city, as a space for work and for life; and therefore the city is a *product* of their labour as well as their workplace. The city is also the space for other struggles of social reproduction. From anti-austerity and anti-neoliberal protests to Black Lives Matter, #NiUnaMenos and Extinction Rebellion, people protest the danger of death and of life made unliveable. In their actions protesting the violence of the state and of capital, on bodies and on the planet, people both produce and defend life. Community organisation and mobilisation is therefore a form of social reproduction labour as much as it is collective action.

Individual/fragmentary strategies

Yet it would be a mistake to confine a discussion of worker agency to its organised or collective expressions. Protest is spectacular and therefore amenable to research and comment; indeed, that is usually its point. But collective organisation is not always possible, for example when workers are separated from each other and dispersed across space, are vulnerable to repression, or do not wish to mobilise together for other reasons. James Scott argued powerfully for agrarian societies that in these kinds of circumstances we should look for 'hidden transcripts' of resistance, as peasants resist extraction from their landlords and other local elites through varied informal measures including 'in resistant mutuality … in the steady, grinding efforts to hold one's own against overwhelming odds'.[6] Some of the slowdowns that Pun Ngai described in her ethnography of a factory in Shenzhen (see Chapter 2) can be viewed in a similar way, as workers resist the excessive demands of them for speed and intensity of work by simply taking a bit longer over tasks and allowing parts to build up on the assembly line.[7]

Workers do not always *resist*, and often their agency can be found in ways that they respond to their conditions of work that are not exactly oppositional, either overtly or covertly. Take the question of bodily responses. Workers' bodies and health can be a focus for collective mobilisation, especially in the demand for better health and safety at work. Health can also be a driver for more individual mobilisation, especially in a system that relies upon very expensive private healthcare: parents become experts at campaigning for medical treatment for their extremely sick children,[8] a fruit picker in California conducts a legal process against her employer to gain appropriate medical care or compensation after an accident at work.[9] Workers and parents cannot usually undertake these campaigns by themselves, so they need support and collective advocacy as well as individual persistence. Also, achieving recognition of responsibility from an employer might create a precedent to benefit others. But the primary goal – the main product of their labour of campaigning – might well be simply to make life liveable for them and their family.

Workers' bodily responses can also be interpreted as a form of agentive resistance or accommodation to work, an experience that is felt within the body and as part of a collective. Aihwa Ong was one of the first anthropologists to recognise this in her discussion of young Malay women workers who experienced spirit possessions in their factory, especially associated with liminal places where their bodies were scrutinised, like toilets and changing rooms. For Ong, the mass possessions were a form of resistance to the factory regime of surveillance and overwork.[10] As well as a spectacular act of resistance, we might also interpret the possessions as a way that the women's bodies turned inwards so that their work was made into an experience that could be understood physically (as traumatic). The suicides in Foxconn and the farmers suicides in India discussed in Chapters 2 and 3 respectively could be similar: where conditions for people were so bad that the workers' minds and bodies became destructive and focused that destruction on the only thing that they had power over.

Suicide could also be interpreted as escape, an extreme version of what is probably one of the most common forms of worker agency. If possible, many simply leave a job that does not suit them, and the conditions that allow employers to fire people easily often also allow workers to find different employment with relative ease.[11] Piecework and day rates can be attractive to workers who want to control when they work (and for whom), and in many sectors of the economy, job mobility ('churn') is quite high. From Silicon Valley to Shenzhen, people move from employer to employer, staying in a job for one-two years at a time. Chinese factory workers go home for New Year and don't return to their factory. In Tiruppur, garment workers go back to their natal village for the holidays and decide that it's a good moment to change job; or they draw on their kinship connections with labour brokers to seek different employment.[12] Fruit pickers in California move to farms where they can pick cane berries so that they do not have to bend down quite as much as strawberry picking;[13] domestic maids leave employers with whom they have fallen out, sometimes agreeing on a story they'll both tell about how the maid is returning home or starting a new life project that requires different hours, such as education.[14] Undoubtedly, people are often stuck – e.g. in situations of debt bondage – but not always. And sometimes, labour mobility has led capitalists to respond with incentives like higher wages, or Diwali bonuses. Or they respond to labour churn with greater automation, as in agricultural sectors of wealthy economies.

At times, workers seem to choose challenging conditions because they can earn more; a choice which brings out the importance of workers' relationship to time as much as to money. Young men in Tiruppur said that they preferred piecework, an option open to them because of their gender and where they are in their life cycle: with few dependents, they wanted to work more to gather money for going home for the holidays at particular times of the year.[15] In Western China, some workers see the factories as a temporary part of life, especially young women who are expected to return home to their village when they are married. While working in the cities, they can experiment with urban life and dormitory friendships.[16] Students also often have a different orientation to temporality than those with dependents, like the student Deliveroo riders of Brighton, who mostly moved on after a couple of years.[17] They were the most willing to engage with activities of union organisation but also less radical than the migrant workers who had families to support as well as experience from back home and so were the ones who actually organised the strikes. Other migrant platform workers in Western cities might see themselves as working hard for a relatively short while to gather together money for a mortgage. Meanwhile, coalminers in Zambia and steelworkers in India aspire to save enough money to start their own business.[18] This temporal orientation to the future is a kind of mental escape before physical escape becomes possible.

The relationship between life cycle and gender also influences how understandings of selfhood shape agency in work. If the work is seen as temporary or subordinate to your primary identity, then conditions are often worse and the power to change them is reduced. Grandmothers caring for their grandchildren while their daughter has migrated overseas carry out that labour as an obligation to their child and as a part of their own identity. As I discussed in Chapter 4, nurses and home care workers can take pride in the quality of care they give, and often go beyond the explicit demands of their jobs to take care of their charges well. These are gendered expectations of women's responsibilities to care. In the case of Filipina nurses in the US, the gendered expectations were combined with ethnicity, as they took pride in the standard of care they provided in comparison with the American nurses they worked with.[19] They saw themselves as more hard working and more caring; they would do more than precisely what they had been asked to do and develop a closer relationship with their patients. American home carers and nurses actually also reported a similar orientation to their patients; and the domestic worker is classically seen as 'part of the family'. When your work is about developing 'deep alliances'[20] with clients, overt actions like a strike are difficult to contemplate, and instead action to improve conditions can be a complex and emotional negotiation within families and between families, clients, carer and employment agency.

Similarly, academics and bureaucrats take pride in a professional identity that defines them as people as well as (or more than) workers. For some this could become even a kind of over-identification that is a dysfunctional counterpart to alienation, where we define ourselves by our work and little else. Whole societies might be caught up in this kind of work ethic, not just professional sectors.[21] It can be hard to mobilise professionals who do not see themselves as workers; or perhaps do not identify a boss external to them. As I argue in Chapter 5, the material metaphors of labour that are still dominant act as a demobilising force.

Thus, our immaterial labour produces selves and it produces relations, as well as the other immaterial products like affect, knowledge and communication. These products of our labour shape what we as workers think is possible and desirable when it comes to our agency to improve our working conditions. To take my own profession: maybe academics are too neurotic to withdraw from the processes of evaluation through metrics in the workplace;[22] maybe some tenured professors think that they are somehow better than precariously employed early career scholars; maybe they think that they had to go through that experience so others can too. Alternatively, maybe academics don't want to go on strike because they worry about the effect it will have on the students, the subjects of our care. Maybe they don't wish to see themselves as an employee, but rather something different, more autonomous, higher status.

Many workers don't resist exploitation. More usually, they accommodate themselves to their situation: through making it temporary, dreaming of alternatives, escaping to something a bit better when the opportunity presents itself and so on. Sometimes they join together to bargain and negotiate for small improvements; only occasionally does that tip over into a protest or riot. Resilience maintains structures of domination but also makes life liveable. We should include it in our analysis of worker agency, not least because it is probably the norm for most of us. The more spectacular moments of collective mobilisation are the exception.

Thus, labour agency is shaped by the organisation of our work and the products we produce as a result of our labour. I have included in the latter immaterial products of labour like communication, knowledge, circulation of goods, love, security, selves and so on. We can even see social reproduction labour as the production of life itself. When we look at work in this way, we see that a complex politics emerges out of our efforts to create, nurture and sustain ourselves and those we love. We experience that politics at multiple scales of action and as part of processes that operate at all levels of social relations, from intimate to global. Capturing that politics analytically is challenging, and this book has attempted to do so by focussing specifically on the relation between type of work and possibilities for agency. What emerges from that relationship is multiplicity. It is precisely that multiplicity which is so important for understanding what people do to make their lives better at work and through their labour.

Coda
The Covid-19 Pandemic and Labour
Continuities and the Potential for Change

What difference is the pandemic making to the scenario just outlined? I wrote most of this coda in the middle of 2021, which is too early to make more than tentative and quite general observations. I also have not been able to conduct ethnographic fieldwork on the topic, so speak instead from a combination of personal experience in my home country of the UK, recently published survey-based reports, newspaper articles and conference presentations of initial research findings. I also draw on the collection *Corona and Work around the Globe*, edited by Andreas Eckert and Felicitas Hentschke, which was mostly written in mid-2020.[1]

In 2020, when the pandemic was young, it felt to me and I think to many others as if everything would change; as if this intensely dramatic historical event must lead to new configurations of society, work and government. Eighteen months later I was more cynical, and I saw more continuity. I suspect that the pandemic will mostly exacerbate trends and cleavages that were prominent in pre-pandemic times, and that feature strongly throughout this book.

One of the most notable of those trends is the vulnerability of migrant workers, both transnational and rural-urban, because of their position in low paying and insecure jobs across the globe. The news pictures of hundreds of thousands of migrant workers from Indian cities walking to their rural villages after the sudden lockdown was declared by the government struck many observers, and were mirrored elsewhere in the world, albeit not to the same scale. These flows of people during the pandemic underlined just to what extent rural areas subsidise capital in the cities. As Alina-Sandra Cucu points out:

> While the uneven geography of capital and labor constantly pushes individuals out of their immediate environment in search of remote

survival opportunities, the pandemic has made it clear how, in the long run, capitalism survives on people's capacity and willingness to fall back on their kinship support structures whenever the elusiveness of these opportunities is revealed.[2]

In countries with large urban informal sectors, poor urbanites who could not return home had little choice but to go to work in crowded street markets, poorly regulated workshops and factories, or in the homes of the wealthy as domestic employees. The first Covid fatality in Rio de Janeiro is thought to be a maid infected by her employer who had picked up the virus on a European ski trip but compelled the maid to come to work nonetheless.[3]

In the UK, migrant workers in low paid jobs couldn't afford to isolate if they contracted the virus because they received little or no sick pay; they were disproportionately employed in sectors that closed down under lockdown, especially retail, hospitality and leisure; or in sectors such as food processing and slaughterhouses where low pay, lack of sick pay, cooling systems and worker proximity contributed to virus outbreaks; not to mention workplaces where employers were lax about safety provisions anyway.[4] Migrant workers also sometimes lived in crowded community housing, where they were stigmatised by the state and left with little support to isolate or socially distance. In Göttingen, an 18-storey building with over 600 residents was put into quarantine in May 2020, with residents suddenly confined to their homes, initially without medical support and food supplies. Residents were stigmatised as members of the Roma community 'known' to be usually uncompliant with the rules of good citizenship, or 'extended families' who had ignored social distancing in order to celebrate the end of Ramadan together.[5] In the UK, similar tropes of stigmatisation operated against 'multi-generational households' in minority urban areas, often implicitly racialised as Muslim.[6] As Sarah Horton's work with agricultural labourers in the US explains, migrant workers also have higher incidences of health conditions like cardiovascular disease that increase their vulnerability to serious illness from coronavirus.[7]

Lockdowns caused temporarily radical shifts in some parts of the economy, and workers in those low paid and less formal jobs that disappeared almost overnight had to switch to jobs that would generate a bit more income. Supurna Banerjee tells Raju's story. When his construction work disappeared, he spent some time trying to survive on assistance from charitable organisations and government rations in Kolkata; but then he switched to selling vegetables. This new work provided some income for him, but vegetable selling was a crowded sector as many others had made similar changes.[8] In Brazil, sex workers switched to webcam platforms as their physical workplaces evaporated.[9] Everywhere, delivery jobs boomed. Electric scooter collectors in Berlin (who are mostly migrants) used their vans to deliver packages during the day and collect scooters at night.[10] In the UK, freelancers including journalists, artists and musicians made ends meet by hiring a van and taking up temporary delivery work for online retailers. For some this was a new experience, but for many people, the rapid switch to alternative income-generating strategies was an expression of what Cucu calls 'compulsory fluidity' that built upon longer-term experiences of flexibility.[11] Platform workers have always combined multiple jobs and platforms, and the strategy of picking up different jobs as they come available and depending on conditions is key to the patchwork living I describe in Chapter 7. For Denisa, in Craiova, Romania, the experience during the pandemic of losing her job and having to search for another one was 'just normal'. By the age of 23, she had already experienced twelve different employment relations between Romania and Italy, even before the pandemic.[12]

Together with migration, another important theme of this book has been the importance of gendered differences for work. During the pandemic in the UK, women have been vulnerable to infection and trauma as the majority of frontline workers in social and healthcare, as well as taking on a larger share of social reproduction labour than men. In most countries of the world, case mortality rates are higher among men than women, while long Covid is, it seems, more prevalent among women.[13] Women were disproportionately affected by the shutdowns in the hospitality, retail and leisure sectors, which are also the three largest low-paying sectors of the UK economy.[14] Globally, healthcare workers experienced an intensification of their work, and we don't yet know what long term effect that will have on their health, mental and physical. Women lost their jobs in greater numbers than men during the lockdowns in Japan, South Africa and France,[15] or found that their hours were cut or increased without increase in pay.[16] In India and Brazil, domestic workers had to fill in for others who could not travel to their workplace, without any increase in their pay.[17] Globally, women took on most of the strain of home-schooling and domestic labour, even as many men working from home did more than they had done previously. The pandemic exposed just how much we rely upon the labour of social reproduction and care, which is feminised and usually unpaid. It was this women's labour that absorbed the shocks of contractions in other parts of the economy. And the home became even more dangerous for women as rates of gender violence rose during lockdowns.

Youth also intersected importantly with gender, ethnicity and class, as young people are especially employed in low paid sectors that shut down, when employers renegotiated their terms of employment or simply fired them. Young people have also experienced an unusual rise in prevalence of mental health problems, especially anxiety and depression disorders, possibly especially driven by the student population, as proportional numbers are much higher among 18–21-year-olds than in the 18–24-year-old category overall.[18] Students found themselves having to switch to online learning (while teachers learnt how to teach online), but also to online internships, graduate placements, job interviews and an extremely uncertain job future. Many were attempting the shift without stable internet connections, their own study space, or laptops. These kinds of shocks may not last for long, but in combination they underline just what we expect of young workers in terms of adaptability and fluidity, confirming the cultural logic that a stable and secure job is something that one must take a few years to grow into, if it is even a realistic possibility at all.

Those who have done quite well out of the pandemic are of course wealthier workers in white collar jobs. They have had the luxury of being able to stay at home when it was the safest place to be; those with the space to work at home perhaps enjoyed not having to commute, having more control over work hours, and spending time with their families; like some of the much less well-paid digital workers discussed in Chapter 6. Some people even threw themselves into the social reproduction labour of DIY, home baking and hobbies. For some, working from home meant a sense of isolation, while others found it difficult to manage full time work and home-schooling together. Remote working and schooling are easier in homes with reliable broadband, sufficient laptops, monitors, and the ability to pay the increased energy and food bills that resulted from a wholesale shift in where we spend our days.

(Potential) changes

It's fair to say that the experience of remote working during the pandemic will change administrative, professional and managerial work, but it is not yet completely clear how. Some corporations, especially in the tech sector, flipped to entirely remote working if their employees desire, while others asked employees to come into the office for one or two days a week but allowed them to work from home for the rest. In mid-2022, a few key employers started to try and enforce more office working. If working from home becomes widespread, the practice will change urban commutes and depopulate some parts of big cities like London, as people cash in and move out to the country. It will raise questions about taxation, as some fully remote employees ask why they can't live in a different country or US state to where their office is located. New working spaces may emerge, based on residence rather than employment: in my village just outside Cambridge, the local village hall opened one morning a week for people working from home to come and work together. Remote work itself will save money for workers on their commute and for employers on buildings costs. Greater entanglements of work and family will have ramifications that we cannot completely foresee. Jürgen Kocka suggests that – for Germany – home will become more regulated, as things like health and safety regulation are applied to home offices. It may become even more difficult to create a distinction between work and non-work time when the spatial distinctions of home and office have broken down; new surveillance mechanisms are likely to emerge, to track how many hours workers spend at their computers, especially those in clerical or administrative jobs. Remote working favours those with space and people they like spending time with at home, and not everyone is in that situation. The experience of the pandemic has also created an appreciation of the importance of social interaction in offices and especially in educational settings.

The pandemic may then open up new opportunities, for good or ill. It made some kinds of work more visible, including migrant labour, and the labour of care and social reproduction. In many countries, some workers were deemed essential, a categorisation that in the UK allowed them to continue sending their children to school during lockdown, and in other countries gave them earlier access to vaccinations. The category of essential workers nearly always included healthcare and social care workers, workers in food delivery and supermarkets, and professions like teachers, police officers; in general, workers associated with care, with provisioning and with public infrastructures. Healthcare workers were applauded once a week for ten weeks in the UK, a practice that started in Wuhan, China, took off in Italy, then spread across Europe.[19] Here in the UK, TV programmes and social media were full of appreciation for the NHS and healthcare workers; and people put signs outside their houses and schools thanking the NHS, often with the symbol of a rainbow. Captain Sir Tom Moore became a 'hero' when he raised nearly £33 million for NHS charities in a much-celebrated endeavour of walking 100 lengths of his garden, no mean feat for a 100-year-old with a Zimmer frame. At one point, I think many of us hoped that all the popular celebration of the NHS would translate into substantive political support for the publicly funded health system; but the announcement of a one per cent pay raise for nurses in early 2021 and proposed restructuring plans in mid-2021 put paid to much of that optimism and by 2022 the service seemed under near-intolerable strain. Yet, there was at least a public conversation about what work we value as a society, which did underline the importance of work as care for others. Some workers have begun to make that explicit in their campaigns for better pay and conditions, like the Sage nursing home care workers organised by UVW, discussed in Chapter 4.

Another conversation that has been amplified by the pandemic is about workplace safety. Although health and safety is clearly a very longstanding issue for union mobilisation, Covid brought to the fore the responsibility of employers to ensure adequate conditions to protect employees from infection. We all had to think about social distancing, about times when in person events were possible and other times when we had to move online, and about what it means for the workers when we open up businesses, transport and schools with and without mandatory mask-wearing and other provisions. Especially early on in the pandemic, there was public outrage in the UK press and social media about healthcare and nursing home workers not being provided with sufficient personal protective equipment (PPE). Photos circulated of nurses using bin bags as protective aprons, and rumours spread of the reuse of some PPE in hospitals. Some nursing homes were woefully understocked at the beginning, contributing to the desperate spread of the virus among the very vulnerable there. Government procurement of PPE was a significant contributor to the several corruption scandals of the pandemic, as ministers gave contracts to friends and/or companies without the capacity to deliver. The challenge (but also opportunity) for workers organisations will be to turn the public outrage into solidarity for campaigns for better conditions.

In our day-to-day life, most of us had to consider workplace safety to an unfamiliar extent. The risk assessment as a form of action and pre-emptive audit took on new salience as the instrument which would determine whether an activity could go ahead; and risk assessments constantly changed as new government guidelines came out. Workers of all kinds got used to masks, protective screens, keeping two metres away from customers, hand sanitisers, etc.; as did students, schoolchildren and customers. Different employers were more or less assiduous in their respect for workplace safety, and some of the breakouts in garment and food processing factories and agricultural settings were associated with employers failing to implement social distancing measures or to allow workers to self-isolate when they came into contact with the virus. The provision of adequate safety measures and PPE was also a significant motivation for the worker mobilisations we saw in 2020, such as Amazon warehouse workers, Instacart shoppers and other platform workers, as described in Chapter 6. Teachers' unions also argued for the importance of their members' safety in the decision about when to re-open schools; and argued that teachers should be vaccinated early on, after health workers and the clinically vulnerable, so that they would be safer in their workplace.

The pandemic has also created specific opportunities for work, from mask manufacturing and PPE sales to the boom in delivery jobs and online retail. The British supermarket Waitrose estimated that online grocery shopping doubled,[20] and many who tried grocery deliveries for the first time will not go back to in person shopping. The retailer Gap closed all its stores in Europe and moved entirely online. The demand for delivery drivers and other workers associated with online shopping did lead to companies increasing wages or introducing bonuses, especially in the run up to Christmas 2021. Amazon offered sign-on bonuses of £1,000–£3,000 for warehouse workers in the UK; almost all of the main UK supermarkets offered similar sign-on bonuses for lorry drivers, while Aldi and Tesco also offered pay increases.[21] In the UK, the supermarkets were responding to the supply chain difficulties that had resulted from the combination of pandemic and Brexit. Companies could not find enough workers to stock shelves and deliver goods. There were also lots of employment opportunities that opened up in the hospitality sector as pubs and restaurants reopened after lockdown without the usual reserve of young Europeans to draw on for their jobs.

At multiple levels of the workforce, churn has increased as people moved to different jobs, or retired early or just resigned. In the US, this has become known as the Great Resignation. In January 2022, the US Bureau of Labor Statistics reported that a record 4.5 million American workers quit their jobs in November 2021, following similarly high numbers in September and October.[22] The UK has seen something similar, and in both countries the loss of people has been especially notable in job sectors that were under particular strain during the pandemic, such as health-care, social care and teaching. Ilana Gershon conducted research with US workers who worked in person during the early stages of the pandemic, and found a strong sense that many had of feeling that their job was just not worth endangering themselves and those they loved. She suggests that an important driver of the resignations has been a sense of betrayal; a sense that their employers simply did not care for them as the social contract between them demanded.[23] As yet (mid-2022), public sector employers have not responded to these trends with the agility of (parts of) the private sector by improving pay and employment conditions in order to attract or keep workers. It is probably a long shot to think that they might do so. Still, there is no doubt that during the pandemic we have seen an increase in mobility and escape as forms of worker agency.

Trends of 'platformisation' of work will probably become more entrenched, as digital platforms effectively mediate remote management and surveillance. This can lead to greater control and exploitation, but it is also the case that gig workers are developing new forms of collective mobilisation and learning how to press their case in both the courts and the streets, as Chapter 6 discussed. Educational labour will transform as 'blended learning' becomes standard and we debate the appropriate balance between lecture recordings and in person requirements. Our relation to our students, which is the main product of our work, is in flux. White collar workers are unlikely to travel as much as they did before, having realised that remote conferencing is possible and effective, as well as being more environmentally friendly. That will have an impact on the aviation industry. Reshaped urban environments will have implications for public administration, maintenance, retail and hospitality workers. All these changes will prompt new forms of adaptation and action for workers.

Meanwhile, politically, we have seen an increase in state expenditure on ordinary people in grant schemes like the UK furlough system and small business support, unemployment payments and other grants in countries as diverse as Germany, Brazil and South Africa.[24] Governments may find it hard to completely roll back to austerity measures, and when I am feeling optimistic, initiatives such as universal basic income feel a little bit closer as we've collectively acknowledged the need for a state that cares for its people. This might enable advocacy for better welfare conditions, but it has also gone alongside authoritarian measures, including the lockdowns themselves, voter suppression initiatives, border closures and curbs on protest. The pandemic is likely more a space of opportunity exploited by anti-democratic politicians than a prompt for such measures. Still, the outcome is the same. This could constitute a period of post-neoliberal governance that combines the recognition of the need for state welfare with authoritarian and illiberal politics of surveillance and control to an unprecedented extent. And even if we were somehow to avoid disruption from future pandemics, the climate crisis means that the post-Covid world will not be stable.

All these tendencies were present before 2020, but the Covid-19 pandemic has brought the uncertainty of life today into focus even for people who usually have the luxury of living with stability. This will require a response from all of us, and whether that response is individual or collective is a political choice. Ethnographers and other researchers will need to consider both continuities and changes when thinking about how work and workers' agency will change in post-pandemic futures. First, the 'post' of 'post-pandemic' is unlikely to indicate a situation where we have fully overcome the pandemic. Globally, countries will come out of the most extreme pandemic situations at different rates, and new diseases could emerge, while new climate-related emergencies are inevitable. It is already evident that the pandemic is exacerbating some cleavages in society: between rich and poor, migrant and non-migrant, along lines of gender and age, perhaps also polarised political differences. In the early stages of the pandemic, workers confronted these processes mostly by accommodating to new difficulties and finding even more fluidity, but more resistant strategies might yet emerge. Meanwhile, the pandemic has made some kinds of work and workers more visible and created a space for people to acknowledge the importance of care, social reproduction, safety at work and state support for the vulnerable. These are potential opportunities for us to fight to orient work more towards life. If we choose to do so, the best chance of success lies in collective action and solidarity.

Notes

Introduction

1. I thank one of the anonymous readers of the book proposal for Pluto Press for this formulation of words.
2. See https://webarchive.nationalarchives.gov.uk/20210104165629/https://www.gov.uk/government/publications/coronavirus-covid-19-maintaining-educational-provision/guidance-for-schools-colleges-and-local-authorities-on-maintaining-educational-provision.
3. See www.bbc.co.uk/news/uk-england-leicestershire-53311548; www.tuc.org.uk/news/women-working-uk-garment-factories-four-times-more-likely-die-covid-19-average-woman-worker.
4. See www.business-live.co.uk/manufacturing/warning-over-food-factories-becoming-19361405.
5. See https://schoolsweek.co.uk/school-staff-wont-be-prioritised-for-vaccine-as-government-continues-with-age-based-approach.
6. Covid mortality rates were higher for men than women. See https://assets.publishing.service.gov.uk/government/uploads/system/uploads/attachment_data/file/965094/s1100-covid-19-risk-by-occupation-workplace.pdf.
7. Corrêa, L. R. & Fontes, P. (2020). Maids in Brazil: Domestic and Platform Workers during the COVID-19 Pandemic. In A. Eckert & F. Hentschke (eds), *Corona and Work around the Globe* (pp. 37–42). De Gruyter.
8. See https://theconversation.com/farmers-in-india-have-been-protesting-for-6-months-have-they-made-any-progress-161101.
9. See www.bbc.co.uk/news/business-59588905.
10. See https://theconversation.com/amazon-starbucks-and-the-sparking-of-a-new-american-union-movement-180293; www.amazonlaborunion.org/
11. Carbonella, A. & Kasmir, S. (2014). Introduction: Toward a Global Anthropology of Labor. In S. Kasmir & A. Carbonella (eds), *Blood and Fire. A Global Anthropology of Labor* (pp. 1–29). Berghahn books.
12. Bear, L., Ho, K., Tsing, A. L. & Yanagisako, S. (2015). Gens: A Feminist Manifesto for the Study of Capitalism. Retrieved from https://culanth.org/fieldsights/gens-a-feminist-manifesto-for-the-study-of-capitalism.
13. Carrier, J. & Kalb, D. (eds). (2015). *Anthropologies of Class*. Cambridge University Press. Kalb, D. (2009). Conversations with a Polish Populist: Tracing Hidden Histories of Globalization, Class, and Dispossession in Postsocialism (and Beyond). *American Ethnologist*, 36(2), 207–223; Kasmir & Carbonella, *Blood and Fire*.
14. Bear et al., Gens.

15. Tsing, A. (2009). Supply Chains and the Human Condition. *Rethinking Marxism, 21*(2), 148–176, here 148.
16. Ibid; Tsing, A. L. (2015). *The Mushroom at the End of the World: On the Possibility of Life in Capitalist Ruins.* Princeton University Press.
17. Tsing, Supply Chains and the Human Condition.
18. Parry, J. (2018). Introduction. In C. Hann & J. Parry (eds), *Industrial Labor on the Margins of Capitalism: Precarity, Class, and the Neoliberal Subject.* Berghahn.
19. Beynon, H. (1973). *Working For Ford.* Penguin Books.
20. I have told a story about 'conventional' narratives that has its own conventional hierarchies (and I thank a reader for Pluto Press for correcting me on this matter). It is important to point out that the development of social democracy after the Second World War did not happen evenly across Europe. Immediately after the Second World War, Spain, Portugal and Greece were subject to fascist dictatorships, while Italy had very active labour unions but not the kind of political stability found further north. Labour unions were powerful under socialism in eastern Europe, but most were utterly subject to the state (although Solidarnosc in Poland is an important counter-example). Soviet industrialisation was heavily influenced by Fordism – both Lenin and Stalin were fans – but labour organisations were not independent of the state. Dunn, E. (2004). *Privatizing Poland: Baby Food, Big Business, and the Remaking of Labor.* Cornell University Press.
21. Shever, E. (2012). *Resources for Reform: Oil and Neoliberalism in Argentina.* Stanford University Press, 58, 59.
22. Federici, S. (2012). *Revolution at Point Zero: Housework, Reproduction, and Feminist Struggle.* PM Press.
23. Carbonella & Kasmir, Introduction; Harvey, D. (2004). The 'New' Imperialism: Accumulation by Dispossession. *Socialist Register, 40.*
24. Li, T. M. (2017). After Development: Surplus Population and the Politics of Entitlement. *Development and Change, 48*(6), 1247–1261. Carbonella & Kasmir, Introduction. Denning, M. (2010). Wageless Life. *New Left Review, 66,* 79–96; Munck, R. (2013). The Precariat: A View from the South. *Third World Quarterly, 34*(5), 747–762.
25. Li, After Development.
26. Muehlebach, A. & Shoshan, N. (2012). Introduction. *Anthropological Quarterly, 85*(2), 317–343; Neilson, B. & Rossiter, N. (2008). Precarity as a Political Concept, or, Fordism as Exception. *Theory, Culture & Society, 25*(7–8), 51–72.
27. Trott, B. (2017). Operaismo and the Wicked Problem of Organization. *Journal of Labor and Society, 20*(3), 307–324.
28. Winant, G. (2021). *The Next Shift: The Fall of Industry and the Rise of Health Care in Rust Belt America.* Harvard University Press.
29. Lopez, S. H. (2004). *Reorganizing the Rust Belt: An Inside Study of the American Labor Movement.* University of California Press.
30. Carbonella & Kasmir, Introduction.
31. Silver, B. (2003). *Forces of Labor. Workers' Movements and Globalization since 1870.* Cambridge University Press; Silver, B. (2014). Theorising the Working Class in Twenty-First-Century Global Capitalism. In M. Atzeni (ed.), *Workers*

and Labour in a Globalised Capitalism. Contemporary Themes and Theoretical Issues (pp. 46–69). Red Globe Press.

32. Harvey, D. (2001). Globalization and the 'Spatial Fix'. *Geographische Revue*, 3(2), 23–30.

33. Robinson, C. J. (2021 [1983]). *Black Marxism: The Making of the Black Radical Tradition*. Penguin.

34. Costa, M. D. & James, S. (1973). *The Power of Women and the Subversion of the Community*. Falling Wall Press; Federici, S. (2012). *Revolution at Point Zero: Housework, Reproduction, and Feminist Struggle*. PM Press.

35. Arruzza, C., Bhattacharya, T. & Fraser, N. (2019). *Feminism for the 99%: A Manifesto*. Verso Books; Federici, *Revolution at Point Zero*.

36. For example, see Vergès, F. (2021). *A Decolonial Feminism*. Pluto Press.

37. For example, see Wolf, E. R. (1971). *Peasant Wars of the Twentieth Century*. Faber & Faber.

38. Scott, J. C. (1985). *Weapons of the Weak: Everyday Forms of Peasant Resistance*. Yale University Press, 29, 350.

39. Gutmann, M. (1993). Rituals of Resistance: A Critique of the Theory of Everyday Forms of Resistance. *Latin American Perspectives*, 20(2), 74–92.

40. Lüdtke, A. (2018 [1995]). *The History of Everyday Life: Reconstructing Historical Experiences and Ways of Life* Princeton, NJ: Princeton University Press, 313–314.

41. Kalb, D. (1997). *Expanding Class: Power and Everyday Politics in Industrial Communities, The Netherlands, 1850–1950*. Duke University Press; Narotzky, S. & Smith, G. (2006). *Immediate Struggles: People, Power, and Place in Rural Spain*. University of California Press.

42. Wright, E. O. (2015). *Understanding Class*. Verso Books, 190, 191.

43. Millar, K. (2018). *Reclaiming the Discarded: Life and Labor on Rio's Garbage Dump*. Duke University Press.

44. Barchiesi, F. (2011). *Precarious Liberation: Workers, the State, and Contested Social Citizenship in Postapartheid South Africa*. State University of New York Press.

45. Weeks, K. (2011). *The Problem with Work: Feminism, Marxism, Antiwork Politics, and Postwork Imaginaries*. Duke University Press, 70, 71, 77.

46. Jaffe, S. (2021). *Work Won't Love You Back: How Devotion to Our Jobs Keeps Us Exploited, Exhausted, and Alone*. PublicAffairs.

47. In making this formulation, I am influenced by David Graeber: Graeber, D. (2018). *Bullshit Jobs: A Theory*. Penguin Books; Graeber, D. (2011). *Debt: The First 5,000 Years*. Melville House. But it is important to acknowledge his debt to the large body of work that takes this kind of approach to labour, especially from a feminist perspective (for example Barbara Ehrenreich's work). See the discussion and references in Chapter 8. See also Narotzky, S. (2018). Rethinking the Concept of Labour. *Journal of the Royal Anthropological Institute*, 24(S1), 29–43; Narotsky, S. & Besnier, N. (2014). Crisis, Value, and Hope: Rethinking the Economy: An Introduction to Wenner-Gren Symposium Supplement 9. *Current Anthropology*, 55(S9), S4–S16.

48. Narotzky, Rethinking the Concept of Labour, 30; Narotsky & Besnier, Crisis, Value, and Hope.

49. Weeks, *The Problem with Work*.

50. Hardt, M. & Negri, A. (2005). *Multitude*. Hamish Hamilton.
51. Virno, P. & Hardt, M. (1996). *Radical Thought in Italy: A Potential Politics*. University of Minnesota Press; Lazzarato, M. (1996). Immaterial Labor. In P. Virno & M. Hardt (eds), *Radical Thought in Italy: A Potential Politics* (pp. 133–148). University of Minnesota Press.
52. Yanagisako, S. (2012). Immaterial and Industrial Labor. *Focaal*, 2012(64), 16.
53. Hardt & Negri, *Multitude*.
54. Hochschild, A. R. (2012 [1983]). *The Managed Heart: Commercialization of Human Feeling*. University of California Press.
55. Graeber, *Bullshit Jobs*, xvi, xvii. See also www.strike.coop/bullshit-jobs.
56. Soffia, M., Wood, A. J. & Burchell, B. (2021). Alienation Is Not 'Bullshit': An Empirical Critique of Graeber's Theory of BS Jobs. *Work, Employment and Society*, online first.
57. Sanchez, A. (2020). Transformation and the Satisfaction of Work. *Social Analysis*, 64(3), 68–94.
58. Scott, *Weapons of the Weak*.
59. Denning, *Wageless Life*.

1   Heavy Industry and Post-Fordist Precarities

1. Mitchell, T. (2009). Carbon Democracy. *Economy and Society*, 38(3), 399–432.
2. Bello, W. (1994). *Dark Victory: The United States, Structural Adjustment and Global Poverty*. Pluto Press; Stiglitz, J. E. (2002). Globalization and its Discontents. London: Allen Lane.
3. Kwan Lee, C. (2018). Varieties of Capital, Fracture of Labor: A Comparative Ethnography of Subcontracting and Labor Precarity on the Zambian Copperbelt. In C. Hann & J. Parry (eds), *Industrial Labor on the Margins of Capitalism: Precarity, Class, and the Neoliberal Subject* (pp. 39–60). Berghahn.
4. Makram-Ebeid, D. (2018). Between God and the State: Class, Precarity, and Cosmology on the Margins of an Egyptian Steel Town. In Hann & Parry, *Industrial Labor on the Margins of Capitalism*, 180–196.
5. See https://researchbriefings.files.parliament.uk/documents/CBP-7317/CBP-7317.pdf.
6. See www.worldsteel.org/en/dam/jcr:80fe4bd6-4eff-4690-96e6-534500d35384/50+years+of+worldsteel_EN.pdf.
7. The concept of the 'spatial fix' is from David Harvey. See Harvey, D. (2001). Globalization and the 'Spatial Fix'. *Geographische Revue*, 3(2), 23–30, for a clear summary and genealogy of his thinking. See also the work of Beverley Silver: Silver, B. (2003). *Forces of Labor. Workers' Movements and Globalization since 1870*. Cambridge University Press; Silver, B. (2014). Theorising the Working Class in Twenty-First-Century Global Capitalism. In M. Atzeni (ed.), *Workers and Labour in a Globalised Capitalism. Contemporary Themes and Theoretical Issues* (pp. 46–69). Red Globe Press.
8. Silver, Theorising the Working Class.

9. Trevisani, T. (2018). Work, Precarity, and Resistance: Company and Contract Labor in Kazakhstan's Former Soviet Steel Town. In Hann & Parry, *Industrial Labor on the Margins of Capitalism*, 85–110.

10. Kesküla, E. (2016). Temporalities, Time and the Everyday: New Technology as a Marker of Change in an Estonian Mine. *History and Anthropology, 27*(5), 521–535.

11. Parry, J. (2013). Company and Contract Labour in a Central Indian Steel Plant. *Economy and Society, 42*(3), 348–374; Parry, J. (2018). Introduction. In Hann & Parry, *Industrial Labor on the Margins of Capitalism*.

12. Kwan Lee, Varieties of Capital; Sanchez, A. (2016). *Criminal Capital: Violence, Corruption and Class in Industrial India*. Routledge India.

13. Hann & Parry, *Industrial Labor on the Margins of Capitalism*.

14. Kofti, D. (2018). Regular Work in Decline, Precarious Households, and Changing Solidarities in Bulgaria. In Hann & Parry, *Industrial Labor on the Margins of Capitalism*, 110–133.

15. Kwan Lee, Varieties of Capital; Makram-Ebeid, Between God and the State; Sanchez, A. (2018). Relative Precarity: Decline, Hope, and the Politics of Work. In Hann & Parry, *Industrial Labor on the Margins of Capitalism*, 218–240.

16. Parry, Company and Contract Labour.

17. Kofti, Regular Work in Decline; Makram-Ebeid, Between God and the State; Sanchez, Relative Precarity; Trevisani, Work, Precarity and Resistance; Kesküla, E. (2018). Miners and Their Children: The Remaking of the Soviet Working Class in Kazakhstan. In Hann & Parry, *Industrial Labor on the Margins of Capitalism*, 61–84.

18. In practice this was usually passed down to sons, but formally it could be a child of either sex, a spouse or a brother-in-law (Sanchez, Relative Precarity).

19. Makram-Ebeid, Between God and the State.

20. Kesküla, E. (2014). Disembedding the Company from Kinship: Unethical Families and Atomized Labor in an Estonian Mine. *Laboratorium, 6*(2), 58–76.

21. Ibid., 64.

22. Lazar, S. (2017). *The Social Life of Politics: Ethics, Kinship and Activism in Argentine Unions*. Stanford University Press; Lazar, S. (2018). A 'Kinship Anthropology of Politics'? Interest, the Collective Self, and Kinship in Argentine Unions. *Journal of the Royal Anthropological Institute, 24*(2), 256–274.

23. Shever, E. (2012). *Resources for Reform: Oil and Neoliberalism in Argentina*. Stanford University Press; Soul, J. (2020). 'The Union is Like a Family Father, the Chief': Working-Class Making and (Re)making and Union Membership Experiences in Two Generations of Argentinian Metalworkers. *Dialectical Anthropology, 44*(2), 137–151; Wolanski, S. (2015). La familia telefónica: Sobre las relaciones de parentesco en la política sindical. *Cuadernos de Antropología Social, 42*, 91–107.

24. This is a kind of care for its affiliates that Argentine unionists often call 'contención', or containment, drawing on therapeutic language, which I have discussed at length elsewhere. See Lazar, *The Social Life of Politics*; Lazar, A 'Kinship Anthropology of Politics'?

25. Soul, 'The Union is Like a Family Father'.

26. Kapesea, R. & McNamara, T. (2020). 'We Are Not Just a Union, We Are a Family': Class, Kinship and Tribe in Zambia's Mining Unions. *Dialectical Anthropology*, 44(2), 153–172, here 157, 167.
27. Keskülä, Disembedding the Company from Kinship, 71–72.
28. Ibid; see also Trevisani, Work, Precarity and Resistance.
29. Sanchez, Relative Precarity.
30. Huws, U. (2014). *Labor in the Global Digital Economy: The Cybertariat Comes of Age*. Monthly Review Press; Parry, J. Introduction. In C. Hann & J. Parry (eds), *Industrial Labor*.
31. Kofti, Regular Work in Decline.
32. Keskülä, Miners and Their Children.
33. Strümpell, C. (2018). Precarious Labor and Precarious Livelihoods in an Indian Company Town. In Hann & Parry, *Industrial Labor on the Margins of Capitalism*, 134–154; Sanchez, A. & Strümpell, C. (2014). Sons of Soil, Sons of Steel: Autochthony, Descent and the Class Concept in Industrial India. *Modern Asian Studies*, 48(5), 1276–1301.
34. Trevisani, Work, Precarity and Resistance.
35. Bear, L. (2014). For Labour: Ajeet's Accident and the Ethics of Technological Fixes in Time. *Journal of the Royal Anthropological Institute*, 20(S1), 71–88, here 73.
36. Thompson, E. P. (1967). Time, Work-Discipline and Industrial Capitalism. *Past & Present*, 38(1), 56–97. Several ethnographers have engaged directly with this piece, in both industrial and non-industrial settings, e.g. see Millar, K. M. (2015). Introduction. *Focaal*, 2015(73), 3; Parry, J. P. (1999). Lords of Labour: Working and Shirking in Bhilai. *Contributions to Indian Sociology*, 33(1–2), 107–140.
37. Dunn, E. (2004). *Privatizing Poland: Baby Food, Big Business, and the Remaking of Labor*. Cornell University Press.
38. Parry, Lords of Labour.
39. Keskülä, Temporalities, Time and the Everyday.
40. Kofti, Regular Work in Decline.
41. Muehlebach, A. (2011). On Affective Labor in Post-Fordist Italy. *Cultural Anthropology*, 26(1), 59–82; Muehlebach, A. & Shoshan, N. (2012). Introduction. *Anthropological Quarterly*, 85(2), 317–343.
42. Muehlebach, A. (2012). *The Moral Neoliberal: Welfare and Citizenship in Italy*. University of Chicago Press.
43. Morris, J. & Hinz, S. (2018). From Avtoritet and Autonomy to Self-Exploitation in the Russian Automotive Industry. In Hann & Parry, *Industrial Labor on the Margins of Capitalism*, 241–264.
44. Hoffmann, M. (2014). Red Salute at Work. *Focaal*, 2014(70), 67–80.
45. Kwan Lee, Varieties of Capital.
46. Keskülä, Miners and Their Children; Morris & Hinz, From Avtoritet and Autonomy.
47. Rose, N. (1989). *Governing the Soul: The Shaping of the Private Self*. Routledge.
48. Sennett, R. (2007). *The Culture of the New Capitalism*. Yale University Press.

49. Rudnyckyj, D. (2018). Regimes of Precarity: Buruh, Karyawan, and the Politics of Labor Identity in Indonesia. In Hann & Parry, *Industrial Labor on the Margins of Capitalism*, 155–179.

50. Cross, J (2010). Neoliberalism as Unexceptional: Economic Zones and the Everyday Precariousness of Working Life in South India. *Critique of Anthropology*, 30(4), 355–373.

51. Lazar, *The Social Life of Politics*.

52. Mitchell, J. C. (1956). *The Kalela Dance: Aspects of Social Relationships among Urban Africans in Northern Rhodesia*. Manchester University Press.

53. Ferguson, J. (1999). *Expectations of Modernity: Myths and Meanings of Urban Life on the Zambian Copperbelt*. University of California Press.

54. Kwan Lee, Varieties of Capital.

55. Sanchez & Strümpell, Sons of Soil.

56. Barua, R. (2015). The Textile Labour Association and Dadagiri: Power and Politics in the Working-Class Neighborhoods of Ahmedabad. *International Labor and Working-Class History*, 87, 63–91.

57. See their website at www.sewa.org. Bhatt, E. (2006). *We Are Poor but So Many. The Story of Self-employed Women in India*. Oxford University Press.

58. Parry, Company and Contract Labour; Sanchez, Relative Precarity; Strümpell, Precarious Labor.

59. Parry, Company and Contract Labour; Sanchez, Relative Precarity.

60. Keşküla, E. & Sanchez, A. (2019). Everyday Barricades: Bureaucracy and the Affect of Struggle in Trade Unions. *Dialectical Anthropology*, 43(1), 109–125; Sanchez, Relative Precarity.

61. Bithymitris, G. & Spyridakis, M. (2020). Union Radicalism versus the Nationalist Upsurge: The Case of Greek Shipbuilding Workers. *Dialectical Anthropology*, 44(2), 121–135.

62. Lazar, *The Social Life of Politics*; Sanchez, *Criminal Capital*.

63. Parry, Company and Contract Labour; Parry, Introduction.

64. Matos, P. (2012). Call Center Labor and the Injured Precariat: Shame, Stigma, and Downward Social Mobility in Contemporary Portugal. *Dialectical Anthropology*, 36(3/4), 217–243.

65. Standing, G. (2011). *The Precariat: The New Dangerous Class*. Bloomsbury.

66. Lazar, S. (ed.). (2017). *Where Are the Unions? Workers and Social Movements in Latin America, the Middle East, and Europe*. Zed Books.

67. Kwan Lee, Varieties of Capital, 55.

68. Kapesea & McNamara, 'We Are Not Just a Union'.

69. Fernandez Alvarez, M. I. (2019). 'Having a Name of One's Own, Being Part of History': Temporalities and Political Subjectivities of Popular Economy Workers in Argentina. *Dialectical Anthropology*, 43(1), 61–76.

70. Silver, Theorising the Working Class.

2 *Light Industry: Gender, Migration and Strategies of Resilience*

1. Collins, J. (2003). *Threads: Gender, Labour, and Power in the Global Apparel Industry*. University of Chicago Press.

2. Mezzadri, A. (2017). *Sweatshop Regimes in the Indian Garment Industry*. Cambridge University Press.

3. Collins, *Threads*.

4. Chan, J., Pun, N. & Selden, M. (2013). The Politics of Global Production: Apple, Foxconn and China's New Working Class. *New Technology, Work and Employment, 28*(2), 100–115.

5. Hou, J., Gelb, S. & Calabrese, L. (2017). *The Shift in Manufacturing Employment in China*. Background paper. Overseas Development Institute (Supporting Economic Transformation Programme).

6. Collins, *Threads*, 7.

7. Rofel, L. & Yanagisako, S. (2018). *Fabricating Transnational Capitalism: A Collaborative Ethnography of Italian-Chinese Global Fashion*. Duke University Press.

8. See http://manufacturingmap.nikeinc.com.

9. Barrientos, S. (2013). Corporate Purchasing Practices in Global Production Networks: A Socially Contested Terrain. *Geoforum, 44*, 44–51.

10. Chan et al., The Politics of Global Production.

11. See www.forbes.com/sites/walterloeb/2015/03/30/zara-leads-in-fast-fashion/#21f463585944.

12. See http://fortune.com/2008/11/24/apple-the-genius-behind-steve; Chan et al., The Politics of Global Production.

13. Chan et al., The Politics of Global Production.

14. Ibid., 108.

15. Chan, J. (2017). Intern Labor in China. *Rural China, 38*, 82–100; Chan, J., Pun, N. & Selden, M. (2015). Interns or Workers? China's Student Labor Regime. *The Asia-Pacific Journal, 13*(36).

16. Collins, *Threads*.

17. Prentice, R. (2017). Microenterprise Development, Industrial Labour and the Seductions of Precarity. *Critique of Anthropology, 37*(2), 201–222.

18. Campbell, S. (2016). Putting-Out's Return. *Focaal—Journal of Global and Historical Anthropology, 2016*(76), 71–84, here 77.

19. Prentice, Microenterprise Development.

20. De Neve, G. (2008). Global Garment Chains, Local Labour Activism: New Challenges to Trade Union and NGO Activism in the Tiruppur Garment Cluster, South India. In G. De Neve, P. Luetchford, J. Pratt & D. C. Wood (eds), *Hidden Hands in the Market: Ethnographies of Fair Trade, Ethical Consumption, and Corporate Social Responsibility* (pp. 213–240). Emerald Insight.

21. Pun, N. (2005). *Made in China: Women Factory Workers in a Global Workplace*. Duke University Press; Carswell, G. & De Neve, G. (2013). Labouring for Global Markets: Conceptualising Labour Agency in Global Production Networks. *Geoforum, 44*(0), 62–70; Carswell, G. & De Neve, G. (2018). Towards a Political Economy of Skill and Garment Work: The Case of the Tiruppur Industrial Cluster in South India. In C. Hann & J. Parry (eds), *Industrial Labor on the Margins of Capitalism: Precarity, Class, and the Neoliberal Subject* (pp. 309–335). Berghahn.

22. Tsing, A. (2009). Supply Chains and the Human Condition. *Rethinking Marxism, 21*(2), 148–176.

23. Elson, D. & Pearson, R. (1981). 'Nimble Fingers Make Cheap Workers': An Analysis of Women's Employment in Third World Export Manufacturing. *Feminist Review*(7), 87–107, here 93.
24. Pun, *Made in China*.
25. Elson & Pearson, Nimble Fingers, 93.
26. Fang, I.-C. (2018). Precarity, Guanxi, and the Informal Economy of Peasant Workers in Contemporary China. In C. Hann & J. Parry (eds), *Industrial Labor on the Margins of Capitalism: Precarity, Class, and the Neoliberal Subject* (pp. 265–288). Berghahn; Pun, *Made in China*.
27. Pun, *Made in China*.
28. Kwan Lee, C. (2007). *Against the Law: Labor Protests in China's Rustbelt and Sunbelt*. University of California Press.
29. Don Kalb, personal communication, 10 September 2021. See also Kalb, D. (1997). *Expanding Class: Power and Everyday Politics in Industrial Communities, The Netherlands, 1850–1950*. Duke University Press.
30. Pun, *Made in China*, 143, 144.
31. Ibid., 83.
32. Chan et al., The Politics of Global Production.
33. Pun, *Made in China*.
34. Prentice, R. (2015). *Thiefing a Chance: Factory Work, Illicit Labor, and Neoliberal Subjectivities in Trinidad*. University Press of Colorado.
35 Carswell & De Neve, Labouring for Global Markets.
36. Ibid., 330.
37. Ibid..
38. Fang, Precarity, Guanxi and the Informal Economy of Peasant Workers, also Pun, *Made in China*.
39. Carswell & De Neve, Labouring for Global Markets, 64.
40. Pun, *Made in China*; Pun, N. (2020). The New Chinese Working Class in Struggle. *Dialectical Anthropology*, 44(4), 319–329.
41. De Neve, G. (2014). Entrapped Entrepreneurship: Labour Contractors in the South Indian Garment Industry. *Modern Asian Studies*, 48(5), 1302–1333, here 1325–1326.
42. Herod, A. (1997). From a Geography of Labor to a Labor Geography: Labor's Spatial Fix and the Geography of Capitalism. *Antipode*, 29(1), 1–31; Carswell & De Neve, Labouring for Global Markets, 63.
43. Mezzadri, *Sweatshop Regimes*.
44. Chan et al., The Politics of Global Production.
45. Pun, The New Chinese Working Class, 322.
46. Chan, Intern Labor.
47. Chan, J., Selden, M. & Pun, N. (2020). *Dying for an iPhone: Apple, Foxconn, and The Lives of China's Workers*. Haymarket Books.
48. Hou et al., *The Shift in Manufacturing Employment in China*.
49. Chan, Intern Labor.
50. Chan, J. (2013). A Suicide Survivor: The Life of a Chinese Worker. *New Technology, Work and Employment*, 28(2), 84–99.
51. Chan et al., The Politics of Global Production.

52. Ashraf, H. & Prentice, R. (2019). Beyond Factory Safety: Labor Unions, Militant Protest, and the Accelerated Ambitions of Bangladesh's Export Garment Industry. *Dialectical Anthropology*, 43(1), 93–107.
53. Chan et al., *Dying for an iPhone*, 159.
54. Pun, *Made in China*.
55. Scott, J. C. (1985). *Weapons of the Weak: Everyday Forms of Peasant Resistance*. Yale University Press.
56. Prentice, *Thiefing a Chance*.
57. Ong, A. (1988). The Production of Possession: Spirits and the Multinational Corporation in Malaysia. *American Ethnologist*, 15(1), 28–42, here 35.
58. Ibid., 34.
59. Pun, *Made in China*.
60. Chan, A Suicide Survivor. The wave of suicides did not change conditions for the better for Foxconn workers: Apple suffered a temporary dent to its reputation and decided to diversify its contracting procedures by finding an additional supplier. Foxconn denied all culpability. They installed nets around buildings to catch those workers who might throw themselves out of high-story windows; and locked the windows, creating stifling conditions in the dormitories. It is difficult now for researchers to gain access to their factories, but the signs are that they have begun to explore automation technologies in earnest.

3 *Agricultural Labour: Exploitation and Collective Action*

1. There are considerable problems with describing 'peasants' as if 'peasant' were a homogeneous subject, even politically. Inhabitants of the countryside who make a living from agriculture might occupy many different positions in class terms, quite apart from any other kinds of differentiation: smallholders, 'middle peasants' (Wolf, E. R. (1971). *Peasant Wars of the Twentieth Century*. Faber & Faber), wage labourers, vagrants, and so on.
2. Davis, M. (2004). Planet of Slums. *New Left Review*, 26. Retrieved from https://newleftreview.org/issues/ii26/articles/mike-davis-planet-of-slums.
3. Federici, S. (2012). *Revolution at Point Zero: Housework, Reproduction, and Feminist Struggle*. PM Press.
4. Besky, S. (2014). *The Darjeeling Distinction: Labor and Justice on Fair-Trade Tea Plantations in India*. University of California Press; Mintz, S. W. (1985). *Sweetness and Power. The Place of Sugar in Modern History*. Elisabeth Sifton Books.
5. Taussig, M. (1984). Culture of Terror – Space of Death. Roger Casement's Putumayo Report and the Explanation of Torture. *Comparative Studies in Society and History*, 26(3), 467–497.
6. Correia, J. E. (2019). Soy States: Resource Politics, Violent Environments and Soybean Territorialization in Paraguay. *The Journal of Peasant Studies*, 46(2), 316–336.
7. Hetherington, K. (2011). *Guerrilla Auditors: The Politics of Transparency in Neoliberal Paraguay*. Duke University Press.

8.   Correia, Soy States; Hetherington, *Guerrilla Auditors*.
9.   Correia, Soy States.
10. Oliveira, G. d. L. T. (2016). The Geopolitics of Brazilian Soybeans. *The Journal of Peasant Studies*, 43(2), 348–372.
11. Murray Li, T. (2014). *Land's End: Capitalist Relations on an Indigenous Frontier*. Duke University Press.
12. Campbell, B. (2018). Moral Ecologies of Subsistence and Labour in a Migration-Affected Community of Nepal. *Journal of the Royal Anthropological Institute*, 24(S1), 151–165.
13. Sopranzetti, C. (2017). *Owners of the Map: Motorcycle Taxi Drivers, Mobility, and Politics in Bangkok*. University of California Press.
14. Besky, *The Darjeeling Distinction*, 55, 7.
15. Guthman, J. (2019). *Wilted: Pathogens, Chemicals, and the Fragile Future of the Strawberry Industry*. University of California Press.
16. de Genova, N. (2005). *Working the Boundaries. Race, Space, and 'Illegality' in Mexican Chicago*. Duke University Press; Horton, S. B. (2016). Ghost Workers: The Implications of Governing Immigration Through Crime for Migrant Workplaces. *Anthropology of Work Review*, 37(1), 11–23.
17. Guthman, *Wilted*, 135.
18. Ibid.
19. Horton, S. B. (2016). *They Leave Their Kidneys in the Fields: Illness, Injury, and Illegality Among US Farmworkers*. University of California Press.
20. Ibid., 25.
21. Bolt, M. (2015). *Zimbabwe's Migrants and South Africa's Border Farms*. Cambridge University Press, 147.
22. Besky, *The Darjeeling Distinction*.
23. Ibid.
24. Holmes, S. (2013). *Fresh Fruit, Broken Bodies: Migrant Farmworkers in the United States*. University of California Press.
25. Horton, *They Leave Their Kidneys*.
26. West, P. (2012). *From Modern Production to Imagined Primitive: The Social World of Coffee from Papua New Guinea*. Duke University Press, 115, 118.
27. Ibid., 121.
28. Ibid., 121.
29. Shield-Johannson. (2013). 'To Work Is to Transform the Land': Agricultural Labour, Personhood and Landscape in an Andean Ayllu. PhD thesis, London School of Economics.
30. Harris, O. (2007). What Makes People Work? In R. Astuti, J. Parry & C. Stafford (eds), *Questions of Anthropology*. Berg, 141. See also West, *From Modern Production to Imagined Primitive*; Shield-Johannson, *To Work Is to Transform the Land*.
31. Shield-Johannson, *To Work Is to Transform the Land*.
32. Murray Li, *Land's End*.
33. West, *From Modern Production to Imagined Primitive*.
34. Harris, What Makes People Work?
35. Pandian, A. (2009). *Crooked Stalks: Cultivating Virtue in South India*. Duke University Press, 166.

36. de L'Estoile, B. (2014). 'Money Is Good, but a Friend Is Better': Uncertainty, Orientation to the Future, and 'the Economy'. *Current Anthropology*, 55(S9), S62–S73, here 568.
37. Scott, J. C. (1985). *Weapons of the Weak: Everyday Forms of Peasant Resistance*. Yale University Press, 29, 37.
38. Guthman, *Wilted*.
39. Horton, *They Leave their Kidneys*.
40. Hetherington, *Guerrilla Auditors*; Hetherington, K. (2013). Beans Before the Law: Knowledge Practices, Responsibility, and the Paraguayan Soy Boom. *Cultural Anthropology*, 28(1): 65–85.
41. Hetherington, Beans before the Law.
42. Hetherington, *Guerrilla Auditors*.
43. Campbell, Moral Ecologies of Subsistence and Labour; Shah, A., Lerche, J., Axelby, R., Benbabaali, D., Donegan, B., Raj, J. & Thakur, V. (2018). *Ground Down by Growth: Tribe, Caste, Class and Inequality in Twenty-First-Century India*. Pluto Press.
44. Reichman, D. R. (2011). *The Broken Village: Coffee, Migration, and Globalization in Honduras*. Cornell University Press.
45. Münster, D. (2012). Farmers' Suicides and the State in India: Conceptual and Ethnographic Notes from Wayanad, Kerala. *Contributions to Indian Sociology*, 46(1–2), 181–208.
46. Ibid.
47. Grisaffi, T. (2019). *Coca Yes, Cocaine No: How Bolivia's Coca Growers Reshaped Democracy* Duke University Press.
48. See https://theconversation.com/farmers-in-india-have-been-protesting-for-6-months-have-they-made-any-progress-161101.
49. See https://thewire.in/agriculture/farmers-protests-agriculture-laws-corporate-interests.
50. See https://viacampesina.org/en/wp-content/uploads/sites/2/2018/03/List-of-members.pdf.
51. See www.sewa.org/About_Us_Structure.asp. Figures from 2016. Gujarat membership is nearly 700,000.
52. Guthman, *Wilted*.
53. Ibid., 136.
54. Besky, *The Darjeeling Distinction*.
55. Raj, J. (2018). Teabelts of the Western Ghats, Kerala. In Shah et al., *Ground Down by Growth*, 49–81.
56. Wilderman, J. (2017). From Flexible Work to Mass Uprising: The Western Cape Farmworkers' Struggle. In E. Webster, A. Britwum & S. Bhowmik (eds), *Crossing the Divide: Precarious Work and the Future of Labour* (pp. 74–98). University of KwaZulu-Natal Press.
57. Ibid.
58. Tarlau, R. (2019). *Occupying Schools, Occupying Land: How the Landless Workers Movement Transformed Brazilian Education*. Oxford University Press.
59. Gilbert, D. E. (2020). Laborers Becoming 'Peasants': Agroecological Politics in a Sumatran Plantation Zone. *The Journal of Peasant Studies*, 47(5), 1030–1051.
60. Ibid., 1048, 1042.

61. Gilbert, D. E. & Afrizal. (2019). The Land Exclusion Dilemma and Sumatra's Agrarian Reactionaries. *The Journal of Peasant Studies, 46*(4), 681–701.

62. See www.theguardian.com/environment/2020/jul/29/record-212-land-and-environment-activists-killed-last-year.

63. Hetherington, Beans before the Law.

64. Gilbert & Afrizal, The Land Exclusion Dilemma.

4 *Affective Labour and the Service Sector: Work as Relations*

1. Hardt, M. & Negri, A. (2005). *Multitude*. Hamish Hamilton, 108.

2. Federici, S. (2020 [2011]). On Affective Labor. In S. Federici (ed.), *Revolution at Point Zero: Housework, Reproduction, and Feminist Struggle* (2nd edition) (pp. 49–56). PM Press; McRobbie, A. (2010). Reflections on Feminism, Immaterial Labour and the Post Fordist Regime. *New Formations, 70*.

3. Federici, On Affective Labor, 49.

4. Ibid., 51.

5. Goodfriend, H. (2018). 'Where You From?': Deportación, identidad y trabajo reciclado en el call center salvadoreño. *Latin American Research Review, 53*(2), 303–317; Huws, U. (2014). *Labor in the Global Digital Economy: The Cybertariat Comes of Age*. Monthly Review Press; Matos, P. (2012). Call Center Labor and the Injured Precariat: Shame, Stigma, and Downward Social Mobility in Contemporary Portugal. *Dialectical Anthropology, 36*(3 4), 217–243; Mirchandani, K. (2012). *Phone Clones: Authenticity Work in the Transnational Service Economy*. Cornell University Press

6. Mirchandani, *Phone Clones*.

7. Ibid.; Mankekar, P. & Gupta, A. (2017). Future Tense: Capital, Labor, and Technology in a Service Industry. *HAU: Journal of Ethnographic Theory, 7*(3), 67–87.

8. Mirchandani, *Phone Clones*; Patel, R. (2010). *Working the Night Shift: Women in India's Call Center Industry*. Stanford University Press.

9. Goodfriend, 'Where You From?' (my translation).

10. Alarcón-Medina, R. (2018). Informational Returnees: Deportation, Digital Media, and the Making of a Transnational Cybertariat in the Mexican Call Center Industry. *Dialectical Anthropology, 42*(3), 293–308.

11. Parreñas, R. S. (2010). Cultures of Flirtation: Sex and the Moral Boundaries of Filipina Migrant Hostesses in Tokyo. In E. Boris & R. S. Parreñas (eds), *Intimate Labors: Cultures, Technologies, and the Politics of Care* (pp. 132–147). Stanford University Press; Peano, I. (2013). Migrant Nigerian Women in Bonded Sexual Labour: The Subjective Effects of Criminalisation and Structural Suspicion, beyond the Trafficking Paradigm. *Africa e Mediterraneo, 79*(2), 44–47.

12. Kang, M. (2010). *The Managed Hand: Race, Gender, and the Body in Beauty Service Work*. University of California Press.

13. Ehrenreich, B. & Hochschild, A. R. (eds). (2003). *Global Woman: Nannies, Maids and Sex Workers in the New Economy*. Granta, 5–6.

14. Ibid.

15. Mather, C. (2015). Domestic Workers in Europe Getting Organised! Retrieved from www.effat.org/wp-content/uploads/2018/11/effat_booklet_domestic_workers_in_europe_en.pdf. The ILO reports that migrant women represent more than 80 per cent of registered domestic workers in Italy in 2011, and they come 'mostly from eastern European countries'. See www.ilo.org/wcmsp5/groups/public/---ed_protect/---protrav/---travail/documents/publication/wcms_436974.pdf.

16. Guevarra, A. R. (2010). *Marketing Dreams, Manufacturing Heroes: The Transnational Labor Brokering of Filipino Workers.* New Brunswick, NJ: Rutgers University Press; Bautista, J. (2015). Export-Quality Martyrs: Roman Catholicism and Transnational Labor in the Philippines. *Cultural Anthropology*, 30(3), 424–447.

17. Guevarra, *Marketing Dreams*.

18. Parreñas, R. S. (2003). The Care Crisis in the Philippines: Children and Transnational Families in the New Global Economy. In B. Ehrenreich & A. R. Hochschild (eds), *Global Woman. Nannies, Maids and Sex Workers in the New Economy* (pp. 39–54). Granta Books; Qayum, S. & Ray, R. (2010). Traveling Cultures of Servitude: Loyalty and Betrayal in New York and Kolkata. In Boris & Parreñas, *Intimate Labors*, 101–116; Yarris, K. (2017). *Care Across Generations: Solidarity and Sacrifice in Transnational Families*. Stanford University Press.

19. Hardt & Negri, *Multitude*.

20. Boris & Parreñas, *Intimate Labors*.

21. Kang, *The Managed Hand*.

22. Hochschild, A. R. (2012 [1983]). *The Managed Heart: Commercialization of Human Feeling* University of California Press.

23. Aneesh, A. (2015). *Neutral Accent: How Language, Labor, and Life become Global.* Duke University Press.

24. Mankekar, P. & Gupta, A. (2016). Intimate Encounters: Affective Labor in Call Centers. *Positions: Asia Critique*, 24(1): 17–43.

25. Mirchandani, *Phone Clones*.

26. Aneesh, *Neutral Accent*; Mankekar & Gupta, Intimate Encounters; Mirchandani, *Phone Clones*.

27. Aneesh, *Neutral Accent*, p. 69, fig 3.4.

28. Mankekar & Gupta, Intimate Encounters.

29. Aneesh, *Neutral Accent*; Mankekar & Gupta, Intimate Encounters; Mirchandani, *Phone Clones*.

30. Aneesh, *Neutral Accent*.

31. Mirchandani, *Phone Clones*.

32. Hoang, K. K. (2010). Economics of Emotion, Familiarity, Fantasy, and Desire: Emotional Labor in Ho Chi Minh City's Sex Industry. In Boris & Parreñas, *Intimate Labors*, 166–182.

33. Kang, *The Managed Hand*, 45–46.

34. Parreñas, Cultures of Flirtation.

35. Koch, G. (2016). Producing Iyashi: Healing and Labor in Tokyo's Sex Industry. *American Ethnologist*, 43(4), 704–716.

36. Aoyama, K. (2009). *Thai Migrant Sexworkers: From Modernisation to Globalisation*. Palgrave Macmillan; Koch, G. (2020). *Healing Labor: Japanese Sex Work in the Gendered Economy*. Stanford University Press.

37. Koch, *Healing Labor*.

38. Hoang, Economics of Emotion, 177.

39. Bernstein, E. (2010). Bounded Authenticity and the Commerce of Sex. In Boris & Parreñas, *Intimate Labors*, 148–165.

40. Hochschild, *The Managed Heart*.

41. Zelizer, V. (2009). Caring Everywhere. In Boris & Parreñas, *Intimate Labors*, 267–279.

42. Federici, On Affective Labor.

43. Guevarra, *Marketing Dreams*; Stacey, C. L. (2011). *The Caring Self: The Work Experiences of Home Care Aides*. Cornell University Press.

44. Rivas, L. M. (2003). Invisible Labors: Caring for the Independent Person. In B. Ehrenreich & A. R. Hochschild (eds), *Global Woman. Nannies, Maids and Sex Workers in the New Economy* (pp. 70–84). Granta.

45. Stacey, *The Caring Self*.

46. Ibarra, M. d. l. L. (2010). My Reward Is Not Money: Deep Alliances and End-of-Life Care among Mexicana Workers and Their Wards. In Boris & Parreñas, *Intimate Labors*, 117–131.

47. Stacey, *The Caring Self*.

48. Guevarra, *Marketing Dreams*.

49. Qayum & Ray, Traveling Cultures of Servitude.

50. Hondagneu-Sotelo, P. (2003). Blowups and Other Unhappy Endings. In B. Ehrenreich & A. R. Hochschild (eds), *Global Woman. Nannies, Maids and Sex Workers in the New Economy* (pp. 55–69). Granta.

51. Ehrenreich & Hochschild, *Global Woman*.

52. Ramos-Zayas, A. Y. (2019). 'Sovereign Parenting' in Affluent Latin American Neighbourhoods: Race and the Politics of Childcare in Ipanema (Brazil) and El Condado (Puerto Rico). *Journal of Latin American Studies*, 51(3), 639–663.

53. Gill, L. (1994). *Precarious Dependencies. Gender, Class, and Domestic Service in Bolivia*. Columbia University Press.

54. Hardt & Negri, *Multitude*; Hardt, M. & Negri, A. (2017). *Assembly*. Oxford University Press.

55. See the special issue Dowling, E., Nunes, R. & Trott, B. (2007). Immaterial and Affective Labour: Explored. *Ephemera. Theory and Politics in Organization*, 7; also Trott, B. (2017). Affective Labour and Alienation: Spinoza's Materialism and the Sad Passions of Post-Fordist Work. *Emotion, Space and Society*, 25, 119–126; Federici, On Affective Labor; McRobbie, Reflections on Feminism.

56. Lopez, S. H. (2004). *Reorganizing the Rust Belt: An Inside Study of the American Labor Movement*. University of California Press; Stacey, *The Caring Self*.

57. Zlolniski, C. (2006). *Janitors, Street Vendors, and Activists: The Lives of Mexican Immigrants in Silicon Valley*. University of California Press.

58. Durrenberger, E. P. & Erem, S. (2005). *Class Acts: An Anthropology of Urban Workers and their Union*. Paradigm.

59. Kang, *The Managed Hand*.

60. See www.theguardian.com/film/2020/aug/12/united-voices-an-inspiring-story-of-workers-grassroots-resistance.

61. See www.uvwunion.org.uk/en/campaigns/sage-nursing-home.

62. See https://vashtimedia.com/2020/12/09/jewish-care-home-workers-strike-sage-golders-green-uvw-jsa-union.

63. See www.uvwunion.org.uk/en/news/2021/11/victory-pandemic-heroes-as-billionaire-trustees-capitulate-at-sage-nursing-home.

64. Boris, E. (2019). *Making the Woman Worker: Precarious Labor and the Fight for Global Standards, 1919–2019*. Oxford University Press.

65. Cobble, D. S. (2010). More Intimate Unions. In Boris & Parreñas, *Intimate Labors*, 280–296.

66. See http://aswaalliance.org; https://apnsw.info; http://plaperts.nswp.org; www.sexworkeurope.org.

67. Aoyama, *Thai Migrant Sexworkers*; Peano, Migrant Nigerian Women in Bonded Labour.

68. Matos, Call Center Labor.

69. Anagnostopoulos, A. & Evangelinidis, A. (2017). The Experience of Grassroots Syndicalism in Greece: Workplace Restructuring and the Role of Traditional Trade Unions in the Tertiary Sector. In S. Lazar (ed.), *Where Are the Unions? Workers and Social Movements in Latin America, the Middle East and Europe*. Zed Books.

70. Stacey, *The Caring Self*.

5 *Professional and Managerial Work: Producing Selves and Processes*

1. The other is Chapter 8, on social reproduction labour.

2. Even international organisations have a central location for their main offices, be that Brussels, New York, Geneva, the Hague, etc.

3. Shore, C. & Wright, S. (2018). Performance Management and the Audited Self. In B. Ajana (ed.), *Metric Culture: Ontologies of Self-Tracking Practices* (pp. 11–35). Emerald Publishing.

4. Depending on the nature of Brexit, London may decline in importance, at least within European finance, in favour of other European centres like Frankfurt and Paris. But the global hegemony of London and New York has a longer history than that of the EU.

5. Chong, K. (2018). *Best Practice: Management Consulting and the Ethics of Financialization in China*. Duke University Press.

6. Hood, C. (1995). The 'New Public Management' in the 1980s: Variations on a Theme. *Accounting, Organizations and Society*, 20(2), 93–109.

7. Born, G. (2005). *Uncertain Vision: Birt, Dyke and the Reinvention of the BBC*. Vintage.

8. Ibid., 234.

9. Ibid., 234.

10. Brown, H. & Green, M. (2017). Demonstrating Development: Meetings as Management in Kenya's Health Sector. *Journal of the Royal Anthropological Institute*, 23(S1), 45–62.

11. Or direction towards specific sectors, as with STEM research in the UK.

12. They also had to demonstrate 'outstanding leadership' according to the University's 'leadership framework'. That framework consisted of five dimensions (Personal Leadership, Setting Direction, Enabling People, Innovating and Engaging, and Achieving Results) each of which required particular capabilities, tightly described. Shore & Wright, Performance Management and the Audited Self.

13. Ho, K. (2009). *Liquidated. An Ethnography of Wall Street.* Duke University Press, 125.

14. Chong, *Best Practice.*

15. Souleles, D. (2020). Trading Options and the Unattainable Dream: Some Reflections on Semiotic Ideologies. *Signs and Society,* 8(2), 243–261, here 245; Souleles, D. (2021). Why Would You Buy an Electric Car on Jetski Friday? Or, a Critique of Financial Markets from an Options Trading Room. *Finance and Society,* 7(2), 113–129, here 115; Pardo-Guerra, J. P. (2019). *Automating Finance: Infrastructures, Engineers, and the Making of Electronic Markets.* Cambridge University Press.

16. MacKenzie, D. (2021). *Trading at the Speed of Light: How Ultrafast Algorithms Are Transforming Financial Markets.* Princeton University Press.

17. Leins, S. (2018). *Stories of Capitalism: Inside the Role of Financial Analysts.* University of Chicago Press; MacKenzie, *Trading at the Speed of Light.*

18. Armelino, M. (2015). Reformas de mercado y reacciones sindicales en argentina: una revisión desde la experiencia de los trabajadores públicos. *Desarrollo Económico,* 55(216): 245–278.

19. Lazar, S. (2012). A Desire to Formalize Work? Comparing Trade Union Strategies in Bolivia and Argentina. *Anthropology of Work Review,* 33(1), 15–24.

20. See www.hesa.ac.uk/data-and-analysis/staff/employment-conditions. See also Loveday, V. (2018). The Neurotic Academic: Anxiety, Casualisation, and Governance in the Neoliberalising University. *Journal of Cultural Economy,* 11(2), 154–166.

21. See www.ucu.org.uk/stampout.

22. See www.timeshighereducation.com/unijobs/article/academic-fixed-term-jobs-changes-germany-split-opinion. See also Peacock, V. (2016). Academic Precarity as Hierarchical Dependence in the Max Planck Society. *HAU: Journal of Ethnographic Theory,* 6(1), 95–119.

23. See www.aaup.org/news/data-snapshot-contingent-faculty-us-higher-ed#.XScYAOhKibg; www.aaup.org/sites/default/files/Academic_Labor_Force_Trends_1975-2015_0.pdf.

24. See www.ucu.org.uk/stampout.

25. O'Keefe, T. & Courtois, A. (2019). 'Not One of the Family': Gender and Precarious Work in the Neoliberal University. *Gender, Work & Organization,* 26(4), 463–479.

26. Ibid.

27. Collins, J. (2012). Theorizing Wisconsin's 2011 Protests: Community-Based Unionism Confronts Accumulation by Dispossession. *American Ethnologist,* 39(1), 6–20, here 8.

28. Eagleton, T. (2015). The Slow Death of the University. *The Chronicle of Higher Education*, 6 April. See also https://reclaimingouruniversity.wordpress.com; www.hyllanderiksen.net/blog/2019/1/25/a-university-is-not-a-factory.

29. Hetherington, K. (2011). *Guerrilla Auditors: The Politics of Transparency in Neoliberal Paraguay*. Duke University Press, 145–146, 149. For other ethnographic discussions of documents, see also Hull, M. S. (2012). Documents and Bureaucracy. *Annual Review of Anthropology*, 41(1), 251–267; Mathur, N. (2012). Transparent-Making Documents and the Crisis of Unimplementability: A Rural Employment Law and Development Bureaucracy in Himalayan India. *Political and Legal Anthropology Review*, 35(2), 167–185.

30. Leins, *Stories of Capitalism*; Souleles, D. (2019). *Songs of Profit, Songs of Loss: Private Equity, Wealth, and Inequality*. University of Nebraska Press.

31. Chong, *Best Practice*.

32. Stein, F. (2017). *Work, Sleep, Repeat: The Abstract Labour of German Management Consultants*. Bloomsbury Academic; Chong, *Best Practice*.

33. Chong, *Best Practice*.

34. E.g. Green, M. (2003). Globalizing Development in Tanzania. Policy Franchising through Participatory Project Management. *Critique of Anthropology*, 23(2), 123–143.

35. See Stein, F. (2018). Anthropology's 'Impact': A Comment on Audit and the Unmeasurable Nature of Critique. *Journal of the Royal Anthropological Institute*, 24(1), 10–29.

36. Loveday, The Neurotic Academic.

37. Gershon, I. (2017). *Down and Out in the New Economy: How People Find (or Don't Find) Work Today*. University of Chicago Press.

38. Mathur, N. (2016). *Paper Tiger: Law, Bureaucracy and the Developmental State in Himalayan India*. Cambridge University Press, 133.

39. Zaloom, C. (2006). *Out of the Pits: Traders and Technology from Chicago to London*. University of Chicago Press, 117, 109.

40. Lewis, M. (2006 [1988]). *Liar's Poker*. Hodder.

41. Ho, *Liquidated*.

42. Lewis, M. (2014). *Flash Boys: Cracking the Money Code*. Allen Lane.

43. Souleles, Trading Options.

44. Leins, *Stories of Capitalism*.

45. Souleles, *Songs of Profit*.

46. Pearson, A. (2020). The Discipline of Economics: Performativity and Personhood in Undergraduate Economics Education. PhD thesis, Department of Social Anthropology, University of Cambridge.

47. Peacock, Academic Precarity as Hierarchical Dependence.

48. Bourdieu, P. (1986). *Distinction. A Social Critique of the Judgement of Taste*. Routledge.

49. Mathur, *Paper Tiger*.

50. Bear, L. (2015). *Navigating Austerity: Currents of Debt along a South Asian River*. Stanford University Press.

51. Yanagisako, S. (2012). Immaterial and Industrial Labor. *Focaal*, 2012(64), 16; Rofel, L. & Yanagisako, S. (2018). *Fabricating Transnational Capitalism: A*

Collaborative Ethnography of Italian-Chinese Global Fashion. Duke University Press.

52. Chong, *Best Practice*, 139.
53. Ho, *Liquidated*.
54. See www.businessinsider.com/amazon-employees-new-compensation-ranges-2022-2?r=US&IR=T.
55. Zaloom, *Out of the Pits*.
56. Isin, E. F. (2004). The Neurotic Citizen. *Citizenship Studies*, 8(3), 217–235.
57. Loveday, The Neurotic Academic.
58. Peacock, Academic Precarity as Hierarchical Dependence.
59. The ILO publishes data on union density but does not disaggregate between public and private sector. Regarding higher rates of unionisation in the public sector in Europe, see the article from the European Trade Union Institute at www.worker-participation.eu/National-Industrial-Relations/Across-Europe/Trade-Unions2. In the UK, the TUC reported union density of 51.8 per cent in the public sector, and 13.5 per cent in the private sector in 2017 (see www.tuc.org.uk/blogs/trade-union-membership-growing-there%E2%80%99s-still-work-do); the US Bureau of Labor reported union density of 33.9 per cent in the public sector and 6.4 per cent in the private sector in 2018 (see www.bls.gov/news.release/union2.nro.htm). In South Africa, union density was 69.2 per cent in the public sector and 24.4 per cent in the private sector in 2013, among formal sector workers (see www.wider.unu.edu/sites/default/files/wp2015-141.pdf).
60. Lazar, S. (2017). *The Social Life of Politics. Ethics, Kinship and Activism in Argentine Unions*. Stanford University Press.
61. See http://allegralaboratory.net/towards-a-transnational-anthropology-union-universitycrisis.
62. Lazar, S. (ed.). (2017). *Where Are the Unions? Workers and Social Movements in Latin America, the Middle East, and Europe*. Zed Books; Thorkelson, E. (2016). Precarity Outside: The Political Unconscious of French Academic Labor. *American Ethnologist*, 43(3), 475–487.
63. See https://easaonline.org/publications/precarityrep.
64. See www.easaonline.org/newsletter/75-0120/guidelines.shtml.
65. E.g. see https://columbiagradunion.org.
66. Lazar, S. (2016). Notions of Work, Patrimony and Production in the Life of the Colón Opera House. *Journal of Latin American and Caribbean Anthropology*, 21(2), 231–253.
67. Compton, M. (2017). 'To Struggle Is Also to Teach': How Can Teachers and Teaching Unions Further the Global Fight for another World? In S. Lazar (ed.), *Where are the Unions? Workers and Social Movements in Latin America, the Middle East, and Europe* (pp. 144–166). Zed Books.
68. Blanc, E. (2019). *Red State Revolt: The Teachers' Strike Wave and Working-Class Politics*. Verso Books. See also www.theguardian.com/commentisfree/2018/dec/11/chicago-acero-charter-school-network-strike-won.
69. Senèn Gonzalez, C., Trajtemberg, D. & Medwid, B. (2009). La expansión de la afiliación sindical: análisis del módulo de relaciones laborales de la EIL. In Ministerio de Trabajo Gobierno de Argentina (ed.), *Trabajo, ocupación y*

empleo. Estudios laborales 2008 (pp. 13–34). Ministerio de Trabajo, Empleo y Seguridad Social.

6 *Platform Labour: Digital Management and Fragmented Collectivities*

1. Estimates from commercial sites: www.statista.com/statistics/617136/digital-population-worldwide and www.internetworldstats.com/stats.htm. For data to 2017 produced by researchers from Oxford University, see https://ourworldindata.org/internet.
2. Graham, M. & Woodcock, J. (2018). Towards a Fairer Platform Economy: Introducing the Fairwork Foundation. *Alternate Routes: A Journal of Critical Social Research*, 29(0); Gray, M. & Suri, S. (2019). *Ghost Work: How to Stop Silicon Valley from Building a New Global Underclass*. HMH Books; Wood, A. J., Lehdonvirta, V. & Graham, M. (2018). Workers of the Internet Unite? Online Freelancer Organisation among Remote Gig Economy Workers in Six Asian and African Countries. *New Technology, Work and Employment*, 33(2), 95–112.
3. Wood et al., Workers of the Internet Unite?
4. Wood, A. J., Graham, M., Lehdonvirta, V. & Hjorth, I. (2019). Networked but Commodified: The (Dis)embeddedness of Digital Labour in the Gig Economy. *Sociology*, 53(5), 931–950.
5. Huws, U. (2014). *Labor in the Global Digital Economy: The Cybertariat Comes of Age*. Monthly Review Press, 44.
6. Data for 9 August to 9 September 2020, retrieved on 9 September 2020 from NYU institute of data science, http://demographics.mturk-tracker.com/#/countries/all. Earlier in the year, figures were lower, between 65 and 70 per cent.
7. Srnicek, N. (2016). *Platform Capitalism*. Polity Press.
8. An extreme version of this is the aggregation of data that each of us produces in our use of social media sites like Facebook, smartphones, gaming and in internet searching. This production of data is also a form of digital labour, as we produce profit for large corporations in the form of advertising revenue, or even help refine Google's machine learning algorithms by identifying the content of images in a reCaptcha puzzle that declares to a web page that 'I am not a robot'. It is a process of the commodification of data, fragmented to the point of where we go (location data), what we click on, who we know, what else is on our phone, what permissions we grant to apps. Our data has become a significant source of profit, both now and potentially in the future.
9. Anwar, M. A. & Graham, M. (2020). Hidden Transcripts of the Gig Economy: Labour Agency and the New Art of Resistance among African Gig Workers. *Environment and Planning A: Economy and Space*, 52(7), 1269–1291.
10. Ravenelle, A. (2019). *Hustle and Gig: Struggling and Surviving in the Sharing Economy*. University of California Press; Rosenblat, A. (2019). *Uberland: How Algorithms Are Rewriting the Rules of Work*. University of California Press.
11. Cant, C. (2019). *Riding for Deliveroo: Resistance in the New Economy*. Polity Press.
12. Rosenblat, *Uberland*, 54.

13. Ravenelle, *Hustle and Gig*, 51, 54.

14. Rosenblat, *Uberland*, 67.

15. Woodcock, J. (2020). The Algorithmic Panopticon at Deliveroo: Measurement, Precarity, and the Illusion of Control. *Ephemera*, 20(3), 67–95.

16. Rosenblat, *Uberland*, 38.

17. Wood, A. J., Graham, M., Lehdonvirta, V. & Hjorth, I. (2019). Good Gig, Bad Gig: Autonomy and Algorithmic Control in the Global Gig Economy. *Work, Employment and Society*, 33(1), 56–75.

18. Gray & Suri, *Ghost Work*.

19. Wood et al., Good Gig, Bad Gig, 67.

20. Ibid., 64.

21. Irani, L. (2013). The Cultural Work of Microwork. *New Media & Society*, 17(5), 720–739; Rosenblat, *Uberland*.

22. Rosenblat, *Uberland*.

23. Woodcock, The Algorithmic Panopticon.

24. Cant, *Riding for Deliveroo*.

25. Anwar & Graham, Hidden Transcripts, 8.

26. de Stefano, V. (2016). *The Rise of the 'Just-in-Time Workforce': On-Demand Work, Crowdwork and Labour Protection in the 'Gig-Economy'*. Conditions of Work and Employment Series. ILO.

27. See www.thenation.com/article/archive/how-crowdworkers-became-ghosts-digital-machine/

28. Wood et al., Networked but Commodified.

29. Irani, The Cultural Work of Microwork; Scholz, T. (2016). *Uberworked and Underpaid: How Workers Are Disrupting the Digital Economy*. Wiley.

30. Wood et al., Networked but Commodified.

31. Gershon, I. & Cefkin, M. (2020). Click for Work: Rethinking Work through Online Work Distribution Platforms. *Ephemera*, 20(2).

32. Wood et al., Networked but Commodified, 940.

33. Rosenblat, *Uberland*, 219.

34. Ravenelle, *Hustle and Gig*.

35. Anwar & Graham, Hidden Transcripts.

36. Gray & Suri, *Ghost Work*.

37. See http://mturkforum.com/index.php.

38. See http://mturkforum.com/index.php?threads/finding-great-hits-09-09-whimsical-wintry-why-not-wednesday.15638.

39. See https://therideshareguy.com.

40. Irani, L. & Silberman, S. (2013). *Turkopticon: Interrupting Worker Invisibility in Amazon Mechanical Turk*. CHI.

41. Gray & Suri, *Ghost Work*; Salehi, N., Irani, L., Bernstein, M. S., Alkhatib, A., Ogbe, E., Milland, K. & Clickhappier. (2015). We Are Dynamo: Overcoming Stalling and Friction in Collective Action for Crowd Workers. In *Proceedings of the 33rd Annual ACM Conference on Human Factors in Computing Systems*, Seoul, Republic of Korea, 135–136.

42. See www.weareplanc.org/blog/a-new-initiative-rebel-roo-1.

43. Moyer-Lee, J. & Chango Lopez, H. (2017). From Invisible to Invincible: The Story of the 3 Cosas Campaign. In S. Lazar (ed.), *Where Are the Unions? Workers*

and Social Movements in Latin America, the Middle East, and Europe (pp. 231–250). Zed books.

44. Williams, E. C. (2013). Invisible Organization: Reading Romano Alquati. *Viewpoint Magazine.* Retrieved from https://viewpointmag.com/2013/09/26/invisible-organization-reading-romano-alquati.

45. Aslam, Y. & Woodcock, J. (2020). A History of Uber Organizing in the UK. *South Atlantic Quarterly,* 119(2), 412–421.

46. See www.ft.com/content/6b28cb8a-da35-4f02-87cd-780984e6a3ad; www.ft.com/content/11e2e1bf-c1dd-47cc-81b2-2147433ff16d.

47. See www.theguardian.com/us-news/2020/nov/11/california-proposition-22-uber-lyft-doordash-labor-laws. Prop 22 was authored by Uber, Lyft, Doordash and Instacart. They proposed a minimum earnings guarantee and limited healthcare provisions based on hours worked. See www.theguardian.com/us-news/2020/oct/15/proposition-22-california-ballot-measure-explained.

48. See http://faircrowd.work/en/index.html.

49. Graham & Woodcock, Towards a Fairer Platform Economy. See also https://fair.work/en/fw/homepage.

50. Borkin, S. (2019). *Platform Co-operatives – Solving the Capital Conundrum.* Nesta. Retrieved from https://media.nesta.org.uk/documents/Nesta_Platform_Report_FINAL-WEB_b1qZGj7.pdf; Scholz, *Uberworked and Underpaid.*

51. See https://medium.com/@GigWorkersCollective/instacart-emergency-walk-off-ebdf11b6995a.

7 Patchwork Living

1. Names are pseudonyms.

2. Hart, K. (1973). Informal Income Opportunities and Urban Employment in Ghana. *The Journal of Modern African Studies,* 11(1), 61–89; Peattie, L. (1987). An Idea in Good Currency and How it Grew: The Informal Sector. *World Development,* 15(7), 851–860; Denning, M. (2010). Wageless Life. *New Left Review,* 66, 79–96.

3. Narotsky, S. & Besnier, N. (2014). Crisis, Value, and Hope: Rethinking the Economy: An Introduction to Wenner-Gren Symposium Supplement 9. *Current Anthropology,* 55(S9), S4–S16, here S6.

4. Ibid., S6.

5. Davis, M. (2004). Planet of Slums. *New Left Review,* 26. Retrieved from https://newleftreview.org/issues/ii26/articles/mike-davis-planet-of-slums; Federici, S. (2012). *Revolution at Point Zero: Housework, Reproduction, and Feminist Struggle.* PM Press.

6. Census data from Instituto Nacional de Estadística Bolivia, retrieved from www.ine.gob.bo/index.php/estadisticas-sociales/vivienda-y-servicios-basicos/censos-vivienda.

7. Ødegaard, C. V. (2016). *Mobility, Markets and Indigenous Socialities: Contemporary Migration in the Peruvian Andes.* Taylor & Francis, 189.

8. Schuster, C. E. (2015). *Social Collateral: Women and Microfinance in Paraguay's Smuggling Economy.* University of California Press.

9. Pinheiro-Machado, R. (2018). The Power of Chineseness: Flexible Taiwanese Identities amidst Times of Change in Asia and Latin America. *The Journal of Latin American and Caribbean Anthropology*, 23(1), 56–73.

10. Schuster, *Social Collateral*.

11. Sopranzetti, C. (2017). *Owners of the Map: Motorcycle Taxi Drivers, Mobility, and Politics in Bangkok*. University of California Press, 109–116.

12. Hart, Informal Income Opportunities.

13. Gandolfo, D. (2013). Formless: A Day at Lima's Office of Formalization. *Cultural Anthropology*, 28(2), 278–298; Millar, K. (2018). *Reclaiming the Discarded: Life and Labor on Rio's Garbage Dump*. Duke University Press; Lazar, S. (2012). A Desire to Formalize Work? Comparing Trade Union strategies in Bolivia and Argentina. *Anthropology of Work Review*, 33(1), 15–24; Standing, G. (1989). Global Feminisation through Flexible Labour. *World Development*, 17(7), 1077–1095.

14. Millar, *Reclaiming the Discarded*.

15. Davis, M. (2004). The Urbanization of Empire: Megacities and the Laws of Chaos. *Social Text*, 22(4(81)), 9–15; Millar, *Reclaiming the Discarded*; Davis, Planet of Slums.

16. de Soto, H. (1989). *The Other Path: The Invisible Revolution in the Third World*. I. B. Tauris & Co.

17. Barchiesi, F. (2011). *Precarious Liberation: Workers, the State, and Contested Social Citizenship in Postapartheid South Africa*. State University of New York Press, 18.

18. Ferguson, J. (2015). *Give a Man a Fish: Reflections on the New Politics of Distribution*. Duke University Press.

19. Ferguson, J. (2013). Declarations of Dependence: Labour, Personhood, and Welfare in Southern Africa. *Journal of the Royal Anthropological Institute*, 19(2), 223–242.

20. Auyero, J. (2001). *Poor People's Politics: Peronist Survival Networks and the Legacy of Evita*. Duke University Press; Bayart, J.-F. (1993). *The State in Africa: The Politics of the Belly*. Longman; Ferguson, *Give a Man a Fish*; Lazar, S. (2004). Personalist Politics, Clientelism and Citizenship: Local Elections in El Alto, Bolivia. *Bulletin of Latin American Research*, 23(2).

21. Roberman, S. (2014). Labour Activation Policies and the Seriousness of Simulated Work. *Social Anthropology*, 22(3), 326–339, here 328.

22. Cruikshank, B. (1999). *The Will to Empower: Democratic Citizens and Other Subjects*. Cornell University Press; Dickinson, M. (2016). Working for Food Stamps: Economic Citizenship and the Post-Fordist Welfare State in New York City. *American Ethnologist*, 43(2), 270–281; Ong, A. (2003). *Buddha Is Hiding: Refugees, Citizenship, the New America*. University of California Press.

23. Dickinson, Working for Food Stamps.

24. Narotsky & Besnier, Crisis, Value, and Hope, S6.

25. Han, C. (2012). *Life in Debt: Times of Care and Violence in Neoliberal Chile*. University of California Press.

26. Auyero, J. (2012). *Patients of the State: The Politics of Waiting in Argentina*. Duke University Press.

27. Dickinson, Working for Food Stamps.

28. Ibid., 275.

29. Diz, A. (2016). The Afterlife of Abundance: Wageless Life, Politics, and Illusion among the Guaraní of the Argentine Chaco. PhD thesis, London School of Economics.

30. Neumark, T. (2014). Caring for Relations – an Ethnography of Unconditional Cash Transfers in a Nairobi Slum. PhD thesis, Cambridge.

31. Diz, The Afterlife of Abundance.

32. See www.bja.gob.bo.

33. This is enabled by allowing payment in food stamps to count towards the requirement to pay the minimum wage. Dickinson, Working for Food Stamps; Cruikshank, The Will to Empower.

34. Neumark, Caring for Relations.

35. Han, Life in Debt.

36. Neumark, Caring for Relations.

37. Cruikshank, The Will to Empower; Ong, Buddha is Hiding.

38. Diz, The Afterlife of Abundance.

39. Millar, Reclaiming the Discarded.

40. Sandel, M. (1984). The Procedural Republic and the Unencumbered Self. Political Theory, 12(1), 81–96.

41. Ferguson, Give a Man a Fish.

42. Wilkis, A. (2017). The Moral Power of Money: Morality and Economy in the Life of the Poor. Stanford University Press, 57; Millar, Reclaiming the Discarded.

43. O'Hare, P. (2022). Rubbish Belongs to the Poor: Hygienic Enclosure and the Waste Commons. Pluto Press.

44. Sopranzetti, Owners of the Map, 116.

45. Ibid., 117.

46. O'Hare, Rubbish Belongs to the Poor.

47. Ødegaard, Mobility, Markets and Indigenous Socialities, 131.

48. Goldstein, D. (2016). Owners of the Sidewalk: Security and Survival in the Informal City. Duke University Press.

49. Stensrud, A. B. (2017). Precarious Entrepreneurship: Mobile Phones, Work and Kinship in Neoliberal Peru. Social Anthropology, 25(2), 159–173, here 160, 162. The nephew was the son of Isabel's second cousin.

50. Ordoñez, J. T. (2015). Jornalero: Being a Day Laborer in the USA. University of California Press. I first saw this practice of workers waiting to be picked up by employers for day work in Bolivia, and thought it to be characteristic of poor countries. It is certainly widespread across the Global South. I was surprised to read that it is common also in California, one of the richest economies in the world. But this speaks to my point about the analytical strategies of formal/informal bringing to the fore unexpected informalities – or informalities in unexpected places.

51. Frequently, contractors fail to pay the agreed upon wages, sometimes not paying at all, or leave their workers in an unfamiliar location at the end of the day, creating transportation problems for those unfamiliar with the wealthy areas of Berkeley where they work. Workers also risk injury in unregulated and dangerous work conditions. However, their undocumented status means that

the workers are reluctant to pursue grievances via the limited official channels available to them.

52. Lazar, S. (2008). *El Alto, Rebel City: Self and Citizenship in Andean Bolivia*. Duke University Press.
53. Forment, C. A. (2015). Ordinary Ethics and the Emergence of Plebeian Democracy across the Global South: Buenos Aires's La Salada Market. *Current Anthropology, 56*(S11), S116–S125.
54. Goldstein, *Owners of the Sidewalk*.
55. Fikes, K. (2009). *Managing African Portugal. The Citizen-Migrant Distinction*. Duke University Press.
56. Lazar, *El Alto, Rebel City*.
57. Gandolfo, D. (2009). *The City at Its Limits: Taboo, Transgression, and Urban Renewal in Lima*. University of Chicago Press.
58. Millar, *Reclaiming the Discarded*, 78.
59. Gibbings, S. L. (2021). *Shadow Play: Information Politics in Urban Indonesia*. University of Toronto Press.
60. Millar, *Reclaiming the Discarded*; O'Hare, *Rubbish Belongs to the Poor*.
61. Lazar, *El Alto, Rebel City*.
62. Millar, *Reclaiming the Discarded*, 173–175. That said, neither formal nor informal collective associations could keep the dump open once the municipality had decided that it was full, and a few years later, only a small number of cooperative members were left.
63. Sopranzetti, *Owners of the Map*, 1.
64. Ibid.
65. Agarwala, R. (2013). *Informal Labor, Formal Politics, and Dignified Discontent in India*. Cambridge University Press.
66. Neumark, Caring for Relations.
67. Manzano, V. (2015). Lugar, Trabajo y Bienestar: La Organizacion Barrial Tupac Amaru en clave de Politica Relacional. *Publicar, 19*(19); Manzano, V. (2017). Dilemmas of Trade Unionism and the Movement of the Unemployed under Neoliberal and Progressive Regimes in Argentina. In S. Lazar (ed.), *Where Are the Unions? Workers and Social Movements in Latin America, the Middle East, and Europe* (pp. 209–230). Zed Books.
68. Wilkis, *The Moral Power of Money*. See also Auyero, *Poor People's Politics*.
69. Roberts, B. R. (1995). *The Making of Citizens: Cities of Peasants Revisited*. Arnold.
70. Narotsky & Besnier, Crisis, Value, and Hope, S6.

8 Social Reproduction Labour

1. Fisher, J. (2018). In Search of Dignified Work: Gender and the Work Ethic in the Crucible of Fair Trade Production. *American Ethnologist, 45*(1), 74–86, here 81.
2. Aulino, F. (2016). Rituals of Care for the Elderly in Northern Thailand: Merit, Morality, and the Everyday of Long-Term Care. *American Ethnologist, 43*(1), 91–102, here 93–95.
3. My concern at the time was that it might be overly heteronormative to focus on childcare in particular, even though having children has been the single

biggest thing to affect my professional life as a woman. Although my partner and I share childcare and cleaning, our usual practice is to employ a cleaner for a few hours a week, and that has probably been the main thing that improved my quality of life once we had children. During lockdown, as a family we returned to doing the weekly clean ourselves, underlining for me just how the privilege of being able to pay for a cleaner gives me the luxury of a weekend. These concerns feel both mundane and hugely consequential to me, and certainly affect the anthropology that I do.

4. Bhattacharya, T. (2017). *Social Reproduction Theory: Remapping Class, Recentering Oppression*. Pluto Press.
5. Fraser, N. (2017). Crisis of Care On the Social-Reperoductive Contradictions of Contemporary Capitalism. In T. Bhattacharya (ed.), *Social Reproduction Theory: Remapping Class, Recentering Oppression* (pp. 21–36). Pluto Press.
6. Bhattacharya, *Social Reproduction Theory*, 2.
7. Hochschild, A. R. & Machung, A. (1989). *The Second Shift: Working Parents and the Revolution at Home*. Viking.
8. Fraser, Crisis of Care, 22.
9. Boris, E. (2019). *Making the Woman Worker: Precarious Labor and the Fight for Global Standards, 1919–2019*. Oxford University Press, 6–7.
10. Fraser, Crisis of Care, 25–26.
11. Boris, *Making the Woman Worker*; Davis, M. (2004). Planet of Slums. *New Left Review*, 26. Retrieved from https://newleftreview.org/issues/ii26/articles/mike-davis-planet-of-slums; Federici, S. (2012). *Revolution at Point Zero: Housework, Reproduction, and Feminist Struggle*. PM Press; Han, C. (2012). *Life in Debt: Times of Care and Violence in Neoliberal Chile*. University of California Press; Mattingly, C. (2014). *Moral Laboratories: Family Peril and the Struggle for a Good Life*. University of California Press; Millar, K. (2018). *Reclaiming the Discarded: Life and Labor on Rio's Garbage Dump*. Duke University Press.
12. Vergès, F. (2021). *A Decolonial Feminism*. Pluto Press.
13. Yarris, K. (2017). *Care Across Generations: Solidarity and Sacrifice in Transnational Families*. Stanford University Press.
14. Boris, *Making the Woman Worker*.
15. Coe, C. (2019). *The New American Servitude: Political Belonging among African Immigrant Home Care Workers*. NYU Press.
16. Boris, *Making the Woman Worker*, 219.
17. Janowski, M. & Kerlogue, F. (2007). *Kinship and Food in South East Asia*. Indiana University Press.
18. Besky, S. (2014). *The Darjeeling Distinction: Labor and Justice on Fair-Trade Tea Plantations in India*. University of California Press.
19. Patel, R. (2010). *Working the Night Shift: Women in India's Call Center Industry*. Stanford University Press; Mirchandani, K. (2012). *Phone Clones: Authenticity Work in the Transnational Service Economy*. Cornell University Press.
20. O'Keefe, T. & Courtois, A. (2019). 'Not One of the Family': Gender and Precarious Work in the Neoliberal University. *Gender, Work & Organization*, 26(4), 463–479.

21. Coe, *The New American Servitude*; Ehrenreich, B. & Hochschild, A. R. (eds). (2003). *Global Woman: Nannies, Maids and Sex Workers in the New Economy*. Granta.
22. Goldstein, D. (2016). *Owners of the Sidewalk: Security and Survival in the Informal City*. Duke University Press.
23. Ibid.
24. See Laura Bear's work for a discussion of this among shipbuilders in Kolkata. Bear, L. (2015). *Navigating Austerity: Currents of Debt along a South Asian River*. Stanford University Press, 70–72; Bear, L. (2018). The Vitality of Labour and its Ghosts. *Terrain*, 69. Retrieved from https://journals.openedition.org/terrain/16728.
25. Lazar, S. (2017). *The Social Life of Politics. Ethics, Kinship and Activism in Argentine Unions*. Stanford University Press.
26. Mattingly, *Moral Laboratories*.
27. Bridges, K. (2011). *Reproducing Race: An Ethnography of Pregnancy as a Site of Racialization*. University of California Press; Davis, D.-A. (2019). *Reproductive Injustice: Racism, Pregnancy, and Premature Birth*. NYU Press.
28. Mattingly, *Moral Laboratories*.
29. Ibid.
30. Han, *Life in Debt*.
31. Mattingly, *Moral Laboratories*.
32. Yarris, *Care Across Generations*, 19.
33. Ibid., 38–39.
34. Yarris points out that it really is mostly the daughter. Sometimes sons leave their children with their mother, but it is quite rare. Sons tend to send less money home in remittances.
35. Yarris, *Care Across Generations*, 77.
36. Verdugo Paiva, M. (2020). *The Work for Another Life: Motherly Labour, Educational Aspirations and a Reconsideration of Social Reproduction*. EASA.
37. Luttrell, W. (2020). *Children Framing Childhoods: Working-Class Kids' Visions of Care*. Policy Press, 97.
38. Nieuwenhuys, O. (2000). The Household Economy in the Commercial Exploitation of Children's Work: The Case of Kerala. In B. Schlemmer (ed.), *The Exploited Child* (pp. 278–291). Zed Books.
39. Kea, P. (2013). 'The Complexity of an Enduring Relationship': Gender, Generation, and the Moral Economy of the Gambian Mandinka Household. *Journal of the Royal Anthropological Institute*, 19(1): 102–119.
40. Leinaweaver, J. (2008). *The Circulation of Children: Kinship, Adoption, and Morality in Andean Peru*. Duke University Press, 127.
41. Jacquemin, M. (2006). Can The Language of Rights Get Hold Of The Complex Realities Of Child Domestic Work? The Case of Young Domestic Workers in Abidjan, Ivory Coast. *Childhood*, 13(3), 389–406.
42. Leinaweaver, *The Circulation of Children*, 127.
43. Coe, C. (2016). Orchestrating Care in Time: Ghanaian Migrant Women, Family, and Reciprocity. *American Anthropologist*, 118(1), 37–48, here 42.

44. Leinaweaver, J. B. (2010). Outsourcing Care: How Peruvian Migrants Meet Transnational Family Obligations. *Latin American Perspectives*, 37(5), 67–87, here 69.

45. Aulino, Rituals of Care.

46. Han, *Life in Debt*; Millar, *Reclaiming the Discarded*.

47. Kosnik, E. (2020). *Caring Agriculture*. EASA; Angé, O. (2018). *Barter and Social Regeneration in the Argentinean Andes*. Berghahn Books.

48. Wages against Housework essay, originally published in 1975, in Federici, *Revolution at Point Zero*, 17.

49. Weeks, K. (2011). *The Problem with Work: Feminism, Marxism, Antiwork Politics, and Postwork Imaginaries*. Duke University Press.

50. Arruzza, C., Bhattacharya, T. & Fraser, N. (2019). *Feminism for the 99%: A Manifesto*. Verso Books.

51. Combahee River Collective. (1974). The Combahee River Collective Statement. Retrieved from https://combaheerivercollective.weebly.com/the-combahee-river-collective-statement.html; hooks, b. (1982). *Ain't I A Woman. Black Women and Feminism*. Pluto Press; Lugones, M. (2010). Toward a Decolonial Feminism. *Hypatia*, 25(4), 742–759; Mohanty, C. (2002). 'Under Western Eyes' Revisited: Feminist Solidarity through Anticapitalist Struggles. *Signs: Journal of Women in Culture and Society*, 28(2), 500–535; Vergès, *A Decolonial Feminism*.

52. Mattingly, *Moral Laboratories*.

53. Nguyen, V.-K. (2010). *The Republic of Therapy: Triage and Sovereignty in West Africa's Time of AIDS*. Duke University Press.

54. Davis, *Reproductive Injustice*, 195.

55. Van Esterik, P. & R. A. O'Connor (2017). *The Dance of Nurture: Negotiating Infant Feeding*. Berghahn Books.

56. Boyer, K. (2011). 'The Way to Break the Taboo Is to Do the Taboo Thing': Breastfeeding in Public and Citizen-Activism in the UK. *Health & Place*, 17, 430–437.

57. Faircloth, C. (2013). *Militant Lactivism? Attachment Parenting and Intensive Motherhood in the UK and France*. Berghahn Books.

58. Zeiderman, A. (2013). Living Dangerously: Biopolitics and Urban Citizenship in Bogotá, Colombia. *American Ethnologist*, 40(1), 71–87.

59. Holston, J. (2008). *Insurgent Citizenship. Disjunctions of Democracy and Modernity in Brazil*. Princeton University Press.

60. Lund, S. (2011). Invaded City. *Focaal*, 2011(61), 33. See also James, D. (2013). Citizenship and Land in South Africa: From Rights to Responsibilities. *Critique of Anthropology*, 33(1), 26–46; Lazar, S. (2008). *El Alto, Rebel City: Self and Citizenship in Andean Bolivia*. Duke University Press.

61. Shever, E. (2012). *Resources for Reform: Oil and Neoliberalism in Argentina*. Stanford University Press.

62. Ibid., 170, 169.

63. Manzano, V. (2013). *La política en movimiento: Movilizaciones colectivas y políticas estatales en la vida del Gran Buenos Aires*. Prohistoria, 45 (my translation).

64. Auyero, J. (2001). *Poor People's Politics: Peronist Survival Networks and the Legacy of Evita*. Duke University Press; Manzano, *La política en movimiento*.

65. Alexander, P. (2010). Rebellion of the Poor: South Africa's Service Delivery Protests – a Preliminary Analysis. *Review of African Political Economy*, 37(123), 25–40.

66. Sinwell, L. (2017). Thembelihle Burning, Hope Rising. In T. Ngwane, L. Sinwell & I. Ness (eds), *Urban Revolt. State Power and the Rise of People's Movements in the Global South* (pp. 15–28). Haymarket Books, 24.

67. Lazar, *El Alto, Rebel City*.

68. Ngwane, T. (2017). The 'Spirit of Marikana' and the Resurgence of the Working-Class Movement in South Africa. In T. Ngwane, L. Sinwell & I. Ness (eds), *Urban Revolt: State Power and the Rise of People's Movements in the Global South* (pp. 29–50). Haymarket Books, 29.

69. Johnston, P. (1994). *Success while Others Fail: Social Movement Unionism and the Public Workplace*. ILR Press; Lopez, S. H. (2004). *Reorganizing the Rust Belt: An Inside Study of the American Labor Movement*. University of California Press; Waterman, P. (1993). Social-Movement Unionism: A New Union Model for a New World Order? *Review (Fernand Braudel Center)*, 16(3), 245–278.

70. Compton, M. (2017). 'To Struggle Is also to Teach': How Can Teachers and Teaching Unions Further the Global Fight for Another World? In S. Lazar (ed.), *Where Are the Unions? Workers and Social Movements in Latin America, the Middle East, and Europe* (pp. 144–166). Zed Books.

71. Blanc, E. (2019). *Red State Revolt: The Teachers' Strike Wave and Working-Class Politics*. Verso Books. See also Collins, J. (2012). Theorizing Wisconsin's 2011 Protests: Community-Based Unionism Confronts Accumulation by Dispossession. *American Ethnologist*, 39(1), 6–20.

Conclusion

1. Nash, J. (1993 [1979]). *We Eat the Mines and the Mines Eat Us* (Centennial edition). Columbia University Press.

2. Zlolniski, C. (2006). *Janitors, Street Vendors, and Activists: The Lives of Mexican Immigrants in Silicon Valley*. University of California Press; Lopez, S. H. (2004). *Reorganizing the Rust Belt: An Inside Study of the American Labor Movement*. University of California Press; Stacey, C. L. (2011). *The Caring Self: The Work Experiences of Home Care Aides*. Cornell University Press.

3. Nash, *We Eat the Mines*.

4. Mollona, M. (2009). Community Unionism versus Business Unionism: The Return of the Moral Economy in Trade Union Studies. *American Ethnologist*, 36(4), 651–666; Moody, K. (1997). Towards an International Social-Movement Unionism. *New Left Review*, I/225 (September–October). Retrieved from https://newleftreview.org/issues/i225/articles/kim-moody-towards-an-international-social-movement-unionism; Waterman, P. (1993). Social-Movement Unionism: A New Union Model for a New World Order? *Review (Fernand Braudel Center)*, 16(3), 245–278.

5. Kapesea, R. & McNamara, T. (2020). 'We Are Not Just a Union, We Are a Family' Class, Kinship and Tribe in Zambia's Mining Unions. *Dialectical Anthropology*, 44(2), 153–172; Lazar, S. (2017). *The Social Life of Politics: Ethics, Kinship and Activism in Argentine Unions*. Stanford University Press.

6. Scott, J. C. (1985). *Weapons of the Weak: Everyday Forms of Peasant Resistance.* Yale University Press, 350.

7. Pun, N. (2005). *Made in China: Women Factory Workers in a Global Workplace.* Duke University Press.

8. Mattingly, C. (2014). *Moral Laboratories: Family Peril and the Struggle for a Good Life.* University of California Press. See also Chapter 8.

9. Horton, S. B. (2016). *They Leave Their Kidneys in the Fields: Illness, Injury, and Illegality Among US Farmworkers.* University of California Press. See also Chapter 3.

10. Ong, A. (1988). The Production of Possession: Spirits and the Multinational Corporation in Malaysia. *American Ethnologist,* 15(1), 28–42.

11. Gershon, I. (2017). *Down and Out in the New Economy: How People Find (or Don't Find) Work Today.* University of Chicago Press.

12. Carswell, G. & De Neve, G. (2013). Labouring for Global Markets: Conceptualising Labour Agency in Global Production Networks. *Geoforum,* 44(0), 62–70. See also Chapter 2.

13. Holmes, S. (2013). *Fresh Fruit, Broken Bodies: Migrant Farmworkers in the United States.* University of California Press. See also Chapter 3.

14. Hondagneu-Sotelo, P. (2003). Blowups and Other Unhappy Endings. In B. Ehrenreich & A. R. Hochschild (eds), *Global Woman: Nannies, Maids and Sex Workers in the New Economy* (pp. 55–69). Granta. See also Chapter 4.

15. Carswell & De Neve, Labouring for Global Markets. See also Chapter 2.

16. Fang, I.-C. (2018). Precarity, Guanxi, and the Informal Economy of Peasant Workers in Contemporary China. In C. Hann & J. Parry (eds), *Industrial Labor on the Margins of Capitalism: Precarity, Class, and the Neoliberal Subject* (pp. 265–288). Berghahn.

17. Cant, C. (2019). *Riding for Deliveroo: Resistance in the New Economy.* Polity Press. See also Chapter 6.

18. Kwan Lee, C. (2018). Varieties of Capital, Fracture of Labor: A Comparative Ethnography of Subcontracting and Labor Precarity on the Zambian Copperbelt. In C. Hann & J. Parry (eds), *Industrial Labor on the Margins of Capitalism: Precarity, Class, and the Neoliberal Subject* (pp. 39–60). Berghahn; Strümpell, C. (2018). Precarious Labor and Precarious Livelihoods in an Indian Company Town. In C. Hann & J. Parry (eds), *Industrial Labor on the Margins of Capitalism: Precarity, Class, and the Neoliberal Subject* (pp. 134–154). Berghahn.

19. Stacey, *The Caring Self.*

20. Ibarra, M. (2010). My Reward Is not Money: Deep Alliances and End-of-Life Care among Mexicana Workers and Their Wards. In E. Boris & R. S. Parreñas (eds), *Intimate Labors: Cultures, Technologies, and the Politics of Care* (pp. 117–131). Stanford University Press.

21. Jaffe, S. (2021). *Work Won't Love You Back: How Devotion to Our Jobs Keeps Us Exploited, Exhausted, and Alone.* PublicAffairs; Weeks, K. (2011). *The Problem with Work: Feminism, Marxism, Antiwork Politics, and Postwork Imaginaries.* Duke University Press.

22. Loveday, V. (2018). The Neurotic Academic: Anxiety, Casualisation, and Governance in the Neoliberalising University. *Journal of Cultural Economy,* 11(2), 154–166.

Coda: The Covid-19 Pandemic and Labour: Continuities and the Potential for Change

1. Eckert, A. & Hentschke, F. (2020). *Corona and Work around the Globe*. De Gruyter.
2. Cucu, A.-S. (2020). 'It was Quiet': Pandemics as Normal Life in a Romanian Town. In A. Eckert & F. Hentschke (eds), *Corona and Work around the Globe* (pp. 10–18). De Gruyter, 10.
3. Corrêa, L. R. & Fontes, P. (2020). Maids in Brazil: Domestic and Platform Workers During the COVID-19 Pandemic. In A. Eckert & F. Hentschke (eds), *Corona and Work around the Globe* (pp. 37–42). De Gruyter.
4. Moore, S., Ball, C., Cari, M., Flynn, M. & Mulkearn, K. (2021). Research into Covid-19 Workplace Safety Outcomes in the Food and Drinks Sector. Retrieved from www.tuc.org.uk/sites/default/files/TUCHSreport.pdf.
5. Mayer-Ahuja, N. (2020). 'Solidarity' in Times of Corona? Of Migrant Ghettos, Low-Wage Heroines, and Empty Public Coffers. In A. Eckert & F. Hentschke (eds), *Corona and Work around the Globe* (pp. 19–27). De Gruyter.
6. Bear, L. et al. (2020). A Right to Care: The Social Foundations of Recovery from Covid-19. Retrieved from www.lse.ac.uk/anthropology/assets/documents/research/Covid-and-Care/ARighttoCare-CovidandCare-Final-1211.pdf.
7. Horton, S. B. (2016). *They Leave Their Kidneys in the Fields: Illness, Injury, and Illegality Among US Farmworkers*. University of California Press.
8. Banerjee, S. (2020). Skill, Informality, and Work in Pandemic Times: Insights from India. In A. Eckert & F. Hentschke (eds), *Corona and Work around the Globe* (pp. 3–9). De Gruyter.
9. Caminhas, L. (2021). Digital Platforms in the Brazilian Sex Markets. Retrieved from http://platformlabour.crassh.cam.ac.uk/2021/04/15/digital-platforms-in-the-brazilian-sex-markets-/index.html.
10. Litschel, L.-S. (2021). *The 'Old' Normal – Digital Day Laborers Stay Mobile 24/7 in Berlin*. (Remote) Work and Covid: Mobility, Safety, and Health at the Time of the Pandemic, Tallinn University, Estonia (online).
11. Cucu, 'It Was Quiet'.
12. Ibid., 18.
13. See https://globalhealth5050.org/the-sex-gender-and-covid-19-project; www.theguardian.com/society/2021/jun/13/why-are-women-more-prone-to-long-covid.
14. Cominetti, N., McCurdy, C. & Slaughter, H. (2021). Low Pay Britain 2021. Retrieved from www.resolutionfoundation.org/publications/low-pay-britain-2021.
15. Kenny, B. (2020). Coronavirus Conjunctures: Waged Work, Wagelessness, and Futures in South Africa. In A. Eckert & F. Hentschke (eds), *Corona and Work around the Globe* (pp. 43–51). De Gruyter; Kott, S. (2020). Work in Times of COVID-19: What is New and What is Not. A Western European Perspective. In A. Eckert & F. Hentschke (eds), *Corona and Work around the Globe* (pp. 225–230). De Gruyter; Tanaka, Y. (2020). State Dysfunction in a 'Fortunate' Japan.

In A. Eckert & F. Hentschke (eds), *Corona and Work around the Globe* (pp. 120–134). De Gruyter.

16. Kott, Work in Times of COVID-19.

17. Banerjee, Skill, Informality and Work; Corrêa & Fontes, Maids in Brazil.

18. Sehmi, R. & Slaughter, H. (2021). Double Trouble: Exploring the Labour Market and Mental Health Impact of Covid-19 on Young People. Retrieved from www.resolutionfoundation.org/publications/double-trouble.

19. See www.washingtonpost.com/world/europe/clap-for-carers/2020/03/26/3do5eb9c-6f66-11ea-a156-0048b62cdb51_story.html.

20. See www.waitrose.com/content/dam/waitrose/Inspiration/HOW%20BRITAIN%20SHOPS%20ONLINE%20FOOD%20&%20DRINK%20EDITION.pdf.

21. See www.theguardian.com/technology/2021/oct/17/small-firms-fury-as-amazon-offers-3000-sign-up-bonus-to-attract-christmas-staff; www.retailgazette.co.uk/blog/2021/08/ms-offers-new-lorry-drivers-2000-sign-on-bonus.

22. See www.theguardian.com/business/2022/jan/04/great-resignation-quitting-us-unemployment-economy.

23. Ilana Gershon, personal communication; see also Gershon, I. (2022). Plague Jobs: US Workers' Schismogenetic Approaches to Social Contracts. *Anthropological Notebooks*, 27(3). Retrieved from http://notebooks.drustvo-antropologov.si/Notebooks/article/view/503.

24. Corrêa & Fontes, Maids in Brazil; Kenny, Coronavirus Conjunctures; Mayer-Ahuja, 'Solidarity' in Times of Corona?

Bibliography

Agarwala, R. (2013). *Informal Labor, Formal Politics, and Dignified Discontent in India*. Cambridge University Press.

Alarcón-Medina, R. (2018). Informational Returnees: Deportation, Digital Media, and the Making of a Transnational Cybertariat in the Mexican Call Center Industry. *Dialectical Anthropology*, 42(3), 293–308.

Alexander, P. (2010). Rebellion of the Poor: South Africa's Service Delivery Protests – a Preliminary Analysis. *Review of African Political Economy*, 37(123), 25–40.

Anagnostopoulos, A. & Evangelinidis, A. (2017). The Experience of Grassroots Syndicalism in Greece: Workplace Restructuring and the Role of Traditional Trade Unions in the Tertiary Sector. In S. Lazar (ed.), *Where Are The Unions? Workers and Social Movements in Latin America, the Middle East and Europe*. Zed Books.

Aneesh, A. (2015). *Neutral Accent: How Language, Labor, and Life Become Global*. Duke University Press.

Anwar, M. A. & Graham, M. (2020). Hidden Transcripts of the Gig Economy: Labour Agency and the New Art of Resistance among African Gig Workers. *Environment and Planning A: Economy and Space*, 52(7), 1269–1291.

Aoyama, K. (2009). *Thai Migrant Sexworkers: From Modernisation to Globalisation*. Palgrave Macmillan.

Armelino, M. (2015). Reformas de mercado y reacciones sindicales en argentina: una revisión desde la experiencia de los trabajadores públicos. *Desarrollo Económico*, 55(216): 245–278.

Arruzza, C., Bhattacharya, T. & Fraser, N. (2019). *Feminism for the 99%: A Manifesto*. Verso.

Ashraf, H. & Prentice, R. (2019). Beyond Factory Safety: Labor Unions, Militant Protest, and the Accelerated Ambitions of Bangladesh's Export Garment Industry. *Dialectical Anthropology*, 43(1), 93–107.

Aslam, Y. & Woodcock, J. (2020). A History of Uber Organizing in the UK. *South Atlantic Quarterly*, 119(2), 412–421.

Aulino, F. (2016). Rituals of Care for the Elderly in Northern Thailand: Merit, Morality, and the Everyday of Long-Term Care. *American Ethnologist*, 43(1), 91–102.

Auyero, J. (2001). *Poor People's Politics: Peronist Survival Networks and the Legacy of Evita*. Duke University Press.

Auyero, J. (2012). *Patients of the State: The Politics of Waiting in Argentina*. Duke University Press.

Banerjee, S. (2020). Skill, Informality, and Work in Pandemic Times: Insights from India. In A. Eckert & F. Hentschke (eds), *Corona and Work around the Globe* (pp. 3–9). De Gruyter.

Barchiesi, F. (2011). *Precarious Liberation: Workers, the State, and Contested Social Citizenship in Postapartheid South Africa*. State University of New York Press.

Barrientos, S. (2013). Corporate Purchasing Practices in Global Production Networks: A Socially Contested Terrain. *Geoforum, 44*, 44–51.

Barua, R. (2015). The Textile Labour Association and Dadagiri: Power and Politics in the Working-Class Neighborhoods of Ahmedabad. *International Labor and Working-Class History, 87*, 63–91.

Bautista, J. (2015). Export-Quality Martyrs: Roman Catholicism and Transnational Labor in the Philippines. *Cultural Anthropology, 30*(3), 424–447.

Bayart, J.-F. (1993). *The State in Africa: The Politics of the Belly*. Longman.

Bear, L. (2014). For labour: Ajeet's Accident and the Ethics of Technological Fixes in Time. *Journal of the Royal Anthropological Institute, 20*(S1), 71–88.

Bear, L. (2015). *Navigating Austerity: Currents of Debt along a South Asian River*. Stanford University Press.

Bear, L. (2018). The Vitality of Labour and its Ghosts. *Terrain, 69*. Retrieved from https://journals.openedition.org/terrain/16728.

Bear, L., Ho, K., Tsing, A. L. & Yanagisako, S. (2015). Gens: A Feminist Manifesto for the Study of Capitalism. Fieldsights – Theorizing the Contemporary. Retrieved from https://culanth.org/fieldsights/gens-a-feminist-manifesto-for-the-study-of-capitalism.

Bear, L., James, D., Simpson, N. & et al. (2020). A Right to Care: The Social Foundations of Recovery from Covid-19. Retrieved from www.lse.ac.uk/anthropology/assets/documents/research/Covid-and-Care/ARighttoCare-CovidandCare-Final-1211.pdf.

Bello, W. (1994). *Dark Victory: The United States, Structural Adjustment and Global Poverty*. Pluto Press.

Bernstein, E. (2010). Bounded Authenticity and the Commerce of Sex. In E. Boris & R. S. Parreñas (eds), *Intimate Labors. Cultures, Technologies, and the Politics of Care* (pp. 148–165). Stanford University Press.

Besky, S. (2014). *The Darjeeling Distinction: Labor and Justice on Fair-Trade Tea Plantations in India*. University of California Press.

Beynon, H. (1973). *Working For Ford*. Penguin.

Bhatt, E. (2006). *We Are Poor but So Many: The Story of Self-Employed Women in India*. Oxford University Press.

Bhattacharya, T. (2017). *Social Reproduction Theory: Remapping Class, Recentering Oppression*. Pluto Press.

Bithymitris, G. & Spyridakis, M. (2020). Union Radicalism versus the Nationalist Upsurge: The Case of Greek Shipbuilding Workers. *Dialectical Anthropology, 44*(2), 121–135.

Blanc, E. (2019). *Red State Revolt: The Teachers' Strike Wave and Working-Class Politics*. Verso.

Bolt, M. (2015). *Zimbabwe's Migrants and South Africa's Border Farms*. Cambridge University Press.

Boris, E. (2019). *Making the Woman Worker: Precarious Labor and the Fight for Global Standards, 1919–2019*. Oxford University Press.

Borkin, S. (2019). *Platform Co-operatives – Solving the Capital Conundrum.* Nesta. Retrieved from https://media.nesta.org.uk/documents/Nesta_Platform_Report_FINAL-WEB_b1qZGj7.pdf.

Born, G. (2005). *Uncertain Vision: Birt, Dyke and the Reinvention of the BBC.* Vintage.

Bourdieu, P. (1986). *Distinction: A Social Critique of the Judgement of Taste.* Routledge.

Boyer, K. (2011). 'The Way to Break the Taboo Is to Do the Taboo Thing': Breastfeeding in Public and Citizen-Activism in the UK. *Health & Place* 17: 430–437.

Bridges, K. (2011). *Reproducing Race: An Ethnography of Pregnancy As a Site of Racialization.* University of California Press.

Brown, H. & Green, M. (2017). Demonstrating Development: Meetings as Management in Kenya's Health Sector. *Journal of the Royal Anthropological Institute*, 23(S1), 45–62.

Caminhas, L. (2021). Digital Platforms in the Brazilian Sex Markets. Retrieved from http://platformlabour.crassh.cam.ac.uk/2021/04/15/digital-platforms-in-the-brazilian-sex-markets-/index.html.

Campbell, B. (2018). Moral Ecologies of Subsistence and Labour in a Migration-Affected Community of Nepal. *Journal of the Royal Anthropological Institute*, 24(S1), 151–165.

Campbell, S. (2016). Putting-Out's Return. *Focaal – Journal of Global and Historical Anthropology*, 2016(76), 71–84.

Cant, C. (2019). *Riding for Deliveroo. Resistance in the New Economy.* Wiley

Carbonella, A. & Kasmir, S. (2014). Introduction: Toward a Global Anthropology of Labor. In S. Kasmir & A. Carbonella (eds), *Blood and Fire: A Global Anthropology of Labor* (pp. 1–29). Berghahn.

Carrier, J. & Kalb, D. (eds) (2015). *Anthropologies of Class.* Cambridge University Press.

Carswell, G. & De Neve, G. (2013). Labouring for Global Markets: Conceptualising Labour Agency in Global Production Networks. *Geoforum*, 44(0), 62–70.

Carswell, G. & De Neve, G. (2018). Towards a Political Economy of Skill and Garment Work: The Case of the Tiruppur Industrial Cluster in South India In C. Hann & J. Parry (eds), *Industrial Labor on the Margins of Capitalism: Precarity, Class, and the Neoliberal Subject* (pp. 309–335). Berghahn.

Chan, J. (2013). A Suicide Survivor: The Life of a Chinese Worker. *New Technology, Work and Employment*, 28(2), 84–99.

Chan, J. (2017). Intern Labor in China. *Rural China*, 38, 82–100.

Chan, J., Pun, N. & Selden, M. (2013). The Politics of Global Production: Apple, Foxconn and China's New Working Class. *New Technology, Work and Employment*, 28(2), 100–115.

Chan, J., Pun, N. & Selden, M. (2015). Interns or Workers? China's Student Labor Regime. *The Asia-Pacific Journal*, 13(36).

Chan, J., Selden, M. & Pun, N. (2020). *Dying for an iPhone: Apple, Foxconn, and The Lives of China's Workers.* Haymarket Books.

Chong, K. (2018). *Best Practice: Management Consulting and the Ethics of Financialization in China.* Duke University Press.

Cobble, D. S. (2010). More Intimate Unions. In E. Boris & R. S. Parreñas (eds), *Intimate Labors. Cultures, Technologies, and the Politics of Care* (pp. 280–296). Stanford University Press.

Coe, C. (2016). Orchestrating Care in Time: Ghanaian Migrant Women, Family, and Reciprocity. *American Anthropologist, 118*(1), 37–48.

Coe, C. (2019). *The New American Servitude: Political Belonging among African Immigrant Home Care Workers.* NYU Press.

Collins, J. (2003). *Threads. Gender, Labour, and Power in the Global Apparel Industry.* University of Chicago Press.

Collins, J. (2012). Theorizing Wisconsin's 2011 Protests: Community-Based Unionism Confronts Accumulation by Dispossession. *American Ethnologist, 39*(1), 6–20.

Combahee River Collective. (1974). The Combahee River Collective Statement. Retrieved from https://combaheerivercollective.weebly.com/the-combahee-river-collective-statement.html.

Cominetti, N., McCurdy, C. & Slaughter, H. (2021). *Low Pay Britain 2021.* Resolution Foundation.

Compton, M. (2017). 'To Struggle Is also to Teach': How Can Teachers and Teaching Unions Further the Global Fight for another World? In S. Lazar (ed.), *Where Are the Unions? Workers and Social Movements in Latin America, the Middle East, and Europe* (pp. 144–166). Zed Books.

Corrêa, L. R. & Fontes, P. (2020). Maids in Brazil: Domestic and Platform Workers During the COVID-19 Pandemic. In A. Eckert & F. Hentschke (eds), *Corona and Work around the Globe* (pp. 37–42). De Gruyter.

Correia, J. E. (2019). Soy States: Resource Politics, Violent Environments and Soybean Territorialization in Paraguay. *The Journal of Peasant Studies, 46*(2), 316–336.

Costa, M. D. & James, S. (1973). *The Power of Women and the Subversion of the Community.* Falling Wall Press.

Cruikshank, B. (1999). *The Will to Empower: Democratic Citizens and Other Subjects.* Cornell University Press.

Cucu, A.-S. (2020). 'It was Quiet': Pandemics as Normal Life in a Romanian Town. In A. Eckert & F. Hentschke (eds), *Corona and Work around the Globe* (pp. 10–18). De Gruyter.

Davis, D.-A. (2019). *Reproductive Injustice: Racism, Pregnancy, and Premature Birth.* NYU Press.

Davis, M. (2004). Planet of Slums. *New Left Review, 26.* Retrieved from https://newleftreview.org/issues/ii26/articles/mike-davis-planet-of-slums.

Davis, M. (2004). The Urbanization of Empire: Megacities and the Laws of Chaos. *Social Text, 22*(4(81)), 9–15.

de Genova, N. (2005). *Working the Boundaries. Race, Space, and 'Illegality' in Mexican Chicago.* Duke University Press.

de L'Estoile, B. (2014). 'Money Is Good, but a Friend Is Better': Uncertainty, Orientation to the Future, and 'the Economy'. *Current Anthropology, 55*(S9), S62–S73.

De Neve, G. (2008). Global Garment Chains, Local Labour Activism: New Challenges to Trade Union and NGO Activism in the Tiruppur Garment

Cluster, South India. In G. De Neve, P. Luetchford, J. Pratt & D. C. Wood (eds), *Hidden Hands in the Market: Ethnographies of Fair Trade, Ethical Consumption, and Corporate Social Responsibility* (pp. 213–240). Emerald Insight.

De Neve, G. (2014). Entrapped Entrepreneurship: Labour Contractors in the South Indian Garment Industry. *Modern Asian Studies, 48*(5), 1302–1333.

de Soto, H. (1989). *The Other Path: The Invisible Revolution in the Third World*. I.B. Tauris & Co.

de Stefano, V. (2016). *The Rise of the 'Just-in-Time Workforce': On-Demand Work, Crowdwork and Labour Protection in the 'Gig-Economy'*. Conditions of Work and Employment Series. ILO.

Denning, M. (2010). Wageless Life. *New Left Review, 66*, 79–96.

Dickinson, M. (2016). Working for Food Stamps: Economic Citizenship and the Post-Fordist Welfare State in New York City. *American Ethnologist, 43*(2), 270–281.

Diz, A. (2016). *The Afterlife of Abundance: Wageless Life, Politics, and Illusion among the Guaraní of the Argentine Chaco*. Retrieved from http://etheses.lse.ac.uk/3460/

Dowling, E., Nunes, R. & Trott, B. (2007). Immaterial and Affective Labour: Explored. *Ephemera. Theory and Politics in Organization, 7*.

Dunn, E. (2004). *Privatizing Poland: Baby Food, Big Business, and the Remaking of Labor*. Cornell University Press.

Durrenberger, E. P. & Erem, S. (2005). *Class Acts: An Anthropology of Urban Workers and their Union*. Paradigm.

Eagleton, T. (2015). The Slow Death of the University. *The Chronicle of Higher Education*.

Eckert, A. & Hentschke, F. (2020). *Corona and Work around the Globe*. De Gruyter.

Ehrenreich, B. & Hochschild, A. R. (eds). (2003). *Global Woman: Nannies, Maids and Sex Workers in the New Economy*. Granta.

Elson, D. & Pearson, R. (1981). 'Nimble Fingers Make Cheap Workers': An Analysis of Women's Employment in Third World Export Manufacturing. *Feminist Review*(7), 87–107.

Fabricant, N. (2012). *Mobilizing Bolivia's Displaced: Indigenous Politics & the Struggle Over Land*. University of North Carolina Press.

Fang, I.-C. (2018). Precarity, Guanxi, and the Informal Economy of Peasant Workers in Contemporary China In C. Hann & J. Parry (eds), *Industrial Labor on the Margins of Capitalism: Precarity, Class, and the Neoliberal Subject* (pp. 265–288). Berghahn.

Faircloth, C. (2013). *Militant Lactivism? Attachment Parenting and Intensive Motherhood in the UK and France*. Berghahn.

Federici, S. (2012). *Revolution at Point Zero: Housework, Reproduction, and Feminist Struggle*. PM Press.

Federici, S. (2020 [2011]). On Affective Labor. In S. Federici (ed.), *Revolution at Point Zero: Housework, Reproduction, and Feminist Struggle* (2nd edition, pp. 49–56). PM Press.

Ferguson, J. (1999). *Expectations of Modernity: Myths and Meanings of Urban Life on the Zambian Copperbelt* University of California Press.

Ferguson, J. (2013). Declarations of Dependence: Labour, Personhood, and Welfare in Southern Africa. *Journal of the Royal Anthropological Institute, 19*(2), 223–242.

Ferguson, J. (2015). *Give a Man a Fish: Reflections on the New Politics of Distribution.* Duke University Press.

Fernandez Alvarez, M. I. (2019). 'Having a Name of One's Own, Being Part of History': Temporalities and Political Subjectivities of Popular Economy Workers in Argentina. *Dialectical Anthropology, 43*(1), 61–76.

Fikes, K. (2009). *Managing African Portugal. The Citizen-Migrant Distinction.* Duke University Press.

Fisher, J. (2018). In Search of Dignified Work: Gender and the Work Ethic in the Crucible of Fair Trade Production. *American Ethnologist, 45*(1), 74–86.

Forment, C. A. (2015). Ordinary Ethics and the Emergence of Plebeian Democracy across the Global South: Buenos Aires's La Salada Market. *Current Anthropology, 56*(S11), S116–S125.

Fraser, N. (2017). Crisis of Care On the Social-Reperoductive Contradictions of Contemporary Capitalism. In T. Bhattacharya (ed.), *Social Reproduction Theory: Remapping Class, Recentering Oppression* (pp. 21–36). Pluto Press.

Gandolfo, D. (2009). *The City at Its Limits: Taboo, Transgression, and Urban Renewal in Lima.* University of Chicago Press.

Gandolfo, D. (2013). Formless: A Day at Lima's Office of Formalization. *Cultural Anthropology, 28*(2), 278–298.

Gershon, I. (2017). *Down and Out in the New Economy: How People Find (or Don't Find) Work Today.* University of Chicago Press.

Gershon, I. (2022). Plague Jobs: US Workers' Schismogenetic Approaches to Social Contracts. *Anthropological Notebooks, 27*(3). Retrieved from http://notebooks. drustvo-antropologov.si/Notebooks/article/view/503.

Gershon, I. & Cefkin, M. (2020). Click for Work: Rethinking Work through Online Work Distribution Platforms. *Ephemera, 20*(2).

Gibbings, S. L. (2021). *Shadow Play: Information Politics in Urban Indonesia.* University of Toronto Press.

Gilbert, D. E. (2020). Laborers Becoming 'Peasants': Agroecological Politics in a Sumatran Plantation Zone. *The Journal of Peasant Studies, 47*(5), 1030–1051.

Gilbert, D. E. & Afrizal. (2019). The Land Exclusion Dilemma and Sumatra's Agrarian Reactionaries. *The Journal of Peasant Studies, 46*(4), 681–701.

Gill, L. (1994). *Precarious Dependencies: Gender, Class, and Domestic Service in Bolivia.* Columbia University Press.

Goldstein, D. (2016). *Owners of the Sidewalk: Security and Survival in the Informal City.* Duke University Press.

Goodfriend, H. (2018). 'Where You From?': Deportación, identidad y trabajo reciclado en el call center salvadoreño. *Latin American Research Review, 53*(2), 303–317.

Graeber, D. (2011). *Debt. The First 5,000 Years.* Melville House.

Graeber, D. (2018). *Bullshit Jobs: A Theory.* Penguin.

Graham, M. & Woodcock, J. (2018). Towards a Fairer Platform Economy: Introducing the Fairwork Foundation. *Alternate Routes: A Journal of Critical Social Research, 29*(0).

Gray, M. a. & Suri, S. (2019). *Ghost Work: How to Stop Silicon Valley from Building a New Global Underclass.* HMH Books.

Green, M. (2003). Globalizing Development in Tanzania. Policy Franchising through Participatory Project Management. *Critique of Anthropology*, 23(2), 123–143.

Grisaffi, T. (2019). *Coca Yes, Cocaine No: How Bolivia's Coca Growers Reshaped Democracy*. Duke University Press.

Guevarra, A. R. (2010). *Marketing Dreams, Manufacturing Heroes: The Transnational Labor Brokering of Filipino Workers*. New Brunswick, NJ: Rutgers University Press.

Guthman, J. (2019). *Wilted: Pathogens, Chemicals, and the Fragile Future of the Strawberry Industry*. University of California Press.

Gutmann, M. (1993). Rituals of Resistance: A Critique of the Theory of Everyday Forms of Resistance. *Latin American Perspectives*, 20(2), 74–92.

Han, C. (2012). *Life in Debt: Times of Care and Violence in Neoliberal Chile*. University of California Press.

Hann, C. & Parry, J. (eds). (2018). *Industrial Labor on the Margins of Capitalism: Precarity, Class, and the Neoliberal Subject*. Berghahn.

Hardt, M. & Negri, A. (2005). *Multitude*. Hamish Hamilton.

Hardt, M. & Negri, A. (2017). *Assembly*. Oxford University Press.

Harris, O. (2007). What Makes People Work? In R. Astuti, J. Parry & C. Stafford (eds), *Questions of Anthropology*. Berg.

Hart, K. (1973). Informal Income Opportunities and Urban Employment in Ghana. *The Journal of Modern African Studies*, 11(1), 61–89.

Harvey, D. (2001). Globalization and the 'Spatial Fix'. *Geographische Revue*, 3(2), 23–30.

Harvey, D. (2004) The 'New' Imperialism: Accumulation by Dispossession. *Socialist Register*, 40.

Herod, A. (1997). From a Geography of Labor to a Labor Geography: Labor's Spatial Fix and theGeography of Capitalism. *Antipode*, 29(1), 1–31.

Hetherington, K. (2013). Beans Before the Law: Knowledge Practices, Responsibility, and the Paraguayan Soy Boom. *Cultural Anthropology*, 28(1): 65–85.

Hetherington, K. (2011). *Guerrilla Auditors: The Politics of Transparency in Neoliberal Paraguay*. Duke University Press.

Ho, K. (2009). *Liquidated. An ethnography of Wall Street*. Duke University Press.

Hoang, K. K. (2010). Economics of Emotion, Familiarity, Fantasty, and Desire: Emotional Labor in Ho Chi Minh City's Sex Industry. In E. Boris & R. S. Parreñas (eds), *Intimate Labors: Cultures, Technologies, and the Politics of Care* (pp. 166–182). Stanford University Press.

Hochschild, A. R. (2012 [1983]). *The Managed Heart: Commercialization of Human Feeling* University of California Press.

Hochschild, A. R. & Machung, A. (1989). *The Second Shift: Working Parents and the Revolution at Home*. Viking.

Hoffmann, M. (2014). Red Salute at Work. *Focaal*, 2014(70), 67–80.

Holmes, S. (2013). *Fresh Fruit, Broken Bodies: Migrant Farmworkers in the United States*. University of California Press.

Holston, J. (2008). *Insurgent Citizenship: Disjunctions of Democracy and Modernity in Brazil*. Princeton University Press.

Hondagneu-Sotelo, P. (2003). Blowups and Other Unhappy Endings. In B. Ehrenreich & A. R. Hochschild (eds), *Global Woman: Nannies, Maids and Sex Workers in the New Economy* (pp. 55–69). Granta.

Hood, C. (1995). The 'New Public Management' in the 1980s: Variations on a Theme. *Accounting, Organizations and Society*, 20(2), 93–109.

hooks, b. (1982). *Ain't I A Woman: Black Women and Feminism*. Pluto Press.

Horton, S. B. (2016). Ghost Workers: The Implications of Governing Immigration Through Crime for Migrant Workplaces. *Anthropology of Work Review*, 37(1), 11–23.

Horton, S. B. (2016). *They Leave Their Kidneys in the Fields: Illness, Injury, and Illegality Among US Farmworkers*. University of California Press.

Hou, J., Gelb, S. & Calabrese, L. (2017). *The Shift in Manufacturing Employment in China*. Background paper. Overseas Development Institute. Supporting Economic Transformation Programme.

Hull, M. S. (2012). Documents and Bureaucracy. *Annual Review of Anthropology*, 41(1), 251–267.

Huws, U. (2014). *Labor in the Global Digital Economy: The Cybertariat Comes of Age*. Monthly Review Press.

Ibarra, M. d. l. L. (2010). My Reward is not Money: Deep Alliances and End-of-Life Care among Mexicana Workers and Their Wards. In E. Boris & R. S. Parreñas (eds), *Intimate Labors: Cultures, Technologies, and the Politics of Care* (pp. 117–131). Stanford University Press.

Irani, L. (2013). The Cultural Work of Microwork. *New Media & Society*, 17(5), 720–739.

Irani, L. & Silberman, S. (2013). *Turkopticon: Interrupting Worker Invisibility in Amazon Mechanical Turk*. CHI.

Isin, E. F. (2004). The Neurotic Citizen. *Citizenship Studies*, 8(3), 217–235.

Jaffe, S. (2021). *Work Won't Love You Back: How Devotion to Our Jobs Keeps Us Exploited, Exhausted, and Alone*. PublicAffairs.

James, D. (2013). Citizenship and Land in South Africa: From Rights to Responsibilities. *Critique of Anthropology*, 33(1), 26–46.

Janowski, M. & Kerlogue, F. (2007). *Kinship and Food in South East Asia*. Indiana University Press.

Jacquemin, M. (2006). Can The Language Of Rights Get Hold Of The Complex Realities Of Child Domestic Work? The Case of Young Domestic Workers in Abidjan, Ivory Coast. *Childhood*, 13(3), 389–406.

Johnston, P. (1994). *Success while Others Fail: Social Movement Unionism and the Public Workplace*. ILR Press.

Kalb, D. (1997). *Expanding Class: Power and Everyday Politics in Industrial Communities, The Netherlands, 1850–1950*. Duke University Press.

Kalb, D. (2009). Conversations with a Polish Populist: Tracing Hidden Histories of Globalization, Class, and Dispossession in Postsocialism (and beyond). *American Ethnologist*, 36(2), 207–223.

Kang, M. (2010). *The Managed Hand: Race, Gender, and the Body in Beauty Service Work*. University of California Press.

Kapesea, R. & McNamara, T. (2020). 'We Are Not Just a Union, We Are a Family': Class, Kinship and Tribe in Zambia's Mining Unions. *Dialectical Anthropology*, 44(2), 153–172.

Kasmir, S. & Carbonella, A. (eds). (2014). *Blood and Fire: Toward a Global Anthropology of Labor*. Berghahn.

Kea, P. (2013). 'The Complexity of an Enduring Relationship': Gender, Generation, and the Moral Economy of the Gambian Mandinka Household. *Journal of the Royal Anthropological Institute*, 19(1): 102–119.

Kenny, B. (2020). Coronavirus Conjunctures: Waged Work, Wagelessness, and Futures in South Africa. In A. Eckert & F. Hentschke (eds), *Corona and Work around the Globe* (pp. 43–51). De Gruyter.

Kesküla, E. (2014). Disembedding the Company from Kinship: Unethical Families and Atomized Labor in an Estonian Mine. *Laboratorium*, 6(2), 58–76.

Kesküla, E. (2016). Temporalities, Time and the Everyday: New Technology as a Marker of Change in an Estonian Mine. *History and Anthropology*, 27(5), 521–535.

Kesküla, E. (2018). Miners and Their Children: The Remaking of the Soviet Working Class in Kazakhstan. In C. Hann & J. Parry (eds), *Industrial Labor on the Margins of Capitalism: Precarity, Class, and the Neoliberal Subject* (pp. 61–84). Berghahn.

Kesküla, E. & Sanchez, A. (2019). Everyday Barricades: Bureaucracy and the Affect of Struggle in Trade Unions. *Dialectical Anthropology*, 43(1), 109–125.

Koch, G. (2016). Producing Iyashi: Healing and Labor in Tokyo's Sex Industry. *American Ethnologist*, 43(4), 704–716.

Koch, G. (2020). *Healing Labor: Japanese Sex Work in the Gendered Economy*. Stanford University Press.

Kofti, D. (2018). Regular Work in Decline, Precarious Households, and Changing Solidarities in Bulgaria. In C. Hann & J. Parry (eds), *Industrial Labor on the Margins of Capitalism: Precarity, Class, and the Neoliberal Subject* (pp. 110–133). Berghahn.

Kosnik, E. (2020, 24 July 2020). *Caring Agriculture*. EASA.

Kott, S. (2020). Work in Times of COVID-19: What is New and What is Not – A Western European Perspective. In A. Eckert & F. Hentschke (eds), *Corona and Work around the Globe* (pp. 225–230). De Gruyter.

Kwan Lee, C. (2007). *Against the Law: Labor Protests in China's Rustbelt and Sunbelt*. University of California Press.

Kwan Lee, C. (2018). Varieties of Capital, Fracture of Labor: A Comparative Ethnography of Subcontracting and Labor Precarity on the Zambian Copperbelt. In C. Hann & J. Parry (eds), *Industrial Labor on the Margins of Capitalism: Precarity, Class, and the Neoliberal Subject* (pp. 39–60). Berghahn.

Lazar, S. (2004). Personalist Politics, Clientelism and Citizenship: Local Elections in El Alto, Bolivia. *Bulletin of Latin American Research*, 23(2).

Lazar, S. (2008). *El Alto, Rebel City: Self and Citizenship in Andean Bolivia*. Duke University Press.

Lazar, S. (2012). A Desire to Formalize Work? Comparing Trade Union Strategies in Bolivia and Argentina. *Anthropology of Work Review*, 33(1), 15–24.

Lazar, S. (2016). Notions of Work, Patrimony and Production in the Life of the Colón Opera House. *Journal of Latin American and Caribbean Anthropology*, 21(2), 231–253.

Lazar, S. (2017). *The Social Life of Politics. Ethics, Kinship and Activism in Argentine Unions*. Stanford University Press.

Lazar, S. (ed.). (2017). *Where Are the Unions? Workers and Social Movements in Latin America, the Middle East, and Europe*. Zed Books.

Lazar, S. (2018). A 'Kinship Anthropology of Politics'? Interest, the Collective Self, and Kinship in Argentine Unions. *Journal of the Royal Anthropological Institute*, 24(2), 256–274.

Lazzarato, M. (1996). Immaterial Labor. In P. Virno & M. Hardt (eds), *Radical Thought in Italy. A Potential Politics* (pp. 133–148). University of Minnesota Press.

Leinaweaver, J. (2008). *The Circulation of Children: Kinship, Adoption, and Morality in Andean Peru*. Duke University Press.

Leinaweaver, J. (2010). Outsourcing Care:How Peruvian Migrants Meet Transnational Family Obligations. *Latin American Perspectives*, 37(5), 67–87.

Leins, S. (2018). *Stories of Capitalism: Inside the Role of Financial Analysts*. University of Chicago Press.

Lewis, M. (2006 [1988]). *Liar's Poker*. Hodder.

Lewis, M. (2014). *Flash Boys: Cracking the Money Code*. Allen Lane.

Li, T. M. (2017). After Development: Surplus Population and the Politics of Entitlement. *Development and Change*, 48(6), 1247–1261.

Litschel, L.-S. (2021). *The 'Old' Normal – Digital Day Laborers Stay Mobile 24/7 in Berlin*. (Remote) Work and Covid: Mobility, Safety, and Health at the Time of the Pandemic, Tallinn University, Estonia (online).

Lopez, S. H. (2004). *Reorganizing the Rust Belt: An Inside Study of the American Labor Movement*. University of California Press.

Loveday, V. (2018). The Neurotic Academic: Anxiety, Casualisation, and Governance in the Neoliberalising University. *Journal of Cultural Economy*, 11(2), 154–166.

Lüdtke, A. (2018 [1995]). *The History of Everyday Life: Reconstructing Historical Experiences and Ways of Life*. Princeton University Press.

Lugones, M. (2010). Toward a Decolonial Feminism. *Hypatia*, 25(4), 742–759.

Lund, S. (2011). Invaded City. *Focaal*, 2011(61), 33.

Luttrell, W. (2020). *Children Framing Childhoods: Working-Class Kids' Visions of Care*. Policy Press.

Makram-Ebeid, D. (2018). Between God and the State: Class, Precarity, and Cosmology on the Margins of an Egyptian Steel Town. In C. Hann & J. Parry (eds), *Industrial Labor on the Margins of Capitalism: Precarity, Class, and the Neoliberal Subject* (pp. 180–196). Berghahn.

Mankekar, P. & Gupta, A. (2017). Future Tense: Capital, Labor, and Technology in a Service Industry. *HAU: Journal of Ethnographic Theory*, 7(3), 67–87.

Mankekar, P. & Gupta, A. (2016). Intimate Encounters: Affective Labor in Call Centers. *Positions: Asia Critique*, 24(1): 17–43.

Manzano, V. (2013). *La política en movimiento: Movilizaciones colectivas y políticas estatales en la vida del Gran Buenos Aires*. Prohistoria.

Manzano, V. (2015). Lugar, Trabajo y Bienestar: La Organizacion Barrial Tupac Amaru en clave de Politica Relacional. *Publicar, 19*(19).

Manzano, V. (2017). Dilemmas of Trade Unionism and the Movement of the Unemployed under Neoliberal and Progressive Regimes in Argentina. In S. Lazar (ed.), *Where Are the Unions? Workers and Social Movements in Latin America, the Middle East, and Europe* (pp. 209–230). Zed Books.

Mather, C. (2015). Domestic Workers in Europe Getting Organised! Retrieved from www.effat.org/wp-content/uploads/2018/11/effat_booklet_domestic_workers_in_europe_en.pdf.

Mathur, N. (2012). Transparent-Making Documents and the Crisis of Unimplementability: A Rural Employment Law and Development Bureaucracy in Himalayan India. *Political and Legal Anthropology Review, 35*(2), 167–185.

Mathur, N. (2016). *Paper Tiger. Law, Bureaucracy and the Developmental State in Himalayan India.* Cambridge University Press.

Matos, P. (2012). Call Center Labor and the Injured Precariat: Shame, Stigma, and Downward Social Mobility in Contemporary Portugal. *Dialectical Anthropology, 36*(3–4), 217–243.

Mattingly, C. (2014). *Moral Laboratories: Family Peril and the Struggle for a Good Life.* University of California Press.

Mayer-Ahuja, N. (2020). 'Solidarity' in Times of Corona? Of Migrant Ghettos, Low-Wage Heroines, and Empty Public Coffers. In A. Eckert & F. Hentschke (eds), *Corona and Work around the Globe* (pp. 19–27). De Gruyter.

McRobbie, A. (2010). Reflections on Feminism, Immaterial Labour and the Post-Fordist Regime. *New Formations, 70.*

Mezzadri, A. (2017). *Sweatshop Regimes in the Indian Garment Industry.* Cambridge University Press.

Millar, K. (2018). *Reclaiming the Discarded: Life and Labor on Rio's Garbage Dump.* Duke University Press.

Millar, K. (2015). Introduction. *Focaal, 2015*(73), 3.

Mintz, S. W. (1985). *Sweetness and Power. The Place of Sugar in Modern History.* Elisabeth Sifton Books.

Mirchandani, K. (2012). *Phone Clones: Authenticity Work in the Transnational Service Economy.* Cornell University Press.

Mitchell, J. C. (1956). *The Kalela Dance: Aspects of Social Relationships among Urban Africans in Northern Rhodesia.* Manchester University Press.

Mitchell, T. (2009). Carbon Democracy. *Economy and Society, 38*(3), 399–432.

Mohanty, C. (2002). 'Under Western Eyes' Revisited: Feminist Solidarity through Anticapitalist Struggles. *Signs: Journal of Women in Culture and Society, 28*(2), 500–535.

Mollona, M. (2009). Community Unionism versus Business Unionism: The Return of the Moral Economy in Trade Union Studies. *American Ethnologist, 36*(4), 651–666.

Moody, K. (1997). Towards an International Social-Movement Unionism. *New Left Review, I/225* (September–October). Retrieved from https://newleftreview.org/issues/i225/articles/kim-moody-towards-an-international-social-movement-unionism.

Moore, S., Ball, C., Cari, M., Flynn, M. & Mulkearn, K. (2021). Research into Covid-19 Workplace Safety Outcomes in the Food and Drinks Sector. Retrieved from www.tuc.org.uk/sites/default/files/TUCHSreport.pdf.

Morris, J. & Hinz, S. (2018). From Avtoritet and Autonomy to Self-Exploitation in the Russian Automotive Industry In C. Hann & J. Parry (eds), *Industrial Labor on the Margins of Capitalism: Precarity, Class, and the Neoliberal Subject* (pp. 241–264). Berghahn.

Moyer-Lee, J. & Chango Lopez, H. (2017). From Invisible to Invincible: The Story of the 3 Cosas Campaign. In S. Lazar (ed.), *Where Are the Unions? Workers and Social Movements in Latin America, the Middle East, and Europe* (pp. 231–250). Zed Books.

Muehlebach, A. (2011). On affective Labor in Post-Fordist Italy. *Cultural Anthropology*, 26(1), 59–82.

Muehlebach, A. (2012). *The Moral Neoliberal: Welfare and Citizenship in Italy*. University of Chicago Press.

Muehlebach, A. & Shoshan, N. (2012). Introduction. *Anthropological Quarterly*, 85(2), 317–343.

Munck, R. (2013). The Precariat: A View from the South. *Third World Quarterly*, 34(5), 747–762.

Münster, D. (2012). Farmers' Suicides and the state in India: Conceptual and Ethnographic Notes from Wayanad, Kerala. *Contributions to Indian Sociology*, 46(1–2), 181–208.

Murray Li, T. (2014). *Land's End: Capitalist Relations on an Indigenous Frontier*. Duke University Press.

Narotsky, S. & Besnier, N. (2014). Crisis, Value, and Hope: Rethinking the Economy: An Introduction to Wenner-Gren Symposium Supplement 9. *Current Anthropology*, 55(S9), S4–S16.

Narotzky, S. (2018). Rethinking the Concept of Labour. *Journal of the Royal Anthropological Institute*, 24(S1), 29–43.

Narotzky, S. & Smith, G. (2006). *Immediate Struggles: People, Power, and Place in Rural Spain*. University of California Press.

Nash, J. (1993 [1979]). *We Eat the Mines and the Mines Eat Us* (Centennial edition). Columbia University Press.

Neilson, B. & Rossiter, N. (2008). Precarity as a Political Concept, or, Fordism as Exception. *Theory, Culture & Society*, 25(7–8), 51–72.

Neumark, T. (2014). Caring for Relations – an Ethnography of Unconditional Cash Transfers in a Nairobi Slum. PhD thesis, University of Cambridge.

Nguyen, V.-K. (2010). *The Republic of Therapy. Triage and Sovereignty in West Africa's Time of AIDS*. Duke University Press.

Ngwane, T. (2017). The 'Spirit of Marikana' and the Resurgence of the Working-Class Movement in South Africa. In T. Ngwane, L. Sinwell & I. Ness (eds), *Urban Revolt: State Power and the Rise of People's Movements in the Global South* (pp. 29–50). Haymarket Books.

Nieuwenhuys, O. (2000). The Household Economy in the Commercial Exploitation of Children's Work: The case of Kerala. In B. Schlemmer (ed.), *The Exploited Child* (pp. 278–291). Zed Books.

O'Hare, P. (2022). *Rubbish Belongs to the Poor: Hygienic Enclosure and the Waste Commons*. Pluto Press.

O'Keefe, T. & Courtois, A. (2019). 'Not One of the Family': Gender and Precarious Work in the Neoliberal University. *Gender, Work & Organization, 26*(4), 463–479.

Ødegaard, C. V. (2016). *Mobility, Markets and Indigenous Socialities: Contemporary Migration in the Peruvian Andes*. Taylor & Francis.

Oliveira, G. d. L. T. (2016). The Geopolitics of Brazilian Soybeans. *The Journal of Peasant Studies, 43*(2), 348–372.

Ong, A. (1988). The Production of Possession: Spirits and the Multinational Corporation in Malaysia. *American Ethnologist, 15*(1), 28–42.

Ong, A. (2003). *Buddha is Hiding: Refugees, Citizenship, the New America*. University of California Press.

Ordoñez, J. T. (2015). *Jornalero: Being a Day Laborer in the USA*. University of California Press.

Pandian, A. (2009). *Crooked Stalks: Cultivating Virtue in South India*. Duke University Press.

Parreñas, R. S. (2003). The Care Crisis in the Philippines: Children and Transnational Families in the New Global Economy. In B. Ehrenreich & A. R. Hochschild (eds), *Global Woman: Nannies, Maids and Sex Workers in the New Economy* (pp. 39–54). Granta Books.

Parreñas, R. S. (2010). Cultures of Flirtation: Sex and the Moral Boundaries of Filipina Migrant Hostesses in Tokyo. In E. Boris & R. S. Parreñas (eds), *Intimate Labors: Cultures, Technologies, and the Politics of Care* (pp. 132–147). Stanford University Press.

Parry, J. (2013). Company and Contract Labour in a Central Indian Steel Plant. *Economy and Society, 42*(3), 348–374.

Parry, J. (2018). Introduction. In C. Hann & J. Parry (eds), *Industrial Labor on the Margins of Capitalism: Precarity, Class, and the Neoliberal Subject*. Berghahn.

Parry, J. (1999). Lords of Labour: Working and Shirking in Bhilai. *Contributions to Indian Sociology, 33*(1–2), 107–140.

Patel, R. (2010). *Working the Night Shift: Women in India's Call Center Industry*. Stanford University Press.

Peacock, V. (2016). Academic Precarity as Hierarchical Dependence in the Max Planck Society. *HAU: Journal of Ethnographic Theory, 6*(1), 95–119.

Peano, I. (2013). Migrant Nigerian Women in Bonded Sexual Labour: The Subjective Effects of Criminalisation and Structural Suspicion, beyond the Trafficking Paradigm. *Africa e Mediterraneo, 79*(2), 44–47.

Pearson, A. (2020). The Discipline of Economics: Performativity and Personhood in Undergraduate Economics Education. PhD thesis, University of Cambridge.

Peattie, L. (1987). An Idea in Good Currency and How it Grew: The Informal Sector. *World Development, 15*(7), 851–860.

Pinheiro-Machado, R. (2018). The Power of Chineseness: Flexible Taiwanese Identities amidst Times of Change in Asia and Latin America. *The Journal of Latin American and Caribbean Anthropology, 23*(1), 56–73.

Prentice, R. (2015). *Thiefing a Chance: Factory Work, Illicit Labor, and Neoliberal Subjectivities in Trinidad*. University Press of Colorado.

Prentice, R. (2017). Microenterprise Development, Industrial Labour and the Seductions of Precarity. *Critique of Anthropology*, 37(2), 201–222.

Pun, N. (2005). *Made in China: Women Factory Workers in a Global Workplace*. Duke University Press.

Pun, N. (2020). The New Chinese Working Class in Struggle. *Dialectical Anthropology*, 44(4), 319–329.

Qayum, S. & Ray, R. (2010). Traveling Cultures of Servitude: Loyalty and Betrayal in New York and Kolkata. In E. Boris & R. S. Parreñas (eds), *Intimate Labors: Cultures, Technologies, and the Politics of Care* (pp. 101–116). Stanford University Press.

Raj, J. (2018). Teabelts of the Western Ghats, Kerala. In A. Shah, J. Lerche, R. Axelby, D. Benbabaali, B. Donegan, J. Raj & V. Thakur (eds), *Ground Down by Growth: Tribe, Caste, Class and Inequality in Twenty-First-Century India* (pp. 49–81). Pluto Press.

Ramos-Zayas, A. Y. (2019). 'Sovereign Parenting' in Affluent Latin American Neighbourhoods: Race and the Politics of Childcare in Ipanema (Brazil) and El Condado (Puerto Rico). *Journal of Latin American Studies*, 51(3), 639–663.

Ravenelle, A. (2019). *Hustle and Gig: Struggling and Surviving in the Sharing Economy*. University of California Press.

Reichman, D. R. (2011). *The Broken Village: Coffee, Migration, and Globalization in Honduras* Cornell University Press.

Rivas, L. M. (2003). Invisible Labors: Caring for the Independent Person. In B. Ehrenreich & A. R. Hochschild (eds), *Global Woman. Nannies, Maids and Sex Workers in the New Economy* (pp. 70–84). Granta.

Roberman, S. (2014). Labour Activation Policies and the Seriousness of Simulated Work. *Social Anthropology*, 22(3), 326–339.

Roberts, B. R. (1995). *The Making of Citizens: Cities of Peasants Revisited*. Arnold.

Robinson, C. J. (2021 [1983]). *Black Marxism: The Making of the Black Radical Tradition*. Penguin.

Rofel, L. & Yanagisako, S. (2018). *Fabricating Transnational Capitalism: A Collaborative Ethnography of Italian-Chinese Global Fashion*. Duke University Press.

Rose, N. (1989). *Governing the Soul: The Shaping of the Private Self*. Routledge.

Rosenblat, A. (2019). *Uberland: How Algorithms Are Rewriting the Rules of Work*. University of California Press.

Rudnyckyj, D. (2018). Regimes of Precarity: Buruh, Karyawan, and the Politics of Labor Identity in Indonesia. In C. Hann & J. Parry (eds), *Industrial Labor on the Margins of Capitalism: Precarity, Class, and the Neoliberal Subject* (pp. 155–179). Berghahn.

Salehi, N., Irani, L., Bernstein, M. S., Alkhatib, A., Ogbe, E., Milland, K. & Clickhappier. (2015). We Are Dynamo: Overcoming Stalling and Friction in Collective Action for Crowd Workers. In *Proceedings of the 33rd Annual ACM Conference on Human Factors in Computing Systems*, Seoul, Republic of Korea.

Sanchez, A. (2016). *Criminal Capital: Violence, Corruption and Class in Industrial India*. Routledge India.

Sanchez, A. (2018). Relative Precarity: Decline, Hope, and the Politics of Work. In C. Hann & J. Parry (eds), *Industrial Labor on the Margins of Capitalism: Precarity, Class, and the Neoliberal Subject* (pp. 218–240). Berghahn.

Sanchez, A. (2020). Transformation and the Satisfaction of Work. *Social Analysis*, 64(3), 68–94.

Sanchez, A. & Strümpell, C. (2014). Sons of Soil, Sons of Steel: Autochthony, Descent and the Class Concept in Industrial India. *Modern Asian Studies*, 48(5), 1276–1301.

Sandel, M. (1984). The Procedural Republic and the Unencumbered Self. *Political Theory*, 12(1), 81–96.

Scholz, T. (2016). *Uberworked and Underpaid: How Workers Are Disrupting the Digital Economy*. Wiley.

Schuster, C. E. (2015). *Social Collateral: Women and Microfinance in Paraguay's Smuggling Economy*. University of California Press.

Scott, J. C. (1985). *Weapons of the Weak: Everyday Forms of Peasant Resistance*. Yale University Press.

Sehmi, R. & Slaughter, H. (2021). *Double trouble. Exploring the Labour Market and Mental Health Impact of Covid-19 on Young People*. Resolution Foundation.

Senèn Gonzalez, C., Trajtemberg, D. & Medwid, B. (2009). La expansión de la afiliación sindical: análisis del módulo de relaciones laborales de la EIL. In Ministerio de Trabajo Gobierno de Argentina (ed.), *Trabajo, ocupación y empleo: Estudios laborales 2008* (pp. 13–34). Ministerio de Trabajo, Empleo y Seguridad Social.

Sennett, R. (2007). *The Culture of the New Capitalism*. Yale University Press.

Shah, A., Lerche, J., Axelby, R., Benbabaali, D., Donegan, B., Raj, J. & Thakur, V. (2018). *Ground Down by Growth: Tribe, Caste, Class and Inequality in Twenty-First-Century India*. Pluto Press.

Shever, E. (2012). *Resources for Reform: Oil and Neoliberalism in Argentina*. Stanford University Press.

Shield-Johannson. (2013). 'To Work Is to Transform the Land': Agricultural Labour, Personhood and Landscape in an Andean Ayllu. PhD thesis, London School of Economics.

Shore, C. & Wright, S. (2018). Performance Management and the Audited Self. In B. Ajana (ed.), *Metric Culture: Ontologies of Self-Tracking Practices* (pp. 11–35). Emerald Publishing.

Silver, B. (2003). *Forces of Labor: Workers' Movements and Globalization since 1870*. Cambridge University Press.

Silver, B. (2014). Theorising the Working Class in Twenty-First-Century Global Capitalism. In M. Atzeni (ed.), *Workers and Labour in a Globalised Capitalism: Contemporary Themes and Theoretical Issues* (pp. 46–69). Red Globe Press.

Sinwell, L. (2017). Thembelihle Burning, Hope Rising. In T. Ngwane, L. Sinwell & I. Ness (eds), *Urban Revolt: State Power and the Rise of People's Movements in the Global South* (pp. 15–28). Haymarket Books.

Soffia, M., Wood, A. J. & Burchell, B. (2021). Alienation Is Not 'Bullshit': An Empirical Critique of Graeber's Theory of BS Jobs. *Work, Employment and Society*, online first.

Sopranzetti, C. (2017). *Owners of the Map: Motorcycle Taxi Drivers, Mobility, and Politics in Bangkok*. University of California Press.

Soul, J. (2020). 'The Union Is Like a Family Father, the Chief': Working-Class Making and (Re)making and Union Membership Experiences in Two Generations of Argentinian Metalworkers. *Dialectical Anthropology*, 44(2), 137–151.

Souleles, D. (2019). *Songs of Profit, Songs of Loss: Private Equity, Wealth, and Inequality*. University of Nebraska Press.

Souleles, D. (2020). Trading Options and the Unattainable Dream: Some Reflections on Semiotic Ideologies. *Signs and Society*, 8(2): 243–261.

Souleles, D. (2021). Why Would You Buy an Electric Car on Jetski Friday? Or, a Critique of Financial Markets from an Options Trading Room. *Finance and Society*, 7(2): 113–129.

Srnicek, N. (2016). *Platform Capitalism*. Polity Press.

Stacey, C. L. (2011). *The Caring Self: The Work Experiences of Home Care Aides*. Cornell University Press.

Standing, G. (1989). Global Feminisation through Flexible Labour. *World Development*, 17(7), 1077–1095.

Standing, G. (2011). *The Precariat: The New Dangerous Class*. Bloomsbury.

Stein, F. (2017). *Work, Sleep, Repeat: The Abstract Labour of German Management Consultants*. Bloomsbury.

Stein, F. (2018). Anthropology's 'Impact': A Comment on Audit and the Unmeasurable Nature of Critique. *Journal of the Royal Anthropological Institute*, 24(1), 10–29.

Stensrud, A. B. (2017). Precarious Entrepreneurship: Mobile Phones, Work and Kinship in Neoliberal Peru. *Social Anthropology*, 25(2), 159–173.

Stiglitz, J. E. (2002). *Globalization and its Discontents*. Allen Lane.

Strümpell, C. (2018). Precarious Labor and Precarious Livelihoods in an Indian Company Town. In C. Hann & J. Parry (eds), *Industrial Labor on the Margins of Capitalism: Precarity, Class, and the Neoliberal Subject* (pp. 134–154). Berghahn.

Tanaka, Y. (2020). State Dysfunction in a 'Fortunate' Japan. In A. Eckert & F. Hentschke (eds), *Corona and Work around the Globe* (pp. 120–134). De Gruyter.

Tarlau, R. (2019). *Occupying Schools, Occupying Land: How the Landless Workers Movement Transformed Brazilian Education*. Oxford University Press.

Taussig, M. (1984). Culture of Terror: Space of Death. Roger Casement's Putumayo Report and the Explanation of Torture. *Comparative Studies in Society and History*, 26(3), 467–497.

Thompson, E. P. (1967). Time, Work-Discipline and Industrial Capitalism. *Past & Present*, 38(1), 56–97.

Thorkelson, E. (2016). Precarity Outside: The Political Unconscious of French Academic Labor. *American Ethnologist*, 43(3), 475–487.

Trevisani, T. (2018). Work, Precarity, and Resistance: Company and Contract Labor in Kazakhstan's Former Soviet Steel Town. In C. Hann & J. Parry (eds), *Industrial Labor on the Margins of Capitalism: Precarity, Class, and the Neoliberal Subject* (pp. 85–110). Berghahn.

Trott, B. (2017). Affective Labour and Alienation: Spinoza's Materialism and the Sad Passions of Post-Fordist Work. *Emotion, Space and Society*, 25, 119–126.

Trott, B. (2017). Operaismo and the Wicked Problem of Organization. *Journal of Labor and Society*, 20(3), 307–324.

Tsing, A. (2009). Supply Chains and the Human Condition. *Rethinking Marxism*, 21(2), 148–176.

Tsing, A. (2015). *The Mushroom at the End of the World: On the Possibility of Life in Capitalist Ruins*. Princeton University Press.

Van Esterik, P. and R. A. O'Connor (2017). *The Dance of Nurture: Negotiating Infant Feeding*. Berghahn.

Verdugo Paiva, M. (2020). *The Work for another Life: Motherly Labour, Educational Aspirations and a Reconsideration of Social Reproduction*. EASA.

Vergès, F. (2021). *A Decolonial Feminism*. Pluto Press.

Virno, P. & Hardt, M. (1996). *Radical Thought in Italy: A Potential Politics*. University of Minnesota Press.

Waterman, P. (1993). Social-Movement Unionism: A New Union Model for a New World Order? *Review (Fernand Braudel Center)*, 16(3), 245–278.

Weeks, K. (2011). *The Problem with Work: Feminism, Marxism, Antiwork Politics, and Postwork Imaginaries*. Duke University Press.

West, P. (2012). *From Modern Production to Imagined Primitive. The Social World of Coffee from Papua New Guinea*. Duke University Press.

Wilderman, J. (2017). From Flexible Work to Mass Uprising: The Western Cape Farmworkers' Struggle. In E. Webster, A. Britwum & S. Bhowmik (eds), *Crossing the Divide. Precarious Work and the Future of Labour* (pp. 74–98). University of KwaZulu-Natal Press.

Wilkis, A. (2017). *The Moral Power of Money: Morality and Economy in the Life of the Poor*. Stanford University Press.

Williams, E. C. (2013). Invisible Organization: Reading Romano Alquati. *Viewpoint Magazine*. Retrieved from https://viewpointmag.com/2013/09/26/invisible-organization-reading-romano-alquati.

Winant, G. (2021). *The Next Shift: The Fall of Industry and the Rise of Health Care in Rust Belt America*. Harvard University Press.

Wolanski, S. (2015). La familia telefónica. Sobre las relaciones de parentesco en la política sindical. *Cuadernos de Antropología Social*, 42, 91–107.

Wolf, E. R. (1971). *Peasant Wars of the Twentieth Century*. Faber & Faber.

Wood, A. J., Graham, M., Lehdonvirta, V. & Hjorth, I. (2019). Good Gig, Bad Gig: Autonomy and Algorithmic Control in the Global Gig Economy. *Work, Employment and Society*, 33(1), 56–75.

Wood, A. J., Graham, M., Lehdonvirta, V. & Hjorth, I. (2019). Networked but Commodified: The (Dis)Embeddedness of Digital Labour in the Gig Economy. *Sociology*, 53(5), 931–950.

Wood, A. J., Lehdonvirta, V. & Graham, M. (2018). Workers of the Internet Unite? Online Freelancer Organisation among Remote Gig Economy Workers in Six Asian and African Countries. *New Technology, Work and Employment*, 33(2), 95–112.

Woodcock, J. (2020). The Algorithmic Panopticon at Deliveroo: Measurement, Precarity, and the Illusion of Control. *Ephemera*, 20(3), 67–95.

Wright, E. O. (2015). *Understanding Class*. Verso.

Yanagisako, S. (2012). Immaterial and Industrial Labor. *Focaal*, 2012(64), 16.

Yarris, K. (2017). *Care Across Generations: Solidarity and Sacrifice in Transnational Families*. Stanford University Press.

Zaloom, C. (2006). *Out of the Pits: Traders and Technology from Chicago to London*. University of Chicago Press.

Zeiderman, A. (2013). Living Dangerously: Biopolitics and Urban Citizenship in Bogotá, Colombia. *American Ethnologist*, 40(1), 71–87.

Zelizer, V. (2009). Caring Everywhere. In E. Boris & R. S. Parreñas (eds), *Intimate Labors. Cultures, Technologies, and the Politics of Care* (pp. 267–279). Stanford University Press.

Zlolniski, C. (2006). *Janitors, Street Vendors, and Activists: The Lives of Mexican Immigrants in Silicon Valley*. University of California Press.

Index

Thanks to our Patreon subscribers:

Andrew Perry
Ciaran Kane

Who have shown generosity and
comradeship in support of our publishing.

Check out the other perks you get by subscribing
to our Patreon – visit patreon.com/plutopress.

Subscriptions start from £3 a month.